Money, Expense, and Naval Power in Thucydides' *History* 1–5.24

Money, Expense, and Naval Power in Thucydides' *History* 1–5.24

Lisa Kallet-Marx

UNIVERSITY OF CALIFORNIA PRESS
Berkeley   Los Angeles   Oxford

The publisher gratefully acknowledges the contribution provided by the General Endowment Fund of the Associates of the University of California Press.

University of California Press
Berkeley and Los Angeles, California

University of California Press, Ltd.
Oxford, England

© 1993 by
The Regents of the University of California

CIP information to come in proofs

Kallet-Marx, Lisa.
    Money, expense, and naval power in Thucydides' History 1–5.24 / Lisa Kallet-Marx.
      p.   cm.
    Includes bibliographical references and index.
    ISBN 978-0-520-30305-8 (pbk. : alk. paper)
    1. Thucydides. History of the Peloponnesian War. 2. Greece—History—Peloponnesian War, 431–404 B.C.—Historiography.
3. Greece—History—Peloponnesian War, 431–404 B.C.—Finance.
I. Title.
DF229.T6K33   1993
938'.05—dc20   92-40904
                                                                                                CIP

*to A. K., T. K.,
and R. K.-M.*

πλούτῳ τε ἔργου μᾶλλον καιρῷ ἢ λόγου κόμπῳ χρώμεθα
—THUC. 2.40.1

CONTENTS

PREFACE / *xi*
Introduction / *1*
1. Financial Resources in the Archaeology / *21*
Appendix: Financial Terminology in the Archaeology / *35*
2. Financial Resources in the Pentekontaetia / *37*
3. Financial Resources on the Eve of the Peloponnesian War / *70*
4. The Early Years of the War, 431–427 (2.19–3.50) / *109*
Appendix: On 3.17 / *150*
5. From the Kerkyraian Revolt to the Peace of Nikias (3.70–5.24) / *152*
6. Athens' Financial Resources in the Archidamian War / *184*
ABBREVIATIONS / *207*
BIBLIOGRAPHY / *209*
GENERAL INDEX / *219*
INDEX OF PASSAGES IN THUCYDIDES / *225*

PREFACE

It seems almost axiomatic that there will always be another book on Thucydides. There is usually a good reason for this, namely, a pressing need to take one more stab at understanding a writer whose intrinsic worth always repays the effort, whatever the result. This study, which originated in a doctoral dissertation completed in 1987 at the University of California at Berkeley, is yet another attempt. While I cannot, unfortunately, attribute the faults of this book to any of those whom I am about to thank for their role at various stages of its life, I can and do hold them personally responsible for the absence of whatever shortcomings it may lack.

The goal of not simply deciphering, but of understanding, Thucydides is a monumental, often impossible, enterprise for the student fighting through the thickets of his gnarled prose. One wants the best guide. As a beginner to Thucydides I was fortunate enough to spend a year reading the *History* in an independent study with Hunter Rawlings at the University of Colorado, whose own perceptiveness illuminated the text at every step and made the whole experience as exhilarating as it was grueling. It has fueled me ever since. One of the great virtues of a dissertation committee consisting of Ronald Stroud, Raphael Sealey, and Erich Gruen is that the three contrasting judgments and reactions which followed every chapter inevitably fostered rethinking from various, often opposed, perspectives; moreover, the impossibility of satisfying all criticism was useful preparation for my professional career, and, especially, for the reception of this study. Deep gratitude is due to my thesis directors: above all to Ronald Stroud, for his sharp and critical eye, ever-helpful comments, and unflagging encouragement; and to Raphael Sealey, for his thoughtful and careful reading of drafts, and constant support. Erich Gruen, a bottomless fount of stimulating criticism, characteristically refused to let a single assumption slip by unscrutinized. I am unable to express how much I really owe to them. Several others subsequently read the dissertation: Robert Connor, Charles Fornara, and Martin Ostwald. Their comments and criticisms helped immeasurably in the process of revision. For their comments on part or all of the manuscript at later stages, I thank Martin Mueller, Mary Whitlock Blundell, and the two readers for the University of California Press.

I had the benefit of starting the project when I was a Regular Member at the American School of Classical Studies at Athens in 1985–86, and of spending many happy hours at the Epigraphical Museum then and in 1988, for which I thank the generous assistance of Dr. Dina Peppas-Delmouzou and her staff. The Fulbright Foundation sustained me during that year, and Smith College provided financial support during the summer of 1988 to return to the EM. I completed the final revisions of the manuscript while a Junior Fellow at the Center for Hellenic Studies in 1991–92, where the relaxing yet productive and mind-nourishing environment, facilitated greatly by Zeph Stewart's directorship, enabled sorely needed scrutiny and reflection.

Finally, thanks from the soul go to Robert Kallet-Marx. Without having read the book, he knows almost everything in it, through his capacity as supporter, sounding board, adviser, and critic at every stage of my ideas; in appreciation of his inspiring acuity and much more, I dedicate this book to him. I also dedicate this book to my father, memory of whose love, and intellectual honesty and vigor has sustained me; and to my brother Tony, whose love of language was a joy, and critical spirit a model.

My method of presenting Greek in the text follows these principles: in general, in the case of key words and phrases that are used repeatedly throughout the work, I have transliterated the Greek, translating it initially, and sporadically later on. Transliterations do not always follow the same principles. In the case of familiar names, I avoid the Latinized transliterations of the Greek, unless the pronunciation would change significantly: thus, Herodotos, but Thucydides. In the case of less commonly used names, transliterations are more faithful to the Greek, even if the pronunciation differs from the Latinized version: thus, Kerkyra. I try to keep the quotation of Greek in the text to a minimum and to provide translations where they would be especially important to the Greek-less reader. Except where otherwise noted, all translations are my own; they are intended to be more literal than polished. For books and articles listed in the Bibliography, I use short titles in the note citations. S. Hornblower's new commentary on Thucydides 1–3 came out while I was finishing the manuscript; I therefore was not able to use it in any comprehensive way.

Introduction

Thucydides and financial resources: Many students of Thucydides and of the Athenian empire consider the coupling incongruous, and it usually provokes a predictable response of dissatisfaction and disappointment, always generously laced with "should have's," "did not's," "failed to's," and "omitted's." It is difficult to resist such negative judgments when they are made by scholars with the authority of, for example, A. W. Gomme, who included the treatment of financial resources among the areas in which one can "unhesitatingly find fault" with the historian.[1] Thucydides has been charged with and found guilty of both ignorance of and indifference toward financial matters, but these verdicts have been rendered in modern courts by modern judges, without an examination of all the evidence. This book attempts to redirect traditional approaches to Thucydides' treatment of financial resources by exploring this aspect of his work in its context in the Archaeology, Pentekontaetia, and history of the Archidamian War. As shall emerge, financial resources play a central role in Thucydides' ideas about naval power and figure prominently, both explicitly and implicitly, in the speeches and narrative of the work.

If the analysis presented here is on the right track, then the reader is justified in asking why Thucydides' treatment of financial resources has not been properly appreciated; for the consensus on the place of finances in his work is not the result of insufficient attention to this aspect. Scholars have scrutinized many relevant passages, mining the *History* for specific financial information which is then extracted from its context and its historical value assayed, often alongside inscriptions. The result

---

1. *HCT* 1:26; cf. also the blanket statement of Stevenson, *JHS* 44 (1924):1: "Finance did not interest Thucydides."

is often apparent conflict with the latter, and the natural interpretation of the Thucydidean passage is usually sacrificed or adjusted,[2] with the conclusion that Thucydides is either wrong, vague, or imprecise because of his alleged lack of interest and knowledge.

The wealth of epigraphic evidence on Athenian public and imperial finance has, perhaps, been the primary influence on most scholars who have examined financial matters in Thucydides. The sheer weight of this evidence—of such paramount importance for modern historians of fifth-century Athens and so damaging to their ancient predecessor—has made it difficult to resist the conclusion that, had Thucydides really been interested in the subject of Athens' finances, he would have manifestly made use of these documents more explicitly and frequently in his work. The more information we have from inscriptions, the greater and more serious Thucydides' "omissions" and lack of interest become. Accordingly, every piece of stone dug up with inscriptions telling of tribute, loans, expenses, and inventories weights Thucydides' failures more heavily. Thus, in providing readers of Warner's Penguin translation with critical guidelines for assessing the reliability of Thucydides, as well as for understanding the historian generally, M. I. Finley charged that there are "astonishing gaps" in his work and "whole chunks of history" left out.[3] The one example chosen for special comment is the famous reassessment of tribute in 425 (*IG* I^3 71).[4]

Underlying this approach, it must be said, are certain modern assumptions, the validity of which needs to be questioned. Most important, the lens through which scholars have scrutinized the *History* is colored by nineteenth- and twentieth-century notions of economy and finance and of what a historian interested in finances in the modern era would surely include. Accordingly, the absence of income-expenditure ratios and the like in the *History* prompts the conclusion that Thucydides' knowledge was faulty and interest lacking. Balance sheets are indeed absent from the pages of Thucydides. But the whole notion that we should expect to find them in a historical work of the late fifth century B.C.—when the genre of history was an unabashed branch of literature—is anachronistic. If we cast out modern assumptions about what financial information Thucydides should have included in his *History*, then we have no basis on which to conclude that he lacked interest in, and was faulty in his writing about, financial matters because of what he does not mention.

The prevailing scholarly opinions about Thucydides and finance ren-

2. E.g., 1.96; 2.13; 3.19.
3. Thucydides, *The Peloponnesian War*, trans. R. Warner, with an introduction and notes by M. I. Finley (Harmondsworth, 1972), 25.
4. I shall examine the intriguing absence of this document from Thucydides' work in chapter 5.

der it perhaps unsurprising, then, that there has never been a comprehensive historiographical examination of the critical relationship of finance to Athenian power in the *History*. Curiously, at the same time, the historian has won an acknowledged place as a brilliant analyst of power and imperialism, well appreciated since de Romilly's landmark study on the role of imperialism in Thucydides.[5] *Dunamis* has rightly been recognized as a key term and concept in the *History*,[6] while a recent work on *paraskeue*, or "preparation," has brought out the importance of this term to the historian as well.[7] Indeed, there is an entire book on power in Thucydides,[8] though it focuses almost exclusively on its moral aspect, and lacks virtually any reference to financial resources as an essential component of *dunamis*.

Yet in the Archaeology, Thucydides meticulously presents arguments about the necessity of financial resources in order to attain and exercise power, especially naval power. Since he chose to elucidate the importance of money (*chremata*) and its relationship to the fleet (*nautikon*) and naval empire (*arche*) immediately in the beginning of his *History*, it would seem patent that they are vital to his perception of the historical development of power, or *dunamis*.[9] Clearly, *dunamis* is an abstract concept in Thucydides; but the term has an abundantly rich range of nuance and reference that includes a specific, concrete military connotation, referring to the result of the accumulation of *chremata* and *nautikon* and the use to which they are put by a ruler or state. *Prima facie*, alleged "Thucydidean indifference" to finance seems confuted by the Archaeology.

Scholars have long recognized that key themes of the Archaeology, especially those concerning *dunamis*, are developed in and inform the rest of the *History*, often through implicit comparison. If other themes presented in the Archaeology adumbrate the history of the Peloponnesian War and help to justify Thucydides' belief in the importance of his subject, then we would expect the role of *chremata* to elucidate the rest of the work as well.

Thucydides' profound interest in power is itself a compelling reason to open an investigation of the role of financial resources in the *History*. Such an examination is only warranted further by the central importance both of Athens' wealth to virtually all aspects of fifth-century Athenian history and of Thucydides' role as a chief source for this period.

5. *TAI*.
6. E.g., Rokeah, *RFIC* 91 (1963):282–86; Immerwahr, "Pathology of Power," 15–31; Bar-Hen, *SCI* 2 (1975): 73–82; Hunter, *PPHT*, 33–34, 44–45, 136–38.
7. Allison, *PPT*.
8. Woodhead, *Nature of Power*.
9. Its significance to the argument of the Archaeology is well noted by Connor, *Thucydides*, 27–28.

Accordingly, we need to understand as fully as possible his views about Athens' financial resources in the projection of power and empire and to assess the value of the evidence he presents in these areas; it is toward these ends that this book is directed.

This study is thus both historiographical and historical in scope, for a historiographical approach opens the way to historical questions and issues. By understanding the nature of Thucydides' interest in financial resources and his principles of selection (and, correspondingly, his reasons for omission), we are then equipped to explore questions concerning the relationship between Athens' financial resources and the course of the Archidamian War: How did considerations of Athens' financial strength affect Athenian decisions and actions regarding its empire and enemies? What light does Thucydides shed on our knowledge of Athens' financial exploitation of its *arche*? Did the Athenian treasuries suffer a devastating depletion by the end of the Archidamian War, or even by 428? This examination may thus complement studies of the economic aspect of Greek warfare, explored especially in the important work of W. K. Pritchett and by the French "sociological" historians of ancient warfare.[10]

My method of presentation is chronological, or sequential, examining Thucydides' treatment of the role of financial resources as it develops throughout the work to the conclusion of the Archidamian War. My approach is simple: I look at the financial information and details Thucydides includes in their context in the work and explore why he has chosen them. At the same time, the study necessarily broadens in scope to include careful scrutiny of other, chiefly epigraphic, evidence, especially on such historical issues as the condition of Athens' revenue and reserve before and during the Archidamian War; the scope and nature of the polis's financial exploitation of its empire; and the focus and development of policy and strategy for insuring financial revenue during the Archidamian War.

For purposes of presentation I have deviated slightly from adhering to the sequence of Thucydides' work by beginning with two chapters on the Archaeology and Pentekontaetia, since these form distinct units in the work and allow a more focused examination of financial resources immediately before the outbreak of war (i.e., 1.24–86, 1.120–2.13), the subject of chapter 3. I then consider in chapters 4 and 5 the role of financial resources in the rest of Thucydides' account of the Archidamian War. A chronological presentation, while the best way to preserve the

---

10. *GSAW* 1–5; see especially Garlan, *War; Guerre et économie;* also collections such as Vernant, ed., *Problèmes de la guerre;* Centre National de la Recherche Scientifique, *Armées et fiscalité*. Garlan notes as recently as 1989 (*Guerre et économie*, 19) that the economic aspect of war has received less attention than other areas.

integrity of Thucydides' treatment of financial resources, has the undeniable disadvantage of making it more difficult to consider particular patterns, themes, and arguments that emerge, especially on historical issues. The final chapter tries to remedy this by presenting, in conclusion, a survey of the Archidamian War as it affected and was affected by Athens' financial resources. The final chapter also attempts to synthesize the main threads of the preceding investigation, together with some evidence not directly addressed in the earlier chapters. Finally, it ends with a few remarks on some chief historiographical results and Thucydides' overall contribution in treating the subject of financial resources.

The terminus of the study demands explanation; it is both substantive and practical. Books 1 through 5.24 form a clearly defined unit, as they treat the first stage of the Peloponnesian War, including the preparatory sections (the Archaeology and Pentekontaetia) that contain the evidence and arguments comprising Thucydides' justification of his subject. Most important, Thucydides viewed 1–5.24 as a discrete part of his *History:* he judged it necessary both to note explicitly his authorship of the period of the Peace of Nikias and the final ten years of war, as if making a second beginning, and to justify his view that the entire period from 431–404 was one protracted war (5.26). By implying that this point formed a natural break in the war, this in itself suggests the usefulness, for historiographical reasons, of considering his history of the Archidamian War separately from what followed. Further, certain arguments and themes developed in his account of the Archidamian War (for example, the condition of Athens' financial resources in the Archidamian War, the immediate effects of a large-scale war on Athenian revenues, and the nature and quality of Athens' political leadership directly after the death of Perikles) are peculiar to it, and therefore suggest the appropriateness of treating the Archidamian War separately from the subsequent years of war.

This study is intended to be the first part of a larger project on the *History* that will examine the role of financial resources in the entire work, explore Thucydides' place in the history of ideas about wealth and power, and the history of economic thought, and look more comprehensively at late fifth-century attitudes toward public wealth and its expenditure to obtain power for the polis. Although these issues can only be adumbrated here, we can gain a clearer understanding of Thucydides' achievement in the history of discourse about wealth and power by briefly considering the background against which to place his ideas.

It was as obvious in antiquity as it is today that Athens' military might consisted in its navy, as Sparta's lay in an unparalleled hoplite force, and that their military preeminence in their respective spheres of activity commanded allegiance and compliance in different degrees: Athens alone achieved an *arche*, usually translated as "empire." The term *arche* is perhaps only slightly less slippery than the word "empire." Its literal meaning, "rule," clearly implied to contemporaries, including Thucydides, considerably greater impact on the autonomy of its constituent members than a *hegemonia*. At the same time, *arche* can embrace a wide variety of forms of dependency.

One highly concrete form of dependency, however, is the requirement to pay a financial contribution, year in, year out, to a greater power which has the capacity, practically speaking, to do what it wants with it. In my view, this expression of dependency is the one most central to Thucydides' thought on the Athenian empire; indeed, what stands out about Thucydides' analysis of Athenian *dunamis* and *arche* is his deliberate focus on the essential precondition of that power, money. Emerging with clarity throughout the *History*, but presented with particular cogency in the first two books is the fact that Athens' power depends absolutely on surplus or excess wealth (*periousia chrematon*) and expenditure (*dapane*).[11] Indeed, the role of expense demonstrates that specifically money, not wealth broadly defined, is the key to power—the continual and massive use of money, raised primarily from the resources of the empire, in order to maintain naval *arche*; in short that financial resources, because of the necessity of expense to naval power, are the sine qua non of Athens' *dunamis*.

This is an argument whose novelty is easy to miss. In fact, this insight appears in literature for the first time in Thucydides' *History*, and not only represents a lesson in the new military realities of the fifth century, but also marks an important stage in the development of thought about state power, wealth, and imperialism. Even today, when it is virtually a commonplace to note that empires cost money, Paul Kennedy's thesis that a state's economic power is the chief factor in its military success arouses lively controversy.[12] Kennedy's overall arguments are remarkably similar to those running explicitly and implicitly throughout Thucydides' *History*, with the necessary substitution of "financial" for "economic" resources.[13] As we shall see, Thucydides' linkage of financial

11. On the meaning of surplus, see below, p. 18.
12. Kennedy, *Rise and Fall of the Great Powers*.
13. Consider this excerpt: "The triumph of any one Great Power ... has usually been the consequence of lengthy fighting by its armed forces, but it has also been the consequence of the more or less efficient utilization of the state's productive economic resources in wartime, and, further in the background, of the way in which that state's economy had been rising or falling ... in the decades preceding the actual conflict.... It sounds crudely mercantilistic to express it this way, but wealth is usually needed to underpin military power, and military power is usually needed to acquire and protect wealth.... If a state overextends itself strategically—by, say, the conquest of extensive territories or the waging

resources to military success and *arche* informs the narrative, analyses, and speeches of the *History*.

This is not to say that in Thucydides' work we can find the earliest analysis of economic imperialism; nor indeed can one easily discern in the Athenian empire such a motive for the control of other poleis. Certainly, the phenomenon to which the term "economic imperialism" is applied today, one in which the imperial power seeks and fosters foreign markets for investment, in addition to varying degrees of political intervention and control, is not applicable to Athens.[14] Although a by-product, so to speak, of Athenian imperialism was the prospect of increased wealth for individual Athenians and for the polis through a variety of means, both in parts of the empire itself and in Athens,[15] most economic theories of imperialism have little relevance for understanding the peculiar nature of the Athenian *arche*,[16] in which wealth created and developed in the local regions of the empire—and not deriving from an initial investment by Athens—came into Athens and indeed sustained the ruling power. Wealth from the resources of others was necessary for the attainment and maintenance of *arche*, but there is no sign that economic enrichment was a conscious, distinct motive, a motive that presupposes a concept of the economy. It still bears repeating that, as Polanyi puts it, "elements of the economy are . . . embedded in noneconomic institutions" and that in the fifth-century Greek polis there was no separable concept or reality of the economy. The motives of the collective, like those of individuals in a private context, "spring as a rule from situations set by facts of a noneconomic—familial, political or religious—order."[17]

It is easy—but misleading—to blur motive with means and suppose a financial explanation for Athenian imperialism since, by the time the *arche* was fully established, control was exerted in one respect in order to insure revenue necessary to maintain that control; moreover, the material benefits to individuals would have had a perceptible effect on attitudes toward the preservation of the empire. Indeed, dependence on the extortion of wealth from others had the effect, at times, of elevating

---

of costly wars—it runs the risk that the potential benefits from external expansion may be outweighed by the great expense of it all. . . . The historical record suggests a very clear connection *in the long run* between an individual Great Power's economic rise and fall and its growth and decline as an important military power." Kennedy, *Rise and Fall of the Great Power*, xv–xvi; xxii.

14. Doyle, *Empires*, 20; see also Boulding and Mukerjee, eds., *Economic Imperialism*, esp. "Concept and Theory," 1–170.

15. See Finley, *Economy and Society*, 51–53.

16. As Starr has noted, *CJ* 83 (1987):118.

17. Polanyi, "Aristotle Discovers the Economy," 70–71; cf. the useful introductory discussion in Austin and Vidal-Naquet, *ESHAG*, 3–11.

the need for money to the status of motive rather than merely result or by-product. Thus, the Athenian envoys at Sparta in 432 speak of the reasons behind their fellow citizens' refusal to relinquish their *arche*, citing "honor, fear, and tangible gain," as "very powerful motives" that make them hold onto their power (1.76.2).[18] Moreover, voices are no less explicit in declaring profit a motive for war.[19]

We need, however, to draw clear lines distinguishing the motives of an *arche* from those of raids and battles, and the motives for the creation of *arche* from those for its continuation. The paramount impetus driving those seeking to exert control through creating an *arche* was the desire for power, with glory and honor not far behind.[20] Therefore, in speaking about the Athenian empire, we need to make, as Thucydides did, a fundamental distinction between the measures that made an empire possible and the very point of *arche*, which was not to increase one's wealth but rather to be most powerful, a consequence of which was enrichment.

The picture becomes considerably more complex when we turn to consider the motives of the weaker poleis in the *arche*. It is not fashionable, of course, even to speak at all of possible motives of those who came under the sway of imperialist powers such as Athens or Rome; with minor exceptions, the relationship is usually regarded as a neat polarity of oppressor and victim. Thucydides' view, however, differed fundamentally from this: he saw distinct motives on the part of weaker members that were key to the development of *arche*. It is on the issue of Thucydides' "theory" of *arche* that the collaborative theory of imperialism developed by Ronald Robinson may shed some useful light.[21]

Much of Robinson's theory of collaboration is foreign and inapplicable to the peculiar *arche* of fifth-century Athens, but it contains a central point that is directly relevant to Thucydides' views on the development of *arche* in general and Athens' empire in particular. Describing modern European imperialism and stressing the mutual economic benefit of the imperial power and objects of imperial control, Robinson notes that imperialism "was as much a function of its victims' collaboration or non-collaboration—of their indigenous politics, as it was of European expansion."[22] Indeed, if we recognize that in the case of Athens'

18. In this context, ὠφέλεια clearly means material advantage, or profit, as in LSJ, s.v. ὠφέλεια II.
19. E.g., Thuc. 6.24.3; Arist. *Pol.* 1256 b23–26; cf. Finley, *Ancient History*, 77, who notes the infrequency with which modern historians appreciate the profit-motive in accounts of ancient warfare; see now Pritchett, *GSAW* 5:439–45, and the table on 507ff.
20. Cf. de Romilly, *TAI*, 79.
21. Robinson, "Collaboration," 117–40; cf. Atmore, "Extra-European Foundations," 106–25. I thank A. M. Eckstein for these references.
22. Robinson, "Collaboration," 118.

arche, the initial flow of wealth was in the opposite direction of that in modern Western imperialism, the basic idea that, put simply, domination is possible only with the support of locals (that is, local elites) is one with which Thucydides is in accord and for which he provides evidence. As Robinson observes in the case of European imperialism in Asia and Africa, "the irony of collaborative systems lay in the fact that although the white invaders could exert leverage on ruling elites they could not do without their mediation. Even if the bargains were unequal they had to recognize mutual interests and interdependence if they were to be kept."²³ Robinson's statement accords well with the case of Athens and its allies in the beginnings of the Delian League and in its subsequent development; for as we shall explore more fully in chapter 2, Thucydides' analysis does not deny interest in control by the potential imperial power, but at the same time it recognizes the importance of the local poleis in accepting and developing an unequal power relationship with Athens; their complicity and self-interest are intelligible functioning within the larger mechanism of *charis*.

One of the more frustrating lacunae for students of the Athenian empire is that, as M. I. Finley reminds us, we simply do not know who paid the tribute in the poleis of the empire.²⁴ Therefore, Robinson's distinction between local elites as collaborators and mediators and the general population cannot, in the absence of hard evidence from any source, be assumed to apply to the *dunatoi* and the demos in the communities under Athens' control.²⁵ Thucydides infrequently (usually in the context of stasis) breaks down interest groups within a polis. Although he does not provide a basis for inferring the existence of distinctly friendly or hostile groups within the local poleis, his observations led to a theory of development in which, as we shall see, the self-interest of the eventual ὑπήκοοι, as much as that of the aggressor, was responsible for the evolution of *arche*.²⁶ But the initial self-interest of the allies of the Delian League was transformed into outright oppression by the Athenians: the bonds of collaboration and *charis* gradually deteriorated when contributions to a common goal were supplanted by a compulsory system of payment for

23. Ibid., 121.
24. Finley, *Ancient History*, 79. However, he supported the view that the burden fell on the wealthy.
25. But the theory of collaboration is intriguing in fostering questions about the common assumption of a clear-cut distinction between the friendly demos and hostile *oligoi*, which rests largely on a loaded remark in a Thucydidean speech—and one in which the orator (Diodotos) has pointedly noted that one must lie in order to persuade, 3.43.2. Relevant to this question is that after revolts were quelled, Athenian vengeance was generally meted out to all alike, suggesting that the Athenians did not draw a distinction between sectors of the community: all were regarded as hostile at that point.
26. See especially 1.8.3 and 1.99 and discussion of these passages in chapters 1 and 2.

service, which changed both the function of tribute—replacing an obligation based on a good-faith bond with a mechanical contract—and the relationship between Athens and its allies.[27] Likewise, Robinson makes the important if unsurprising observation that when the collaborative mechanism has broken down, imperial control is heightened, whereas it can be very slight in an overt sense when willingness to cooperate is strong, that is, when local mediators have ascendancy over resisters.[28]

Robinson's theory of imperialism has important points in common with what I shall argue is at the center of Thucydides' theory of the development of *arche* and stimulates questions about the nature of the Athenian empire; at the same time, we should not force Athens' *arche* to conform in detail to a model whose applicability to the Athenian empire has clear limits. We need now to return to the late fifth century and set Thucydides' insights about naval *arche* in their historical and literary/historiographical context.

The historian's ideas about empire and power and his presentation of his subject were both shaped by his observations and reflections on the unprecedented nature of Athens' *arche*; necessarily, they jarred with centuries-old traditions about the conduct of war, the projection of power, and the relationship between wealth and military strength. What were the chief differences between traditional ways of exerting power and naval *arche* that are important for appreciating the broader military and conceptual background for the *History*?

The most significant difference is that traditional land-based warfare did not, generally speaking, require the outlay of money by the polis. The individual citizen-soldier was responsible for his own equipment and sustenance, the acquisition of which required individual wealth, but not necessarily money. Whatever the form of wealth used by an individual to procure weaponry and food, it is important to stress that the polis traditionally did not play a role in acquiring the necessary prerequisites of military campaigns. Not until the Peloponnesian War are state pay and the hiring of mercenaries to any significant extent attested.[29] There is no better proof of the unimportance of money in the military sphere than the demonstrable and acknowledged supremacy in hoplite warfare of Sparta, a community with no public financial resources to speak of. If a campaign dragged on beyond a certain limit, state support might be expected;[30] but what we describe as campaigns and wars before the

---

27. Thucydides lays no stress on any moral obligation in the beginning of the Delian League; but as we shall see, this is because it is irrelevant to his purpose in 1.95–96.

28. "Collaboration," e.g., 122–23.

29. See Pritchett's discussion, *GSAW* 1:3–14.

30. Cf. Ar. *Acharn.* 197; *Peace* 312, where three days' rations appears to be the normal expectation for individually supplied provisions; and Anderson, *Military Theory and Practice*, 45.

Peloponnesian War consisted, for the most part, of short, episodic, battles, and sieges and extended fighting were rare.³¹

One should by no means deny or devalue the importance of acquiring wealth on the other end of battle, so to speak, through the accumulation and distribution of spoils by the victors and through raids for the purpose of plunder; obtaining wealth through violent means was a crucial—and normal—aspect of ancient life, acknowledged explicitly by ancient authors.³² In this respect, warfare was (what today would be called) "as much an economic activity . . . as it was a political one."³³ Or, put differently, the sphere of warfare, like that of agriculture, religious life, and gift exchange, had a crucial economic aspect embedded in it. Booty, or perhaps better, "profits" of war,³⁴ constituted one of the "essential processes for the growth of wealth in the Graeco-Roman economy."³⁵

It cannot be overstressed, however, that the expenditure of money to wage war, or even the very idea that money was necessary for success in war, was not part of the experience of land-based warfare in the Greek world. The role of money as a prerequisite for warfare—the "sinews of war," as Cicero puts it³⁶—developed later out of two phenomena: the spread of coinage and the growth of naval warfare. Garlan ties the increased use of money in warfare to its availability and diffusion.³⁷ While this is an important factor, it is insufficient by itself; in my view, it was the introduction not of naval power per se (which was not new to the fifth century) but rather of naval *arche*, that is, naval mastery on the scale of the Athenian naval empire, that required the massive infusion of money into the military sphere.³⁸ By the fifth century, Greeks would have rec-

---

31. Hanson, *Western Way of War*, 35.

32. E.g., Homer *Ody.* 14.233–34; Arist. *Pol.* 1256 b23. As Plato's Phaedo says, "all wars are fought for the possession of wealth" (διὰ γὰρ τὴν τῶν χρημάτων κτῆσιν πάντες οἱ πόλεμοι γίγνονται) (66c). See also Finley, *Economy and Society*, 76; Garlan, *Guerre et économie*, 35.

33. Snodgrass, *Archaic Greece*, 130, with reference to warfare in the archaic period.

34. Aymard, *Revue historique* 217 (1957):233–49.

35. Finley, *Comp.Stud.Soc.Hist.* 19 (1977):321. However, this statement can mislead by casting the accumulation of booty in anachronistic economic terms, while ignoring the social, political, and religious role of wealth, particularly, the prestige value of amassing, displaying, and expending wealth—"symbolic capital"—discernible from Homer through the classical period. See Redfield, "Economic Man"; cf. Davies, *Wealth*, 88–114; for a useful discussion of symbolic capital, see Bourdieu, *Theory of Practice*, esp. 171–83.

36. Cic. *Phil.* 5.5; *De Imp. Cn. Pomp.* 17.

37. Garlan, *Guerre et économie*, 56–57.

38. I have borrowed the phrase "naval mastery," which I shall use from time to time, from Paul Kennedy, who defines it as "a situation in which a country has developed its maritime strength so that it is superior to any rival power, and that its predominance is or could be exerted far outside its home waters, with the result that it is extremely difficult for other, lesser states to undertake maritime operations or trade without at least its tacit consent" (*Rise and Fall of British Naval Mastery*, 9).

ognized that money facilitated the waging of war by making such operations as the provisioning of troops easier;[39] but money was not indispensable before the fifth century, and understanding that it was so with the advent of naval *arche* would not have been self-evident or immediate. In particular, Greeks familiar only with short campaigns and temporarily assembled fleets would not have appreciated the need for surplus cash (*periousia chrematon*)—that is, funds beyond what was expected for immediate exigencies—now critical to the operation of a standing navy.

Two final differences between land and naval warfare should be noted: first, the absence of time-consuming drilling and preparation from land-based warfare (except in the case of Spartan hoplite training).[40] This lack is not surprising, given the short duration of battles and the overlapping of the fighting with the agricultural season, since hoplites typically were farmers. Second, even though military land-based alliances may have been long-lasting, such as the Peloponnesian League, troops were mustered for short periods, only when the need arose. Both of these points are relevant for understanding the novelty of and contemporary reactions to the Athenian *arche*. With them in mind, we can better appreciate the fundamental change that occurred in the fifth century when the Athenians achieved naval *arche*, as well as the consequences for the history of ideas about power.

It was the introduction of naval power on a large scale and the creation of a standing navy that transformed the requirements of war permanently. To be sure, Greeks did not awaken suddenly in the fifth century to the idea of navies and using money in naval war. Even the Spartans themselves had ventured out on the waters quite readily in the sixth century.[41] The pressing need for money and, therefore, the recognition of its importance in the naval arena were patent in the Ionian fleet's ill-fated activities in the beginning of the fifth century.[42] Rather, the scale, the concentration of surplus financial resources in the hands of one polis, and the sheer expense of a permanent, standing navy needed to achieve naval mastery were the novel elements, the consequences of which were previously unknown, perhaps unthinkable. The conditions necessitating large expenditures—building and maintaining ships, hiring rowers and sailors, and provisioning men—all coalesced for the first time during the Athenian empire.

The unprecedented nature of Athens' *arche*, made possible by the massive outlay of money, had an enormous impact on the way that Thu-

---

39. Garlan, *Guerre et économie,* 57, catalogs the facilitating effect of money in the military sphere.
40. Hanson, *Western Way of War,* 32; Anderson, "Hoplite Weapons," 28.
41. E.g., against Samos, Hdt. 3.46–47, 54–56.
42. Hdt. 5.34.3, 36.2–4.

cydides thought about the relationship between wealth and power in the military realm. Individual Athenians had long obtained political power and prestige through lavish expenditure, an important aristocratic measure of personal value. Now, for the first time, the polis itself adopted the similar approach of achieving *dunamis* through expenditure of money.[43] To Thucydides, the novelty of the Athenian naval *arche* fostered, indeed demanded, a new definition of power; it had to be recast into a new framework that elevated its principal components, money and ships, to the position previously reserved for combat skill, bravery, and heroism.[44]

Thucydides' treatment of the relationship between wealth and power, and his originality in reformulating traditional conceptions, can best be appreciated through a brief comparison with his literary predecessors. The primary function of wealth that emerges in literature from Homer through Herodotos is to signify and confirm power; in the milieu of battle in these early works, wealth is not connected to preparation for and conduct of war or to military success.[45] Indeed, the *Iliad* as a whole illustrates the point. Power itself is won through martial prowess, but the honor and respect attendant on it are expressed by the possession of wealth. This is central to the traditional attitude toward wealth: although Agamemnon demonstrates his power and, in a limited sense, maintains alliances through gift giving, the most spectacular instance being the treasure offered to Achilles (*Il.* 9.120–57), military success is achieved through fighting prowess, bravery, and, often, the help of the gods (which expresses one's power as well). In such a world, wealth is an essential and concrete confirmation of power, which it helps to maintain through display and exchange.[46]

Wealth as a sign of power and greatness is prevalent in much literature after Homer,[47] and it is intimately linked with morality; usually present is a decided ambivalence.[48] For example, Herodotos sets before his

43. See Davies, *Wealth*, 88–114; cf. also Kurke, *Traffic*, 163–94, 225–39.
44. The novelty of naval *arche* and the importance of Athens' power to the "truest explanation" of the war (ἀληθεστάτη πρόφασις, 1.23.6) explain why Thucydides spends almost no time analyzing the basis of Spartan power. It is not because he is an Athenian, with a tendency to concentrate on Athens to the exclusion of others, but rather because Spartan power was thoroughly traditional, wholly self-evident, and uncontroversial in its composition and extent. Moreover, it does not play a role in the ἀληθεστάτη πρόφασις, which necessitates the extensive explanation of Athenian power in the Pentekontaetia.
45. I am drawing a distinction, that is, between the active, direct use of money to exert military power and the indirect use to confirm and demonstrate power through display and gift exchange.
46. See Donlan, *AJAH* 6 (1981):101–17, who examines in particular the function of gift exchange, rather than gift possession; see also Mauss, *Gift*.
47. E.g., Hes. *W&D* 313; Archil., Diehl fr. 22; Theog. 667, 718; Pind. *Ol.* 2.59–88.
48. *Contra* Finley, *Ancient Economy*, 35: "the judgment of antiquity about wealth was fundamentally unequivocal and uncomplicated."

readers repeated instances of rulers and cities at the height of their power, evidenced by their wealth, often described in impressive detail.[49] Notable in every case is the absence of reference to the expenditure of money specifically, or use of wealth generally, to attain power. Wealth is, in an important sense, an end in itself. It is implicit to suppose that Polykrates' wealth, for example, must have been used to build up his power, part of which was naval; but what is so revealing is that Herodotos does not demonstrate interest in this aspect.[50] Indeed, the few times that Herodotos does explicitly draw attention to the need for money and wealth in order to achieve military success both demonstrates his awareness of this fact and confirms, by the infrequency with which wealth appears in such a context, that for him, the significance of wealth lay elsewhere.[51]

Herodotos was, like his historiographical successor, interested in the development of power: he evinces his interest particularly in his accounts of the rise of the Mermnadai dynasty, of Cyrus and the Persian empire, of Athens and Sparta. Immerwahr has noted the essentially "static" quality of power in Herodotos, in contrast to Thucydides. For the latter, power is a "direct causal factor for historical action, whereas in Herodotos it is possible for a ruler to enjoy his power by 'sitting still,' to use a phrase commonly employed by the historian."[52] This expresses aptly the manner in which Herodotos treats power, viewing prosperity as a way to illustrate power already achieved, rather than as a means to that end.

Herodotos' treatment of wealth and power is intimately linked with his overall historical theory of the rise and fall of states and rulers, spe-

---

49. Cf. especially, e.g., that of Croesus, 1.50–53 (dedications to Apollo and to Amphiaraios); 3.89–97 (wealth of Darius' realm in tribute and gifts); Babylon, 1.192; Darius, whose power is demonstrated by an extensive catalog of gifts that accrued to him from all parts of his domains (3.89–97), introduced by the comment, "everything was full of the power (*dunamis*) of Darius," δυνάμιός τε πάντα οἱ ἐπιμπλέατο, 3.88.3; Polykrates, 3.39–42.

50. Power in Herodotos, though, as in Thucydides, can have a physical, concrete meaning, referring to wealth, armies, ships, or sometimes territory (*contra* H. Immerwahr, *Form and Thought*, 207, who thinks that Thucydides uses *dunamis* in an abstract, rather than a physical sense), e.g., 7.9a.1; 3.88.3.

51. That the "need for money" existed and served as an important motivating factor on specific occasions (rather than for the broader achievement of power and empire) is made clear in various episodes in the narrative, though it is significant that Herodotos often leaves unexpressed specifically for *what* the money is needed; see his account of the Samian exiles at Siphnos, 3.57–58; cf. also Hekataios' advice to seize the temple treasures at Branchidai on the eve of the Ionian Revolt, 5.36, and Herodotos' reference to the expense of the siege of Naxos, 5.34.

52. Immerwahr, *Form and Thought*, 207.

cifically, with his conception of hubris caused by excessive prosperity. In this context, wealth is an indicator of impending doom.[53] Thus, when he opens his account of a certain ruler or polis by noting that it was at the height of its prosperity, the reader acquainted with this pattern knows immediately that doom is just around the corner. In other words, Herodotos' attention to wealth as a symbol of power reflects his concern with the moral complexities accompanying prosperity, greed, and the volatility and uncertainty of mortal affairs.[54]

In contrast to these traditional assumptions about the place of money and riches in the military sphere of power, a consistent theme in Thucydides' *History* is that naval supremacy (*arche*) depends on excess wealth, or *periousia chrematon*. In earlier authors, as we have seen, wealth is inextricably linked with morality. Herodotos exploits this link in his *History*, in order to demonstrate the folly of equating wealth with happiness and to illuminate the slippery path that a wealthy ruler treads, only to fall despite his attempts to dodge Nemesis by disguising his inherent hubris.

In Thucydides, the ingredients for moral disaster are all there: excess wealth gained from exploiting the resources of other Greeks, used in turn to deprive them of their freedom; the power and prosperity of the Athenians; the catalog of wealth on the eve of war (2.13.3–5); the majestic boasting of the Funeral Oration. Consider the hyperbolic rhetoric of Perikles in his final speech on the extraordinary nature of Athens' naval mastery, a passage of great importance not only for the insight it gives into Athenian views of power, but also, as we shall see, for the light it casts on the ἀληθεστάτη πρόφασις, "the most genuine explanation," of the Peloponnesian War. Athenian naval power, Perikles insists, is a phenomenon of such staggering proportions and is so unprecedented that its implications have not been fully recognized or articulated (cf. 1.23.6: ἀφανεστάτην λόγῳ).

> You [Athenians] think that your *arche* is confined to power over your allies; but I declare that of the two manifest spheres of use, land and sea, you have absolute mastery of the latter, to such an extent that it is over not only what you hold at present but also anywhere you wish to extend it [in future]. There is no one, neither king nor any other race in existence today, who can prevent you, with your current naval *paraskeue* ("preparation" or "preparedness"), from the use of the sea. This *dunamis* itself is not revealed

---

53. de Romilly, *Rise and Fall*, 42.
54. Hdt. 1.5.4; cf. 1.32; 3.39–43. Concerns about the dangerous consequences of prosperity, such as greed, hubris, the jealousy of the gods, and ultimately, Nemesis, were frequently voiced in early Greek literature; cf., e.g., Homer *Ody.* 4.78–99; Hes. *W&D* 319–26; Solon, fr. 13; Theog. 227; see also Immerwahr, *Form and Thought*, 206–7; Jaeger, *Paideia* 1, esp. 70, 201–2.

by our ability to use our farms and land, the loss of which you consider so important. (2.62.2)[55]

In an author such as Herodotos, all of the above would have led inevitably to disaster. But Thucydides rejects such a traditional view in treating the wealth of Athens, and his novel approach is especially remarkable given the disquiet that the existence of the *arche* itself could occasion and the strong moral elements of the *History*, which have been a focus of Thucydidean scholarship, particularly within the last few decades. Although the idea of taking wealth from others for one's own power and prestige would have raised few eyebrows in antiquity,[56] the existence of a massive surplus of wealth alone would have caused moral unease. Indeed, Thucydides' effective detachment of wealth from morality is one of the most conspicuous features distinguishing his work from earlier literature such as Hesiod, Solon, Theognis, and Herodotos. We need to try to explain this. I would like to suggest that several considerations converge to account for Thucydides' treatment, although the discussion that follows is necessarily speculative.

Our starting point is the relationship between the polis and the *oikos*. The conception of the polis as an assemblage of *oikoi*[57] leads readily to comparisons between οἰκονομική and πολιτική and to the idea that one who manages his household well will administer the state effectively.[58] As the *oikos* consists of family and property, some important implications emerge when attitudes about wealth in the private domain of the *oikos* are transferred to the public sphere of the polis. Much ambivalence about money in the hands of individuals fills the part of the first book of

---

55. See [Xen.] *Ath.Pol.* 2.2–8, on the differences between land and sea power. The extraordinary and unsettling nature of naval mastery has always been a challenge to define, since it is more, as Perikles makes clear, than simply a different method of waging war to reach the same end as hoplite warfare. An apposite and useful definition comes from a discussion not of Athens, but of later examples: "Sea power . . . [is] a highly complex factor, defensive as well as offensive; economic or, more specifically, financial as well as military; achieving its greatest effects not so much by its own intrinsic strength as by its skilful exploitation of the weaknesses of its opponents. By its aid first the Portuguese, then the Dutch, and finally the British were able to wield an influence out of all proportion to their size, resources, and manpower" (H. Rosinski, "The Role of Sea Power in Global Warfare of the Future," in *Brassey's Naval Annual* [1947], 105).

56. Cf. the famous and highly problematic anecdote preserved in Plut. *Per.* 12 about the use of allied money in the building program. Significantly, the anecdote concerns the propriety of the use of money taken from the allies, not of the appropriation itself. If the story is true, Perikles' political opponents tried—and failed—to make political hay by suggesting impropriety.

57. E.g., Arist. *Pol.* 1252 b28ff: the polis is an assemblage of villages, which are composed of households; cf. 1280 b32ff., a polis is ἡ τοῦ εὖ κοινωνία καὶ ταῖς οἰκίαις καὶ τοῖς γένεσι.

58. Plato *Polit.* 259b; cf. also Xen. *Mem.* 4.4.1; 4.10–11.

Aristotle's *Politics* which concerns the specific end to which the acquisition and expenditure of money are put, for there are good and bad ways of acquiring wealth and good and bad uses of wealth (*chrematistike*). Aristotle directs his sharpest criticism at those who use money for the purpose of acquiring more money and thus elevate money to the same level as the ends money was introduced to procure.[59]

Aristotle is, however, in accord with Xenophon that wealth produced for τὸ εὖ ζῆν, "living well," or "the good life," is acceptable. "Riches are a collection of tools for the householder and the statesman," and are part of the natural order of things.[60] Money exchange is both necessary and natural when it is put toward the goal of self-sufficiency.[61] Most important, this goes beyond wealth for subsistence needs to the accumulation of surplus wealth, as long as it is directed toward τὸ εὖ ζῆν. Indeed, Xenophon's Ischomachos regards securing surplus wealth as a desirable goal for the household manager;[62] accumulating wealth in the *oikos* beyond subsistence and for the purpose of τὸ εὖ ζῆν can even be regarded as a responsibility.[63]

Surplus wealth acquired for this purpose is acceptable, even laudable, because it has a limit. The desire to amass unlimited wealth, however, contradicts the notion of "the good life," for it implies the pursuit of wealth for its own sake; while wealth acquired to secure "the good life"—the only acceptable end, in Aristotle's view—would necessarily have a limit.[64] The idea of "natural limit" therefore allows for the creation of surplus as a means of achieving τὸ εὖ ζῆν. Not only is surplus—within limits—for the *oikos* acceptable, but surplus in the *oikos* for expenditure on the city is also desirable and worthy of praise.[65]

Thucydides' treatment of surplus and expenditure for power fits this conceptual framework well; indeed, the discernible Greek attitudes toward surplus and expenditure in the realm of the *oikos* may shed light on the acceptability of these aspects of wealth in the public sphere and in Thucydides' *History*. For if wealth used for the benefit of the city has a positive value attached to it, and Athens' wealth is used this way, then Athens' wealth is acceptable. Moreover, although Athens' wealth was vast, it had limits, as Perikles' specification of the extent of the city's

---

59. Usury receives Aristotle's sharpest criticism, for it involves the use of money to get more money ("currency, son of currency"); see Lowry, *Archaeology of Economic Ideas*, 224–26.

60. Arist. *Pol.* 1256 b37–39; ὁ δὲ πλοῦτος ὀργάνων πλῆθός ἐστιν οἰκονομικῶν καὶ πολιτικῶν.

61. See Lowry's discussion, *Archaeology of Economic Ideas*, 224–26.

62. Xen. *Oik.* 11.8.

63. Ibid., 1.4; cf. 2.10.

64. Arist. *Pol.* 1257 b1–29; cf. also Plato *Rep.* 330a–331b.

65. Xen. *Oik.* 11.8; Arist. *Nik. Ethics* 1122 b19–23a4; see Kurke, *Traffic*, 167–70.

wealth in 2.13.3–5 illustrates neatly. But was Athens' wealth acquired by acceptable means and put to "good use"?

As we have seen, wealth accumulated through violent conflict was acceptable and desirable; even Aristotle classifies piratical raids as a natural mode of acquisition.[66] The appropriation of tribute and other moneys as a result of war would not then have aroused concern; what about their use? Their very utility provides a key. The fact that money was essential to Athens' military success explains the acceptability of *periousia chrematon*. It is important to define *periousia chrematon* as precisely as possible and to be clear about its implications. The phrase is usually translated as "surplus wealth," "abundance of wealth," "reserves," or the like. A typical and acceptable formulation of the word *surplus* is an excess "over the minimum demands of necessity,"[67] that is, wealth remaining after necessary disbursements have been made, wealth not to be put to immediate use. It need not mean "excessive wealth." Yet in the context of the Athenian empire, that which remained in the reserve was necessary, and not beyond minimum needs, even though, as mentioned above, it far exceeded what was required for immediate use: the very survival of the *arche* demanded huge stores of wealth that were ready to be expended, if necessary. Thus, for the Athenians, *periousia chrematon*, which in other contexts might be viewed as excessive and hubristic, was merely necessary for the preservation of the polis. That Athens' wealth was spent on the military needs of the polis, then, would have been a compelling argument in favor of its continued accumulation and expenditure. As was made perfectly clear, to relinquish or slacken the *arche* when it was most detested would have resulted in sure destruction.[68]

The expenditure of money—as opposed to its mere display—is a prominent theme in Thucydides, reflecting above all the new realities of naval power; and the possession of wealth for that use renders it acceptable: such wealth is fundamentally different from accumulated wealth in Herodotos. But Thucydides broadens the conception of the possession of wealth for (good) use when he accords it a place as a hallmark of Perikles and Periklean Athens. Thus, when the statesman implies on the eve of war (2.13.5) that all of Athens' wealth could be spent in the coming conflict, he confirms that its value lies in exchange, not in accumulation and display. His attitude toward the function of wealth emerges explicitly in the Funeral Oration: wealth is to be spent, not seen in itself as a sign of greatness (2.40.1). Thucydides' overall treatment of the use of wealth constitutes an implicit rejection of traditional and contemporary

---

66. Arist. *Pol.* 1256 a36.
67. Herskovits, *Economic Anthropology* (New York, 1952), 395.
68. This could be used to good rhetorical purpose, as in Thuc. 1.75 (by the Athenians at Sparta); 2.63.2 (by Perikles).

attitudes toward the display of wealth, which were demonstrated into the late fifth century in both the private and public spheres—for example, in the procession of the year's tribute onto the stage at the Greater Dionysia.[69]

Expenditure for the good and power of the city through the maintenance of its *arche* becomes part of the exchange of *charis* that was fundamental to aristocratic values, further confirming its acceptability; once again, public and private run in parallel. Moreover, the kind of public expenditure at issue links aristocratic values with the people as a whole: they are given the opportunity of participating in aristocratic ideology by means of their role in voting expenditures for the city's military and domestic affairs.

The goal of self-sufficiency—for both *oikos* and polis—further justifies Athens' accumulation of wealth from the empire. For the *oikos*, self-sufficiency includes the necessity to preserve the property of the *oikos*, to add to what was inherited if possible, and, finally, to pass it on to the next generation.[70] In the *History*, concern with inherited power, the need to preserve it, and the desire to increase it corresponds neatly with this view of the desired aim of the *oikos*: the idea of self-sufficiency at the level of the *oikos* can be extended to the polis. In the Funeral Oration, Perikles asserts that Athens has achieved the highest self-sufficiency (2.36.3). This is a remarkable comment applied to a city that relied on imports for its survival, and much of whose financial resources was extracted from outside the polis. What does he mean? He could mean that the city with the power to obtain what it needs and wants, regardless of the source, can be considered self-sufficient.[71] The comment may also simply reflect, like almost everything in the Funeral Oration, the ideal of the Athenian polis, corresponding to the ideal of the *oikos* as opposed to the reality.

There may be more to the comment, however, that ties in with the Athenians' own appraisal of the nature of their *arche*. One of the striking aspects of the Athenians' self-image is their frank acknowledgement of their rule for what it is: Perikles' and Kleon's link between Athens and tyranny in Thucydides, as well as documents which offer a stark image of Athens as ruler, all warrant the conclusion that Athenians considered

---

69. Isok. 8.82, on Raubitschek's interpretation, *TAPA* 72 (1941):356–62; Meiggs, *AE* 433–34; for the display of private wealth in the latter half of the fifth century, e.g., Plut. *Alk.* 4; cf. also Attic Stele VI.172 with the discussion by Amyx, *Hesp.* 27 (1958):208; for modern discussion, see, e.g., Vickers, *JHS* 105 (1985):112–17; Garland, *BSA* 77 (1988):127, suggests, from the lack of evidence to the contrary, that the Athenians began to build enclosures around private tombs in the last decades of the fifth century. See also Stupperich, *Staatsbegräbnis und Privatgrabmal*, 239–50.

70. Arist. *Pol.* 1252 b29; 1280 b35.

71. So, e.g., Arist. *Pol.* 1256 b1–10 makes clear that self-sufficiency includes exchange with others.

the poleis of the empire to be the property of the city.[72] Allusion to Athens' former allies not only as "subjects" but also as "slaves" reinforces the notion of property ownership.[73] Accordingly, if Athens' wealth comes from its own property (that is, the *arche*) and is used for the preservation of that *arche* and, in turn, for the preservation of the polis, then there can be nothing morally wrong with such wealth. Although this line of reasoning may have a sophistic resonance, there is no indication in any contemporary source that plundering the wealth of the Aegean was considered a heinous act for which the Athenians would necessarily pay dearly.

We can clearly appreciate now how the notion of utility, which occupies such a prominent place in the *History* in general, is key to understanding Thucydides' treatment of wealth, with its paramount emphasis on expenditure, *dapane*, together with surplus, *periousia chrematon*. A final important consideration is the repository for most of the city's wealth, namely, its sacred treasuries. As the bulk of Athens' vast surplus was not merely stored in sacred treasuries but was actually considered the property of the gods, there could be neither impropriety nor hubris—especially if when money was removed, it was taken as a loan, repaid with interest. Indeed, this would reasonably be an effective way of insuring against hubris.[74]

In briefly exploring Thucydides' unique treatment of wealth and power, I have attempted to suggest what may have been a complex blend of factors underlying the historian's distancing of wealth from morality. In this context, I have offered what seem to me to be important considerations in understanding the historical and historiographical background for Thucydides' views on money and power. We are now ready to begin the investigation into the role of financial resources in the *History*, 1–5.24.

72. Thuc. 2.63.2; 3.37.2; *IG* I³ 156.2, 15; *IG* I³ 19.9 (κρατδσιν restored).
73. E.g., Thuc. 1.121.5, 122.2; 4.87.3; cf. 1.8.3; 2.63.
74. Cf. Plato *Laws* 745a: individuals who possessed more wealth than allowed in Plato's state would avoid prosecution by giving over their surplus to the state and the gods.

CHAPTER ONE

Financial Resources in the Archaeology

Any study of Thucydides' thought must begin with the Archaeology, the opening chapters of the work (1.1–23), in which the historian analyzes the most notable earlier attempts at power as evidence to support his claim that the Peloponnesian War was "the greatest disturbance" in history, "more worthy of making a *logos* about" than any previous event (1.1).[1] In an important respect, these chapters are the key to the work as a whole; for, as has long been recognized, the Archaeology introduces many of "the formative ideas of the *History*."[2] It is of considerable importance, therefore, that one consistent, developed thread running throughout the Archaeology is the function of financial resources in the development of power. This has not gone unnoticed. De Romilly noted the emphasis in the Archaeology on the underpinnings of Athenian power, its navy and wealth.[3] Thucydidean scholars and Greek historians generally have recognized the author's rejection of the heroic and his

---

1. That the Archaeology as a whole is written as an argument intended to support Thucydides' view of the "greatness" of the Peloponnesian War compared with earlier conflicts (as J. H. Finley, Jr., observed long ago, *Three Essays*, 167) and that he therefore draws support only from those previous conflicts and powers that were commonly believed to be the greatest explain the lack of comprehensiveness troublesome to those who ascribe to Thucydides the intention of generally surveying ancient history or of writing a "history of progress"; e.g., Täubler, *Archaeologie;* de Romilly, *Histoire et raison,* 240–41; de Romilly, *TAI,* 67; Canfora, *REG* 90 (1977):460; Hunter, *Klio* 62 (1980): 205–7; Hunter, *PPHT,* 167–68.

2. J. H. Finley, Jr., *Thucydides,* 87; also e.g., de Romilly, *Histoire et raison,* 260–62; Woodhead, *Nature of Power,* 12–13; Schneider, *Information und Absicht,* 118–19; French, *G&R* 27 (1980):26; Hunter, *PPHT,* 45.

3. de Romilly, *Histoire et raison,* 247; see her important discussion of the Archaeology generally, 240–98.

"unsentimental approach," as W. R. Connor puts it, in which attention to *Machtstellung* reveals the significance, emphasized by repetition, of "self-interest and fear in individual conduct, of naval might and financial reserves in military matters, and of imperialism as a source of power and greatness."[4] The full significance, however, of the role of financial resources in the Archaeology itself and, more so, its implications for the *History* proper, have perhaps not been sufficiently appreciated. Accordingly, this chapter will examine Thucydides' treatment of the role of financial resources in the Archaeology, in order to understand better his perspective on finances in the development of power generally.

In the Archaeology, Thucydides selects the greatest and most noteworthy of previous, mainly military, enterprises in order to compare them to his subject and prove them wanting by means of new criteria that he lays out. What determined his starting point? He chose the episodes from the past that his contemporaries believed to be the most significant,[5] but he actually begins his argument (1.2.1) much earlier than these examples. Why would Thucydides, keenly attuned to the precariousness of establishing the accuracy of ancient history (1.1.3, 1.20), begin in the shadowy, virtually irretrievable past? An answer may lie in his attention to the development of the preconditions of power.

In the opening of the *History*, Thucydides explains how he knew even at the beginning of the war that it would be great and worthy of recording: "I took as indicators that both sides were at their height in every preparation" (*he pasa paraskeue*, *1.1.1*).[6] His measure, that is, was the conditions at the beginning of the war rather than its results; his prescience, however, was confirmed by the length of the war and the suffering it inflicted. Moreover, he was not interested simply in the fact of the level of preparedness of both sides on the eve of the conflict, but also in the origins and development of military preparation that culminated in extraordinary *dunamis*.

This interest may explain why Thucydides began where he did. In his view, the unsurpassed preparedness of both Athens and Sparta in 431 resulted from the convergence of several crucial components of *dunamis*.[7] Thus, Thucydides likely began the Archaeology at the point in history when at least one of these components could be traced to any signif-

---

4. Connor, *Thucydides*, 27. See also Kleingünther, ΠΡΩΤΟΣ ΕΥΡΕΤΗΣ, 131–35.
5. I infer this implicitly since Thucydides in the Archaeology seeks to minimize the relative greatness of previous conflicts commonly regarded as most significant, e.g., the Trojan War, Persian Wars. Accordingly, tradition is as useful as verifiable fact for Thucydides' purpose. Thus, he can reasonably base an argument on events known only by tradition (ἀκοῇ, e.g., 1.4).
6. For a comprehensive study of this key term in Thucydides, see Allison, *PPT*.
7. Cf. Allison, *Hermes* 109 (1981):119; and Allison, *PPT*, 11ff.

icant extent. From there, the historian could begin to analyze the conditions that ultimately led to the events chosen as comparative examples for his argument on the magnitude and importance of the Peloponnesian War. In other words, Thucydides began this work by plotting the stages in the development of *paraskeue*. The factors he focuses on initially make clear the criteria used to judge the ability to achieve power (*dunamis*), growth (*auxesis*), and the state of preparedness. Let us now briefly follow these stages.

In 1.2.2, Thucydides notes the reason for the insecurity and instability of early settlements and, consequently, their continual migrations:

> It was because there were no commercial centers, nor did people even communicate with each other without fear either by land or sea; instead, each inhabited and reaped from the land just enough to subsist, without accumulating a store of *chremata* nor by sustaining agriculture, since it was unclear when someone would attack them and, given the lack of walls, deprive them of their land. Accordingly, harboring the belief that they could get their necessary daily subsistence anywhere, they moved from one place to another readily, and therefore built no cities of any great size nor had any other resources.

Even for this early stage of civilization, Thucydides is thinking of the accumulation of *chremata;* already, in other words, he considers these early Greeks not merely as subsistence dwellers but as potential amassers of surplus wealth, a precondition, he argues, of stability. From the connection between geographical location and wealth, it follows that communities on trading routes would be the strongest. It is important to recognize the concern in this passage with external relations, clear from reference to the lack of *emporia* and the need for security. An abundance of *chremata* would enable one's polis to become strong and secure and to withstand attack. Thus, in this analysis of early settlements, Thucydides focuses on the negative elements that impede stability and security; stated in positive terms, he is arguing that wealth, among other factors, is necessary for lasting strength.[8] This grants immediate prominence to *chremata* as a precondition of power.

In chapters 2 through 4 of book 1 generally, Thucydides details not what we may call the "indices of civilization," but rather the hindrances to strength and *auxesis*.[9] As in 1.2.2, he focuses on what was missing from these loosely defined early communities: they lacked strong cities, settled agriculture, fortifications, *periousia chrematon*, and common effort and unity. Arguments are presented for both the failure of pre-Trojan

---

8. I shall consider below Thucydides' definition of *chremata*, where we can examine his usage more broadly. For now, it is sufficient to translate as "wealth."

9. The phrase is from Hunter, *Klio* 62 (1980):205; *PPHT*, 21.

peoples to grow in strength in 1.2.4–6 and the view that stasis prevents *auxesis*. Fertile land produces stasis, but as Attica lacked fertile land, it was therefore free from stasis and became a haven for refugees from regions in internal unrest. Immigration resulted in overpopulation and, as a consequence, colonization. Most important, Attica was an exceptional region in which *auxesis* did occur, unlike other parts of Greece.[10]

A further deficiency of these early peoples emerges in 1.3: lack of unity and common effort. Weakness and isolation prevented common enterprises before the expedition to Troy, and underlying this event were two preconditions: a sense of identity as Greeks and the use of the sea. The latter is crucial to Thucydides' next subject, Minos, who is introduced to provide the earliest evidence of the kind of naval activity that made possible such later expeditions as the Trojan campaign (1.4.1, explaining 1.3.4).

MINOS

Minos, Thucydides begins, was "the earliest ruler known from tradition to have acquired a fleet and gained control over most of what is now called the Hellenic Sea: he ruled the Kykladic islands and was himself the first colonizer of most of them, after expelling the Karians and establishing his sons as leaders." Thus, Thucydides starts to analyze the first positive example of the development of power, in sharp contrast to the earlier negative instances designed to show the factors responsible for its absence. His intention to determine the origins of naval activity is made clear by references to "the most ancient" (παλαίτατος) and "the first" (πρῶτος), as is his attention only to significant ventures, that is, those undertaken by the greatest power of the time.

Thucydides, then, introduces Minos as the earliest example of a ruler whose power derived from mastery on the sea.[11] He focuses, therefore,

---

10. For a detailed discussion of the text of 1.2, see Marshall, *CQ* 25 (1975):26–40; Biraschi, *PP* 39 (1984):5–22, with earlier bibliography on this controversial passage.

11. Herodotos mentions Minos as well, in his treatment of Polykrates (3.122.2), using language of which Thucydides' own remarks are strongly reminiscent. Thucydides, too, mentions Polykrates later (1.13.6) for "possessing naval strength and rendering the islands subject," and for having taken Rheneia and dedicated it to Apollo. Chapter 4, however, directly contrasts with Herodotos 3.122 in relating the early thalassocracy of Minos. Herodotos is often thought here to be more critical than Thucydides (e.g., by How and Wells, *Comm.* 1, on 3.122; Gomme, *Greek Attitude*, 117; Vidal-Naquet, *Revue de l'histoire des religions* 157 [1960]:65–69. Hunter, *PPHT*, 19); cf. also M. I. Finley, *Use and Abuse*, 18. One should note, however, that Herodotos relates Minos' adventures and death elsewhere (1.171.2–3, 173.2; 7.169.2, 170.1), suggesting that he accepts the basic historicity of Minos, and he notes in 3.122 that Polykrates was the first one known of *besides* Minos. Of relevance in

on those factors that he has judged, partly from probability, essential to the Kretan king's power: his navy, colonization, and island empire and also the likelihood that Minos eradicated piracy, which Thucydides ties to the control of revenue.[12] The very exploitation of an argument based on probability (ὡς εἰκός) in this instance is important testimony to Thucydides' belief in the connection between revenue and power. Indeed, the link with piracy explains the usefulness of Minos to Thucydides' argument on the close relationship between wealth, fleet, and empire. For it was, in his view, likely that Minos' continued suppression of piracy[13] increased his wealth by insuring the flow of revenue to himself.[14] The significance of piracy, therefore, is that it constituted a threat to a crucial component of Minos' power, his wealth. As Garlan notes, Thucydides ties piracy directly, positively and negatively, to the development of (state) power.[15]

Thus far there has been no explicit statement about the precise connection between the use of revenue and the achievement of naval power; but in presenting a picture of regional power stabilized and extended by the elimination of piracy, by the increase in revenues, and by the control of the sea, Thucydides implies a causal relationship among regular revenue, naval power, and control over others (*arche*). The link between sea power and colonization is also clear: only the ability to navigate and to

---

3.122 is that Polykrates was the first human, whereas Minos, as Herodotos and everyone else knew, was of divine descent (as the son of Zeus and Europa [*Iliad* 13.450–54; 14. 321–22]). Cf. also de Romilly, *Histoire et raison*, 274–75.

12. Whether there was a traditional association between Minos and piracy or a tradition about piracy in the age before Minos must remain unknown. Minos was a frequent figure on the Athenian stage in the fifth century, most often portrayed as evil and cruel, especially by the tragedians ([Plato] *Minos* 318d; as Plutarch comments [*Thes.* 16.3]: "assuredly it reasonably is difficult for a man to bear when detested by a city which has a language and literature"), and he was the subject of several (lost) works (Ais. Κρῆσσαι; Soph. Μάντεις ἢ Πολύιδος; Δαίδαλος; Καμίκιοι; Eur. Κρῆτες; also, Ar. Κώκαλος and Δαίδαλος) in which one would not expect any connection with piracy. Plutarch does note Kleidemos' account that Jason purified the sea of pirates (Plut. *Thes.* 19). Cf. de Romilly, *ASNP* 35 (1966):161, who states that Thucydides used Homer to prove that piracy was normal before Minos. Hunter, *Klio* 62 (1980):193–94, assumes that the inferences Thucydides draws about Minos are all his own.

13. As is clear from the imperfect καθῄρει.

14. τοῦ τὰς προσόδους μᾶλλον ἰέναι αὐτῷ. The traditions about Minos' thalassocracy were widespread but probably did not include explicit reference to the means by which he obtained his wealth. Herodotos (1.171.2) insists that, to the best of his knowledge, Minos did not collect tribute from, at least, the Karians. Thucydides does not contradict this; Minos obtains *prosodoi* generally, not *phoros*. Although tribute can be included in the term "revenue," since the latter is used with reference both to the pirates and Minos, it is reasonable to suppose that here, as elsewhere, *prosodos* is not restricted to *phoros*.

15. Garlan, *DHA* 4 (1978):10.

use the sea safely allowed the establishment of colonies. Furthermore, colonization is a means of spreading one's own power over a larger area, with either direct or indirect benefit, as Thucydides later demonstrates in Minos' case: at the same time that the Kretan king was colonizing most of the islands, he was able to expel Karian and Phoinikian pirates from them.[16]

It is evident that piracy is of more than casual interest to Thucydides, as he follows his analysis of Minos' naval power with a discussion of piracy in general and its suppression (chapters 5, 7, and 8). The efficacy of this earliest type of "sea power" for acquiring goods and wealth, as well as its pervasiveness, is well brought out by the historian as he notes that pirates, operating with no hindrances, derived most of their livelihood (τὸν πλεῖστον τοῦ βίου) by this means (1.5.1). Accordingly, Minos' achievement is all the more significant. Thucydides explicitly ties the suppression of piracy not only to the resulting security but also to the ability to acquire *chremata* (especially 1.8.2–3).[17] It is worth looking closely at his discussion.

In 1.8.2, Thucydides examines the consequences of Minos' thalassocracy and suppression of piracy, noting an increase in navigation due to security on the seas. He then continues, "Those who lived by the sea had a more secure existence, now better able to obtain wealth (*chremata*) for themselves; some also walled [their cities] because of their increased wealth."[18] Greater use of the sea, thus, brings more wealth, which in turn prompts a community to build circuit walls and thereby stimulate the development of the polis itself. Thucydides then explains the circumstances that allowed for the concentration of wealth: "For the weaker, desiring gain, submitted to enslavement by the stronger; while the stronger, since they possessed surplus wealth (*periousias*), made the weaker cities subject" (8.3).

As in the case of his argument from probability about Minos, piracy, and revenue, Thucydides here interprets the traditions, deduces, and explains, his views shaped (it is reasonable to suppose) by his understanding of Athens' naval *arche*. It is becoming easy to discern a pattern:

16. Cf., among many later examples, Amphipolis, 4.108.1; cf. below, chapter 5, p. 175–76. Noting colonization here is therefore purposeful and part of the historian's evidence for an increase in power, *contra*, e.g., Ridley, *Hermes* 109 (1981):39–40, 44.

17. Piratical naval raids and their effect are not insignificant in the *History* proper, e.g., 2.32, 69.1; 3.51.2; 4.9.1, 53.3, 67.3; see McDonald, *AJP* 105 (1984):77–84. On Mediterranean piracy generally and its effectiveness as a way of acquiring wealth, see Garlan, *DHA* 4 (1978):1–16 (the same as, with a few changes, Garlan, *Guerre et économie*, 173–201), and Pritchett, *GSAW* 5:312–63.

18. καὶ οἱ παρὰ θάλασσαν ἄνθρωποι μᾶλλον ἤδη τὴν κτῆσιν τῶν χρημάτων ποιούμενοι βεβαιότερον ᾤκουν, καί τινες καὶ τείχη περιεβάλλοντο ὡς πλουσιώτεροι ἑαυτῶν γιγνόμενοι, 1.8.2–3.

a direct connection is once again made between power and wealth; it is implicit in the analysis that the powerful attained their strength through their wealth, that is, wealth is a means to power.

This analysis stands out as a fine illustration of Thucydides' conception of the development of power and the emergence of unequal relationships. It also reflects his view of human nature and behavior, in which those who are stronger will exert power over others, while those who are weaker will agree to submission (literally, "enslavement," δουλεία) because of a desire for gain (κέρδος). The common thread uniting the interests of both sides of the relationship is wealth: it enables power to be exerted and it motivates willingness to submit to a stronger power. This comment is revealing in its acknowledgment of the shared responsibility of ruler and subject in the development of an *arche*[19] and reflects a theory of behavior similar to Robinson's theory of collaboration, which was noted briefly in the Introduction.[20]

Thucydides generalizes about the period between the reign of Minos and the Trojan War and focuses on the use of the sea, the accumulation of wealth, and the control of the weaker by the stronger. His comments, however, easily lend themselves to further generalizing; this is surely not fortuitous. The historian is predisposed to see patterns of behavior, given his understanding of human nature. Thucydides' presentation in 1.8 allows the inference that the weak are party to their own subjugation *in general* because of a desire for gain; the reader likewise draws the conclusion that those who possess *periousiai* [*chrematon*] will generally use them to control others. We shall encounter this argument again.

AGAMEMNON AND THE TROJAN EXPEDITION

Thucydides' perspective on Agamemnon and Troy is similar to that of the preceding analyses. Beginning in chapter 9, he transmits the essentials of the Trojan legend, but he revises the reasons for Agamemnon's preeminence, presenting a novel interpretation of the Trojan War, and especially its protracted length. As in the case of Minos, hearsay or tradition is as important, in a sense, as verifiable fact, since what matters is what people believe.[21] Because the Trojan expedition was considered

19. Rabel, *CJ* 80 (1984):9, n. 8, brings out this point.
20. "Collaboration"; see above, p. 8–9.
21. One cannot argue, on the basis of a comparison between Herodotos' and Thucydides' treatment of the Trojan legend, that Thucydides is less critical than Herodotos (2.118–120); the authors' purposes in dealing with the legends are fundamentally different, *contra* Hunter, *Klio* 62 (1980):192–93. To Thucydides, the λόγοι about the ἔργα προγεγενημένα (viz. 1.1.1) have already been made; this applies to that transmitted ἀκοῇ as well. In the Archaeology he will show that the reasoning by which they have been judged

one of the greatest events of the Greek past, Thucydides had to demonstrate its weakness to support his own argument. He did so through his own opinion (μοι δοκεῖ) and deduction, through a cold, dispassionate rationality which derived from, but ultimately rejected, the epic tradition of his day. Thus, Agamemnon was able to assemble the expedition to Troy not because of the oaths of Tyndareos but because of his superior *dunamis*, which made him preeminent among his contemporaries. From what did this *dunamis* stem? His predominance was derived originally, Thucydides states, from Pelops, who arrived from Asia "with a store of money" (*plethei chrematon*) and thereby acquired power.

It is characteristic of Thucydides not only to focus on power, but also to inquire into its origins. In tracing the origin of Agamemnon's *dunamis* to Pelops' *plethos chrematon*, Thucydides completely overrides a fundamental traditional belief in the authority of oaths in favor of an argument that makes the decisive factor strength through wealth.[22] The explicit statement in 1.9.3–4 that Agamemnon added to his inherited power by acquiring a fleet and ruling over many islands further confirms for the reader Thucydides' argument that wealth and ships must be linked in order to produce *arche* and achieve *dunamis*. Indeed, Thucydides' treatment of Agamemnon is reminiscent of that of Minos: both possessed the necessary ingredients of *dunamis*, namely, *chremata* and *nautikon*.

Thucydides' analysis of the Trojan War forms part of his argument about Agamemnon's power; here the historian's perspective on *chremata* is especially striking. At the end of chapter 10, he concludes that the Greek force assembled at Troy was modest in number (οὐ πολλοί). However, this was not, he explains, from a shortage of men (ὀλιγανθρωπία), but rather from a lack of *chremata* (ἀχρηματία):

> For due to insufficient supplies they brought a smaller army, thinking that they could acquire what they needed from the land while they were at war; but when, having arrived, they prevailed in battle (as they must have, for otherwise they would not have been able to construct fortifications around their camp), they appear not even from that point to have used all their strength; rather, they turned to farming the Chersonese and to plundering due to their insufficient supplies. . . . Whereas if they had come with plentiful supplies and, having drawn together their entire force, had waged

---

great is faulty, not that the ἔργα themselves did not occur. It is to be noted that neither does Herodotos dispute the "historicity" of the Trojan War itself.

22. On the link between the rejection of the importance of oaths here and the absence of mention of oaths in Thucydides' treatment of the origins of the Delian League, see below, p. 58.

war continuously, without resorting to pillaging and farming, they would easily have prevailed in battle and been victorious; this is certainly evident from the fact that even when they were not all together in a body but had only part of their force available, they were able to resist the Trojans. Thus, if they had settled down to a siege, they would have taken Troy in less time and with less trouble. (1.11.1–2)

The argument of this chapter, presented in rather elegant chiastic form, may be reduced thus: the problem at Troy was *achrematia*, for the Greeks lacked supplies (*aporia trophes*). If they had come with an abundance of supplies (*periousia trophe*), they would easily have won early on. But what does *achrematia* mean here? Is it equivalent to *trophe*—that is to say, is it being used with reference to goods and supplies, or in a financial sense?[23]

First, if *chremata* in 1.11 is synonymous with *trophe*, the resulting redundancy is difficult to accept in an analysis clearly sensitive to style and presentation of argument. But there is also a more substantive objection. Thucydides uses the same term, *achrematia*, again at the end of chapter 11 to sum up the difficulties encountered not only in the Trojan expedition but in all other early ventures as well. Although he is not explicit, the instances of *chremata* are most intelligible as conveying the idea of financial resources in that *chremata* is accumulated and connected with naval power. In 1.2.2, a reserve, *periousia chrematon*, is clearly something distinct from *trophe*, and its absence helps to explain the instability of early settlements. Further on, in 1.7, *periousiai chrematon* belonging to those on or near the sea are linked with the building of walls; this context again suggests financial resources, not supplies. Similarly, in 1.8.3–4, Thucydides connects the acquisition (*ktesis*) and accumulation (*periousia*) of *chremata* with the building of defensive walls and suggests a causal link between *chremata* and naval power. Finally, Thucydides argues that the source of Pelops' power was his *plethos chrematon;* this context confirms that the historian is referring to wealth, though not necessarily financial in nature.

The problem is one of translation, not, I think, of Thucydides' meaning. I have shown that, in 1.11, *chremata* differs in nature from *trophe*, in other words, that *chremata* is not equivalent to "supplies." To get from there, however, to determining whether in the Archaeology, *chremata*

23. This is a different problem from that of the synonymity of *trophe* and *misthos*, and *sitos* and *misthos*, discussed by Pritchett, *GSAW* 1:4–6; there military pay in the form of rations is at issue. Pritchett argues that the distinction between pay and money for rations did not exist in the fifth century, as it did later on. But in the Archaeology, at least, Thucydides does distinguish between money and supplies. ἀχρηματία is an unusual term, occurring only here in 1.11 in Thucydides; cf. also Dion. Hal. 7.24; Eus. Mynd., fr. 7.

means "money" or other forms of wealth is a difficult step to take, but one which becomes easier as the Archaeology proceeds.[24] In general, the instances of *chremata* thus far suggest a concern above all with usable wealth: in particular in 1.11, as in 1.8.3, Thucydides' discussion necessitates the idea of expenditure, whether put in positive or negative terms. In the case of the Trojan expedition, the Greeks did not have the *chremata* to acquire *trophe;* he calls this condition *achrematia*. It is significant that, once again, as in the analyses of Minos and Agamemnon, Thucydides probes back to the origins, in this case, tracing the cause of failure or weakness not simply to *aporia trophe*, but ultimately to a state of *achrematia*, which explains why the Greeks could not procure the necessary supplies (*trophe*). Therefore, Thucydides found the Trojan expedition deficient in complete *paraskeue*.

TYRANNY

Having established the central importance of *chremata* and *nautika*, or financial resources and ships, Thucydides goes on to consider the phenomenon of tyranny (1.13):

> As Hellas was becoming more powerful and the acquisition of *chremata* a greater possibility than before, tyrannies were set up in poleis in many areas, since revenues were increasing (before this there had been hereditary kings with fixed prerogatives); Hellas was fitted out with ships and turned more to the sea. (1.13.1)

Tyranny merits inclusion in the chronological progression of Thucydides' argument for two reasons, both related to financial resources: wealth is the tyrants' means to power, and the tyrants occupy a pivotal place, in his view, in the development of poleis attached commercially and militarily to the sea.[25] That is, the most significant result of the acquisition of *chremata*, in Thucydides' view, is the building of fleets. Thus, financial resources, maintained and replenished through revenue, are a crucial prerequisite for naval power.

During the rule of tyrants, according to Thucydides' analysis, two of the essential criteria for extraordinary *dunamis*—money and ships—were present for the first time in history. Yet, as he brings out in 1.17, a third element of *dunamis* was absent, namely, unity, for the tyrants were concerned primarily with maintaining the security of their own position in a polis. Thus, they could not accomplish anything notable, except con-

---

24. See appendix to chapter 1.
25. As Gomme noted: "The tyrants are mentioned because the increasing wealth was their chief cause, and because in turn they added to it, and paid especial attention to naval power" (*HCT* 1, ad loc.).

trolling their neighbors, an area in which the tyrants in Sicily were most successful. The Sicilian tyrants represent a development in the use of wealth for power, as M. I. Finley observes, "whereby military commanders obtained control of substantial financial resources and used them for personal, political ends, for the seizure or the expansion or the stabilization of power."[26] It is here that the similarity between these archaic tyrannies and the Athenian empire begins and ends; for, as Connor points out, Thucydides' depiction of early tyrannies as unable to accomplish much and excessively concerned with security suggests contrast, not comparison.[27]

KORINTH AND NAVAL WARFARE

In analyzing the significance of tyranny in 1.13.1, Thucydides perceives a cause-and-effect relationship between the acquisition (*ktesis*) of *chremata*, increased *prosodoi*, and naval strength; he immediately considers more closely one specific historical example that illustrates his arguments about the combination of reserve, revenue, and ships. The Korinthians, he notes, are said to have been the first to use near-modern ship technology and to build triremes. He cites a tradition giving credit to a Korinthian, Ameinokles, for building four ships for the Samians and identifies the earliest sea battle as having occurred between the Korinthians and Kerkyraians some 260 years before (1.13.2–4). Finally, he explains the reasons for Korinth's early nautical achievements: Korinth had always had an *emporion* because of its geographical position on overland trading routes, and thus it was very wealthy (*chremasi dunatoi*), as the poets confirm in referring to the place as "rich" (ἀφνειόν). Furthermore, as navigation increased generally, the Korinthians built ships and eliminated piracy, and with an *emporion* able to take advantage of sea as well as land routes, they made their city powerful (*dunaten*) by means of revenue (*chrematon prosodo*) (1.13.5).

This analysis is the positive counterpart of the arguments presented in 1.2 detailing the causes of weakness in early Greece. The Korinthians' *dunamis* is explicitly tied to their wealth in the form of reserve and revenue, which enabled them to attain naval power. Thucydides drives home the extent of their revenues not only by drawing attention to their near monopoly of commerce but also by mentioning their suppression of piracy. Characteristically, the historian goes beyond the mere fact of wealth and its link to naval power to seek the origins of Korinthian wealth; he finds that geography was the crucial determinant. Finally, he highlights

26. Finley, *Ancient History*, 83.
27. Connor, "Tyrannis Polis," 105–6.

the Korinthians' obvious vigor in exploiting their natural advantage and in gaining preeminence in the Greek world as a commercial and naval power, thus stressing their active role in developing *dunamis*, as he had done earlier in the examples of Minos and Agamemnon. Here, however, for the first time, the polis emerges as the beneficiary of this prosperity and consequent power. This marks a decisive stage of development: previously, power was concentrated in the hands of a single ruler.

In 1.13.6–1.14, Thucydides identifies the most powerful navies following the Korinthians' achievement, citing those of the Ionians, Polykrates, and the Phokaians; the importance of these three, he adds, was diminished by their lack of triremes. He notes that the Sicilian tyrants and Korinthians began to maintain a significant fleet of these warships only shortly before the Persian Wars. Thus, evidently measuring naval power by numbers of triremes, not ships in general, he traces the first navy of any real account to the Athenian fleet built at Themistokles' instigation for the war with Aigina and defense against the anticipated Persian attack. Even this navy, he comments, was limited by the lack of complete decks (1.14.3). Thucydides summarizes the preceding argument in 1.15.1:

> Such, then, were the fleets of the Hellenes, those of both ancient and later times. Those possessing them, nevertheless, derived great strength from them, both from the revenue of *chremata* which came in, and from ruling over others.

Strength comes from *prosodos chrematon* and from *arche*. But the strength of the great rulers or poleis before the Peloponnesian War could not compare to the power mustered at the beginning of that event, for the reason given at the end of 1.17: they did nothing in common.

SPARTA AND ATHENS

In 1.18–19, Thucydides turns to the development of Sparta and Athens, to the growing division between them despite the Persian Wars, and to the military preparation through which both cities achieved unprecedented power in Greece. The analysis presented in the Archaeology has not only provided the evidence to support Thucydides' assertion about the weakness of *kineseis* before the Peloponnesian War but has also established the historical context for the development of Athenian power in the fifth century. Since the historian has already directly linked the origins of naval military activity to the acquisition of financial resources, we expect to be informed likewise about the role played by financial resources in the development of Athenian power. Sparta, however, does not fit into the same historical pattern. In 1.18, Thucydides notes that the key to Sparta's power is its influence over others; the significance of this becomes clear in 1.19, which discusses the concrete means by which Sparta and Athens were able to exert their control:

> And so the Lakedaimonians held the leadership of allies who did not pay tribute but insured that they were governed by oligarchies so that they would work in the Spartan interest, while the Athenians, on the other hand, having gradually taken over their allies' fleets, with the exception of Chios and Lesbos, rendered the rest tributary.

The external measure of *dunamis* is the ability to compel; this demonstrates in practical terms the importance of both Athens' naval *arche* and Sparta's authority by virtue of its unsurpassed military superiority on land maintained by a stable *politeia* and the ability to impose similar *politeiai* on its allies.

* * *

We need now to consider the overall argument and its implications presented in these opening chapters of the *History*. In his treatment of the power of Minos, Pelops, and Agamemnon, as well as in his discussion of the weakness of early communities, Thucydides manipulates and reworks traditions in order to make repeatedly a central point about naval power and also to demonstrate the method and criteria by which he analyzes power. The pattern that emerges illumines the purpose of the Archaeology as a whole and its relationship to the rest of the *History*. In 1.1, Thucydides presents no specific reasons for asserting the primacy of his subject other than the general magnitude and all-encompassing scope of the Peloponnesian War. However, as he begins in the Archaeology to support his contention with evidence from past events considered to be "great" from the standpoint of military might and scale, we quickly learn the precise criteria by which he reveals, analyzes, and judges their significance. These are financial resources (consisting of revenue and reserve), navy, *arche*, and consequently unity; together, these lead to superior *dunamis*. Of these criteria, the one that is of central importance as the sine qua non of naval power is financial resources, consisting not simply of *chremata* itself, but rather of *periousia chrematon*, supplemented by *prosodos*.

Thucydides, then, in reworking the traditions concerning power, presents a view of military success that differs fundamentally from the customary explanations derived chiefly from the epic, heroic conventions. He does not reject the events embedded in traditions; rather, he considers the reasoning underlying earlier accounts to be faulty.[28] Thus, ele-

---

28. That is, as already noted (n. 21, above), he attempts to demonstrate that the *logoi* about past events (τὰ προγεγενημένα, 1.1.1) are faulty, not that those events did not occur.

ments such as individual prowess, bravery, or *nomoi* to which military success is often ascribed, for example, divine favor, retribution, or oaths, have no place in his dissection of power. *Dunamis*, in this context, is material and tangible, not abstract. Success and failure are measured by the presence or absence, respectively, of *periousiai chrematon;* the greatest *kineseis* of the past had as their basis the goal and/or use of profits and power.

Given the purpose of the Archaeology, in support of which Thucydides rejected traditional beliefs about the great military events of the past partly by redefining the criteria by which they were implicitly judged, its polemical tone is not surprising. Thucydides intends to set the record straight on the question of what precisely does power consist. We cannot know whether his particular kind of "nuts and bolts" analysis of heroic traditions was unique or in what specific respects it was highly original. Certainly, the rationalizing spirit of the Archaeology has much in common with other literary products of the late fifth-century sophistic climate.[29] It may be similar in spirit to other contemporary *archaiologiai*, but our knowledge is too meager for a fruitful discussion.[30] We know that Hellanikos wrote an *Archaiologia* as part of his work on the history of Athens, as did other Atthidographers as well. Their treatment of myths especially popular in tragic works, for example, those dealing with Minos, put into prose rationalized accounts that reduced the fantastic to the realistic, the heroic to the mundane.[31] According to Jacoby, the Atthidographers "very audaciously made an historical narrative of the τραγικώτατος μῦθος," though often not entirely eliminating the wondrous or surreal.[32]

It is reasonable to suppose that Thucydides went further, taking an even more ostentatiously revisionist, analytical stance on the use of myth, extracting from the traditional materials the minimum elements necessary as evidence for his new treatment of power. Most important, unlike other treatments of the past, Thucydides' Archaeology is not an end in itself, a reinterpreted history of early civilization, an excursus on progress, or a general introduction to the work, but rather an analysis of a group of events carefully selected to support his views on revenue, fleet, and *arche*.[33]

With a clinical eye, Thucydides analyzes the *phusis* of power empiri-

29. De Romilly, *ASNP* 35 (1966):159.
30. See Connor, *Thucydides*, 22–23, and the references in n. 8.
31. Such as Hellanikos' account of the treaty between Athens and Minos (323a F14).
32. Jacoby, *Atthis*, 136.
33. As Erbse has noted, *AA* 10 (1961):19–34. Indeed, given the purpose of 1.1–19, the term "Archaeology" is hardly warranted and is certainly misleading.

cally and breaks it down into discrete, nonsupernatural components that must be combined and exploited by human agency in order for power to result. Then, based on a conviction of the consistency of human nature in accordance with circumstances, he draws conclusions about the anatomy of *arche* and *dunamis* that could be applied universally. What are his conclusions?

In these early chapters of the *History*, Thucydides presents several important lessons about power, in such a way as to suggest their universality: that revenue and wealth are tied to naval power (Minos, Agamemnon, tyrants, Korinth, Athens); that might derived from *chremata* compels unity (Agamemnon, Athens); that naval power through the accumulation (and use) of wealth can be increased in a way that land power cannot (Minos, Korinth, Athens); that reserves, not emergency provisioning, are necessary for success in long wars (Trojan expedition); and, finally, that exploitation of inherited power can be key in developing overall strength (Pelops). The principles of selection used by Thucydides in producing this extended comparative argument reveal the criteria he thinks are crucial for assessing and explaining naval power historically. His method, moreover, is designed to promote a particular response: it conditions the reader to expect similarities between the examples presented in the Archaeology and Athens' *arche*. Indeed, the emphasis on financial resources in the Archaeology surely is explained by an abiding concern with the intimate link between financial resources and naval power in his own day, and this fosters a strong presumption that he will be attentive to this relationship in the rest of the work. We shall explore in the following chapters whether and, if so, how, these expectations are met. For as we shall see, the argument developed systematically in the Archaeology directly informs the narrative to come. This will become especially clear as we consider the origins of the Delian League, the focus of much of the next chapter.

APPENDIX: FINANCIAL TERMINOLOGY IN THE ARCHAEOLOGY

It is important to try to determine what Thucydides means when he mentions *chremata* in reference to early Greek societies. In his analysis of ancient warfare and power, he expresses himself in such a way as to stress the connection between the past and present; thus, when he arrives at the fifth century, he uses the same terminology and method as for the earlier periods (cf. the remarks of Jacoby, *Atthis*, 87). Accordingly, he speaks in 1.19 of the state of preparation (*paraskeue*) on both the Lakedaimonian and Athenian sides and refers to the *chremata* that the Athenians received from their allies as assessed tribute. But in Thucydides' conception, has the definition of *chremata* changed from that used elsewhere in the Archaeology?

In Thucydides' time, *chremata* could refer not only to coined money but also to objects of monetary value and, for example, sacred treasure generally; it is therefore an ambiguous term, and the context must provide its specific application. In 1.19, *chremata* clearly refers to coined money; but what about earlier instances? The contexts for the word earlier in Archaeology fairly consistently suggest expenditure with the aim of acquiring power and, therefore, something distinct from supplies or provisions. This seems to me to be its meaning in chapters 2.2, 7, 8.3, 9.2, 11.1, 11.2, 13.1, 15.1, and 19. Its meaning in 13.5 in connection with the wealth of the Korinthians ([οἱ Κορίνθιοι] χρήμασί τε δυνατοὶ ἦσαν, ὡς καὶ τοῖς παλαιοῖς ποιηταῖς δεδήλωται. ἀφνειὸν γὰρ ἐπωνόμασαν τὸ χωρίον) is not certain in itself. But taken in its overall context (in particular with the sense of the following sentence, ἐπειδή τε οἱ Ἕλληνες μᾶλλον ἔπλῳζον, τὰς ναῦς κτησάμενοι τὸ λῃστικὸν καθῄρουν παρέχοντες ἀμφότερα δυνατὴν ἔσχον χρημάτων προσόδῳ τὴν πόλιν) it seems likely that the definition of *chremata* here too implies expenditure. To argue on the basis of other passages would only be circular; except at the reference to tribute in 1.19, it cannot be proved that Thucydides intends only this restricted meaning for *chremata*. But one can draw support from the use of *trophe*, which seems to me distinct from *chremata*, as well from the fact that Thucydides' analysis consistently poses the problem of one's ability to obtain something, either food (1.11.1), or a fleet (1.13.1), to cite just two examples. This suggests that he is concerned with one's financial competence and, especially, one's financial surplus (*periousia*). The term *prosodos*, on the other hand, is more ambiguous in meaning. In 1.13.1, in connection with tyranny, *prosodoi* apparently refers to financial income. Explicit reference to financial revenue occurs in 1.13.5, with the phrase *chrematon prosodo*. But in chapter 4, where he speaks of Minos' revenues, certainty is, I think, impossible.

CHAPTER TWO

Financial Resources in the Pentekontaetia

"I regard it as the truest explanation [for why the war began], although the one least able to be articulated, that the Athenians, increasing their power and engendering fear in the Lakedaimonians, made recourse to war necessary."[1] This sentence, polemical in its implied opposition to common beliefs about the causes of the war, informs the Pentekontaetia in the same way that Thucydides' initial assertion about the merit of his subject did the Archaeology. For just as the Archaeology contained the argument and evidence to support the premise that no previous war was as great as the Peloponnesian War, so the Pentekontaetia attempts to present a cogent argument to support the ἀληθεστάτη πρόφασις, the "truest explanation" of the war.[2] Both of these highly analytical, argumentative

---

1. 1.23.6. The translation and meaning of this sentence will always be controversial. See Ostwald, ΑΝΑΓΚΗ, 1–5, for a useful summary of the various interpretations and important bibliography. Ostwald, whose starting point is the absence of an object after the verb ἀναγκάσαι, argues that the ἀληθεστάτη πρόφασις was an abstract ἀνάγκη, necessity "imposed by external factors over which one has no control," but which does not mean that they are not "intelligible and rationally explicable" (8); the series of events that culminated in the Peloponnesian War "followed a necessary course, which was in itself not self-evident" (4). One difficulty with this interpretation, in my view, is that Thucydides makes "the Athenians" the subject of the verb ἀναγκάσαι; he does not seem to be thinking in abstract, but in concrete, terms about the "truest explanation"; that is to say, he places responsibility for the war on the Athenians, not even "Athenian imperialism" generally (so de Romilly, TAI, 18). The growing power of the Athenians and the consequent fear that it instilled in the Spartans explain what precisely about the Athenians drove the participants to war, but Thucydides states neither that δύναμις nor that ἀνάγκη caused the war. His focus is instead on human behavior and action.

2. The main support for the ἀληθεστάτη πρόφασις only comes now in the narrative, beginning at 1.89, since Thucydides first takes the reader through the events and speeches that pertain to his other preliminary task, to give an account of the αἰτίαι καὶ διαφοραί,

sections of the *History* help to define, clarify, and expand upon key statements such as 1.1.2 and 1.23.6 and, in the process, reveal Thucydides' central ideas about power.³

In the Archaeology, Thucydides analyzes power by tracing its origins to the points in history when it surfaced, isolating its essential preconditions and criteria (or their absence to explain the lack of significant military achievement) in *periousia chrematon*, *prosodos*, and *nautikon*, and thereby demonstrating the factors necessary for its increase (*auxesis*). As noted in the last chapter, Thucydides' approach has larger implications and aims: the historian was so consistent in singling out these same elements in his analyses of events he ultimately dismissed as mere flirtations with military greatness compared to the Peloponnesian War that the reader expects him to judge Athenian power by identical criteria. In this chapter we shall examine Thucydides' approach to the relationship of financial resources and naval power in the Pentekontaetia; for it is especially in this section of the work that we should be able to determine his views on the anatomy of power and to assess the value of the Archaeology as an introduction to the historian's ideas and methodology informing the work as a whole.

The Pentekontaetia, and especially 1.89–96, is introduced by an assertion made in 1.88. Thucydides has, between the Archaeology and Pentekontaetia, presented the grievances and disputes that finally set off the conflict of 431 and has completed relating the relevant *logoi* on the eve of war, which dealt both with these specific complaints and with issues of the Athenian empire more generally.⁴ The immediate consequence was that the Lakedaimonians voted to go to war, but not, accord-

---

"grievances and disputes," which explain the timing of the war and which help to illustrate the focus on these problems in prewar discussions rather than on what Thucydides believed to be the real issue.

3. The need to support his view of Athens' *dunamis* and of the reason for its effect on the Spartans explains the selective nature of this section of the *History* and the strict focus on Athenian, rather than on both Athenian and Spartan, power. It is Athenian power that inspires the fear crucial to Thucydides' theory of the origins of the Peloponnesian War (on the importance of fear in the work generally, see de Romilly, *C&M* 17 [1956]:119–27). Moreover, the basis and nature of Spartan power were obvious and uncontroversial, while Thucydides, as he makes clear, regarded Athenian power as something unprecedented in the context of traditional Greek military experience. The Pentecontaetia is, therefore, not intended as a historical sketch of the fifty years intervening between the Persian and Peloponnesian wars, though it is commonly regarded as such and thus criticized for omissions; Proctor, *Experience*, 185, puts his dissatisfaction more metaphorically: "The Pentecontaetia is like a badly loaded shopping-basket from which a number of sorely needed articles are missing;" cf. also, e.g., Gomme, *HCT* 1:361–413; Meiggs, *AE*, 444–46; McGregor, "Athenian Policy," 67; Lenardon, "Thucydides and Hellanikos," 60; Gabba, *JRS* 71 (1981):51.

4. On which see chapter 3, below.

ing to Thucydides, because of the persuasiveness of the *logoi;* rather, "they feared the Athenians, lest their power increase further, as they saw that much of Greece was already subject to them" (1.88). This recalls directly the ἀληθεστάτη πρόφασις of 1.23.6. Thucydides' judgment of the "truest cause," or "explanation," of the decision to go to war requires support, and 1.89 begins the extended argument of the Pentekontaetia (with the explanatory γάρ) to demonstrate "in what kind of manner (τρόπῳ τοιῷδε) the Athenians came to the circumstances in which their power was increased ηὐξήθησαν" (1.89.1). The phrase τρόπῳ τοιῷδε has a wider range of nuances than simply specific actions taken or decisions made; it also suggests Athenian character and habits in general, which allow them to accomplish extraordinary things. The sense is, therefore, that the Athenian disposition is key to their attainment of power.[5] The verbal form of *auxesis* is deliberate, recalling the attention Thucydides gave to *auxesis* in the Archaeology and his interest in the historical development of power, not merely in the eventual results. Thucydides thus signals that in the Pentekontaetia, as in the Archaeology, he intends to analyze the means by which power developed.

The first circumstance that enabled the Athenians to increase their power was the rebuilding of their walls. Thucydides offers an extensive description of the manner in which the Athenians successfully refortified their city after the destruction of the Persian invasion in 480 (1.89–93), including a detailed account of Themistokles' ruse designed to forestall Spartan opposition to the Athenian project. The historian comments on the speed with which the walls were built around the city and then describes the completion of the walls in the Piraieus; this brings him back to Themistokles, who emerges as the architect of Athens' naval *arche* and *dunamis* (1.93), a visionary who foresaw that Athens' power would rest on the sea.[6] We then learn briefly of the military campaigns

5. Emphasis on the character of the Athenians and its link with their extraordinary achievements recurs prominently throughout the *History;* see especially the Korinthians' speech, in which they find it necessary to explain to the Spartans πρὸς οἴους 'Αθηναίους ... ὄντας (1.70.1); see also 2.36.4, 41.2–3, etc.; cf. Rawlings, *Prophasis*, 89, on Thucydides' use of the phrase μεγάλους γιγνομένους in 1.23.6 instead of δύναμις: "It was not the power itself which caused fear, but the way (τρόπος) that power was established." Cf. the emphasis on "national character" as a precondition for achieving sea power in A. T. Mahan's classic study, *The Influence of Sea Power upon History, 1660–1783* (Boston, 1890), 50–58; his typology occasions discomfort and objections in the post–World War II mind, but the Athenians would have been in full accord with it.

6. He does not, interestingly, mention the revenue from the mines at Laureion with which the Athenians built their fleet prior to Xerxes' invasion (Hdt. 7.144); this may be because it concerns a point anterior to that which marks the real beginnings of Athens' *dunamis*, or because Herodotos mentions it and Thucydides generally avoids repetition of other treatments unless he deems them inaccurate. Reference to the campaigns of 478 recalls Herodotos; but these directly relate to Athenian *dunamis*.

of 478 B.C. (1.94), which had also been reported by Herodotos (with whose fuller account Thucydides undoubtedly agreed, insofar as he makes no corrections here). But in 1.95 the focus narrows and the pace of narrative adjusts to concentrate on the detail of events. Chapters 1.95–96 are especially crucial for understanding Thucydides' conception of the development of power, and as we begin to explore them in depth, our goal will be to unpack as much as possible the historian's underlying assumptions, purpose, and criteria for inclusion.

At the end of 1.94, Thucydides begins to identify as precisely as possible each stage in the process by which allies in the Hellenic League grew dissatisfied with Pausanias, the Spartan commander of the expedition, and requested a change in the leadership of the hegemony from Sparta to Athens.[7] The meticulous attention to chronology is often attributed to a desire to correct inaccuracies in other accounts, such as that of Hellanikos, whom Thucydides singles out in 1.97.2.[8] But this explanation, though plausible, is not complete: there are other, internal reasons underlying the narrative which emerge as he describes the events that led to the transfer of leadership.

In fact, the need to fix each decision and action as it unfolded arises from Thucydides' very purpose in writing this section: to isolate each significant step in the evolution of Athenian power. The painstaking nature of this chapter is necessary to allow Thucydides to bring out clearly what he regards as a crucial factor, namely, the role of the allies. The transfer of hegemony became possible at this specific juncture only because the allies so intensely disliked their leader's medizing and generally obnoxious behavior that they appealed to the Athenians to replace him. The egregiousness of Pausanias, then, which greatly antagonized others in the Hellenic League, was responsible for at least the timing of the transfer, a point reiterated by Thucydides further on (1.96.1, 1.130.2).[9]

Is Thucydides' account, pointing out that the Athenians became the new hegemon on the initiative of the allies, also intended to correct Herodotos, who presents a different version?[10] In the latter's brief mention (8.3.2), it was the Athenians who instigated the transfer of hegemony by

---

7. ἐν τῇδε τῇ ἡγεμονίᾳ (1.94.2); ἤδη δέ (1.95.1); φοιτῶντες (1.95.1); ἐν τούτῳ δέ (1.95.3); ἅμα (1.95.4).

8. For a discussion of Thucydides' use of Hellanikos in general throughout the Pentekontaetia, see Lenardon, "Thucydides and Hellanikos," 58–67; also Ziegler, *RhM* 78 (1929), 59, 62, 66–67. See also below, p. 59.

9. That Thucydides genuinely believed the charge of medism can be inferred from 1.95.5: κατηγορεῖτο δὲ αὐτοῦ οὐχ ἥκιστα μηδισμὸς καὶ ἐδόκει σαφέστατον εἶναι.

10. Herodotos' version is seen as contradictory to Thucydides' by, e.g., Sealey, "Origins of the Delian League," 236–37; Rawlings, *Phoenix* 31 (1977):8.

using Pausanias' behavior as an excuse (πρόφασις).¹¹ Although Herodotos does not deny Pausanias' behavior, it was not the real reason for the change of leadership. The issue, then, is one of motive and responsibility. According to Herodotos, the Athenians were responsible for the transfer; they had aimed all along at assuming the leadership, and Pausanias' behavior provided them with a convenient excuse or opportunity. In Thucydides' account, responsibility falls on the allies, who proposed the transfer of leadership. As Larsen noted, the contradiction is only apparent: "Undoubtedly the Athenians desired the *hegemonia*, and undoubtedly the Ionians, even if the formal initiative came from them, did not act without knowledge that their proposal was acceptable to the Athenians."¹²

The story, then, is told from two different perspectives, the Athenians' (Herodotos) and the allies' (Thucydides). Herodotos' account, while emphasizing the underhanded nature of the Athenians' action, need not contradict the notion that the allies grievously resented Pausanias' obnoxious conduct, nor does Thucydides' account preclude the possibility that the Athenians themselves by that time desired the leadership of the allies. As Thucydides notes, they readily accepted the proposal to assume the command (1.95.2).

Nevertheless, it is undeniable that the two accounts produce appreciably different effects. Thucydides, emphasizing the role of the allies, appears less judgmental and less cynical about Athenian motives in the transfer than does his predecessor. Both accounts are of course retrospective, viewing the origins of the Delian League from a time when virtually the entire membership of the alliance had been reduced to subjection by Athens. Thucydides' intention, however, is hardly to absolve the Athenians. We need to keep in mind the aim of the Pentekontaetia. It is not simply a narrative of events, filling in the gap from the end of Herodotos' account to the advent of the Peloponnesian War. On the contrary, it has the objective of demonstrating the means by which Athens' power evolved and increased. There is an important point to recognize: the polis had not emerged from the successes of 480–479 with sufficient power—or popularity—to explain the result of the events of 478, namely the transfer of hegemony and the measures which directly followed. Let us take a closer look.

In 480 the majority of the Greeks were opposed to the idea of Athe-

11. But cf. Sealey, "Origins," 236–37 and 253 n. 8, who translates πρόφασις simply as "occasion" and interprets the passage differently. For a general discussion of Herodotos and his attitude toward Athens, see Strasburger, *Historia* 4 (1955):1–25; also Fornara, *Herodotos*, 37–58.
12. Larsen, *HSCP* 51 (1940):184–85.

nian leadership in the Hellenic League and preferred that of the Spartans.[13] According to Herodotos, the Athenians, though desirous of the leadership, waited for an opportune moment to show their hand; Pausanias' behavior was a gift. Sparta's greater strength and popularity underlie the decision to deny Athens, still a minor, relatively weak power in the Greek world, the leadership at that time. How much did the allies' attitude change by 478?

The Athenians' reputation was improved by their contribution in the war; on the other hand, the Spartans also demonstrated extraordinary bravery and skill, no doubt enhancing their own standing among the Greeks. Moreover, Themistokles' method of extorting money from the islanders who had not supported the Hellenic cause could only have made many uncomfortable.[14] It is difficult to believe that, by 478, sentiment so strongly favored the Athenians that on their initiative alone the command would have passed to them. It is significant that no move in that direction had yet been made; the Spartans continued to exercise their leadership until Pausanias' authority became intolerable to the allies.

Let us return to Thucydides. His version of the transfer was the result, I suggest, of solving a puzzle: to explain how Athens was able to move so quickly from a state of insufficient power and popularity to a position of unprecedented potential, at the head of an alliance whose members paid an annual contribution of which the Athenians had charge. This stage, the transfer of hegemony, was critical to Thucydides, who was interested in the precise way in which a new kind of power evolves. Accordingly, the reasons for emphasizing the validity of the charges against Pausanias and the μῖσος felt by the allies become clear. Thucydides wrote chapters 94–95 to show how the free Greek poleis came not only to accept but even to court the Athenians as hegemons, a move that ultimately resulted in their gradual subjection to the hegemonic city.

The overall issue Thucydides addresses here is how a single polis could acquire the means to achieve naval *dunamis*. The steps are clearly indicated: the rebuilding and completion of the fortifications, followed by the promotion of the city to the head of a naval alliance, the terms of which immediately put Athens in such an extraordinary position to exploit its allies that Thucydides could not explain this outcome by Athens' own real power at this juncture. Thus, he attributes it to the strength of the hatred felt toward Pausanias—and, not negligibly, to the Spartans' own willingness to wash their hands of naval leadership in distant parts

13. Hdt. 8.2.2.
14. Hdt. 8.111–12.

(1.95.7). He then moves to the next stage of the argument, in 1.96, to demonstrate how the Athenians set in place the very mechanism that would make possible their naval *arche*.

This important chapter, high on the list of intensively scrutinized and controversial passages in the *History*, has always been regarded as a description of the purpose, general arrangements, and constitution of the Delian League.[15] On that basis, its deficiencies are patent, and it is often criticized for its many omissions, for example, the absence of any reference to the oaths taken to cement League loyalty attested in other authors.[16] However, chapter 96 is not intended purely as a description of the arrangements of the Delian League; rather, its precise and single-minded function is to provide the evidence and analysis for a specific stage in a larger argument about the origin and development of Athenian power. We will begin to explore its contents and implications by first looking at the passage as a whole:

> After the Athenians received the hegemony in this way, since the allies were willing [for them to do so] because of their hatred of Pausanias, they assessed which cities should provide *chremata* and which should contribute ships against the barbarian—a pretext being retaliation for their suffering by plundering the King's land. Moreover, then, for the first time, the Athenians established the office of Hellenotamiai, who received the *phoros;* this was the term used for the payment of *chremata*. The first assessment of *phoros* was 460 talents. The treasury was on Delos, and the meetings were held in the temple.

Following the participial phrase reiterating the explanation for the transfer of hegemony, Thucydides immediately places the Athenians in control of all that follows: they assessed (ἔταξαν) which cities should furnish *chremata* "against the barbarian" and which should supply ships. He then comments that "a pretext (πρόσχημα) given was to punish [the barbarians] for their suffering by plundering the King's territory." The interpretation of these lines and especially of the word πρόσχημα, meaning a "cloak" or "screen," rendered here as "pretext," has prompted vigorous debate among scholars on the purpose of the Delian League.[17]

---

15. Some important treatments in which, in addition, more extensive bibliography may be found are: Larsen, *HSCP* 51 (1940):175–213; *ATL* 3, esp. 234–43; Chambers, *CP* 53 (1958):26–32; Meyer, *Historia* 12 (1963):405–46; Sealey, "Origins of the Delian League," 233–55; McGregor, "Athenian Policy," 67–84; Jackson, *Historia* 18 (1969):12–16; Meiggs, *AE*, 42–47; Raaflaub, *Chiron* 9 (1979):1–22; French, *Antichthon* 22 (1988):12–25.

16. Giovannini and Gottlieb, "Thukydides und die Anfänge," 7–45, use that particular omission to overthrow the idea that the Delian League was a new organization separate from the Hellenic League. Reasons for finding this unpersuasive will emerge below.

17. Larsen, *HSCP* 51 (1940):175–213; Meyer, *Historia* 12 (1963):405–46; Sealey, "Origins," 233–55; Jackson, *Historia* 18 (1969):12–16; Rawlings, *Phoenix* 31 (1977):1–8; Raa-

Discussion has been guided by the prevailing belief that the πρόσχημα refers to a publicly avowed intention (whether true or untrue) about the purpose of the Delian League generally. The antecedent referent of the word πρόσχημα has always been taken as "the Delian League." However, nowhere is this stated or implied in Thucydides. The antecedent reference for *him* is clearly indicated in the main clause of the preceding sentence: "[the Athenians] assessed which of the cities should provide *chremata* against the barbarian and which should furnish ships."

The πρόσχημα, then, concerns strictly the assessing of money and ships, not the purpose of the Delian League generally. Chapter 96 begins with a long participial phrase describing in brief how the Athenians took over the hegemony; it is a summary of events just detailed (in 1.95) and is subordinate to the main clause of the sentence, which, beginning with ἔταξαν, concerns the *assessment* of *chremata* and ships. It is to this that the explanatory γάρ refers, and not what is in the participial phrase; the latter's purpose is to emphasize once again (not for the last time) that Pausanias' medism was instrumental in the transfer of hegemony.

An objection might be raised against this seemingly excessive pedantry on the grounds that, even if the πρόσχημα, strictly speaking, refers to the assessment of tribute, still the Delian League is generally assumed to have been formed for the same purpose and, therefore, that the distinction is not significant. An immediate response is that recognizing that the πρόσχημα concerns something other than the general purpose of the League eliminates the problem of reconciling statements elsewhere in Thucydides that suggest that the League's aim was to "free the Greeks from the Persians."[18] But there is a more important issue. For if we explore the implications of taking the πρόσχημα to refer strictly to the institution of tribute, we will find that the distinction is not at all trivial; indeed, to overlook it is to miss part of Thucydides' argument about the novelty and significance of tribute. We need to consider the circumstances more closely so that we can appreciate the reasons why a pretext—or even a stated explanation at all—was required at the time.

Military alliances were common in the Greek world, and, in cases where the impetus for their formation was an obvious threat, one wonders whether an explicitly stated purpose was ever necessary. This seems especially true of the Delian League, whose initial aim was self-evident: to continue the operations of the naval arm of the Hellenic League.[19]

---

flaub, *Chiron* 9 (1979):1–22; Robertson, *AJAH* 5 (1980):64–96; French, *Antichthon* 22 (1988):12–25.

18. 3.10.3; 6.76.3–4. Whether these assertions, all in highly tendentious contexts, are to be taken at face value is another matter, but they at least suggest an ostensible, well-known purpose of the League.

19. That the Delian League was a new alliance, and not simply the continuation of the

What required clarification and explanation when a League was formed were its terms and obligations, especially if a novel arrangement was introduced. Indeed, the Delian League had several unprecedented features, stemming from the fact that it was a naval alliance: first, the institution of *phoros*, a system whereby the hegemon demanded regular payments from each polis in the League. As we saw in the Introduction, as a rule, individuals were required to equip and provision themselves for military campaigns;[20] public support was the exception. Moreover, not only was the providing role of the polis absent from or minimal in the military sphere, but even money itself did not have a significant presence in the functioning of alliances and war. Therefore, the very idea of introducing money on any large and regular scale, implicit in the systematic institution of *phoros*, would have been unfamiliar, and its necessity unclear.[21] Furthermore, the notion of assessment, that is, a system of projected regular payments, was novel enough within a polis without adding the unprecedented aspect of removing a polis's portion from the city to an extra-polis fund.[22] Wherever the Athenians got the idea to establish this system of financial obligations, its originality in a purely Greek context should not go unappreciated.[23]

The central point is that innovations require explanation, hence the πρόσχημα. But can we say more about the reception that such a proposal to institute *phoros* would have been given? There can be no doubt that an open-ended arrangement as unprecedented and potentially burdensome to local economies over the long, if not the short, term would have aroused some concern in the poleis that would have to pay it.[24] Beyond

---

old Hellenic League, is clear, even though Thucydides does not speak explicitly of a new league and refers in 1.95–96 to the mere change in hegemony of an existing league, especially in light of Thucydides' later comment that the Athenians withdrew from "the existing alliance against the Mede" after the Spartans rejected their help at Ithome (1.102.4), which can refer only to the Hellenic League; but cf. Giovannini and Gottlieb, "Thukydides und die Anfänge."

20. Pritchett, *GSAW* 1:30–34.

21. See below for a discussion of the reasons for maintaining that *phoros* consisted entirely of money. I am drawing a distinction between the temporary need for money that occurred especially in naval ventures, e.g., during the Ionian Revolt and the campaigns of 480–479, and the institution of a systematic, regularized procedure of compulsory financial obligations.

22. In Athens during our period, no regular, direct taxation, as opposed to extraordinary, irregular taxes, existed; Andreades, *HGPF*, 366, n. 2.

23. I shall return to this presently.

24. We do not know whether the members of the Delian League knew that it was to be permanent; Thucydides' discussion in 1.99 suggests at the least that, whether or not the alliance itself was permanent, the allies did not really expect or understand at the outset that the Athenians had in mind a standing navy. The widespread assumption in the scholarship is that the rich bore the burden of tribute payment, but even those who share this assumption have to recognize that, in the end, we do not know how the obligation was met

this statement, we are on slippery ground. It is difficult, if not impossible, to reconstruct the collective attitude of League members in 478 to *phoros* in a Greek military context. However, although we must recognize the speculative nature of the attempt, it is important to try to determine the implications of tribute assessment so that we can appreciate fully the significance of the measure and of the necessity for the πρόσχημα.²⁵

We can start with some probable comparisons and associations. After the battle of Salamis, a Greek fleet under Themistokles' command visited various places in the Aegean with the purpose of extorting money from medizers (Hdt. 8.111–12).²⁶ The context is specific—retaliation for support of Persia—but Herodotos leaves open the possibility that Themistokles' action instilled fear in those who had not openly supported either side. Recollection of the earlier Athenian demands for money, "or else," could have had one of two effects (or a combination) on a member of a League under Athenian hegemony in 478 facing the prospect of *phoros:* concern, or relief at having a regular system imposed on all regardless of one's loyalty during the war.

Second, contributions for military ventures in the Hellenic world were neither unprecedented nor unacceptable. We have the evidence of Plu-

---

(e.g., Finley, *Ancient History,* 79); see Nixon and Price's discussion, "Size and Resources," 151. Even if the assessment and distribution of the requirement within the polis were equitable, it still meant parting with local resources in an exchange of uncertain financial return; I shall be concerned with this question below.

25. Plutarch's story (*Arist.* 24.1) that the Greeks desired a regular assessment and entrusted the task to Aristeides is not convincing. It is true, as maintained in *ATL* 3, 185, that the need for "some such contribution" existed, yet tribute assessed every year, in amounts which exceeded what was merely necessary for immediate disbursement, differed demonstrably in nature and scope from the type of contribution envisaged in Plutarch. One could still argue, of course, that Plutarch's story about the allies' desire to be assessed is true, while conceding that the Athenians had something rather different in mind which they imposed on the allies. But the main objection that stands in the way of accepting Plutarch is that a πρόσχημα for assessing tribute was necessary: this vitiates the idea that the allies wanted to be assessed.

26. The question of whether Themistokles did demand "contributions" in an arbitrary manner is important for determining whether, in fact, this influenced writers who explicitly or implicitly contrasted Themistokles to Aristeides. Herodotos is our main source for these activities (8.111–12). There is also the additional contemporary evidence of Timokreon (Plut. *Them.* 21.2–3), who has Themistokles coming as far as Rhodes and other places as well, ἀργυρίου δ' ὑπόπλεως. Timokreon and Themistokles were no friends, yet there is no good reason to reject the evidence that Themistokles went at least to Ialysos. Timokreon suggests that not all of those whom Themistokles visited were actually medizers; whether this should be believed is more difficult to determine. Some scholars have criticized Herodotos' account on the grounds of anti-Themistoklean bias, e.g., How & Wells, *Comm.* 2:272. Automatic rejection of Herodotos' account is hasty. On Herodotos and Themistokles, see Fornara, *Herodotus,* 66–74; Frost, *Themistocles,* 5–11.

tarch (*Arist.* 24.1) that the Greeks made a contribution (*apophora*) to the war effort of the Hellenic League (significantly, the context is largely naval); these contributions, however, need not have consisted solely of money. As need occasionally arose, allies could expect to offer financial assistance in addition to meeting their regular requirements. Naval activities, however, necessarily changed the exception to the rule. Naval warfare, and a standing naval alliance, required a stable financial source to build, equip, maintain, and repair ships, as well as to provision rowers.[27] Therefore, in 478 the Greeks in the new league were being asked to comply with an arrangement rather different from one-time payments in a time of emergency. Indeed, the implications of an assessment—something regular, systematized, and long-term—sharply contrast with the notion even of annual levies based on the needs of war; they suggest that what was envisioned was a permanent standing navy.

Finally, perhaps the most important issue is whether the *phoros* of the Delian League bore a similarity, so obvious later on, to tribute imposed on a subject by a ruler outside of the Greek world.[28] The only precedents for systematic obligations of tribute come entirely from non-Greek powers, though they occurred in areas of Greek contact (for example, Persia, Lydia, Skythia, Thrace, and Egypt). Non-Greeks were known to pay tribute to non-Greeks, and even Greeks to non-Greeks, but not Greeks to other Greeks.[29] Near-contemporary evidence shows that tribute was an effective signifier of barbarian despotism.[30] Some, possibly the majority, of the original members of the Delian League had themselves been subject to Persian domination, which included the requirement of tribute. What would their reaction have been to the apparently fixed requirement now established by the Athenians? Would the contribution called *phoros* have evoked barbarian connotations?

Oswyn Murray has argued that the word the Greeks used for Persian

27. The most thorough treatment of naval finances is that of Blackman, *GRBS* 10 (1969):179–216; see also Jordan, *Athenian Navy*, 56–116 (though much of the evidence collected comes from the fourth century).

28. Certainly in its developed form, when the treasury was moved to Athens and the symbolism of subjugation was made concrete by the procession of allies and their tribute to the Akropolis, the similarity was unmistakable; cf. Thucydides' own implicit equation of the two in his account of tribute and gifts in the Odrysian kingdom, below, chapter 4, pp. 125–26.

29. Barbarians to barbarians, e.g.: to Darius, Hdt. 3.89–96; Skythia, Hdt. 1.106.1. Greeks to barbarians: to Cyrus, Hdt. 7.51.1; to Croesus, 1.6.2; to Darius, 6.42 (Artaphernes' assessment); to Xerxes, 7.108.1.

30. Ais. *Pers.*, produced in 472: "Not now for long will they that live through Asia / live under the sway of the Persians, / nor will they pay tribute anymore / by the compulsion of their master, / nor will they prostrate themselves on the earth / in reverence; for the royal / power has perished utterly" (584–90) (Smyth [Loeb], adapted); the term used to refer to tribute is δασμοφοροῦσιν.

tribute was likely *dasmos* and that the term *phoros* was meant to distance it from the Persian practice; similarly, when the Athenians launched their second naval alliance in the fourth century, they favored, with good reason, the innocuous-sounding *suntaxis*, "contribution," over *phoros*.[31] Murray's suggestion has much to commend it; certainly Thucydides' remark on the term *phoros*, "for that was what the payment of *chremata* was called," does require explanation. It is also possible, given the likely difficulty of imagining a time when the word was neutral in tone, that the historian wants to point out that the now-distasteful word had been used all along. This would be consistent with his frankness in characterizing the new League as an *arche*, rather than a *hegemonia*, even at its inception (1.97.2).[32] Thus, Thucydides states that the empire was always an empire, and the *phoros* was always called *phoros*.[33]

It is usually assumed that Persian tribute was the model for both the idea and the amount of *phoros*.[34] But it needs to be made clear that this is pure speculation, and the question of how the institution of *phoros* appeared in 478 must not be confused by the obvious similarities between barbarian tribute and Athenian *phoros* after the *arche* was mature.

In the end, we cannot be certain what connections the charter members of the Delian League drew between Persian tribute and *phoros;* nor should we assume a uniform reaction. Greeks who had previously been under Persian control may have felt a suspicion that the *phoros* now demanded of them was something like the tribute they had been paying to the Persians. However, the Athenian *phoros* differs significantly from Persian tribute in the voluntary nature of the contribution in the case of the Delian League and the stated use to which it was to be put (that is, the πρόσχημα). For as we have already seen, the Athenians would not have had the power to force tribute on the poleis initially; in fact, this point is crucial to understanding the πρόσχημα. Whatever the connotations of *phoros*, it is unlikely that such an unfamiliar imposition would have been agreed upon unless it were made palatable. An explanation of its necessity was critical; thus, the πρόσχημα.

Still other questions remain concerning the πρόσχημα—for example, why Thucydides regarded the explanation for tribute and ships as in-

---

31. *Historia* 15 (1966):150, 154. Cf. Eddy, *CP* 63 (1968):185–87, who argued that φόρος was a word used primarily by prose writers, and δασμός, a more elegant and poetic word, by tragedians. One should note, however, that *dasmophoros* appears not infrequently in Herodotos (3.97.1; 5.106.6; 6.48.2, 95.1; 7.51.1, 108.1).

32. As Winton rightly notes, *MH* 38 (1981):147–52, though he finds *hegemonia* to be synonymous with *arche*.

33. Cf. 1.75.2, αὐτὴν τήνδε [ἀρχὴν] ἐλάβομεν; 1.76.2, εἰ ἀρχήν τε διδομένην ἐδεξάμεθα.

34. See, recently, Nixon and Price, "Size and Resources," 145–46, with bibliography in n. 8, 145; on Persian tribute and taxation, see Tuplin, "Achaemenid," in Carradice, *Coinage*, 137–58.

herently fraudulent, and in what way would the pretext given have satisfied Delian League members—but it will be best to return to them after we have considered fully Thucydides' comments following his reference to the assessment of money and ships.

Thucydides continues by noting that then, for the first time, the Athenians established the office of Hellenotamiai, who received the *phoros*, and he adds an exegetical comment on *phoros:* "this was the term used for the payment (*phora*) of *chremata.*" The context and wording make it likely that the Athenians filled the board from their own ranks;[35] they would in any case have maintained ultimate control as hegemon of the League. It is notable that Thucydides not only explains the term *phoros* but also defines it as consisting of *chremata.* Here *chremata* is money, not supplies or provisions, for *phoros* not only was assessed in money but also was to be housed in a common treasury (I shall return to the significance of this later). Moreover, Thucydides expressly states that the *phoros* was to be received by the Hellenotamiai, whose purview included only items of monetary value, but not supplies. This too may have set it apart from the Persian system of taxation and compulsory gifts.[36]

Many scholars have doubted, or at least have been uncomfortable with, the figure of 460 talents for the total of the first assessment, despite the limitations of our knowledge about the founding membership of the League and the fact that the accuracy of an assessment figure cannot necessarily be fairly tested by reference to estimated totals for later periods. Nevertheless, the flood of scholarship on this one sentence has attempted primarily to account for the figure in any way other than by taking Thucydides' statement at face value. It will be useful to summarize the main lines of approach and argument. The editors of *ATL*, for example, supposed that the figure, because of its magnitude, must include both money and the monetary value of ships.[37] Chambers, on the other hand, argued that the *phoros* could only mean cash and not the cash equivalence of ships, and concluded that Thucydides was in error on the amount of the first assessment.[38] Robertson also believes that the figure is incorrect and, further, may even have been a "deliberate fiction" given to Thucydides by Athenian informants, a figure which "would pal-

---

35. So the schol. to 1.96; Meiggs, *AE*, 234, treats it as fact; cf. Thompson, *C&M* 28 (1967):216, who thinks that it was a Delian magistracy before 454; against his view, also see, e.g., Gomme, *HCT* 1:86, 272–73, 279; *ATL* 3:230 with n. 26; Woodhead, *JHS* 79 (1959):149.

36. Cf. Wallinga, *Mnem.* 37 (1984):401–37, who argues that Darius at least, and perhaps Cambyses, monetized the Persian tribute; cf. also Tuplin, "Achaemenid," esp. 137–45.

37. *ATL* 3:236–43; cf. also McGregor, "Athenian Policy," 67–84. Eddy, *CP* 63 (1968):186

38. Chambers, *CP* 53 (1958):28, 29–30.

liate Athens' exactions in later days."[39] The view of Gomme, and then French, that the tribute quota lists do not accurately reflect the total tribute collected, has been revived by R. K. Unz, who argues that not all tribute reached Athens and only out of that which did was quota paid to Athena.[40] Finally, Meiggs suggests that tribute assessments were higher in the beginning of the League than later on.[41]

Of what can we be certain? First, as we noted above, the assessment must refer only to cash. How much further can we go in accepting Thucydides' testimony? The sum of 460 talents has been called into question solely on the basis of the evidence of the tribute quota lists (which do not begin until almost twenty-five years later) or, more accurately, on inferences drawn from the lists, which suggest lower actual totals of tribute for later periods when (it is thought) League membership was higher and tribute increased. There is no reason to dispute the credibility of Thucydides' figure. His impressive attention to details about the institution of tribute as a whole in 1.96 suggests careful research; in addition, it is clear that the first assessment was still generally well known in the later fifth century.[42] It is best, then, to draw the most cautious conclusions that we can from the tribute quota lists: they allow the inference that the actual tribute collected about twenty-five years after 478 was less than 460 talents.[43] Second, there is no reason to assume from Thucydides' narrative that the first assessment required only minimal amounts from individual poleis;[44] value terms such as "moderate" or "low" are meaningful only in later periods, after the precedent of *phoros* had been set. Moreover, the financial burden on each polis depended on the number of members in the original League and the nature of distribution among them, neither of which can be determined definitively. That the first assessment was adopted as the standard in the terms of the Peace of Nikias may suggest only that Aristeides' settlement seemed moderate in comparison with subsequent ones. It may also have had political rather than financial value: as the first assessment hearkened back to the League's inception, it recalled a time of voluntary unity, general consent, and goodwill. Perhaps the most important consideration, however, is the difference between assessment and collection: the former is an ideal or standard to which reality probably rarely corresponded. In this case, the

---

39. Robertson, *AJAH* 5 (1980):68.
40. Gomme, *HCT* 1:273–79; French, *Historia* 21 (1972): 1–20; Unz, *GRBS* 26 (1985):21–42, esp. 21–28.
41. Meiggs, *AE*, 58–67 (with the exception of that in 425).
42. Thuc. 5.18.5.
43. Ca. four hundred talents on the estimate in *ATL* 3:265–74.
44. *Contra* Robertson, *AJAH* 5 (1980):68, in whose opinion Thucydides "harp[s] on the moderation and equity of the first assessment."

disparity between the 460 talents assessed in 478 and the estimated tribute collected, based on the quota lists, does not actually prove that Thucydides' figure is too high. Rather, it is most sensible to infer that, as a matter of routine and practice, the Athenians always assessed a higher amount than they actually expected to collect.

Another factor that has strongly influenced the view that the first assessment must in fact have been "moderate" is the reputation of the man credited for it, Aristeides, whose constant companions were justness and fairness.[45] What is the evidence for the mildness of Aristeides' assessment?

Both Plutarch and Diodoros state that Aristeides' nickname, "the Just," arose from his general reputation for justice. According to Diodoros, he won this renown by dividing the tribute "exactly and justly" (ἀκριβῶς καὶ δικαίως). In Plutarch, Aristeides acquired the epithet through his continual exercise of justice, including his assessment of the tribute, which Plutarch explicitly contrasts to subsequent ones. The Aristeides who appears in Diodoros and Plutarch could do no wrong. From the fourth century on, Aristeides became virtually a type, the epitome and paradigm of justness, and this characterization should warn us to treat most cautiously the particulars of his life and actions. What of more contemporary evidence about Aristeides and his assessment?

Plutarch's amusing story (*Arist.* 7.5–6) about the illiterate man who asked Aristeides to write his name on the ostrakon because he disliked hearing Aristeides referred to constantly as "the Just" may suggest that Aristeides had acquired that nickname by the 480s, that is, before the first assessment; but one is reluctant to give too much credence to either this story or its implied chronology. Contemporary opinions about Aristeides were more equivocal than those in later sources. Herodotos' view was that Aristeides was "the best and most just man in Athens" (8.79.1), an opinion based, he points out, on information about Aristeides' character. He reiterates his view several chapters later (8.95). Meiggs suggests that Herodotos "may be taking sides in a controversy," because of the manner in which he introduces his opinion.[46] Furthermore, his portrayal of Aristeides is contrasted against that of Themistokles, whom Herodotos treats much less favorably than does Thucydides, for example. Alongside Herodotos' assessment we may place the contemporary view of Kallaischros, who called Aristeides "fox by deme and fox by nature."[47]

None of these largely anecdotal indications brings us much closer to determining precisely how the assessment itself was regarded. But it is

---

45. Plut. *Arist.* 24; Arist. *Ath.Pol.* 23.3; Diod. 11.47.2.
46. Meiggs, *AE*, 42, n. 3.
47. ἀλώπηξ ᾿Αλωπεκῆθεν ([Them.] *Ep.* 4 [743 Hercher]); the translation is Meiggs', *AE*, 42.

useful to recognize when considering the nature of the original assessment that, first, any judgment is relative: it would not have looked the same to Athens' allies in 478 as it did in 421. Moreover, Aristeides' subsequent reputation for determining an assessment that could be called "just" (and "exact") may mean no more than that it was distinguished by its lack of arbitrariness, being arranged according to specific guidelines and principles. Finally, Aristeides' reputed justness, which seems to be rooted mainly in his conduct in Athens, does not necessarily tell us much about his attitude and policy toward non-Athenians.[48]

We have not found adequate reason to reject the evidence of Thucydides that the first assessment was 460 talents. But let us pursue a different line of inquiry from that usually taken to see if we can explain a figure as high as 460 talents. It is possible that the sum reflected an ambitious program, in support of which the allies were asked to contribute an amount that was higher than what we infer was actually collected at a later date. Here we meet the πρόσχημα again. Retaliatory raids on Persian-held territory, the "pretext" given for the assessment of tribute (and ship contributions) reflect its offensive nature, strategically speaking, and imply regular, vigilant activity. Moreover, the very nature of an assessment, requiring more time, effort, and calculation than an emergency war levy, further suggests an ongoing operation of a regularly assembled—and, therefore, costly—fleet. Finally, the Athenians could have made a convincing case for having sufficient financial reserve to cover the unexpected and thus insure the new League's success. But we now have to ask what the allies expected in exchange for the obligatory contributions that they agreed to pay regularly in the form of *phoros* or ships.

Consider the institution of *phoros* and the stated explanation against its historical background: following the final battle of the Persian Wars at Mykale the preceding summer, the Greek victors, with the exception of the Peloponnesians, laid siege to Sestos by the Hellespont. The undertaking proved a test of perseverance and endurance, lasting some ten months into the winter until the city finally surrendered. Two lessons would have been apparent: first, that such operations could be expensive, especially if they lasted a long time (and they certainly would without sufficient resources); and second, that they could also be extremely lucrative. For example, Herodotos tells the story of the satrap Artayktes, who plundered the nearby sanctuary of Protesileos containing numer-

---

48. Thus, I am arguing that the substantial nature of the first assessment does not provide evidence that the original membership of the League was larger than scholars have estimated, so that the assessment should be viewed as distributed among many states and the burden on each would thereby be considered "equitable." Cf. Chambers, *CW* 57 (1963):10; French, *Historia* 21 (1972):6; Huxley, *PRIA* 83 (1983):198.

ous items of gold, silver, and bronze, and who said that, in return for his life, he would give two hundred talents to the Athenians (and one hundred to Protesileos for looting his sanctuary) (9.116, 120.3). But Artayktes met instead with a grisly end, and the Athenians sailed home with the rest of the booty (*ta alla chremata*), which, by inference from the description of the wealth of the sanctuary alone, not to mention that of Sestos itself, was worth a king's ransom.

It is likely that League members anticipated tangible rewards for their efforts as a result of ravaging Persian territory;[49] indeed, it is probable that such a prospect would have been necessary to convince the allies to part with their own financial resources, pool them in a common fund, and not even to have any surplus redistributed to them at the end of a campaigning season. The Athenians would have had persuasive grounds on which to base their case for *phoros*. Aggressive campaigns in territory held by the Persians could be costly and, in order to insure success, not only anticipated funds but those *in excess* of expectations would be necessary so that in the event of emergency and unforeseen difficulties, the League would be able to draw on immediately available and expendable—thus cash—financial reserves (and so avoid the problems faced, in Thucydides' analysis, by the Greeks at Troy). The chief lure enticing League members would be the prospect of rich rewards like those they had seen the preceding year at Sestos—but they could benefit only if they agreed to pay out systematically and in larger amounts than might have been necessary simply for minimal success.[50]

This reconstruction of motivation and considerations at the inception of the Delian League seems to me to explain reasonably, without an unduly procrustean approach to Thucydides' words, the relationship between the surprisingly large figure of 460 talents and the stated purpose of *phoros* and ships. Why did Thucydides regard the explanation as fraudulent? The reality as he appraised it convinced him that the rhetoric was a lie: from the start, tribute and the navy were used for purposes other than those expressed to the new members.

The interpretation proposed here—that the allies were led to believe that revenge would be sweetest and rewards greatest if they were willing to invest, perhaps heavily, in the League navy—strikes an insidious chord, reminding us of Thucydides' comment in the Archaeology that

---

49. Blackman, *GRBS* 10 (1969):186; Finley, *Economy and Society*, 50 (= "Fifth-Century Athenian Empire," 113); cf. also Sealey, "Origins of the Delian League," 233–55, whose argument about booty may have more merit in it than scholars have been willing to admit; see Pritchett's collection of evidence on booty in *GSAW* 5:363–401.

50. I owe this idea of a "corporate" model of "investment" and "dividend" to W. R. Connor, whose stimulating comments at an earlier stage of the manuscript were beneficial to my thinking about the beginnings of the Delian League.

the stimulus of gain (κέρδος) explains acceptance of oppression on the part of the weak as much as it does the rule of the weak by the strong (1.8.3). As yet, the allies are not under that kind of compulsion, but the relevance of the observation to the events of 478 is clear: it is the desire for gain that sets in motion a development of oppression and submission.

Thucydides concludes his discussion in chapter 96 by noting that "the treasury was on Delos, and the meetings were held in the temple [of Apollo]" (1.96.2). This sentence provides another financial detail, one which many modern readers doubtless pass over quickly. Yet as it occurs in a passage so highly selective in content, Thucydides' reference to the treasury demands careful attention; for on closer scrutiny, it reflects on the nature and novelty of the arrangements made by the Athenians.

Why did Thucydides consider that this detail about the League treasury merited inclusion? It may not seem surprising at first that he would complete a discussion of the financial arrangements of the Delian League by giving the location of the treasury. But Thucydides did not pursue comprehensiveness simply for its own sake; one of his hallmarks, often a great source of frustration for historians of the fifth century who wish for more evidence, is his ability to eliminate what is extraneous or insignificant to his purpose.[51] Moreover, it is unusual in literary works to be told even the general location of a treasury, even in historical works whose authors relate financial matters. For this reason we know regrettably little about the location of many funds of money, sacred and other. Therefore, mere mention of such information is noteworthy, especially when it occurs in a highly selective description of certain features of the Athenians' new hegemony.

On a basic level, its very inclusion confirms the degree of Thucydides' interest in the financial arrangements of the early League. It also may provide an implicit contrast between past and present; that is, at that time the tribute was housed on Delos, not in Athens. Indeed, in a sense Thucydides does not fail to mention the transfer of the League treasury to Athens; rather, he supplies this information in a way other than that which we expect.[52]

---

51. Note that in the Pentekontaetia itself (1.97), Thucydides finds it necessary to defend in the first person his reason for including *as much* as he does of details which, from the standpoint both of structural narrative and of his purpose, would not seem entirely germane to his thesis.

52. Much weight is given in discussion of Thucydides' "omissions" to his failure to state explicitly when the treasury was moved, or even that it was moved. Although I think that in 1.96 he is alluding to the change in location of the treasury, he still does not mention when it occurred. But is it a serious omission in that he neglected something relevant to his argument (so, e.g., Gomme, *HCT* 1:370; de Romilly, *TAI*, 91; Meiggs, *AE*, 444)? The

Most significant, however, is the institution of a common extra- and inter-polis treasury in which a part of the coined financial resources of separate, independent Greek poleis were amalgamated, with League-authorized treasurers charged with their oversight. This arrangement bears no substantive resemblance to panhellenic dedications at sanctuaries such as Delos, Delphi, and Olympia, in which valuables offered to the god by various cities were housed side by side. The idea of a centralized, common treasury intended for use in military activity was an innovation with highly significant implications: first, it testifies concretely to the existence of fundamental, though ultimately ephemeral, cooperation. The poleis gave over to a common purpose precious resources that would be used to benefit not just themselves (so the expectation would have been held out) but also one other; moreover, if my hypothesis is correct that estimates exceeding minimum campaigning costs were used in the first assessment in order to create a surplus and thus necessitate a proper treasury with its own board of officials, the allies were being asked to forgo the return of any surplus at the end of the annual campaign. If the allies understood this clearly at the outset, this too is an important indication of their initial commitment.

Whether or not a surplus was envisioned from the start, it is clear that a reserve must have begun to accumulate early on.[53] This *ktesis* and *periousia* in the League treasury over the course of the fifth century testify to an important change both in policy and attitude from the traditional way of dealing with surplus by distributing it among the citizenry and, in the context of the Delian League, among League members.[54]

The League treasury served as a focus of unity among its members; this is not, however, simply a conceptual issue. The creation of a treasury signals recognition of the importance of financial power in the military sphere, for the centralization of wealth was necessary to enable an *auxesis* in power. The importance of this factor is brought out clearly in Archidamos' speech before the assembled Spartans on the eve of war, especially when he reminds the Spartans of their lack of public wealth and the difficulty of putting scattered resources to use.[55] Archidamos' words, in such close proximity to the beginning of the Pentekontaetia, have a

---

historian leaves the reader no doubt that the Athenians controlled the League funds from the beginning. Given this fact, the treasury's location is not significant. This is not to deny the symbolic importance of the transfer of the League treasury to Athens; it is probable that the allies regarded the move as a significant step toward oppressive control. But Thucydides was not much concerned with symbols; what mattered to him, especially in the area of finance, was the money itself and who controlled it.

53. Thuc. 2.13.3 (reserve at its height).
54. Themistokles first departed from the usual practice in Athens, Hdt. 7.144.1; cf. Plut. *Them.* 4.1–2; Nepos *Them.* 2; distributions on Siphnos, Hdt. 3.57.2.
55. 1.80.4. For a detailed discussion of this speech, see below, pp. 81–85.

special resonance in the context of 1.96; for the reader already is aware of the significance of centralized resources to naval power and, therefore, can well appreciate the perspicacity in creating a centralized treasury for League funds. This was a novel example of the kind of common effort (*koine*), in its financial as well as naval manifestation, of which Thucydides establishes the importance in the Archaeology. The Athenians had developed a solution to the problem of *achrematia* that, the historian argued earlier, frustrated the Trojan expedition (1.11).

Thus, a standing naval alliance engendered institutional and administrative developments—a common treasury, new system of revenue (*phoros*)—which accompanied the need for surplus and expenditure that constitute an advancement beyond a rudimentary concept of money and reserve.[56] The financial structure of the League presupposes the idea of deposits and accounting and shows clearly the Athenians' full appreciation of the efficiency of money in the naval sphere; there is no indication that those who were assessed tribute could make a contribution in kind by providing supplies and provisions. Why not? The tributary system (and, gradually, naval *arche*) was founded on the idea of preparedness, as was land-based military activity. But unlike hoplite warfare, in which needs were predictable, actual fighting was of short duration (until the Peloponnesian War), and money was not necessary, naval warfare made unexpected and longer-term demands; a reserve of money was essential because needs could not be precisely anticipated and the ability to procure what was necessary immediately was key to success.

Obviously, I have discussed the creation of the League treasury in inverse proportion to the length of Thucydides' comment on its location. However, this attention is justified, for understanding the unfamiliarity of the arrangements of the League, the fundamental recognition of the need for money, and the apparent goodwill at the time is essential for appreciating the extraordinary step taken by the poleis that voluntarily parted with and forfeited control over their own financial resources. In this treasury, then, lie the origins, both practical and symbolic, of an imperialism created and maintained by one power's exploitation of others' resources. That it happened initially without force is an important feature of Thucydides' understanding of the evolution of Athens' *arche*.

This scrutiny of chapter 96 reveals Thucydides' paramount concentration on the finances of the League. In order now to grasp fully the

---

56. Cf. the surplus theory, which—through the idea that surplus fosters the development of economic institutions and enables social and economic changes—has some relevance for the Delian League if one understands that only financial developments on the polis level with broader political effects (for both Athens and its allies) are at issue, not economic developments; cf. the useful discussion of the history of the development of surplus theory by Pearson, "The Economy Has No Surplus."

point of such attention, let us enumerate its contents and appreciate the specificity and detail. Thucydides states, after noting in a participial phrase that the Athenians took possession of the hegemony, that: (1) the Athenians decided who should pay money and who should furnish ships; (2) they said they were doing this for the purpose of retaliation by ravaging the King's land; (3) they created the board of Hellenotamiai, who received the tribute; (4) for thus the payment of money was called; (5) the first *phoros* was assessed at 460 talents; (6) the treasury was on Delos, and the meetings were held in the temple.

Every sentence, every clause, in this chapter concerns the institution of *phoros*. It is a tightly defined, extraordinarily detailed, exegetical description of the financial measures taken by the Athenians on their accession to the hegemony. This single-minded focus, combined with the absence of general constitutional arrangements, stipulations, and initiating oaths, such as we find in other authors,[57] alerts us to the presence of a different aim altogether. Chapter 96 is the decisive stage in, and the centerpiece of, Thucydides' argument about the creation and development of Athens' power; in other words, it constitutes the chief support for the purpose of the Pentekontaetia. It is of great significance that, following the comment that the Athenians first decided who should pay money and who should contribute ships, Thucydides proceeds to focus solely on the financial resources of the League, demonstrating his deeply penetrating analysis of power: he probes below the level of gods, warriors, or method of warfare, down to the concrete financial foundation of naval power. This kind of analysis of power is remarkable in the context of earlier ancient literature; its argument gives prominence not so much to the means by which war was waged (that is, the navy) as to the financial resources that underpin military success on the sea.

Chapter 96, then, is composed of a deliberate selection of carefully and cogently presented evidence that Athens' *auxesis* originated in the imposition of tribute and the creation of a centralized treasury in Athenian hands.[58] It is no more a general description of the League's origins than was the historian's account of Agamemnon and the Trojan expedition a general description of that great event of the past. I bring up Agamemnon not as a random case in point; for Thucydides' treatment of that chieftain offers additional insight into the approach taken in 1.96 and demonstrates the importance of the Archaeology in introducing the

---

57. Arist. *Ath.Pol.* 23.5; Plut. *Arist.* 25.1.
58. *Contra*, e.g., McGregor, "Athenian Policy," 69–70: "What we have in [1.96] is a selection made by Thucydides of the results of the congress.... Thucydides incorporates in his *History*, although not comprehensively, what happened in consequence; but the order of composition in this chapter is almost accidental, it has no special historical meaning.... It comprises the stage-setting."

principles of selection and the focus of attention in the rest of the work. Thucydides' explicit rejection of the importance of oaths with respect to the acquisition and maintenance of power in his analysis of Agamemnon's ability to compel unity and obedience gains additional significance in connection with 1.96 and vice versa. The oaths of Tyndareos, he argues, had nothing to do with the real basis of Agamemnon's power; rather, the *dunamis* of this "big man" derived from Pelops, to whose wealth Thucydides explicitly alludes. In 1.96, Thucydides chooses to omit any reference to the oaths the allies took at the inception of the League. Why? Because it is implicit here as it was made explicit in 1.9 that *dunamis* is built on concrete, material resources; naval *dunamis*, specifically, rests on financial resources, not on symbolic *foci* of unity.

In an important sense, the account of 1.94–96 mirrors Thucydides' treatment of the origins and explanation of the Peloponnesian War. He differentiates between the events critical for understanding the timing of the war (the αἰτίαι καὶ διαφοραί) and the larger explanation of why the war was fought at all (the ἀληθεστάτη πρόφασις). To put it another way, the Peloponnesian War could have and would have occurred even without the specific disputes involving Kerkyra and Poteidaia—some other direct stimulus would have been as effective—but it would not have occurred in the absence of the ἀληθεστάτη πρόφασις. Such an extraordinary and unprecedented conflict, however, required a careful analysis of its immediate origins—something crucial for those "who want to understand" such phenomena.[59] Indeed, an explanation of the role of these disputes in stimulating the greatest conflict that the Greek world had ever seen was perhaps especially necessary precisely *because* they were intrinsically lacking in larger significance. A similar consistency of method, approach, and presentation can be found in the chapters that we have been examining here. Something as extraordinary as Athens' naval *dunamis* is based on, in Thucydides' view, a unique capability inherent in the character of Athenians that allows them to exploit advantages;[60] consequently, they would likely have achieved naval *arche* without the specific circumstances of 478. But these circumstances were immediately elevated to primary importance because of their instrumental role in the creation of something unprecedented; as in the case of the events of 433–432, Thucydides' point is that circumstances unremarkable in themselves can generate remarkable results, but only if they occur in a matrix that allows such potential.

Thucydides has now completed his account of the means by which the Athenians were able to capitalize on the conditions following the Persian

---

59. 1.22.4: ὅσοι δὲ βουλήσονται τῶν τε γενομένων τὸ σαφὲς σκοπεῖν.

60. Cf. among Mahan's six criteria for sea power, "national disposition," *Influence of Sea Power*, 50–58.

Wars. Chapter 97 marks a change: it, and the rest of the Pentekontaetia, does not, strictly speaking, continue the argument of 1.89–96. To be sure, although much remains to be added to the analysis of the development of and increase in Athenian power, an additional goal now emerges. The chief purpose of the Pentekontaetia is, as we have seen, to present an argument. Mere tracing of events per se is not precisely germane to the historian's goal in this section of the work. Accordingly, when Thucydides signals that in what follows, he will be relating *erga* from the period between the inception of the Delian League and the beginning of the Peloponnesian War with a more general aim of recounting events both in war and in the administration of affairs involving the Persians, their own allies, and the Peloponnesians—in short, adopting a procedure less rigidly oriented to the purpose introduced in 1.88—he finds it necessary to step out of the narrative expressly to explain his reasons for doing so: authors of *Hellenika* omitted this period, concentrating on the time before the Persian Wars or on the wars themselves. Hellanikos, the only writer who touched on the period between the Persian and Peloponnesian wars in his Attic history, did so only cursorily and with inaccurate chronology (1.97.2).

The very presence of such a comment made in the first person (ἔγραψα) demonstrates the historian's self-conscious awareness that his narrative will deviate somewhat from its primary aim; now his purpose will shift slightly from an analysis of the foundations of Athenian power to an exposition of the way in which the *arche* itself was established.[61] Thucydides' remarks on his procedure in the rest of the Pentekontaetia are instructive as much for the light they shed by implication on what preceded as they are for what follows 1.97. Words such as ἀπόδειξις, "exposition," with reference to the following narrative, and the allusion to treating the events between the wars on a broader canvas confirm a fundamental difference from the earlier chapters 1.89–96. It is significant, that is, that Thucydides places these remarks on his approach at this point in the Pentekontaetia, and not earlier. However, we should bear in mind as we proceed that Thucydides does not suggest the intention of providing a comprehensive narrative of events; his need to explain the departure from his primary purpose, now an exposition and analysis of the establishment of Athens' *arche*, confirms that he will, in true Thucydidean fashion, keep the events chosen for inclusion to the minimum. Therefore, it will be instructive, as always, to mark what he isolates as worthy of inclusion, especially what warrants detailed attention.

61. ἅμα δὲ καὶ τῆς ἀρχῆς ἀπόδειξιν ἔχει τῆς τῶν Ἀθηναίων ἐν οἵῳ τρόπῳ κατέστη, 1.97.2. The use of *tropos* recalls the opening of the Pentekontaetia, 1.89.1.

Thucydides begins by relating early League activities in a way that emphasizes their function in enhancing Athens' strength at the expense of the League as a whole. As in 1.96, he pointedly focuses on the Athenians, not the League collectively, as the initiators of aggression against primarily Greek targets, whose defeat brings tangible, concrete benefit to the Athenians themselves, with nothing said explicitly about that to the allies.[62] The inference is not necessarily that the allies in fact derived no advantage from the early campaigns of the League; rather, that Thucydides' narrative is constructed to demonstrate the falsehood of the πρόσχημα, a word that, especially in an author as fond of antitheses as Thucydides, begs to be balanced, explicitly or implicitly, by the true reason for instituting tribute and a standing navy. Thucydides answers this implicit antithesis in 1.98: while the first League campaign is directed against a town held by the Persians, Eion on the Strymon, in none of the other League activities are League moneys and fleet directed πρὸς τὸν βάρβαρον; the narrative unfolds with examples of the use of the fleet to increase directly and gradually the power of the Athenians. Of direct benefit, they gain a new colony as a result of the seizure of Skyros, a pirate haven.

Explicit reference to the suppression of piracy and colonization recalls the use to which the naval power of Minos was put; there Thucydides spelled out the probable concrete benefits of thalassocracy and the suppression of piracy in terms of economic gain, and a connection was suggested between revenue and naval power, and colonization as a means of extension and consolidation of naval power. Singling out in both cases the significance of naval power for acquiring wealth through the eradication of piracy and other means is deliberate; once again, as in 1.96, the Archaeology informs substantively the selection of material and analytical criteria.

Thucydides' treatment, then, of the uses to which League moneys and navy were immediately put demonstrates the Athenians' ability to employ the allies' voluntary efforts and contributions in the process of *auxesis*. League membership is gradually expanded by coercion, as the Karystians and Naxians are forced by siege into the alliance, while League wealth increases from such expansion, from slavery, and presumably revenue from piracy and from tribute from the new members. Thucydides then moves from specific examples of the treatment of uncooperative Greeks to a general analysis of the significance of dissatisfaction and revolts. His approach is familiar: he is not interested in disaffection and revolt simply as a reflection or consequence of *arche*, but rather in their relevance for understanding the *auxesis* of empire.

62. This is brought out well by Rawlings, *Phoenix* 31 (1977):1–8.

First, he suggests a pattern of revolts that resulted in "enslavement" in violation of "the established agreement" (τὸ καθεστηκός), of which the subjugation of the Naxians was only the first, and cites inadequate tribute payments and ship contributions, and a failure to serve on campaigns, as the chief points of contention fostering rebellion. The Athenians used coercion against those who failed to comply entirely with their obligations in these areas, and their exacting and belligerent stance toward the allies sparked revolts.

Thucydides next analyzes the specific means by which the general climate of dissatisfaction led to a decisive increase in Athens' naval *dunamis*. He continues to present a subtle and complex picture of the evolution of an unequal power relationship between Athens and its allies, while at the same time offering insight into his own thinking about the nature of naval power. Let us look closely at the passage, introduced by a general comment:

> No longer were the Athenians otherwise at all agreeable [to the allies] as leaders, nor did they serve on campaigns on an equal basis,[63] and it was accordingly easier to compel to submission those who revolted. For this [inequality] and its consequences, the allies were themselves responsible. For it was because of their reluctance to serve on campaign that a good number, in order to remain at home, had themselves assessed to pay a proportionate amount of money instead of ships, and the navy increased in strength [verbal form of *auxesis*] to the Athenians' benefit from the expense (*dapane*) incurred by the allies; while the allies, whenever they would revolt, went into war unprepared (*aparaskeuoi*) and untrained. (1.99.2–3)

Thucydides thus plots the next decisive stage of the *arche*: he argues that, as in the transfer of hegemony, the allies once again facilitated the growth of Athenian power—unwittingly, but not without their own self-interest in mind. In this case, the process was insidious: by preferring to pay tribute over serving on campaign, they financed an Athenian fleet at their own expense, and that, ultimately, brought about their own subjugation. As the institution of tribute is regarded as the foundation of Athens' *dunamis*, it is likewise the mechanism of *auxesis*. The revenue-expense-power ratio could not be more precisely defined than it is in this passage, in which the necessary use (*dapane*) of money to sustain a fleet is presented by the historian in its most explicit form; while it is itself an elaboration of an earlier remark by Archidamos (1.83.2), which concisely makes the same point that the function of money in the sphere of naval power lies in expense. Indeed, the increase in requirements of money

---

63. I understand by the phrase "on an equal basis" (ἀπὸ τοῦ ἴσου) not an equality of power but rather, especially from what follows, a reference to the equal application of campaign obligations on all.

over manpower would have crystallized the fact that money was the basis of the Delian League's *dunamis*. Thucydides, thus, continues to analyze naval power not on an abstract or static plane in which, for example, the institution of tribute would be used to indicate the deteriorated status of the allies; rather, tribute is the key to understanding the anatomy, the very *phusis*, of naval power.

The role of the allies in the Athenians' *auxesis* thus continues to be of crucial importance to Thucydides, who argues that the Athenian *arche* cannot be understood simplistically as a one-way relationship between oppressor and victim. Additionally, his analyses of 1.95–96 and 1.99 in particular reveal an astute understanding of embryonic power and the nature of *auxesis:* power does not burst forth fully formed. To put it in Thucydidean terms: the phenomenon of the Athenian *arche* cannot be explained simply by the use of force; such power requires massive expenditure that no one polis from its own internal resources could possibly have sustained; it depends on the concentration of money pooled from a large area under the control of one polis. It was self-evident that Athens could not exert power before acquiring power; that is why the relationship between Athens and its allies is central to Thucydides' analysis, for the financial resources necessary for naval *arche* had to come voluntarily from them. The phenomenon of voluntary change of status, then, acquires a larger, fundamental significance in the growth of Athenian power. Indeed, this unique aspect of Athens' *arche*, namely, that it was developed largely without the direct use of force, is a point remarked on explicitly by the Athenians at Sparta, partly as a justification for its existence.[64]

Thucydides suggests, then, a general trend of conversion to tributary status. Quantification is difficult, if not impossible, both of those who voluntarily changed their status and of those who became tributary as a result of revolt. His account of voluntary change, however, has elicited serious doubt chiefly because of its presumption of an initially sizable number of ship contributors in the League and the motivation he offers for the change. Some scholars have gone so far as to reject the entire chapter, but the reasons advanced are ultimately unpersuasive.[65] More serious objections to taking 1.99 as good historical evidence have been proposed by E. Ruschenbusch in a series of articles concerned with citi-

---

64. 1.75.2, 76.2.

65. Robertson, *AJAH* 5 (1980):65, finds that the conversion to tributary status "strains credulity" because it is impossible, he argues, to suppose that there could be a fixed, standard monetary value of a trireme. Yet there is no reason to suppose this. Robertson is making an assumption about how monetary payments would have been assessed in relation to ship payments and then using that assumption to discount Thucydides on the grounds of impossibility; I shall return to this shortly.

zen population figures in many small communities, mainly islands, in the Delian League.[66] Ruschenbusch has concluded that the number of citizens in practically all of these communities would have been too small ever to have been sufficient to man one trireme, much less more than one.[67] How strong are the grounds for this view?

First, it presupposes a direct parallel between ancient population figures and those between the years 1879–1940; in other words the population in most of these small communities would have remained basically stable over a long period of time. While one can accept the premise that fewer dramatic changes might have occurred over time in these communities compared to larger ones, this view does not adequately take into account many significant variable factors such as disease, emigration and immigration, depletion of land resources, and changes in the arability of land due to drought. Second, ancient testimony other than that of Thucydides tells against Ruschenbusch's thesis: numbered among the Greek poleis contributing ships to the Hellenic cause in the Persian Wars are many which likely were original members of the Delian League—the Eretrians, Keans, Naxians, Styrians, Kythnians, Seriphians, and Siphnians (Hdt. 8.46.2–4). In addition, there were many Greeks in the Persian fleet who contributed both men and ships, detailed also by Herodotos: the Ionians alone furnished one hundred ships (7.94), the islanders, seventeen ships (7.95.1), and those from Pontos, one hundred ships (7.95.2). And as Blackman has noted, the losses of ships in the Persian Wars were probably not tremendously large.[68] It is clear that Ionian and Hellespontine allies had their own ships, which would have been necessary to sail to their respective homes following the siege of Sestos.[69]

66. Ruschenbusch, ZPE 53 (1983):125–43, 144–48; "Modell Amorgos," 265–71; ZPE 59 (1985):253–63. Cf. also Merkelbach and Varinlioglu, ZPE 59 (1985):264.

67. He bases his population estimates on two factors: believing, first, that there is a close relation between amounts of tribute, citizen population, and an agricultural livelihood, he arrives at a figure of 1 talent of tribute per 800 citizens, 3,000 dr. per 400, and so on; and second, that population figures between the years 1879–1940 establish limits applicable to the fifth and fourth centuries B.C. (ZPE 53 [1983]: 126). Difficulties in estimating occur (1) in the case of naval, nonagricultural cities, since agricultural potential and yield are the criteria used in the estimates; (2) in the case of cities whose tribute exceeded 1 talent, because they may have had other sources of income that were considered when the tribute was assessed. Thus, if one accepts the conclusion that only a very small number of cities would have been able to contribute manned ships, then one is compelled to question the accuracy of Thucydides' statement in 1.99, which carries the implication that many states had contributed ships in the early years of the League. One is forced, therefore, to choose between population estimates based on modern analogy and the ancient testimony of Thucydides.

68. Blackman, GRBS 10 (1969):180–81.

69. Thuc. 1.89.2; Blackman, ibid. Herodotos, however, does not mention that the allies took part in the siege; still, they had participated in the earlier campaigns.

But there is another consideration as well: Ruschenbusch rejects the idea of ship contributors among the majority of allies on the grounds that they would have lacked the necessary complement of two hundred to man a single trireme; yet nowhere does Thucydides or any other source state that triremes alone were eligible for the League fleet. Indeed, there is every reason to suppose that some of the ships contributed were pentekonters, which at least Melos, Seriphos, and Siphnos are known to have supplied in the Persian War campaigns (Hdt. 8.46). Accordingly, many of the smaller communities could easily have contributed ships and men, even if we were to accept Ruschenbusch's estimates. In addition, merchant ships (ὁλκάδες) would have been used for transporting troops and provisions, and πλοῖα as messenger boats, though these latter perhaps not on any large scale.[70] Finally, those providing ships need not have manned them solely from the citizenry; slaves may also have been used as rowers.[71]

We would like to be able to quantify more precisely Thucydides' vague οἱ πλείους, "many," partly so that we could test the validity of the interpretation advanced here that the voluntary aspect is critical to the historian's analysis of Athens' *auxesis*. "Many" was apparently sufficient for his analysis; he may not have known the precise number. The vagueness does not, however, suggest lack of confidence that in fact there were many—and no *eikos* argument is presented, the absence of which is the historian's implicit guarantee of accuracy. Although his accuracy cannot be proven, there are insufficient grounds for rejecting Thucydides' testimony wholesale; certainly his interest in the collective responsibility of Athenians and allies alike in the creation and development of Athens' *arche* implies corresponding diligence in research, given the historian's propensity to buttress his views with concrete evidence.

The reason that Thucydides supplies for the allies' preferring to pay tribute, "in order not to be away from home," is credible, though its implication that paying tribute entirely exempted allies from military service does not inspire complete confidence. However, his explanation may suggest that in the absence of a large war (during which time we know that allies served alongside Athenians), it was possible for service on campaigns to be minimal. But if we accept Thucydides, are we compelled to reject Plutarch (*Kim.* 11), who describes the initiative as coming from the Athenians (and specifically Kimon)? The difference between sources here is rather similar to that between Thucydides' and Herodotos' treatment of Pausanias, which we examined earlier in this chapter. In both cases, Thucydides explores the question of the allies' responsi-

---

70. As in, e.g., Thuc. 6.22 (explicitly allied boats), 30.1, 44.1; 7.7.3, 17.3, 18.4, 19.3.
71. As in the case of Chian ships, 8.15.2.

bility, while not, in my view, discounting the possibility of Athenian motives. In this case, Thucydides' account permits an eagerness on the part of the Athenians that allies contributing ships change to the tributary category.

Let us return to the terms of the adjustment in the relationship between Athens and the allies who changed their status. The Athenians arranged for them to pay a sum of money which Thucydides describes as a "proportionate" or "corresponding cost," an amount that the allies "had coming to them."[72] What does the phrase mean? We are not to suppose one fixed sum for everyone who converted to a monetary payment. Rather, just as the various poleis were assessed different amounts of tribute depending on their individual circumstances, and had likely contributed different numbers of ships, so for each, the "corresponding cost" would also have varied. But we have no reason to assume that the Athenians attempted directly to correlate the cost of a trireme and tribute payment[73] nor that the amount would have been lower than a rough equivalent of the cash outlay on a trireme (or other kind of ship).[74] First of all, as Thucydides puts it, the issue was not one of lightening a polis's financial or equivalent burden but of reducing the time spent away from home (which could have a financial effect). We should not overlook the possibility that subjective criteria such as time, travel, and effort would have been taken into account. Those who chose voluntarily to change their category, after all, were paying money for others to perform the service and take on the burden which they had previously carried. That is, the ἱκνούμενον ἀνάλωμα may not have been made on objectively quantifiable grounds alone.

We can see how the change described in 1.99 is crucial for understanding the development of the relationship between Athens and its allies from the standpoint of exchange. At the beginning of the League, allies contributed to a common effort. A fundamental change occurred, as described in 1.99, when the relationship transformed into a cash payment by one party (the allies) for a service by another party (the Athenians). Thus, the operation becomes, in a limited but important sense, a strictly economic act or contract. Payment of cash for a service re-

---

72. τὸ ἱκνούμενον ἀνάλωμα, 1.99.3. The bibliography on 1.99 and specifically on the states involved is extensive. A useful place to start is *ATL* 3:244–52, and Woodhead, "West's Panel of Ship Payers," 170–78, for commentary and bibliography. See also Gomme, *HCT* 1, ad loc.

73. *Contra* Robertson, *AJAH* 5 (1980):65.

74. Blackman, *GRBS* 10 (1969):184; cf. Finley's suggestion, *Economy and Society*, 49 (= "The Fifth-Century Athenian Empire," 112–13), that, following the battle of Eurymedon, the prospect of a reduced financial burden offered by tribute would have contributed to the change in category, with his general discussion on 49–50.

moves entirely the good-faith element of a common contribution and roughly equal exchange; from the perspective of *charis*, the Athenians, as Perikles points out in the Funeral Oration, always have the upper hand (2.40.4).[75]

In 1.94–99, Thucydides highlights the Athenians' alacrity in using their position to their decided advantage; but in cases that also involved actions or decisions motivated by the allies' self-interest, the historian shapes his account accordingly to give prominence to this aspect, which he judged essential to the development of Athenian power. His attention to the allies' responsibility clearly ties in with an earlier discussion about developing power in the period sandwiched between the "second account" of Minos and Troy (1.8.3) that we examined in the previous chapter. The connection is deliberate; indeed, the parallels are striking.[76] Recall the linear progression from Minos to Agamemnon: the result of Minos' naval rule, by which he expelled pirates and colonized the islands, was a general increase in the use of the sea, and the *ktesis* of wealth. Stronger and weaker alike were party to the development of a profoundly unequal relationship that fed the self-interest of both: the weak were motivated by the expectation of advantages which would make the price of subjugation tolerable, while the strong, by possessing *periousiai*, won for themselves the weaker as subjects. In the course of time, the numbers of those on one side were great enough to mount a campaign the size of the Trojan expedition. It follows, therefore, that Agamemnon as the head of this campaign had power through inherited wealth, not through oaths (1.8.2–9.2).

This parallels remarkably the account of 1.96–99: the hegemony of Athens in the Delian League led to the expulsion of pirates and colonization (Skyros). It insured the *ktesis* of wealth (the League treasury, tribute, and other revenue). Athens and the allies both had reasons to develop an unequal relationship: the weaker allies were willing to endure subjection for the benefits first of plunder, then of protection without personal sacrifice; while the stronger Athenians, in control of the *periousiai* of the League, were able to render the allies subjects. The result was a naval power extensive enough to undertake a war of the scope of the Peloponnesian War.

The coherence of the two analyses both confirms and offers additional insight into 1.94–99. For we can appreciate how the treatment of the evolution of Athens' rule in those chapters fits into a larger historical

---

75. See Bourdieu, *Outline of a Theory of Practice*, 171–73, for the implications of an increasingly "economic" character of a contract.

76. Scholars have noted general similarities between the account of the Trojan expedition and the Athenian empire and have suggested other specific correspondences; e.g., Rabel, *CJ* 80 (1984):8–10; Hunter, *Klio* 62 (1980):203–5.

conception about the development of power and power relationships. It is also clear that Thucydides' method of focusing alternately on the allies and the Athenians is not intended to lay blame at key stages on one side and thus remove it temporarily from the other, but rather to show that both sides are intertwined in a complex relationship, with each expecting to gain something tangible. Thucydides presents a dispassionate analysis, making no moral judgments on either the Athenians or the allies. It is tempting at first glance to read implicit condemnation of the Athenians into this account because of its careful attention to their use of the League to develop their own power at the allies' expense in money and freedom; but it is important to remember Thucydides' purpose in writing these chapters. We have examined them with the utmost scrutiny and have found a strict adherence to the aim of analyzing rationally the concrete stages by which the Athenian *arche* evolved—and this purpose precludes moral judgment and criticism.

In Thucydides' account of the increase in tributary members of the alliance and its role as a catalyst in the development of *arche*, the beauty of the Athenian *arche* emerges in elegant and simple form. The Athenian *arche* rested on the use (*dapane*) of the resources of the allies; moreover, the allies' regular contribution of money to the League treasury enabled the Athenians not only to sustain but also to increase (thus, *auxesis*) their fleet. The connection between *chremata* and *nautikon* through expense could not be more clearly expressed. That it was not an obvious connection is suggested by the fact that Thucydides judged it important to explain the relationship. The additional ingenuity of the arrangement was that at decisive stages cooperation, not compulsion, was responsible for *auxesis*, a remarkable circumstance in the history of power and *arche* (cf. Xen. *Por.* 5.5). The consequence was the nonviolent acquisition by one polis of the precious wealth of others; that it was for the purpose of maintaining power over those same poleis that supplied the wealth is a great irony.

Thucydides has marked distinct stages in the increase in Athens' power after establishing its initial foundations. Thus, the imposition of tribute upon some of the allies was the fundamental basis on which the Athenians built the phenomenon of the *arche*. The next stage was the change to tributary status of most of the ship-contributing members. Thucydides emphasizes a crucial result of this: the allies were the ones who paid for the Athenian navy. The necessity and function of expense, *dapane*, will echo throughout the work, linked with the need for revenue. In war, as Archidamos notes, expense is the constant factor. In the development of naval *arche*, it is the sine qua non.

In the rest of the Pentekontaetia, Thucydides points out other ways by which Athens' *dunamis* increased as well. Revolts turned out to the advantage of the Athenians, because their suppression usually resulted in the imposition of tribute, if the polis was not already tributary. Such was the case with Thasos (1.101.3). In addition, the Athenians would compel the state to pay an indemnity, so that they ultimately suffered no serious financial loss, as in the case of both Thasos and Samos (1.101.3, 117.3). Furthermore, Thucydides' account of the revolt of Thasos is illuminating also for pointing to financial benefits other than tribute derived from the empire even in the early years of the League. The revolt was prompted, he tells us, by a dispute concerning the mines under the control of the Thasians, and after the revolt was suppressed, the Athenians gained control of the mines. This testifies to a considerable source of income over and above tribute which presumably benefited the Athenians alone and, furthermore, which would have made its way directly to Athens, rather than the League treasury on Delos.[77] Finally, Thucydides specifies the financial gain which resulted when Athens forced new members into the League, as they did Aigina (1.108.4). In all of these cases, Athens gained not only money but also ships, for the states were required to surrender their fleets.

In the Pentekontaetia, therefore, Thucydides has applied the same method and criteria used in the Archaeology to illuminate and to judge the development of Athenian power. Thus, the reader is given the means by which to weigh Athens' strength against that of the most notable previous rulers and states: Minos and Agamemnon, for example, also possessed a fleet, *periousiai chrematon*, and empire, but of a lesser degree compared to the Athenians in the fifty years before the war. In addition, the emphasis on inherited power in the Archaeology also continues in the Pentekontaetia: the Athenians took over an existing League and built on it.[78] As has also emerged, the Archaeology is instrumental in adumbrating the chapters in the Pentekontaetia that treat the development of the *arche;* in particular, Thucydides' account of Minos and Agamemnon informs and enriches the reader's understanding of the nature of Thucydides' analysis of Athenian power.

Our examination of these two analytical sections of the work, the Archaeology and the Pentekontaetia, has sought to lay out the historian's approach to and conception of the role of financial resources with re-

---

77. Herodotos, 6.46.3, estimates the amount of revenue extracted from the mines at Skapte Hyle at eighty talents, and the total from the island and mainland ranging from two hundred to three hundred talents annually.

78. This perhaps explains why Thucydides does not portray the Delian League as a *new* alliance, but rather, more the continuation of what was already created, in contrast to later sources who do present the Delian League as something new and separate from the Hellenic League led by the Spartans.

spect to naval power. It should be clear that this is not simply an aspect that Thucydides was aware of and noted, but rather, that it is at the very core of his understanding of the historical development of power, to such an extent that he gives it prominence in the section of the work which penetrates to the foundation of Athens' naval *arche*. In his analyses of earlier powers, for which evidence was lacking, the historian had recourse to *eikos* arguments and similar deductive reasoning, which addressed, significantly, the role of financial resources in their development as well. We now have the conceptual framework to turn to Thucydides' main subject, the Peloponnesian War itself, to continue to explore the historian's treatment of financial resources.

CHAPTER THREE

Financial Resources on the Eve of the Peloponnesian War

We have seen in the arguments of the Archaeology and Pentekontaetia consistent attention to the connection between *chremata* and *nautikon*, and to the relationship of revenue, reserve, and expense (*prosodos, periousiai chrematon, dapane*). The historian's analyses are intended to demonstrate that naval *arche* on Athens' scale is possible only through the accumulation and immediate, continual expenditure of *chremata*, from a reserve supplemented regularly by revenue. As Thucydides' intention in both the Archaeology and the Pentekontaetia was to present arguments and evidence to justify key thematic statements on the magnitude both of Athens' naval *arche* and of the Peloponnesian War compared to earlier military engagements and attempts at naval power, and as the role of financial resources was of explicit, paramount importance in his analysis, the reader expects the historian to continue with this focus and purpose. Yet it is precisely in Thucydides' account of the Peloponnesian War itself that scholars have detected little interest in the area of finances. As we have seen, the relationship between finances and external military power is woven more tightly into the fabric of the Archaeology and the Pentekontaetia than has been recognized; is it integral as well to the history of the Archidamian War?

In this chapter we shall examine the historian's account of the outbreak of the war using the same approach as in the previous two chapters, following Thucydides' narrative, argument, and speeches in the account of this period. In doing so, we shall consider (1) whether Thucydides highlights the same elements in analyzing his main subject as he did in the Archaeology and Pentekontaetia, thus drawing attention to the connection between *chremata, nautikon,* and *arche;* (2) if he does shape his material and analysis in such a manner, whether it is general or specific in nature; (3) the implications of his analyses concerned with financial resources for our understanding of his conception of Athenian *dunamis* and military strategy.

THE *AITIAI* AND *DIAPHORAI* OF THE PELOPONNESIAN WAR

The Epidamnian affair and the Korinthian/Kerkyraian conflict

Let us begin by considering the Kerkyraian and Korinthian conflict over Epidamnos, the first of the disputes which led to the Peloponnesian War. This conflict is also the first instance in which the *History* treats specific, contemporary events of causal importance to the main subject, the war itself. Thucydides recounts briefly the history of Epidamnos and its relationship to both Korinth (one of whose citizens was the founder of Epidamnos) and Kerkyra (the mother city), and the latter's refusal to help the demos of Epidamnos in stasis. He notes the Epidamnians' query to Delphi whether to hand over their city to Korinth and the oracle's favorable response, armed with which the Epidamnians turned to the Korinthians, reminded them that the founder of Epidamnos was a Korinthian, and told them of the oracle's pronouncement (1.24–25.2). The Korinthians accepted the appeal "according to justice" (κατὰ τὸ δίκαιον, that is, because of their relationship to the colony through the founder) and also because of their hatred (μῖσος) of the Kerkyraians for their contempt of Korinth, their mother city (1.25.3). Thucydides continues with the reason for the hatred:

> For neither did [the Kerkyraians] give the customary honors due to Korinth in their common festivals nor did they give precedence to Korinthians in the sacrifices just as the other colonies did; instead, they disdained them, since in wealth (*chrematon dunamei*) they were equal to the richest of the Hellenes and more powerful in military resources (*te es polemon paraskeue dunatoteroi*), while their navy (*nautiko*) was greatly superior, owing partly to the fame of the great sailors, the Phaiakians, who previously dwelled on Kerkyra; indeed, this encouraged them to build up a fleet (*nautikon*) which was not inconsiderable in power (*ouk adunatoi*), comprised of 120 triremes when the war broke out. (1.25.4)

In addition to their sense of responsibility, the Korinthians were also motivated to heed the Epidamnians' appeal because of their hatred caused by a slight to their honor;[1] Thucydides thus provides a rare glimpse into the complexities of the relationship between metropolis, colony, and founder in his discussion of the causes of the Epidamnian

---

1. The precise nature of the obligations and honors scorned is somewhat uncertain; see Graham, *Colony*, 161; on relations between Korinth and Kerkyra generally, see Salmon, *Wealthy Corinth*, 270–80.

affair. He alludes to the role of the oracle and the issue of justice and responsibility, and it is chiefly on these aspects that scholars have focused.[2] But a further element—the Kerkyraians' superior power, the result of their wealth and fleet—provides another manifestation of the Kerkyraians' arrogance and thus another reason for the μῖσος.[3] Recall the detail and choice of words with which Thucydides defines the specific elements of the Kerkyraians' power: their *chrematon dunamis, nautikon,* and *paraskeue,* key terms that he has linked in the Archaeology and Pentekontaetia as well as here, where he ties the Kerkyraians' wealth directly to their ability to make war.[4]

Thucydides' emphasis on justice, honor, and even hatred as causal factors comes as no surprise to students of Greek literature and, more relevant here, Greek historiography. Indeed, Herodotos described in great detail the enmity between Korinth and Kerkyra in the time of Periander, in which retaliation and revenge are presented as prominent motives (3.48–53). But while Herodotos might have described the Kerkyraians' arrogance as hubris, because they scorned their obligations to their mother city and had excessive wealth, or have concentrated on personal motives, Thucydides not only attributes the Kerkyraians' attitude partly to their wealth but also is specific about its role in generating strength and power (*dunamis*). It is this kind of detail and analysis of power on the basis of *chremata* and *nautikon* which, as we can begin to appreciate, marks Thucydides' originality.

Indeed, Herodotos' story of Croesus and Solon is instructive in illuminating the difference in approach between the two historians to the meaning and importance of wealth and its role in historical events. To Herodotos, Croesus' belief that he was "most blessed" (ὀλβιώτατος, 1.30.3) because of his great wealth was sheer hubris.[5] Herodotos' purpose is to illustrate the dangers of hubris, the jealousy of the gods, and the misguided equation of wealth with happiness. These messages are couched in words such as εὐδαιμονίη and ὀλβιώτατος. Though Herodotos alone of the two historians formulates the notion that great wealth leads to evil and destruction (especially if one's prosperity is not tempered by some bad luck) and makes it inseparable from belief in divine

---

2. Gomme, *HCT* 1, ad loc.; Graham, *Colony,* 26–27, 147–51, 153; Kagan, *Outbreak,* 205–21, 223–26; Ste. Croix, *OPW,* 66–70, 77–79; Salmon, *Wealthy Corinth,* 280–85.

3. Hatred is clearly an important motive which deserves explanation as here; cf. also 1.96, where hatred of Pausanias is the direct cause of the formation of the Delian League; also 1.103.4 (Korinth toward Athens: τὸ σφόδρον μῖσος); 2.64.5; 3.67.5; 4.128.5; 5.27.2; 6.17.6.

4. τῇ ἐς πόλεμον παρασκευῇ, 1.25.4.

5. Polykrates' wealth was also implicitly one of the components of his good fortune (3.39–43).

retribution, the idea that great wealth may cause arrogance is present in both works; yet there is a profound difference between the two authors' definition and expression of the idea.

In Thucydides' account, which treats a typical Herodotean theme of the causes of a long-standing feud, the significance of wealth as a basis for the animosity is treated analytically in relation to ships, preparation for war, and power. The Kerkyraians, then, have enormous power because of their wealth and fleet of triremes, and in addition they possess an impressive heritage which brings them fame.[6] All of these factors combine to breed arrogance and arouse the Korinthians' μῖσος.

The Korinthians' awareness of the need for money follows immediately on the heels of their acceptance of the Epidamnians' appeal. After the initial land force they dispatched to Epidamnos proved insufficient to defend the Epidamnians in the city against the Kerkyraians, the Korinthians made preparations to send an army and, at the same time, "proclaimed that a colony would be sent out to Epidamnos and that anyone who wished could go on an equal basis; but if anyone wanted to join the colony but did not wish to sail immediately, he could pay fifty Korinthian drachmas and remain behind" (1.27.1). This passage has often been discussed but only with reference to the colony itself, that is, Epidamnos' relationship to Korinth and Kerkyra, and not in regard to the clause on the payment (καταθέντα) whereby those who wished to take part in the colony later could buy into it now and remain behind.[7] Was this a common option, and whatever the answer, why does Thucydides choose to tell us about it?

First, what precisely is envisioned? κατατίθημι can mean "deposit," that is, something put down which would be returned upon arrival in the colony; but this sense occurs usually only in the middle voice,[8] whereas καταθέντα is here more likely a down payment, not a refundable deposit.[9] This practice seems to be unusual, although one cannot be

---

6. Cf. 1.13.2: the *Korinthians* λέγονται . . . τριήρεις ἐν Κορίνθῳ πρῶτον τῆς Ἑλλάδος ναυπηγηθῆναι, and they themselves had an impressive heritage and fame due to their wealth: χρήμασί τε δυνατοὶ ἦσαν, ὡς καὶ τοῖς παλαιοῖς ποιηταῖς δεδήλωται· ἀφνειὸν γὰρ ἐπωνόμασαν τὸ χωρίον (1.13.5).

7. Graham, *Colony*, esp., 134, 147–50, 153, and for earlier bibliography; Salmon, *Wealthy Corinth*, 387–88 (and for bibliography), who, although he discusses the question of reinforcements sent by Korinth to its colonies, makes no note of this monetary alternative. Gomme, *HCT* 1, ad loc., mentions the fifty Korinthian drachmas, but only to translate the amount into Attic currency.

8. LSJ II. 4; Thucydides uses the verb several times in reference to hostages, e.g., 1.115.3; 3.102; 8.3.

9. Cf. 7.82.3 for another example of money handed over and not to be returned. Perhaps in 1.27.1 the issue is not Thucydides' usage, but rather the use and meaning of the verb in official language, since Thucydides' description reads very much as the actual proclamation (κήρυγμα) would have, cf. below.

certain. At least, such an option does not appear in any of the foundation decrees extant or in literary accounts of foundations of colonies, where, given the degree of detail in the arrangements related, one might well expect to find it.[10] Its absence suggests that it was not a common occurrence.

Thucydides records the precise amount of the payment (*pentekonta drachmas . . . Korinthias*) and also the result: many chose to sail immediately to the colony, and many paid down money and remained at home. The historian also specifies "silver" (*argurion*), rather than the more general *chremata*. Indeed, the entire description of the request for participants in the colony has a decidedly documentary character, suggested especially by the phrasing of the proclamation.[11] This points to careful research as well as interest in the specific financial arrangements. What then was the significance of the colony and the "deposit" to Thucydides? One could argue that the effect on the actual military conflict was minimal: the next battle was a decisive victory for the Kerkyraians, who, with their allies, besieged Epidamnos and forced the city to surrender. It was not its effectiveness in the development of events that is notable, though the measure doubtless raised money for the Korinthians: as noted, Thucydides remarks that many chose to pay a deposit of silver, fifty Korinthian drachmas each.[12] Thucydides' narrative has conditioned the reader's awareness of the financial aspect of military ventures; its presence in this, a minor, low-cost episode compared with what will soon follow, has the effect of highlighting what will be a critical issue in the coming war and will crystallize in the course of Thucydides' account, namely, that military success depends on financial resources, not from quickly raised funds but from accumulated reserves.[13]

That the Korinthians not only recognized their financial weakness relative to Kerkyra but also regarded it as an obstacle to military success is clear from the down payment for participation in the new colony and is further suggested by their requiring money from the Thebans, Phleiasians, and Elians, allies who accompanied the settlers to Epidamnos (1.27.2).[14] Epidamnos' location on the coast meant that armed engagements would be primarily naval, and this explains the need for *chremata*, which would have been much less relevant for land engagements alone.

---

10. Cf. the most complete foundation decrees, *IG* I³ 46 (Brea); ML 5 (Cyrene); cf. also ML 20 (Naupaktos); cf. also Graham, *Colony*, 40–68.
11. τὸν βουλόμενον, εἰ δέ τις, etc.; cf. also 1.26.1, τὸν βουλόμενον.
12. 1 Korinthian drachma = ⅔ of an Attic drachma.
13. Cf. 1.141.5; cf. 1.80.4.
14. This suggests that their decision to send out a colony to Epidamnos had a practical, military goal, to defend Epidamnos by sea. The Korinthians' need for money is attested also by an Epidamnian issue at this time to finance Korinthian aid, Kraay, *ACGC*, 84.

What is most important for our present purposes is that Thucydides chose to include these specific details about levying cash for naval war.

The naval battle off Aktion was won by the Kerkyraians, who then proceeded to retaliate against Kyllene for aiding the Korinthians; Thucydides specifies the nature of their aid: *naus kai chremata* (1.30.2).[15] The Korinthians, on the other hand, turned their attention with zeal and fervor (ὀργή) toward building up their fleet, in preparation for renewing the fight against the Kerkyraians.[16] The historian notes that their efforts lasted two years (1.31.1). They used their resources (*mistho peithontes*) to lure rowers from throughout Greece (1.31.1). This is the first of several instances in which reference to mercenaries and *misthos* appears in the years before the war. At first glance, such references do not seem to warrant special notice; yet Thucydides makes a point of noting when soldiers have been hired for pay, particularly in the period preceding the outbreak of war, and a connection appears between the need for money and procuring soldiers. Hired soldiers were common in the archaic period and in the fourth century but were relatively rare in the fifth century, at least until the Peloponnesian War.[17]

Thus, Thucydides is documenting a new development in the arena of war. The Korinthians' preparations in building ships and hiring rowers have a decisive effect on the Kerkyraians, who grow frightened and ask the Athenians for an alliance, a move which causes the Korinthians in turn to send an embassy to Athens. Let us consider their respective arguments, keeping in mind the obvious point that Thucydides has chosen purposely to present these speeches in such a way as to highlight the factors that he has judged central.[18]

---

15. This reference is directly causal: the Kerkyraians burned the land of Kyllene because the inhabitants had helped the Korinthians.

16. Just as they had accepted the Epidamnians' appeal out of μῖσος for the Kerkyraians, they now worked furiously to build up their fleet out of ὀργή.

17. Parke, *GMS*, 14–17; Garlan, *War*, 94. See Pritchett, *GSAW* 1:7–13, for a thorough discussion of the evidence for the introduction of military pay in the fifth century; he concludes that pay was almost certainly instituted prior to the Peloponnesian War, though not necessarily much before. See also, above, p. 10.

18. Since these are the first speeches to be examined here, it will be useful to express as succinctly as possible my views on the "authenticity question" (1.22.1), not in order to engage in controversy but rather to convey as simply as I can my understanding of Thucydides' principles of composition, since it will obviously underlie the analysis of speeches in this and later chapters. Thucydides regarded the *logoi* of the war as part of the entire *erga* of the war; his concern for accuracy extends in 1.22 to both speeches and narrative, as he makes clear. The difficulties of ascertaining or remembering exactly what was said, however, were substantial: as he comments, it was impossible to recall perfectly a speech that he himself heard, let alone to guarantee the accuracy of those reported by others. What was his method, then, if he was concerned about accuracy but unable to reproduce the original speech? We need not deal here with the various problems of interpretation of

When the Kerkyraians ask the Athenians for an alliance, they begin with reference to what is right and just;[19] then they move on to the tangible, concrete benefits of an alliance. They ask:

> What good service could be rarer, or what more detrimental to your enemies, than that the power (*dunamis*) that you value above much money (*pollon chrematon*) and favor arrives of its own free will, offering itself without danger and expense (*dapane*)? In addition, this alliance would confer *arete* on you in the eyes of many, while also bringing gratitude from those whom you have helped, and strength to you yourselves. (1.33.2)

Significantly, part of what the Kerkyraians specify that they have to offer is material and put in financial terms (*chremata, dapane*). Moreover, they begin this part of their argument by drawing attention to their fleet, which they note is the largest besides the Athenians'. Next, they cite the advantage of the voluntary addition of the Kerkyraian fleet to the Athenian navy, by making a point that we have seen has special weight in Thucydides' own ideas about money and power. They allude to the indirect financial gain accruing to the Athenians, since they, the Kerkyraians, would be assuming the expense (*dapane*). Thus, they address explicitly this essential mechanism linking *chremata* and *nautikon*. Furthermore, they draw attention to the great expense required to acquire new allies by force. Finally, the Kerkyraians offer the possibility that the Korinthians might gain an advantage over them by hiring sailors (*misthophorous*) from the Athenian alliance as well as elsewhere (1.35.4). The idea of the

---

Thucydides' Greek in this passage, in particular, in the sentence ὡς δ' ἂν ἐδόκουν ἐμοὶ ἕκαστοι περὶ τῶν αἰεὶ παρόντων τὰ δέοντα μάλιστ' εἰπεῖν, ἐχομένῳ ὅτι ἐγγύτατα τῆς ξυμπάσης γνώμης τῶν ἀληθῶς λεχθέντων, οὕτως εἴρηται. Whatever the precise meaning of the ambiguous τὰ δέοντα and τῆς ξυμπάσης γνώμης (on ἡ ξύμπασα γνώμη, see the useful comments of Badian, *Athenaeum* 80 [1992]:187-90), the historian is clearly implying that he had knowledge of the contents of speeches and stating that he is rendering them as accurately as possible. At the same time, he is plainly acknowledging that the speeches as they appear in his *History* are, ultimately, his own product (ἐδόκουν ἐμοί) based on the principles that he has noted (in contrast to the *erga*, which were written down οὐδ' ὡς ἐμοὶ ἐδόκει, 1.22.2) and not the speeches actually delivered. The important point to recognize is that Thucydides does not intend to rewrite history; fundamentally altering the actual speeches would have been diametrically opposed to his purpose and his conception of the value of the understanding to be gained from history. Yet the source material—that is, what he remembered himself and what he heard about from others—would have varied. His stated principles about the speeches and the literary nature and historical purpose of his work allow, if not require, that, as in the case of the *erga*, he will make choices about what is significant to his subject and to his own interpretation and analysis. This last point has particular importance for the present work, for what Thucydides includes in speeches about financial resources reflects both his knowledge and his view of their significance.

19. Cf. the comments of Connor, *Thucydides*, 34-35, n. 33.

Peloponnesians' hiring soldiers and sailors from Athenian-controlled cities surfaces here for the first time; its appearance so soon after the earlier mention of hiring mercenaries generally (1.31.1) not only suggests that it was a serious issue in the deliberations leading up to the war but also weakens further the reader's perception of the superiority even of the Peloponnesians' chief strength, their manpower.

We have seen how fundamental these arguments—that extended naval enterprises necessitate considerable expense and are by implication altogether different in nature and degree from traditional land warfare or short-term naval expeditions—are to Thucydides' analysis of power. The conclusion to be drawn is not that Thucydides was simply imposing his own ideas about the role of expense in naval war, but rather that he judged the issue of money and expense in these debates before the outbreak of war to be particularly important and, accordingly, featured them in his speeches. Whatever one's view on the composition of the speeches in the *History*, the fact is undiminished that financial resources occupy a central place in these *logoi*.

The Kerkyraians' arguments are sound and practical; yet the Athenians do not seem convinced of the advantages at this juncture:[20] they neither make overtures to the Kerkyraians themselves nor seize the opportunity to ally with them upon the Kerkyraians' offer. Thucydides tells us that when the speeches on both sides had been heard, the Athenians inclined toward accepting the Korinthians' arguments (1.44.1); only later did they change their minds. Clearly, they were not persuaded by the material benefit they would reap through an alliance with Kerkyra, either now or before.[21] The point is made especially forceful by the Kerkyraians' use of one of the most compelling arguments they could make, namely, that the Athenians could gain Kerkyra as an ally without expense—*dapane*. That the Athenians failed to be impressed by this, at least initially, attests to the confidence they had in their own *dunamis*, based on *periousia chrematon* and *nautikon*.

In the Korinthian and Kerkyraian war, what we would expect to happen does happen: first, the Kerkyraians have superior resources, and they emerge victorious throughout their confrontation with the Korinthians. Indeed, even after the Korinthians spent two years in vigorous preparation, they still failed to win decisively: at Sybota, both sides claimed victory (1.54.2). Second, the Korinthians realize that they need more money and ships but cannot acquire them in sufficient quantities

---

20. Cf. Stadter, *GRBS* 24 (1983):134.
21. Cf. Connor, *Thucydides*, 34. Cf. Bloedow, *Athenaeum* 79 (1991):199, who disputes the idea that the Kerkyraian navy would have affected significantly Peloponnesian naval strength.

suddenly, or even in two years, a comparatively brief period.[22] The Korinthian-Kerkyraian conflict illustrates implicitly the increasingly familiar theme that *periousiai chremraton* are necessary for naval warfare, because the latter entails immediate and continual expense, *dapane*.[23]

We have seen the attention Thucydides pays to the importance of superior financial resources for naval success already in this narrative of the first of the αἰτίαι καὶ διαφοραί precipitating the Peloponnesian War. Let us now continue to the second crucial "grievance and dispute."

The revolt of Poteidaia

In the Kerkyraian-Korinthian conflict and in their decision to accept the offer of an alliance with the Kerkyraians, the Athenians are portrayed by Thucydides as hesitant and cautious, concerned not to demonstrate hostility toward Korinth. The decision to form a defensive alliance with Kerkyra came only after great initial doubt and uncertainty. When Athenian ships did sail to the aid of the island, it was with the express instruction to avoid direct conflict with the Korinthians, unless absolutely necessary to prevent the Korinthians from landing on Kerkyra itself (1.45; cf. also 1.53).[24] By contrast, the Athenians react immediately and aggressively to events involving Poteidaia, the first threat to the Athenian empire in the period immediately preceding the Peloponnesian War. Thucydides points out the change in response by stressing the speed with which the Athenians decided to make their demands on the Poteidaians and to send a fleet to the area.[25] It is not that all hope of avoiding war was now lost, although the Athenians knew that the Korinthians were now hostile toward them for aiding Kerkyra. The reason for the change from hesitation to swift and decisive action lies elsewhere.

Thucydides tells us that immediately after the battle of Sybota, the Athenians, convinced of the imminence of Korinthian retaliation, took steps to protect the security of Poteidaia, a subject of the empire but also a Korinthian colony. They instructed the Poteidaians to tear down part of their fortifications, give hostages, dismiss the Korinthian officials cur-

---

22. Korinth sent 30 ships to Epidamnos (1.27.2); they had a combined force of 75 ships at the battle of Leukimme, and 15 Korinthian ships were destroyed there (1.29.5). After preparing for two years, they had a combined force of 150 ships, 90 of which were Korinthian (1.46.1). Thucydides does not specify whether they were triremes; he simply calls them νῆες (this opens the possibility that not all were triremes).

23. Cf. 1.83.2 and below, pp. 184–85.

24. Thucydides underscores awareness of the seriousness of this order in 1.49.4 (πανταχῇ μὲν οὖν πολὺς θόρυβος . . . 'Αθηναίων).

25. μετὰ ταῦτα δ' εὐθύς (1.56.1), and repeated in 1.57.1: ταῦτα δὲ περὶ τοὺς Ποτειδεάτας οἱ 'Αθηναῖοι προπαρεσκευάζοντο εὐθὺς μετὰ τὴν ἐν Κερκύρᾳ ναυμαχίαν; *contra* Gomme, *HCT* 1, ad loc., who thought that εὐθύς may be simply a way of indicating "the next possible event," which could even be months away.

rently there, and finally not to admit any more of these magistrates in the future (1.56.2).[26] Fearing not only a revolt in Poteidaia but the possibility that other cities in the area might rise up as well, the Athenians quickly dispatched thirty ships to the region (1.57.6), only to find upon their arrival that the Poteidaians and other poleis had already revolted, appeals to Athens having failed (1.59).

Much attention has been given to the question of the validity of the Athenians' justification in making demands on the Poteidaians and the responsibility of both the Athenians and Peloponnesians in the ensuing events.[27] It is also important to appreciate Athens' reaction to the threat to its empire, specifically to the income from the Thraceward allies now at stake. Thucydides notes that the Poteidaians are *phorou hupoteleis*, "subject to tribute" (1.56.2), a point which he includes among the Athenians' grievances against the Peloponnesians, namely that they had given support to a polis that was allied with and paid tribute to Athens.[28] Large-scale defections in the region as feared (1.56.2, 1.57.5) would have meant the potential loss of revenue and the enormous expense of siege operations; these were doubtless crucial factors in the decision to anticipate such a result by imposing demands on Poteidaia that proved only to spark the revolt they were intended to avert.

For the Korinthians, the issue of resources to hire soldiers emerges once again as it had in the conflict with Kerkyra: they collect a force of volunteers from Korinth and soldiers from other parts of Greece whom they attract by the lure of pay, for a total of sixteen hundred hoplites and four hundred light troops (1.60.1). Thus far, the Athenians have both money and sufficient manpower and ships, while the Korinthians have had continued concerns about money, men, and ships.

Accordingly, there is a clear sense of imbalance in respective *paraskeue* brought out by Thucydides' attention to financial details in his account

---

26. It is of considerable interest that up to this point, 432, there were annual magistrates from Korinth in this tributary subject of the Athenians. There are a number of intriguing implications; one is that the Athenians did not judge war with Sparta (or Korinth, specifically) as imminent until 432.

27. E.g., de Romilly, *TAI*, 21; Graham, *Colony*, 136–41; Kagan, *Outbreak*, 273–85; Ste. Croix, *OPW*, 79–85; Salmon, *Wealthy Corinth*, 292–97, 299, 302–5.

28. Poteidaia's tribute was (apparently) consistently six talents in the years preceding 433/2 (445/4: *IG* I³ 267, II.4; 443/2: *IG* I³ 269, III.31; 442/1: *IG* I³ 270, III.30 (amount restored; name mostly restored); 440/39: *IG* I³ 272, II.50; 434/3: *IG* I³ 278, V.21 (amount restored, name almost completely restored). It paid fifteen talents in 433/2 (*IG* I³ 279, II.70); when it was raised to fifteen talents is problematic; cf. Meiggs, *AE*, 528–29. Tribute of fifteen talents was a substantial amount proportionately. Thucydides' emphasis on the suddenness of the Athenian response when they sensed impending danger is fully in accord with the indications from the quota lists, and we may believe him when he stresses the speed of their reaction.

of these small-scale engagements involving Epidamnos and Poteidaia,[29] in which the Korinthians' scramble for military resources is implicitly contrasted with both the Athenians' initial indifference to the idea of acquiring the impressive naval might of Kerkyra without expense and their ease in immediately dispatching a naval force to Poteidaia judged sufficient for the task.

THE DELIBERATIONS AND PREPARATIONS PRECEDING THE WAR

Archidamos' and Sthenelaidas' speeches (1.80–86)

Having implicitly suggested an assessment of imbalance, Thucydides next brings us to the deliberations at Sparta. Many took the floor to voice complaints against Athens, among them the Aiginetans, the Megarians, and the Korinthians, a version of whose speech Thucydides chose to present. The speech is a remonstrance of Sparta's hesitation to act against Athens (1.68–71); its centerpiece is an eloquent and vigorous analysis of the respective character of the Athenians and Spartans (1.70). Indeed, this section of the speech itself contains elegant illustrations of the unique disposition, the *tropos,* of the Athenians that underlies and makes possible their exploitation of key advantages and their achievement of *arche.* Significantly, as we noted in the last chapter, it links up with the opening of the Pentekontaetia, which will describe and analyze this specifically.

The Korinthians' speech is followed by that of the Athenians, who happen to be at Sparta "on other business" (1.72.1). They bring out in their remarks the significance of sea power and its critical role in the history of Hellas during the Persian Wars.[30] They follow this with justifications of their right to empire, citing their role in the Persian Wars, the Spartans' unwillingness to continue the command at sea, and the allies' request for the change of leadership in the hegemony. The Athenians pointedly note that they acquired the *arche* without force[31] and that they were motivated to increase their power primarily by fear, and secondarily by honor and self-interest, the same motives now preventing them from relinquishing their empire.

The envoys follow up with a further general rationalization that it has "always been established that the weaker should be subject to the

---

29. The siege of Poteidaia, of course, will become a major operation in time and cost for the Athenians.

30. 1.73.4–74.2. Cf. 1.14.3.

31. This is a point of great importance that Thucydides will follow up in his discussion of the evolution and development of Athens' *arche* in 1.95–99 (see above, p. 67). The idea is implicit in 1.8.3, on which see above, pp. 26–27.

stronger." This bald assertion about human nature, one which is elaborated in the Melian Dialogue, almost suggests a historical determinism. However, the analogy does not hold, for while determinism suggests a continuum over which humans have no control, the point here and elsewhere in Thucydides is precisely that people do have control but that they also behave in certain predictable ways, according to circumstances.[32] Thucydides offers *in propria persona* more specific formulations at several points in his work, two of which we have already examined and which are set off from the rather simple expression in 1.76.2 (1.8.3, 1.99.3) that lies between them. For as we have seen, he elaborates on the specific motives that impel both weak and strong consistently to behave in a manner that justifies the categorical statement made by the Athenian envoys. The Athenians, thus, advance the argument that others in their position necessarily would act the same way. However, at the same time, this broad statement is diminished by the singular nature of Athens; the idea that anyone else could have been in their position rings false. The Athenians alone are "worthy" of *arche*, a point repeated in 1.75.

We now come to Archidamos' speech, which seeks to dissuade the Spartans from deciding precipitously in favor of war. Its contents differ dramatically from the preceding speeches of the Korinthians (1.68–71) and the Athenians (1.73–78), which were made in an open assembly of the Peloponnesians. In a closed session, Archidamos speaks to the Spartans. Some of his opening remarks are reminiscent of the Korinthians' in their allusions to the vast gulf between the Athenians and Spartans;[33] Archidamos, however, focuses not on character but on material and military disparity:

> Against the Peloponnesians and their neighbors, our respective power is similar, and it is possible to strike quickly; but attacking the Athenians means going against men who live far away and, even more so, have great experience at sea and are extremely well equipped in all other areas, in both public and private wealth (*plouto te idio kai demosio*), and ships and cavalry and soldiers and a larger population than any other single region in Hellas. Furthermore, they also have plentiful allies who pay tribute (*pollous phorou hupoteleis*). How could we rashly start a war with them, and trusting in what would we attack them unprepared? In our fleet? But it is inferior to theirs; and if we work on improving it to the point of equivalent strength, much time will elapse. In our wealth (*chremasin*), then? There we are at an even greater disadvantage, since we possess neither public funds nor accessible private resources. (1.80.3–4)[34]

32. 1.22.4, 76.2; 3.82.2; cf. 1.8.3; 2.52–53.
33. Whereas in 1.84.3–4, he brings out the similarities.
34. οὔτε ἐν κοινῷ ἔχομεν οὔτε ἑτοίμως ἐκ τῶν ἰδίων φέρομεν, 1.80.4.

Archidamos' description of the disparities in resources between Athens and Sparta offers insight on a number of points as well as having intriguing implications from the standpoint of both perspective and substance. The contrast between the Spartans' fiscal poverty and deficiency in naval strength and the Athenians' financial might and relative economic sophistication coupled with their fleet illumines in concrete military terms the consequences of Athenian character so brilliantly described earlier by the Korinthians; but it also demonstrates that the prerequisites and methods of war have suddenly, drastically (and irrevocably) changed. The Athenians, by virtue of having achieved naval *dunamis* themselves, have necessarily affected fundamentally the way in which the Greek world would now wage war. Naval power was de facto the superior form of warfare, to which any opponent would have to conform. So that, as is implicit in Archidamos' speech, it is not a question of Sparta's need and ability to marshal greater manpower, or even to muster and pool existing ships from their allies; something fundamental is missing, something no less than the insurmountable essential precondition, financial resources.

The profundity of the Spartans' financial disability is revealed by Archidamos' blanket assertion that the Spartans have no public wealth,[35] nor could it be created by amassing usable private wealth. Finally, the absence of wealth within Sparta is not compensated for by the contributions of its allies—they are not tributary. It therefore becomes impossible to match Athenian naval power and its ability, through Athens' financial strength, to be exerted over a long period of time.

Archidamos' presumption of the inherent superiority of naval power offers no way around this impediment: the Peloponnesians will have to match the Athenians' naval might in order to succeed, for the Athenians' naval power will not be undermined by the Spartans' formidable prowess on land. Accordingly, what stands out clearly and without qualification is the indispensability of usable wealth in a war with Athens; the precise relationship, that wealth is inextricably linked to the very ability

---

35. Aristotle (*Pol.* 2.1271 b13) echoes this. Newman, *Politics*, ad loc., suggests that Aristotle had the Spartan king's words in mind; but note that Aristotle includes the definite article (ἐν τῷ κοινῷ), omitted by Archidamos. In any case, Aristotle's remark demonstrates the continued lack of concentrated and movable public wealth in the fourth century. Possibly, Archidamos may be alluding to the absence of taxation of Spartans and the hesitancy to do so; see also Gomme, *HCT* 1:247; Andreades, *HGPF*, 58–61. Left open, in my view, is the question of whether the Spartans even had a public treasury. Taxes on land went to individuals (Andreades, 58–59) and not to a state treasury, an important distinction in connection with the polis's financial capability for naval war. Cf. also Bogaert, *Banques*, 99, who notes the lack of a public bank until the Roman Empire.

to make war, underlies Archidamos' discussion and will shortly emerge explicitly.[36]

More than a simple acknowledgment of the need for money in connection with waging war is revealed in this speech: in particular, that attention is paid to the sources and accessibility of wealth reflects understanding on a deeper level and suggests the intrinsic value of these allusions to the persuasiveness of the argument. The reference to public and private wealth shows an awareness that what is necessary is immediately accessible money; therefore, the importance of centralized financial resources is implicit—scattered wealth cannot be put straight to use, while wealth in land or kind is useless. Wealth at hand, furthermore, must be supplemented by steady revenue; thus, the significance of tribute to military power is also patent from Archidamos' reference to Athens' allies "who pay tribute." The importance of revenue emerges as Archidamos continues: "What kind of war," he asks, "can the Spartans expect with the Athenians? Unless we prevail with our navy or deprive them of the revenues (*tas prosodous*) which support theirs, we shall be severely harmed" (1.81.4).

Archidamos thus explicitly points to the intimate link between money and ships: the Athenians' revenues are essential to the existence of the fleet, because naval power requires the expense of money. The Spartans' deficiencies thus are increased when one looks at the respective resources of Sparta and Athens beyond the borders of their poleis, for the tremendous strength in manpower of the Peloponnesian League sudenly becomes insignificant when set beside the revenue-contributing allies of Athens. The critical role of revenue and of tribute in waging naval, as opposed to land, war thus crystallizes; the issue is not only the Athenians' total monetary resources but also their entire system of acquiring money and building up reserve, to which the Spartans have nothing comparable. In order to compete, the Spartans must either acquire a superior navy or deprive the Athenians of theirs by cutting off their *prosodoi*; each of these options, however, requires money, the very resource which the Spartans lack.

Archidamos continues to address specifically the problem of resources in his suggestions for improving Sparta's military capability, advising the Spartans to acquire new allies from among both Greeks and barbarians, not so much to gain additional manpower as to increase their naval and financial strength (*nautikou e chrematon dunamin*, 1.82.1). The Athenians have *chremata* and a *nautikon* by virtue of their empire, specifically, their "allies who pay tribute" (*xummachoi phorou hupoteleis*); Archi-

---

36. See the echoes of this in Perikles' first speech, 1.141.5, 142.1, 143.1–2.

damos warns, in effect, that the Spartans must acquire allies who can supply the same, if they are not to suffer greater harm. Again, the fundamental weakness of the Peloponnesian League in a conflict with a naval power is clear.

Although Archidamos has now illuminated the necessity for financial resources by connecting money, expense, and naval power, he has not yet finished impressing upon the Spartans the significance of *chremata* to war. His already compelling argument on the importance of financial resources in war culminates in perhaps the clearest and most consummate statement on the role of *chremata* in Thucydides' work:

> Let no one call us cowards because we, in all our numbers, decide not to attack immediately a single city. For their allies are as numerous as ours, and they pay money (*chremata*). Make no mistake: war is not so much a matter of men as of expense (*dapane*), by means of which men are put to use, especially when it is a matter of a land power against a sea power. Let us therefore first provide for the expense and not get carried away by the speeches of our allies. (1.83.2)

These comments, and in particular Archidamos' hard-nosed statement on the ultimate prerequisite for fighting a war, provide the most explicit statement in the *History* of why money is absolutely crucial: because war, especially naval war, is a matter of *dapane*, and by implication, victory depends upon the expenditure of tremendous amounts of money. The direct connection between *chremata* and *dapane* lends still firmer support to a definition of "cash" or "money" for the former. The *chremata* are immediately disbursed, an action possible only if, in general, they consist of liquid assets. Archidamos' clear, succinct observation recalls the theme of resources and their connection, through expense, with naval power present in the Archaeology and in the accounts of the Kerkyraian-Korinthian war and the Poteidaian revolt, and points ahead to the analysis in the Pentekontaetia on money, expense, and naval *arche*. It will continue to be a familiar refrain.

Finally, Archidamos counsels his fellow Spartans to avoid a hasty decision about a matter that concerns "many bodies and money and poleis and renown,"[37] thereby conveying unequivocally that financial resources in war in general, and in the imminent struggle in particular, are elevated to the same plane of importance as human lives (σώματα), poleis, and fame (δόξα).

Thucydides presents Archidamos as perspicacious and knowledgeable about the connection between the use of reserve and revenue and war with a naval power. The Spartan king's speech is unusual in the degree of attention devoted to financial resources: more than any other in the *History*, it provides a lucid and cogent explanation of the necessity of

---

37. περὶ πολλῶν σωμάτων καὶ χρημάτων καὶ πόλεων καὶ δόξης (1.85.1).

chremata to the coming war. Indeed, the nature of his remarks and the conspicuous emphasis on usable wealth, revenue, and expenditure raise questions about both text and audience.

First, we have seen that the focus on financial resources in this speech is indispensable to Archidamos' argument that the Spartans are unprepared for war. Its obvious resonance with Thucydides' analyses and narrative thus far is not fortuitous: Archidamos' speech, as related by Thucydides, fits into and forms part of the historian's larger argument about wealth and power developed in the *History*. The conclusion to be drawn from the similarities between speech and narrative is not that Thucydides puts his own historical views into Archidamos' mouth, but rather that he judged Archidamos' arguments to be right on target and insured their prominence in the speech that he composed. Finally, it hardly needs stating by this point that Thucydides, in order to write this speech and convey properly and persuasively Archidamos' points, had himself to possess a keen appreciation of the role of financial resources in naval war.

Second, the dramatic milieu of the *logos* makes it a highly effective instrument to communicate a critical point not only about the reality of military preparedness but as much, as we shall see, about the Spartan audience. The basic level and recurrence of allusion and explanation in the speech carry an important implication. They suggest that Archidamos is making points and providing exegeses that were not self-evident to his listeners in order to educate them about unfamiliar concepts. It is reasonable to suppose a general lack of awareness on the part of land powers concerning the use of money for war, and especially the extent to which expenditure of ready cash is necessary. The military superiority of the Spartans on land and their ability to exert control did not derive from financial resources;[38] additionally, naval *arche*—in contrast to the possession and use of a fleet—was a new phenomenon in the Greek world, and it therefore makes sense that its requirements would not have been at all obvious to those without direct experience of it. Its absence from the Spartans' military theater is confirmed by their total lack of centralized wealth suitable for expenditure.[39]

Moreover, if it is experience that precedes and breeds understanding, then a vast gulf separated the Spartans and the Athenians on the conceptual level. Unfamiliar even with the idea of using money for military power, the Spartans were so unprepared to meet a naval opponent that they could not even recognize the problem, much less give it sufficient

---

38. See above, Introduction, pp. 10–11.

39. Fliess, *Bipolarity*, 38, suggests that the view that a fleet would have led to democracy was responsible for the Spartans' failure to build a sizable fleet. This begs the question of Sparta's ability to pay for a navy as much as it ignores the important differences between Athens' and Sparta's own peculiar political/social history.

attention. In particular, it would have been especially difficult for them to accept the clear implication of Archidamos' remarks that preeminent manpower is not the key issue in the new sphere of war and that Sparta and its allies no longer have what is critical to military success. That they were unable fully to comprehend this point is suggested by the result of the assembly. Furthermore, as long as the Spartans failed to grasp the ultimate significance of money, as indeed was the case throughout the Archidamian War, the strategy both of acquiring financial resources to try to match the Athenians and of depriving them of their revenues would have little thrust.

Thucydides highlights the gulf between the mentalities underlying new and old warfare throughout his account of the Archidamian War, demonstrating that the Spartans continued to think about logistics and strategy in much the same way as they always had, with corresponding uncertainty about the new requirements of war with a naval power. But it is the dramatic context of *logoi* that reveals the problem in its greatest clarity, as Sthenelaidas, a Spartan ephor, follows Archidamos with a short, plain, yet impassioned speech, which is, in the end, most effective. Consider his response to the king's arguments: "they [the Athenians] may have considerable money and ships and cavalry, but we have good allies" (1.86.3). He is thus arguing that effective manpower—ξύμμαχοι ἀγαθοί—can offset a lack of money, ships, and cavalry and that current Spartan resources are equivalent to or better than the resources, financial and other, of the Athenians. Ignored is Archidamos' view that the Spartans need more allies as a means to an end—as a way of obtaining ships and money.

Sthenelaidas, instead, bases his argument on the injustice (ἀδικία) of the Athenians; and his appeal primarily to the sense of injury and the retaliatory instinct of the Spartans ultimately prevailed: the Spartans voted to go to war, doing so, according to Thucydides, also out of fear (consistent with the ἀληθεστάτη πρόφασις).[40] In fact, the impression that Archidamos tried to give of the magnitude of Athenian resources as an argument against joining battle at that time was turned on its head by Sthenelaidas to support an immediate declaration of war: "Vote justly for war, Lakedaimonians," he adjured; "do not allow the Athenians to grow greater still nor betray completely our allies. Let us advance against the wrongdoers with the gods on our side!" (1.86.5; cf. 1.88).

On the heels of Archidamos' speech, Sthenelaidas' words sound naive and misguided; indeed, he seems to miss the point.[41] This is surely inten-

---

40. On Archidamos' and Sthenelaidas' speeches, see Bloedow, *Historia* 30 (1981):135–43; Allison, *Hermes* 112 (1984):9–16; and, in response, Bloedow, *Hermes* 115 (1987):60–66.

41. But cf. Stahl, *Thukydides*, 56, for a more favorable assessment.

tional on Thucydides' part: Archidamos' elementary lessons on the need for money in war, followed by the thoroughly traditional stubbornness of Sthenelaidas, are designed to underscore the conceptual gap between traditional land, and innovative naval, warfare. Accordingly, they suggest the distance that the Spartans would have to go before understanding, much less meeting, the requirements of the imminent war. Significantly, the ephor's arguments accorded with the majority view; Thucydides notes, however, that they encouraged a response based more on emotion (fear) than on reason. Nevertheless, even if Archidamos had made as compelling a case as Thucydides presents, the Spartan king's discourse on the problem of resources and the nature of the coming struggle had little impact: when war broke out and the Peloponnesians, for the first few years under the command of Archidamos, implemented their military strategy, it was entirely conventional.[42] Both Archidamos' failure to convince the Spartans and their receptiveness to Sthenelaidas' words, combined with the implementation of a traditional strategy, underscore their unfamiliarity with the new warfare.

The full scope of their ignorance about the requirements of engaging a naval power will emerge as we examine Thucydides' account of the course of the Archidamian War. Archidamos' arguments are left behind, as if irrelevant, as the Spartans repeatedly seem to miss the whole point of financial resources, specifically how they fit into the strategy of initiating revolts and impeding the flow of revenue to Athens. As the first ten years of war unfolded, even when the Spartan commanders were presented with sensible opportunities to change the nature of their strategy and respond more successfully to naval warfare (as in 428, when Mytilene revolted), their decided reluctance to do so suggests a fundamental failure of understanding.

Archidamos' remarks about Athenian *dunamis* and *paraskeue* suggest most fully thus far its nature and extent. The reader knows already that the Athenians were at their height in preparedness (as Spartan resources were also) on the eve of war, learns from the Archaeology that the coming struggle dwarfed all earlier conflicts—easily, according to Thucydides' criteria, even the Persian Wars—and, finally, is informed that Athens' *dunamis* itself is of immeasurable importance in accounting for the war's outbreak. So far, discussion and allusions to Athenian power

---

42. Moreover, they thought that they could win that way within a few years (5.14.3). Cf. in 2.7.2 the Spartans' order to allied cities from Italy and Sicily to contribute five hundred ships and a fixed sum of money. While the number of ships is practically impossible, it is important to recognize that Thucydides is reporting a Spartan order, and thus Spartan thinking, not what was actually sent; see Gomme, *HCT* 2, ad loc.; cf. Hornblower, *Comm.*, ad loc., who, after Jowett, takes the number to refer to the Peloponnesian fleet as a whole.

have been fairly general; but when, in 1.88, Thucydides recalls the ἀληθεστάτη πρόφασις by commenting that the fact and potential of Athens' *dunamis* were far more important in the decision to go to war than the specific complaints of Sparta's allies, it becomes necessary for him to provide specific evidence to justify the significance he ascribes to Athens' *dunamis*. Thus begins the Pentekontaetia, examined in the preceding chapter, which offers evidence and analysis to demonstrate the formidable and fearful nature of Athenian power, and of the Athenians themselves.

Thucydides makes a transition from the Pentekontaetia back to his account of the *erga* and *logoi* immediately preceding the outbreak of war in 1.118, where he notes that during the period between the Persian and Peloponnesian wars, the Athenians strengthened their *arche* and advanced themselves to a height of power.[43] Then he addresses the Spartans' reaction to this development: although they were aware of it, they had done nothing significant to stop it, because of both their general propensity to move slowly into wars unless forced and their involvement in their own wars. This accounts for their immobility up to 432. But at that point, with Athens' *dunamis* obviously (σαφῶς) increasing and encroaching on their alliance, the situation finally became intolerable to the Spartans. The strength (ἡ ἰσχύς) of the Athenians had to be destroyed, if possible, through war.

As Gomme noted (ad loc.), this passage is directly relevant to the ἀληθεστάτη πρόφασις; indeed it elucidates and elaborates on it. For here, Thucydides brings out more fully the complexities of the Spartans' approach to Athens over a period of time, the reasons for their unwillingness to confront the Athenians directly, and especially, the motives for their change in attitude toward Athens' *arche* from 446 to 432. At that earlier time, they accepted an *arche* within certain limits. What changed, Thucydides seems to be saying, was the Spartans' perception of the *arche* more than the *arche* itself: the potential of Athens' *dunamis* to affect the stability of the Spartan sphere of power became evident in 432. Thus, the issue is greater than mere disputes between Athens and *individual* allies of Sparta, the standard stuff of interpolis relations. Now, in 432, the Spartans apparently accepted the difficulty of setting limits on naval power.

By this interpretation, then, the ἀληθεστάτη πρόφασις is something specifically tied to the period immediately before the outbreak of war, not some remote, underlying cause. Complaints had been lodged at Sparta against the Athenians by Spartan allies for a long time, but Sparta

---

43. ἐν οἷς οἱ Ἀθηναῖοι τήν τε ἀρχὴν ἐγκρατεστέραν κατεστήσαντο καὶ αὐτοὶ ἐπὶ μέγα ἐχώρησαν δυνάμεως, 1.118.2.

had not yet felt compelled to act. Something else had to account for the change. Thucydides drew two inferences: first, the complaints and disputes of 433–432 were not different from those of earlier times; they did not directly involve Sparta, and, most important, they by themselves failed to explain the wholeheartedness of the Spartans' resolve in this war to try to destroy Athens' *dunamis*. Second, they were not sufficient to force Sparta into war. Thus, it was not the Korinthians or Megarians or Aiginetans who *ultimately* persuaded the Spartans to go to war; it was the Athenians themselves, paradoxically, who forced the decision upon the Spartans that an *ergon*, war, was necessary to put down another *ergon*, Athens' *dunamis*. A poignant irony in Thucydides' History is the role of *logoi* in an *ergon* consisting of war with unlimited objectives: *logoi*, the indispensable handmaidens of *erga*, could not themselves destroy an *ergon* and thus were ultimately useless.

The Korinthians' speech (1.120–24)

The Spartans, though they had determined by vote that the Thirty Years' treaty had been broken and that the Athenians were in the wrong, nevertheless consulted Delphi and convened their allies once again. Thucydides resumes his account of the debates preceding the war, beginning with the speech made by the Korinthians at Sparta to the members of the Peloponnesian League.

The Korinthians address many of the points made by Archidamos concerning the imbalance in the resources of the Athenians and Spartans. They connect money with the fleet, recognizing the necessity of expense:

> We will equip our own fleet, the area in which [the Athenians] are strong, from existing resources in our respective possession as well as from the moneys (*chremata*) in Delphi and Olympia; we can take the latter out as a loan with which to lure away by the prospect of greater pay the foreign sailors in their navy. You know that Athenian *dunamis* results from hired rather than native efforts; we would not have this problem, since our advantage lies in manpower rather than money (*chremasi*). (1.121.3–4)

Thus, in their recognition of the need for money, the Korinthians respond to Archidamos' call for greater funds in order to build up a fleet, but they have a different plan: in addition to contributing themselves, they suggest the idea of borrowing from the sacred moneys at Delphi and Olympia.[44] It is unclear whether in fact they ever did borrow such

---

44. This comment constitutes the oldest evidence of (intended) recourse to monetary loans; Migeotte, *L'Emprunt,* 89; see his brief discussion of this passage and its echo in 1.143.1, pp. 89–90 with notes. The proposal to borrow money from international sanctuaries like Delphi and Olympia could doubtless be expressed in various terms, from being

money.⁴⁵ But the suggestion alone demonstrates, by its recognition of the inadequacy of the Peloponnesians—even combined—to meet the financial demands of naval warfare with Athens, awareness of the extraordinary quantity of cash needed in this sphere against this opponent. Such wealth existed only in the fabulously wealthy panhellenic sanctuaries—and in the single polis of Athens. The Korinthians, then, directly connect money and the fleet, in this case, concerning the hiring of sailors.⁴⁶ Archidamos had admitted the Athenians' clear superiority of wealth and fleet over the Spartans and argued that the only way to compete with them was by attempting to match their preparation and power with the same kind of resources. The Korinthians, on the other hand, cleverly attempt to turn Athens' strength into a weakness when they argue that the Peloponnesians are better off than the Athenians in not having to rely on foreign sailors. One side is strong in men, the other in money; but ultimately, the Korinthians suggest, it is preferable to have men rather than money. Their argument is intended to obscure Athenian superiority in both manpower and money by implying the instability of foreign manpower and the ease of procuring money. Their proposed strategy is noteworthy for its focus on manpower as the goal, as if to suggest that once the sides achieve parity in ships and men, the Spartans would gain the edge. One would be inclined to judge even this proposal, which after all connects money and ships, as shortsighted in ignoring the ultimately paramount importance of money. But in 1.121.5, they immediately add to their argument:

> With practice we can match the superior skill at sea that the Athenians currently possess; so let us collect money (*chremata*) to this end. For it would be outrageous if their allies continually pay money to insure their own slavery, while we should balk at running up expenses (*dapanesomen*) for vengeance and survival in order to keep it from being taken away from us and used by the Athenians for our harm!

---

called a simple "loan" (δάνεισμα) to temple robbing, depending on the speaker's point of view. Perikles comes close to implying the latter when referring to the Korinthians' suggestion (1.143.1). For a similar proposal to "borrow" sacred money, cf. Hekataios' advice before the Ionian Revolt to take the money from the temple at Branchidai (Hdt. 5.36). The advice was not followed, although it was sound and reflects a solid understanding of the need for money to be put toward becoming "masters of the sea." In 356, the Phokians actually did remove sacred treasures from Delphi; the reaction was not favorable (Diod. 16.23–39, 56–64). For other references and discussion, see Parker, *Miasma*, 170–75. The Athenians borrowed money from their gods, but that was a case of borrowing from one's own patron goddess and other local deities, not from an international sanctuary. Would the Korinthians be taking money out of their own treasuries at these sanctuaries?

45. On this question, see Parke and Wormell, *Delphic Oracle* 1:191.
46. As Thucydides tells us they did in 1.31.1 during their conflict with Kerkyra. Significantly, the Korinthians, a naval power themselves, alone of the Peloponnesians are presented as being quite accustomed to the use of *chremata* in naval war.

Now the Korinthians connect money not only with the initial construction and equipping of a fleet but also with its continued maintenance and operations. They also bring out the link specifically between revenue, expense, and power. They further suggest the possibility that what happened to Athens' allies could also happen to the Peloponnesians: Athens could use the Peloponnesians' resources as a means to power over them.

The Korinthians have just suggested ways to increase the Peloponnesians' financial basis by internal contributions and by loans from the great sanctuaries of Delphi and Olympia in order to match the Athenians' fleet and to gain the necessary naval experience. Next, they address an additional two-pronged strategy, inciting revolts and placing a fort in Attic territory. They spell out the particular effectiveness of the first component: revolts would result in the loss of the revenues "by which [the Athenians] are strong" (*ton prosodon hais ischousi*) (1.122.1). Thus, the issue is no longer put in terms so much of manpower as of money. The phrase "the revenues by which they are strong" is reminiscent of Archidamos' similar expression, although the latter is more specific, making explicit the connection between revenues and fleet.[47] It is significant that, although both the Korinthians and Archidamos recognize the strategy necessary to defeat a naval power, that is, depriving it of its financial basis, many years will pass before the Spartans actually attempt to implement this strategy.

Thus, like Archidamos, the Korinthians confront squarely the issue of *chremata*. They draw attention to the fundamental causal connection between *chremata* and *nautikon*, and consequently *dunamis*. When they address the practical considerations of preparing for and engaging in the coming war, money is key: it figures in every aspect of the development of naval power, shipbuilding, wages for rowers, maintenance of the fleet, and the exercise of naval mastery.

The Peloponnesians' preparation for war (1.125.2)

The Korinthians' speech was effective: the Peloponnesians voted to go to war, despite recognizing their lack of preparedness. They resolved to improve their resources individually; "nevertheless," Thucydides comments, "less than a year elapsed before they invaded Attica and began the war openly."[48] This remark is usually taken to mean that, even though the Spartans resolved immediately to go to war, nevertheless they *delayed so long* that almost a (whole) year passed. The sentence as a whole would therefore be rendered as follows: "They immediately decided upon war but because of their unprepared state undertook to

---

47. τὰς προσόδους ἀφ' ὧν τὸ ναυτικὸν τρέφουσι (1.81.4; cf. ἡ πρόσοδος δι' ἣν ἰσχύομεν, 3.39.8).

48. ὅμως δὲ καθισταμένοις ὧν ἔδει ἐνιαυτὸς μὲν οὐ διετρίβη, ἔλασσον δέ, πρὶν ἐσβαλεῖν ἐς τὴν Ἀττικὴν καὶ τὸν πόλεμον ἄρασθαι φανερῶς (1.125.2).

make the necessary preparations individually. Yet as much as almost a year elapsed before they invaded Attica and declared open war." Thucydides' comment, then, would accord well with the stereotypical Spartan reputation for dilatory action. But those who consider delay the thrust of Thucydides' remark have at the same time been disturbed by the syntax of the sentence, which yields such an interpretation only with a fight.[49] Our examination of the significance of financial resources to naval power in Thucydides is relevant to this problem of interpretation. For the historian's treatment thus far of financial resources in general, and Athens' in particular, is intended to demonstrate not only the magnitude of Athens' usable, concentrated wealth but also the extent to which this kind of financial strength requires years to achieve because of the level of expenditure necessary to its very existence. Athens' naval *dunamis* resulted from its ability to insure enormous revenue over time so that, despite continual annual expenditure, a vast reserve could accumulate; indeed, Athens' *periousia chrematon* and naval mastery developed over fifty years. By its very nature, this preparedness could not be equaled or approached quickly.

The implications of this analysis for 1.125.2 should be clear. As Gomme noted, it is possible that Thucydides, rather, is marking the relative speed with which the Peloponnesians completed their preparations, and this is, in my view, correct.[50] Thus, Thucydides comments, "Even though it was impossible for the Peloponnesians to attack immediately because they were not prepared, it did not even take a year, but (rather) *less*, before they invaded Attica and began the war openly." The contrast, then, is not between the immediate decision to declare war and the delay of about a year before the Peloponnesians invaded, but between their unpreparedness for war and the fact that, nevertheless, it was *only* approximately one year before they attacked.[51] Thucydides was, I suggest, noting the celerity of the Peloponnesians' invasion of Attica, given their plan to match Athens in the naval sphere with its necessary preconditions.

But even if the sentence were less clear in meaning syntactically, still other reasons, which relate to the progression of the narrative, give cre-

---

49. E.g., Gomme (*HCT* 1:420) notes that if delay is the point and the correct meaning, as he thinks it is, one might prefer to find "οὐ πολλῷ δὲ ἔλασσον or the like"; cf. Steup: "nach dem Zusammenhang kann an dieser offenbar verdorbenen St. *nur* [my emphasis] gesagt sein: 'trotz des Beschlusses, nicht zu zögern, verging, wenn auch kein Jahr, so doch auch nicht viel weniger, d.i. beinahe ein Jahr'" (Classen/Steup, 1:325).

50. The δέ that belongs to the εὐθὺς μέν of 1.125.2 is to be found in the following clause of the same sentence, ἐκπορίζεσθαι, not in ὅμως δέ of the beginning of the next sentence.

51. *Contra* Gomme, if Thucydides had meant to emphasize the delay, he would not have written οὐ διετρίβη, which emphasizes rather less time having elapsed.

dence to the view that Thucydides is stressing the speed, not the delay, of the Peloponnesian invasion of Attica. The historian's remark in 1.125.2 follows on the heels of the Korinthians' lengthy discussion of resources, which in turn comes directly after the description of the development of Athens' financial and naval power over a fifty-year period (the Pentekontaetia); the Pentekontaetia, finally, follows Archidamos' attempts to bring out the enormous disparity in the resources of the Athenians. If we recall further that the Korinthians had previously spent two years preparing to fight the Kerkyraians alone (1.31.1), then Thucydides' comment in 1.125.2 not only becomes fully intelligible but is considerably enhanced in meaning when approached from the standpoint of preparedness for war.

It is true that Thucydides often throughout his work contrasts Spartan inertia with Athenian celerity, and this may have led scholars to assume that he is alluding to their characteristic sluggishness here.[52] But in fact, this seems to be a rare illustration of the relative swiftness of Peloponnesian action, consistent with, and supportive of, Thucydides' claim that the Peloponnesians had come to fear greatly Athenian power, manifest in *chremata* and *nautikon*.

If Thucydides had meant to emphasize the delay and imply that the Peloponnesians should have invaded Attica immediately, the preceding deliberations and concern about building up resources to match the Athenians' would, in a sense, have been trivialized. Thucydides has presented the reader with the argument, in narrative, speeches, and personal comment, that Athenian power was vast and growing, and he demonstrated it in the Pentekontaetia by showing its development over the course of nearly fifty years. Furthermore, he makes clear that the Spartans recognized this development—after all, it is the reason they were going to war in the first place. Preparation of less than a year would significantly diminish the effect that has been building up, unless the point is a sense of surprise that it took only that long; this itself, I think, emphasizes the urgency and the degree of fear with which the Peloponnesians viewed the impending conflict.

Perikles' speech (1.140–44)

After the Spartans decided to declare war on the Athenians, they sent embassies to Athens with several demands. The final embassy delivered a single ultimatum: "The Lakedaimonians want peace, and there will be, if you let the Hellenes be autonomous" (1.139.3). The Athenians met to debate the matter, and Perikles addressed his fellow citizens with the

---

52. Mention of μέλλησις in the preceding sentence may also have prompted this interpretation.

purpose of convincing them not to accede to the Spartans' demands and of persuading them that they were well prepared for war, should it break out. Having dispensed with the terms of the ultimatum in the opening remarks, he turns to examine the reasons for Athens' superiority in power over the Spartans:

> Regarding the war and the respective resources of both sides, mark, as you hear what each side has, that we are not the weaker power. The Peloponnesians work the land themselves, and they have neither private or public moneys (*oute idia out' en koino chremata*); next, they are inexperienced when it comes to long wars and those fought across the sea and so, owing to their poverty, they launch brief attacks against others. Such people have the capacity neither to man ships nor dispatch land expeditions with any frequency, since both entail absence from home and the expense of their own resources (*dapanontes*); besides, they are prevented from the sea by us. It is the case that reserves of wealth (*hai periousiai*) maintain wars, not forced [irregular] taxes (*eisphorai*). Those who work the land themselves are more prepared to wage war with their bodies than with their wealth (*chremasi*), and while they are confident that they will survive the risks physically, they lack the assurance that their money will not have run out beforehand, especially if, contrary to expectation, but rather the more likely, the war lasts a long time. (1.141.2)

Perikles' remarks about the Spartans' poverty, which allude to the absence of both private and public wealth, recall Archidamos' like observation (1.80.4). The Athenian statesman, too, stresses both the amount of wealth and expense involved in a war such as that likely to occur, and he proffers a general statement that serves as a kind of corollary to that expressed by Archidamos (namely, that war is a matter of expense, not men at arms), that accumulated reserves are what matters in war, not forced irregular contributions.[53] That Perikles regards the necessity of financial resources as paramount in the coming struggle is confirmed when he returns but a moment later to the matter:

> But most important in all this is that the Peloponnesians will be hindered by their lack of money (*chrematon*) when they have to take time procuring it. The opportunities of war, however, wait for no one, and further, we need not fear either their building a fort in our territory, or their navy. (1.142.1)

---

53. αἱ δὲ περιουσίαι τοὺς πολέμους μᾶλλον ἢ αἱ βίαιοι ἐσφοραὶ ἀνέχουσιν. This sentence is especially pointed when one reads further on to 3.19. Perikles continues by relating the disadvantages of the lack of centralized authority in times of war, which reminds the reader also that the Athenians have a centralized League treasury, while the Peloponnesians do not.

Perikles also responds to one of the Korinthians' proposals (1.121.3), that of borrowing money from Delphi and Olympia in order to hire away the foreign sailors serving in the Athenian navy:

> Suppose they make off with (κινήσαντες) moneys (*chrematon*) from Olympia or Delphi in an attempt to lure away the foreign sailors in our navy by offering greater pay; it would be a weighty concern were we not a match for them by ourselves supplemented by our metics who could serve on board. (1.143.1)[54]

Although, as many have noted, there are striking verbal parallels with the Korinthians' original suggestion, the tenor of Perikles' rejoinder is, not surprisingly, a little different. Whereas the Korinthians represent the possibility of borrowing sacred funds as an unequivocally legitimate option, Perikles implies that it is somewhat underhanded (and therefore sacrilegious) by using the verb κινέω.[55] Perikles' response to every point made by the Korinthians focuses on the superior resources which Athens has at its disposal, among which are *chremata*.[56] As Connor observes, "While refuting [the Korinthians'] arguments, Pericles can drive home the importance of finances and of naval power which emerges from the analysis of the Archaeology and has been affirmed by Archidamus."[57]

---

54. See Connor, *Thucydides*, 49–50 and especially n. 58 for a good discussion on this passage. The question of the identity of the foreigners to whom the Peloponnesians allude has some important ramifications. Rowers primarily would come from the lowest social stratum, but whether slaves were used in the Athenian navy is a matter of lively controversy; for evidence and discussion, see Jordan, *Athenian Navy*, especially 240–68; Garlan, *War*, 78–82; see Gomme, *HCT* 5 on 8.15.2 and 40.2; Graham, *TAPA* 122 (1992):257–70. The foreign sailors whom Perikles seems to have in mind are not metics, since he remarks that even if the Peloponnesians succeed in luring away these men, the Athenians alone with their metics could suffice. Perikles states that if the *xenoi nautai* fought on the Peloponnesian side, they stood to be exiled. If so, then they are citizens, not slaves. Furthermore, if we take Perikles' remark strictly (as we perhaps should not necessarily do—in this context, exaggeration would certainly not be out of place to make the point more persuasive), the cities whence the *xenoi* came would likely have been those in the empire. If this is the case, we need to consider this fact in view of Thuc. 1.99.3, where the chief motive for electing to pay money instead of contributing ships was the desire *not* to be away from home on campaigns. This therefore has possible implications for the literal truth of Thucydides' claim in 1.99. But in addition, it would mean that many allies were *voluntarily* serving in the Athenian navy. We may qualify the degree of voluntarism by supposing that many needed employment and felt compelled to serve in the League fleet—but the fact remains that, strictly speaking, on this view, allies were sailing in the Athenian fleet by choice.

55. Cf. 1.93.2; 2.24.1; 4.98.5; cf. Classen-Steup on 1.93.2; also, the result of the Phokians' recourse to the sacred treasures at Delphi, Diod. 16.23–39, 56–64.

56. The word is repeated often in this speech: 1.141.3, 141.5, 142.1, 143.1; Connor, *Thucydides*, 50, n. 60.

57. Connor, *Thucydides*, 50.

Perikles describes the reasons for the primacy and superiority of Athenians' naval power in comparison with land-based power in 1.143.4, noting the preeminence of sea power in a war.[58] He has already made abundantly clear that this kind of power depends absolutely on the accumulation and expense of money. The burden, then, clearly lies on the Spartans to meet the Athenians on their own turf, not vice versa. It is thus evident from Perikles' remarks, as it has been in the speeches of Archidamos and the Korinthians, that the state of preparedness and the kind of war that will be fought stem from money, the inherently superior position awarded to the side with greater financial resources.

Athenian financial resources on the eve of war (2.13.3–5)

The war between Sparta and Athens is poised on the threshold: Archidamos invades Attica with the Peloponnesian army. Thucydides has indicated clearly the scale of the plans and designs of both sides, and he summarizes the resources contributed to them by their respective allies (2.7–8). He then presents the final, exhortatory speeches, the first to the Peloponnesian army. Archidamos notes that the strength of the Peloponnesians lies in the size and quality of their numbers (2.11.1), reinforcing a point which is true, but has a rather hollow ring coming from the same Spartan who recognized the inadequacy of this asset. Thucydides then moves to the center of Athens. Perikles exhorts his fellow Athenians by repeating a point also familiar to the reader that their strength derives from their fleet (2.13.2) and from the revenue of their allies (*ton chrematon tes prosodou*). He notes that victory in war depends on intelligent judgment (*gnome*) and financial resources (*chrematon periousia*) (2.13.2). He continues by specifying the nature and quantity of Athens' financial resources, giving in effect a catalog not of ships, but of money. Thucydides, relating this speech in indirect oration, writes:

> He urged them to be encouraged by the knowledge that they had six hundred talents, for the most part consisting of tribute, coming in annually to the city from the allies, apart from the other revenue; moreover, they currently had on the Akropolis even then six thousand talents of coined silver (for at its height, the treasury contained ninety-seven hundred talents, from which funds had been drawn for the Propylaia of the Akropolis and the other buildings and for Poteidaia), apart from the uncoined gold and silver both in private and public dedications, and as many sacred objects for the festivals and games and the Persian spoils and other such items, all of which add up to no less than five hundred talents. And what's more, he estimated that there was a considerable amount of money (*chremata ouk oliga*) from the other temples, which they could use, and in the worst extremity, they could even use the gold affixed to the statue of the goddess:

---

58. 1.143.3–5; N.B.: μέγα γὰρ τὸ τῆς θαλάσσης κράτος, 1.143.5.

he pointed out that the statue had forty talents' weight of refined gold, all of it removable. It could be used for purposes of survival but would have to be replaced. Thus he emboldened them with respect to their wealth (*chremasi*) and then noted that they had thirteen thousand hoplites without counting those on garrison duty, and sixteen thousand defending the walls. (2.13.3-6)[59]

This passage, which has been quoted at length because of its singular importance, has been a veritable treasure trove of information for historians and epigraphists concerned with Athenian public, imperial, religious, and war finance.[60] Since this speech provides rich detail on the amount of revenue and reserve that Athens had available in the beginning of summer 431, it has been one of the most important pieces of evidence in the reconstruction of Athenian finances, otherwise reliant primarily on often fragmentary and undated epigraphic evidence. In contrast, 2.13.3-5 is dated, not fragmentary, nor compromised by restored figures. Despite this apparent blessing, however, the text in one place has been attacked as corrupt and the interpretation of several items is hotly contested, particularly in the light of various inscriptions, chiefly the tribute quota lists and the financial decrees of Kallias, *IG* I³ 52.

Virtually all scholars, energetic controversy notwithstanding, share a similar approach to 2.13.3-5, examining specific financial information in the passage and discussing various interpretations of the text in order to learn something about Athens' financial resources on the eve of war and to understand other information which seems either to complement or to conflict with Thucydides. The passage has much to offer for these purposes. But its historiographical significance is also important to appreciate. Why did Thucydides bother to include 2.13.3-5? What significance, if any, does it have to the historian's overall argument? What does

---

59. θαρσεῖν τε ἐκέλευε προσιόντων μὲν ἑξακοσίων ταλάντων ὡς ἐπὶ τὸ πολὺ φόρου κατ' ἐνιαυτὸν ἀπὸ τῶν ξυμμάχων τῇ πόλει ἄνευ τῆς ἄλλης προσόδου, ὑπαρχόντων δὲ ἐν τῇ ἀκροπόλει ἔτι τότε ἀργυρίου ἐπισήμου ἑξακισχιλίων ταλάντων (τὰ γὰρ πλεῖστα τριακοσίων ἀποδέοντα μύρια ἐγένετο, ἀφ' ὧν ἔς τε τὰ προπύλαια τῆς ἀκροπόλεως καὶ τἆλλα οἰκοδομήματα καὶ ἐς Ποτείδαιαν ἀπανηλώθη), χωρὶς δὲ χρυσίου ἀσήμου καὶ ἀργυρίου ἔν τε ἀναθήμασιν ἰδίοις καὶ δημοσίοις καὶ ὅσα ἱερὰ σκεύη περί τε τὰς πομπὰς καὶ τοὺς ἀγῶνας καὶ σκῦλα Μηδικὰ καὶ εἴ τι τοιουτότροπον, οὐκ ἐλάσσονος [ἦν] ἢ πεντακοσίων ταλάντων. ἔτι δὲ καὶ τὰ ἐκ τῶν ἄλλων ἱερῶν προσετίθει χρήματα οὐκ ὀλίγα, οἷς χρήσεσθαι αὐτούς, καὶ ἢν πάνυ ἐξείργωνται πάντων, καὶ αὐτῆς τῆς θεοῦ τοῖς περικειμένοις χρυσίοις· ἀπέφαινε δ' ἔχον τὸ ἄγαλμα τεσσαράκοντα τάλαντα σταθμὸν χρυσίου ἀπέφθου, καὶ περιαιρετὸν εἶναι ἅπαν. χρησαμένους τε ἐπὶ σωτηρίᾳ ἔφη χρῆναι μὴ ἐλάσσω ἀντικαταστῆσαι πάλιν. χρήμασι μὲν οὖν οὕτως ἐθάρσυνεν αὐτούς . . . (2.13.3-6).

60. The reader is referred to the following standard treatments for bibliography and discussion: *ATL* 3:118-32; Lewis, *Historians' Text*, 81-82; Gomme, *Historia* 2 (1953/54):1-21; *HCT* 2:26-33, and ad loc.; Wade-Gery and Meritt, *Hesp.* 26 (1957):188-97; Mattingly, *BCH* 92 (1968):456-57.

its inclusion indicate about Thucydides' appreciation of the role of financial resources in the war?

This section of Perikles' speech comprises a full accounting of Athens' resources on the eve of war. Thucydides stated in 1.1.2 that Athens' (and Sparta's) resources were at their height in 431. He then provided evidence that just as the resources were greater at this time than any other[61] so the Peloponnesian War was greater than any of the most impressive conflicts or military achievements of the past. Next, he supplied, in the Pentekontaetia, the evidence to demonstrate how Athens' power became so great. Furthermore, there have been numerous testimonies to the wealth of Athens expressed by Archidamos, the Korinthians, and Perikles. Now, in 2.13.3–5, as the war is about to begin, Thucydides presents to the reader, as Perikles had presented to the Athenians, hard evidence concerning the basis of Athens' naval power, its vast financial resources, here enumerated and described *in extenso*. This passage has an important function in the work in giving specific details of what previously had been asserted or elaborated only in general terms (such as, "We have an abundance of money"). Thus, it is significant as part of the justification for writing about the Peloponnesian War. As we turn to examine the passage, it bears repeating that the very inclusion of such material in a work of literature is hardly casual and tells us something important about the historian, his viewpoint, interests, and approach.

The passage is singular in the degree of detail with which the sources of Athens' income and capital are delineated. For Thucydides has not merely summarized or omitted much of the specific information, as would be expected of a writer who lacked interest in financial matters. Rather, consider how the historian introduces and ends Perikles' testimony to the greatness of Athens' financial resources: "He [Perikles] urged them to take heart," and he closes this section, "Thus he cheered them up with respect to their money."[62] Thucydides thus notes that Perikles encouraged and cheered the Athenians by specifying and enumerating amounts of money in revenue and reserve, their location, their nature. He does not embolden them by referring to their prowess, bravery, glory, honor, or pride, but by giving an account of their financial status. It is surely a most unusual exhortatory speech, though its focus is not surprising given that Perikles opened by asserting that the Athenians would win with sound judgment and financial resources. Its detail is striking in large part for what it suggests about the average citizen's ability to appreciate the contents. That Perikles regarded Athens' finances

---

61. As mentioned earlier, p. 38, n. 3, Thucydides does not provide a lengthy account of Spartan strength and its development for two reasons: first, because it does not figure in the ἀληθεστάτη πρόφασις; and second, because it was completely self-evident and patent.

62. θαρσεῖν τε ἐκέλευε (2.13.3); χρήμασι μὲν οὖν οὕτως ἐθάρσυνεν (2.13.6).

as something that would hearten the Athenians testifies to the psychological effect that money had on them in this context of power and war. Money has such a powerful effect because it is spent in attaining power and is tied up with the positive self-image of the city through the projection of power; its value is therefore enhanced—it acquires "plus-value," as Baudrillard would term it, that is, beyond its basic function of use.[63]

Perikles begins with the annual imperial income, which he claims totals six hundred talents "for the most part consisting of tribute" (*hos epi to polu phorou*). This is a natural starting point, since he has just noted that the Athenians' strength lay in their revenue from the allies.[64] The phrase ὡς ἐπὶ τὸ πολύ and the figure of six hundred talents have invited two different interpretations: either Thucydides means that on average about six hundred talents of tribute came in annually or that six hundred talents came in annually from the allies, the greater part of which was tribute. Uncertainty is caused not simply by the Greek, which can support both renderings, but also by epigraphic evidence, which appears to conflict with the first alternative, that on average six hundred talents of tribute were collected annually. What is that evidence?

Examination of the tribute quota lists has led scholars to estimate that the maximum annual intake ever reached in any year approximated four hundred talents. Accordingly, acceptance of the first possibility necessitates rejecting the number six hundred or positing that the term *phoros* included imperial income other than tribute, in other words, that "tribute" is used loosely to describe any revenue derived from the empire. The only other ancient evidence (though six hundred years later) that would support the first rendering as it stands in Thucydides' text comes from Plutarch, who infers (*Arist.* 24.3) that the tribute had been increased by the late fifth century, but this has not won acceptance, so influential are the inferences and assumptions made on the basis of the quota lists.[65] Is the idea supportable that more than tribute, strictly

---

63. Baudrillard, *Pour une critique de l'économie politique du signe*, 131–32; on the positive psychological function of money, cf. Simmel's remarks, *Philosophy of Money*, 171; see Parry and Bloch, eds., *Money and the Morality of Exchange*, 2–7, for a useful concise discussion of the "liberating" versus socially deteriorating function of money; cf. also Boeckh, *Public Economy*, 205.

64. τὴν ἰσχὺν αὐτοῖς ἀπὸ τούτων [ξυμμάχων] εἶναι τῶν χρημάτων τῆς προσόδου. . . . (2.13.2).

65. At the risk of sounding overly pedantic, I must stress that the tribute quota lists do not provide *evidence* of tribute totals; they record only the amount of money given out of a city's tribute to be dedicated to Athena, from which one can try to calculate actual totals of tribute. Virtually all of the lists are fragmentary, with many figures either missing or incomplete, and often restored on the basis of parallels from other lists, which may or may not be accurate for other years, especially those outside of a given four-year assessment period. Even within the same assessment period, totals of tribute might vary, and therefore quota, depending on whether a polis actually paid its full assessment.

speaking, is reflected in the word *phoros*? The editors of *ATL* suggested that Thucydides may well have used the term *phoros* loosely to include all imperial income or that "he may have been misinformed,"[66] but they inclined toward a third alternative, that *phoros* is a gloss.[67]

In light of the scrappy state of our knowledge about actual tribute totals over a period long enough to be meaningful, the idea that they were significantly higher than scholars have thought seems preferable to the possibility that *phoros* includes money other than tribute. It is unlikely, I think, that Thucydides (or Perikles, since it is just as much his usage here that is at issue) would have used the word in this way, especially given the precision of the historian's first reference to and careful definition of *phoros* in 1.96.2. He is also exact in 3.50.1, where he records the Mytilenaian settlement. He writes, "Later on, they [the Athenians] did not assess the Lesbians *phoros*, but they divided up the land into lots (κλῆροι)." Such income as Athens derived from this settlement would have been included in 2.13.3 (that from klerouchies, rents from sacred land, and so on) as general imperial income. Yet Thucydides specifies that such income was not considered *phoros*, and he did not call it that. Whereas *chremata* can comprise or include *phoros*,[68] in Thucydides *phoros* has a restricted meaning, defined in 1.96.2, as *chremata* that are assessed.[69]

If, then, we dispense with the translation "six hundred talents on average of tribute accrued to Athens annually" as unlikely, what about the second possibility, that Thucydides and Perikles were referring to six hundred talents of imperial revenue, "for the most part consisting of tribute"? Some scholars have objected to this alternative,[70] while others have favored it,[71] and it is with the latter group that I am inclined to concur. Objections raised are not decisive,[72] and in view of the evidence that imperial revenue apart from tribute was far from insubstantial and

66. *ATL* 3:132. This latter suggestion seems extremely unlikely; moreover, would not Perikles' knowledge have been at issue as well?

67. *ATL* 3:132. Cf. also Meiggs, *AE*, 258, for acceptance of the possibility that ὡς ἐπὶ τὸ πολὺ φόρου refers to an average annual income of tribute of six hundred talents and, therefore, that φόρος is being used loosely; cf. also Rubincam, *AJAH* 4 (1979):78.

68. As in 1.99.3.

69. The aspect of assessment is important here and also militates against taking *phoros* to include such moneys as all other kinds of imperial revenue, not all of which would have been subject to assessment.

70. Gomme, *HCT* 2, ad loc., asserts that ὡς ἐπὶ τὸ πολύ cannot be translated, with φόρου, "the greater part of it tribute," citing parallels in Isok., 4.154, 8.35; Plato *Polit.* 294a, and Thuc. 1.12.2, 5.107, and 6.46.4.

71. Kolbe, in Nesselhauf, *Klio* Beiheft 30 (1933):117; Huxley, *PRIA* 83 (1983):198.

72. For example, in none of the parallels in Thucydides cited by Gomme of the phrase ὡς ἐπὶ τὸ πολύ is the phrase followed by a genitive, and therefore they are not, in my view, convincing.

has been underappreciated, it is most likely that the phrase "for the most part" should be taken with what follows, that is, "for the most part consisting of *phoros*." This would mean that every year, six hundred talents came in from the allies, for the most part consisting of tribute. Of what the other imperial revenue consisted has been discussed often,[73] and we shall return to this important issue later. For now it suffices to note the existence of imperial revenue such as that from mines, klerouchies, and rent from sacred land.

Perikles, then, in his accounting of revenue, begins with imperial income, consisting of both tribute and other *chremata*, and then mentions "the other revenue" (*he alle prosodos*), which must refer to domestic revenue. He then turns to capital,[74] beginning with ὑπαρχόντων δέ, which introduces another problematic section of the passage. We need only summarize and address briefly the difficulties. The matter, simply put, is this: Thucydides' text of the passage, "They currently had on the Akropolis, even then, six thousand talents of coined silver (for at its height, the treasury contained ninty-seven hundred talents, from which funds had been drawn for the Propylaia of the Akropolis and the other buildings and for Poteidaia),"[75] has been called into question by a variant preserved in a scholium to Aristophanes' *Ploutos* 1193, which substitutes αἰεί ποτε for ἔτι τότε, περιεγένετο for μύρια ἐγένετο, and ἐπανηλώθη for ἀπανηλώθη (followed by a colon instead of a comma after the verb περιεγένετο), so that the sentence would read: "And there was, he said, a regular standing amount of 6,000 talents on the Akropolis. (The greater part of this, actually 5,700 talents, was in fact still there. There had been extra disbursements from it for the Propylaia and other buildings and for Poteidaia.)"[76]

The main case for acceptance of this version was made by the editors of *ATL*;[77] Gomme in particular objected to their view.[78] Huxley has revived the case for accepting the "book text" of Thucydides over this quotation, and I am in agreement with his arguments and discussion.[79] The

---

73. See, e.g., Huxley, *PRIA* 83 (1983):198–99 (though his inclusion of the revenue from the silver mines at Laureion is not relevant); also Nixon and Price, "Size and Resources," 140, who suggest that other revenue besides tribute "may have totalled 200 talents in the years before the Peloponnesian War"—perhaps on the basis of this passage.

74. As Gomme notes, *HCT* 2, ad loc., Thucydides is careful to distinguish between "revenue and capital"; see also Lewis, "Public Property," 248.

75. ὑπαρχόντων δὲ ἐν τῇ ἀκροπόλει ἔτι τότε ἀργυρίου ἐπισήμου ἑξακισχιλίων ταλάντων (τὰ γὰρ πλεῖστα τριακοσίων ἀποδέοντα μύρια ἐγένετο . . .), 2.13.3.

76. As translated in *ATL* 3:131.

77. *ATL* 3:118–32; cf. also Lewis, *Historian's Text*; Rhodes, *Thucydides. History II*, ad loc.

78. Gomme, *Historia* 2 (1953/54); *HCT* 2, 26–33. Cf. also Oliver, *AJP* 79 (1958):188–90; Hammond, *CR* n.s. 8 (1958):31.

79. Huxley, *PRIA* 83 (1983):200f., to which the reader is referred for details.

grounds for rejecting the book text are unpersuasive for substantive as well as methodological reasons (that is, quotations in scholia are inferior in authority to the manuscript tradition): for the case rests heavily on the premise that Athens could never have accumulated as much as ninety-seven hundred talents and on the restoration and interpretation of the problematic Papyrus Decree (Strasbourg Papyrus Graeca 84: *Anonymus Argentinensis*) advanced in *ATL,* a document which, because its date is disputed and contents heavily restored with insufficient control, has little authority as strong evidence.[80] Many of the difficulties with the Greek of the scholiast's text have been noted;[81] more can be added, however, especially to bring out the implications of the scholiast's version for understanding Thucydides' viewpoint.

As the scholium reads, Thucydides is stepping in to correct Perikles: whereas Perikles said that there was a regular standing amount of six thousand talents on the Akropolis, Thucydides notes that, as a matter of fact, there were only fifty-seven hundred talents, from which additional disbursements had been made. This can only be understood as an intention to undermine seriously Perikles' confident assertion about the total reserve: not only were there actually three hundred talents less than Perikles had just stated (which is rather a pedantic point by itself) but there would also be the additional subtraction from Perikles' total for the Propylaia, other buildings, and Poteidaia. The latter point implies further exaggeration on Perikles' part. Thucydides would thus be bringing Perikles' six thousand down several sizable notches—the clear implication being that Perikles was feeding the Athenians quite a line. We should not dismiss out of hand the possibility that Thucydides' comment is meant to detract from Perikles' optimism; but the chief difficulty is that, as it stands, the scholiast's comment makes little sense as it is translated.

The editorial comment begins with γάρ, which clearly introduces an explanation of the figure of six thousand talents, not a correction.[82] Thucydides sets out to explain, not to dispute, the figure. Moreover, it is not

---

80. The assumption that the Athenians could never have amassed as much as ninety-seven hundred talents has been called into question for some time: see Ferguson, *Proc.Mass.Hist.Soc.* 64 (1930–32):350–51; Ferguson, *Treasurers of Athena*, 153; Pritchett, *GSAW* 1:101–4; see also Kallet-Marx, *CA* 8 (1989):265–66. The most comprehensive study of the papyrus fragment, in which the standard interpretation is most fully expressed, is by Wade-Gery and Meritt, *Hesp.* 26 (1957):163–88; cf. Sealey, *Hermes* 86 (1958):440–46; see Meiggs, *AE*, 515–18, for a concise discussion on the history of the scholarship and problems of restoration; cf. Huxley, *PRIA* 83 (1983):200ff., for arguments for placing the decree in its apparent "original" year, 431, and for a good discussion of the difficulties with the usual date and interpretation; cf. also Kallet-Marx, ibid. 254–56.

81. See Gomme, *HCT,* ad loc.

82. The rare use of γάρ to introduce a dissenting comment appears only in the case of answers; Denniston, *Greek Particles*, on γάρ, V.2.

easy to see how the Athenians' reserve could possibly have been maintained at the same level at all times (as is required by accepting ἀιεί ποτε), especially with expenses required by, for example, the building program on the Akropolis and costly campaigns such as that against Samos in 440.

We therefore should accept the contents of 2.13.3 as we have them in Thucydides. With the controversy relegated to the background, what remains important for us (and holds true regardless of whichever text one prefers) is the fact that, in the midst of relating Perikles' exhortation to the Athenians, Thucydides includes a parenthetical remark of explanation of his own. First, it suggests that the surrounding text represents what Perikles actually said and that Thucydides judged that, in particular, ἔτι τότε ("even then") required exegesis; he therefore inserts a comment explaining how it was that they had *only* six thousand talents. Second, it displays Thucydides' interest in Athens' public finances; otherwise, he would not have bothered to explain at all, much less have even reproduced the information Perikles supplies.

After giving the total of the reserve in Athens, consisting of six thousand talents of coined silver, Perikles turns to sacred moneys and treasures (2.13.4), providing meticulous detail on their nature, closing with their total in talents. Then, in 2.13.5, he cites the *chremata ouk oliga* from the other temples available for use. This section of the "inventory" differs in nature from what has preceded. In 2.13.3–4, Perikles catalogs income and reserve, and the reserve, or capital, is introduced by the words ὑπαρχόντων δὲ ἐν τῇ ἀκροπόλει; that is, Perikles gives its location. The individual components which he then describes all depend on ὑπαρχόντων and contain specific figures. But in 2.13.5, the discussion becomes less exact: now, Perikles is estimating (προσετίθει) when he refers to the *chremata* from the other temples, and for the first time, he does not provide a precise figure for the total, or even a rounded-off figure (as surely the previous sums were). This suggests that he is no longer referring to treasure on the Akropolis itself, as is also clearly implied by the phrase "from the other temples," which seems to be a reference to shrines *not* on the Akropolis, that is, those of the city and Attica. He ends by noting that, if the Athenians had to, they could even resort to forty talents' worth of gold on the statue of Athena. Perikles, then, did not stop with the known, ready, and usual revenue and reserve but went on to identify additional resources in 2.13.5, as if to assure the Athenians that the total resources were not only sufficient to win the war (specified in 2.13.3–4) but that they even exceeded the requirements.

Perikles' confidence is intended to instill corresponding confidence among the Athenians that they had more than ample resources to maintain their power and win the war (if they also exercised *gnome*). An immediate question is whether Perikles' prediction was correct or whether he underestimated the drain on the reserve that would be caused not just by the war itself but also by the maintenance of the empire during a costly war. For even before the war began, Poteidaia revolted, and the cost of the siege of the polis, we learn later (2.70.2), amounted to a staggering two thousand talents. Although the question cannot be answered absolutely, it is still appropriate to consider whether Perikles would have appraised realistically the drain on Athens' reserve by revolts.

By summer 431 the siege of Poteidaia had already consumed a year; by its conclusion in winter 430/29, a year and a half later, the expense had run up to two thousand talents. Almost half of the siege had taken place by the time Perikles spoke, and, as he notes, money had already been drawn from the reserve to pay for it, which may have run as high as approximately 750 talents. There was, moreover, another expensive enterprise against a recalcitrant ally of recent enough memory to be useful as a measure: that against Samos in 440, a siege that lasted ten months and cost in excess of fourteen hundred talents, and a campaign of which Perikles was one of the ten generals (*IG* I³ 363; Thuc. 1.116.1). We can accordingly allow that Perikles' estimates took into account the possibility of sizable drains such as those occasioned by revolts and that he still considered that with their current *periousia chrematon*, which was yet, even then, at six thousand talents, coupled with *gnome* (and we are left with no doubts as to whose judgment is of concern), the Athenians could win.

Perikles was not speaking generally about the Athenians' public wealth; he knew the amount of their *periousia chrematon* and used this information to encourage the Athenians and to impress upon them their superiority, which depended directly and fundamentally on those very resources.[83] The copiousness of description and elaboration, the quantities that were immediately accessible and expendable, combined with the great area throughout which more wealth existed and could come into the city, would have created an impression of near invincibility. The wealth outside of the city walls, however, would be of little use unless it was brought together, especially since Perikles next proposed that all Athenians living outside the city walls move within them as part of his

---

83. Linders, "Gods, Gifts, Society," 115–22, objects to the idea that the treasure of a god would have been regarded as a financial reserve and views it purely in the context of prestation and piety. This creates what seems to me an unnecessary division and either/or proposition. Clearly, the Athenians did not consider their sacred treasuries as, in effect, a financial reserve bank; but their opinion about the money and other precious metal belonging to the gods was that it was there to be used. It was not there, that is, merely in its function "to demonstrate, in the most convincing manner they knew, the piety, wealth, and power of their city" (122).

strategy (2.13.2). The availability of wealth not yet concentrated is clearly implied; how specifically this would have been insured is omitted. We are fortunate in being able to supplement and complement Thucydides' picture not only of Athens' financial strength but also of the decisions about strategy in preparation for and engagement in the war. An important decree, the first of the two famous "Kallias Decrees," *IG* I³ 52, may well fit into this context and, prescribing the procedure for concentrating the treasures of the local gods and goddesses of Athens and Attica, reflect the appreciation of the need to centralize wealth that is assumed in Perikles' strategy.

Both decrees have been the subject of vigorous controversy and are usually dated to the year 434/3; interpretations of their provisions must vary according to the dates proposed for their passage. I have argued against the likelihood that either decree was passed in 434/3 and instead have suggested the year 431/0 for the first.[84] Since the decrees are not themselves dated, no year can be proved; but there are, as I have suggested, strong reasons for supposing that the first decree was passed at the beginning of the Peloponnesian War.

We know that the treasures of the local divinities were concentrated certainly by 429, from an inscription (*IG* I³ 383) which records the inventory of the treasury of the "Other Gods." It also seems most likely, from the procedures and wording of the first Kallias Decree, that the treasures had not yet been concentrated at the time that the decree was passed.[85] Finally, the very passage we have been examining in Thucydides, 2.13.3–5, suggests that the local treasures of the gods and goddesses were, at that time, early summer 431, still in their respective shrines that dotted the landscape of the city and countryside.

Recall that Perikles began his reassurance to the Athenians about the state of their financial resources with reference to income and then turned to the sacred treasures. As we saw, in contrast to the moneys and other sacred treasure on the Akropolis, for which Perikles had specific figures, he has to make an estimate (προσετίθει) about what is available "from the other temples," which suggests that the treasures of the local deities were still in their individual shrines. If they had already been concentrated and, therefore, inventoried, Perikles would not likely have limited himself to the vague and general *chremata ouk oliga*, "not inconsiderable moneys," but would have been specific: it would only have added to the strength of his argument about Athenian financial capability (*peri-*

---

84. Kallet-Marx, *CQ* 39 (1989):94–113, in which a summary of the controversies and bibliography can be found.
85. Ibid., 105–8.

ousia chrematon). In short, if exact figures had been available, which would have been the case had the treasures been concentrated a few years before, then Perikles would have made use of them.[86]

Sensible as the decision was from the standpoint of security to bring in the scattered treasures of Athens and Attica,[87] what was more important, it reflected a factor essential to military success, as Thucydides has already made abundantly clear: naval power rests on the immediate and continual expense of money; the latter must, therefore, be immediately accessible and usable. This exigency alone would have overridden any unease at removing sacred moneys from their homes in order to concentrate them for use. To insure the greatest amount of expendable wealth, then, as well as for protection, the local sacred treasures of Athens and Attica were brought to the Akropolis, a treasury was created for them, as was a board of treasurers responsible for their oversight; the Kallias Decree outlines the procedure to accomplish all this. The document also offers additional insight into the decisions made before the war attesting to awareness of the need for massive centralized financial resources. Kallias, the proposer of the decree, called for the repayment of debts owed to the local gods of Athens and Attica (lines 2–3), a measure which presumably also aimed at accumulating in one place the most money possible (as well as of settling accounts before the new procedure of centralizing the treasures took place, after which it would undoubtedly prove more difficult to keep track of old debts owed to individual gods). Furthermore, he specified the precondition of the repayment to the local gods that was about to begin, that three thousand talents of Athena had been brought up to the Akropolis.[88]

The details of these three thousand talents, such as their composition, source, and manner in which they were "brought up" (in stages or all at once, over what period of time) are unknown. But the very existence of this decision to increase Athena's treasury by such an amount is of great importance in connection with what we can determine about the city's financial strength, consisting not just in the continued reliance on exploiting the wealth of its subjects as a means of maintaining power over

---

86. Mattingly, *BCH* 92 (1968):457.

87. As it happened, the Spartans seem to have made a point of avoiding Attic sanctuaries, Hanson, *Warfare and Agriculture*, 121–22; see Holladay's remarks in Goodman and Holladay, *CQ* 36 (1986):152–60 on Sparta's religious scruples in general. Note also that Demosthenes deposited the spoils given him by the Akarnanians ἐν τοῖς 'Αττικοῖς ἱεροῖς (Thuc. 3.114.1), demonstrating a certain degree of confidence in the security of the sanctuaries.

88. ἀποδόναι τοῖς θεοῖς / [τ]ὰ χρέματα τὰ ὀφελόμενα, ἐπειδὲ τει 'Αθεναίαι τὰ τρισχίλια τάλαντ/[α] ἀνενένεγται ἐς πόλιν, ἁ ἐφσέφιστο, νομίσματος ἡμεδαπό (lines 3–4).

them but, as important, in the accumulation and centralization of financial resources, which could be supplemented and maintained by regular revenue. If the decision to build up the reserve by three thousand talents goes back a number of years, as it well might, then it is not necessarily connected with an anticipated war with Sparta but may only reflect recognition of the need for centralized resources (*periousia chrematon*) for naval *arche* in general. It may have been prompted by a depletion of the reserves caused, for example, by the Samian expedition in combination with the building program, to which Athena's treasury contributed the most.[89] The significance of the decision to bring the three thousand talents to the Akropolis, and of the amount itself for the total of Athens' reserve, emerges when one appreciates the recognition in Thucydides' work of the need for financial resources for power and the prominence given this by Perikles.

The Kallias Decree and Thucydides 2.13.3–5, then, supplement each other and together confirm a broad awareness, reflected in political decisions, of the relationship between money and power. The three thousand talents mentioned in the Kallias Decree would have comprised half of the available cash reserve to which Perikles alludes. Let us return specifically to Thucydides. In 2.13.2, Perikles claims that victory in the war would come through *gnome*, and *periousia chrematon*, the most important source of which came from the allies. He provides evidence of the Athenians' *periousia chrematon* in 2.13.3–5. It is the eve of war: Athens is about to embark on what will be the κίνησις μεγίστη (1.1.2). Thucydides wrote that he knew the conflict would be so great because both sides were at their peak in resources. For Athens, this meant a combination of the strongest navy and enormous financial resources with which to sustain it. Athens' public and imperial finances, therefore, are a crucial component of Thucydides' argument for the justification of the greatness of his subject and of his conception and analysis of power; furthermore, they are central to his view of the ἀληθεστάτη πρόφασις. Section 2.13.3–5 is the culmination of this argument and provides a significant part of the evidence that confirms Thucydides' thesis. Moreover, 2.13 as a whole gives the most detailed definition in the entire work of the ultimate basis of Athens' *dunamis* in its material sense. For Thucydides, Athens' power is not an abstraction but rather the concrete result of the accumulation of tangible resources: money, ships, and men.

---

89. Kallet-Marx, *CQ* 39 (1989):111–12, especially n. 83; cf. Giovannini's suggestion, *Historia* 39 (1990):137, that the three thousand talents include the repayment of the loan from Athena for the Samian expedition.

CONCLUSIONS

What role have financial resources played in the years immediately preceding the war and on the eve of war itself? In the narrative and speeches preceding the war we find such familiar aspects as the antithesis between ships and money, on the one hand, and men, on the other, when reference is made to the "native resources on both sides" (1.19.1, 82.1, 83.2, 86.3). Related to this is the explicit recognition of the necessity for *chremata* in connection with a fleet (1.25.4, 30.2, 31.1, 81.4, 86.3, 121.3–4; cf. 1.4 [Minos], 1.9 [Agamemnon], 1.13 [effects of tyrannies], 1.13 [Korinth]). In addition, in the Korinthian and Kerkyraian conflict (1.24–55), there is clear concern with expense, *dapane*, and recognition of the immediate purpose to which *chremata* is put, namely, expenditure, something inherent in the Archaeology as well. There is additional emphasis on the extent of and need for financial reserves in discussions about the impending war between Athens and Sparta. Moreover, in the speeches, the importance of money, the connection between *chremata* and *nautikon* through *dapane*, receives its most explicit and comprehensive elucidation in the *History* as a whole.

These observations confirm the continuation of the central role played by finances in the Archaeology and Pentekontaetia into Thucydides' treatment of his main subject, the Peloponnesian War. Thucydides brings out in both general and specific ways the necessity of financial resources for success in war and for *dunamis*. In presenting Perikles' accounting of Athens' financial state *in extenso,* Thucydides provides detailed evidence of Athens' unprecedented power and shows concretely the critical area of preparation, the sine qua non of naval power, financial resources. The image of the historian as ignorant of and uninterested in finances has been erased from the mind.

CHAPTER FOUR

The Early Years of the War, 431–427 (2.19–3.50)

At the end of Perikles' exhortation, the reader is left with a strikingly vivid and concrete image of Athens' public wealth, most of it ready at hand for the Athenians to use in the war. Money, ships, and men were all immediately deployable.[1] The Spartans, on the other hand, have tried to build up similar resources, but their true strength lay rather in manpower (ξύμμαχοι ἀγαθοί, 1.86.3). The Athenians needed no outside help; in contrast, the Peloponnesians had to call constantly for allied assistance. We are, then, conditioned to read the following narrative with the expectation of an easy victory for the Athenians, precisely because Thucydides has brought out their financial *dunamis* so clearly and has maintained the reader's presumption that it is up to the Spartans to meet the Athenians on the latter's terms. In this chapter, we shall be exploring the development of Thucydides' treatment of Athens' financial strength, to see how it challenges or conforms to such expectations.

After Perikles encouraged the Athenians by recounting their resources in money, men, and ships, most of the inhabitants of Attica moved within the city walls, as the statesman had advised. He had laid out his strategy in 2.13.2: the Athenians should come inside the city and guard it, and not venture out to fight the Spartans on land; rather, they should rely on their navy for virtually all military action against the Peloponnesians.[2] This strategy testifies unequivocally to Perikles' view

---

1. They instantly send out forces to help Kerkyra, 1.45.1, in contrast to the Korinthians, 1.31.1, 48.1; and forces to Poteidaia, 1.57.6, and especially 1.61.1, in contrast to the Korinthians, who had to call in help from outside, 1.60.1.

2. Cf. 1.143.5; 2.62.2–3; 2.65.7. For discussion of Perikles' policy and strategy for the war, see Knight, *Mnem.* 23 (1970):150–61; Garlan, *Recherches de poliorcétique grecque,* 44–65; Cawkwell, *YCS* 24 (1975):53–70; Holladay, *Historia* 27 (1978):399–427; Allison, *Histo-*

that the foundation of the city's strength was its *chremata*, through the expense of which it possessed its *nautikon:* for all the Athenians' *chremata* was to be guarded in the city. This suggests not that the land of Attica was insignificant in its wealth on the private level but that, for the purposes of the war and military expenditure, what mattered was public, centralized money.

THE PELOPONNESIAN INVASION AND ITS RESULT

The Peloponnesians under the command of Archidamos invaded Attica in midsummer 431 (2.19), probably to the surprise of many Athenians, who had been unconvinced that the invasion would actually occur.[3] When the Spartan king and his army did finally cross the border, they devastated Acharnai for some time (2.19.2). Thucydides describes the effect on the Athenians: "It was unbearable for them to see their land ravaged before their eyes, for the young men had never seen it happen before, while the older men had not witnessed such a thing since the Persian invasion" (2.21.2). It was in this state of shock that the Athenians decided "to set aside one thousand talents from the moneys on the Akropolis, neither to use it, nor propose to use it, under penalty of death, for any purpose other than defense against an attack by sea. They also voted to set aside one hundred ships for this purpose as well."[4] The connection between money and the fleet could not be clearer nor the conscious recognition by the Athenians of the extraordinary expenditure required for naval operations, especially sieges.

The timing of the decision to create this "iron reserve" is important, for it suggests something about Athenian expectations going into the war; not only was there doubt about whether an invasion would indeed occur but also about whether Perikles really meant it when he proposed that no attempt be made to meet the Peloponnesians on land and protect

---

ria 32 (1983): 14–23; Ober, "Thucydides, Pericles, Strategy," in Eadie and Ober, *Craft*, 171–88; Spence, *JHS* 110 (1990):91–109.

3. 2.21.1: they recalled the time when Pleistoanax had invaded Attica, only to leave when his army reached Eleusis and Thria.

4. καὶ χίλια τάλαντα ἀπὸ τῶν ἐν τῇ ἀκροπόλει χρημάτων ἔδοξεν αὐτοῖς ἐξαίρετα ποιησαμένοις χωρὶς θέσθαι καὶ μὴ ἀναλοῦν, ἀλλ' ἀπὸ τῶν ἄλλων πολεμεῖν· ἢν δέ τις εἴπῃ ἢ ἐπιψηφίσῃ κινεῖν τὰ χρήματα ταῦτα ἐς ἄλλο τι, ἢν μὴ οἱ πολέμιοι νηΐτῃ στρατῷ ἐπιπλέωσι τῇ πόλει καὶ δέῃ ἀμύνασθαι, θάνατον ζημίαν ἐπέθεντο (2.24.1–2). Thucydides seems in part to reproduce the actual wording of the decree which directed the establishment of the reserve, especially in the phrase "neither to use it, nor propose to use it, under penalty of death, for any purpose," etc. This suggests that he took pains to examine the document containing the *psephisma* or to remember its precise contents; cf. also other instances dealing with decisions of a financial nature, 1.27.1; 3.70.4; 4.116.2; 5.18.5; cf. also 1.143.1, in which Perikles uses the verb κινέω with reference to the Korinthians' proposal to "borrow" sacred money.

Attic property. It is likely that only then, after the invasion and the insistence that no defense be put up, could many appreciate that if the Athenians were consistently judged impervious to land attacks, it would be only a matter of time before they could expect an attack by sea. Thus, the Athenians seem only now to have been collectively sobered by the gravity of their present circumstances, by the possibility that the war could indeed drag on for a long time if they adhered to Perikles' strategy, and by the corresponding potential for an even greater drain on the reserve. Their response is significant, since it confirms acceptance of Periklean strategy and suggests that, already in 431, the Athenians foresaw the possibility of serious depletion of their reserves.

The first summer of the war passed with no decisive action against the Peloponnesians. The Athenians sailed around the Peloponnese (2.23.2), sent out thirty ships to Lokris and the area around Euboia (2.26.1), expelled the Aiginetans, and colonized the place themselves (2.27.1). They also turned their attention northward to Thrace and took steps to contract an alliance with Sitalkes, king of the Odrysians, so that he might help Athenian interests by controlling Perdikkas and the Thracian towns (2.29).[5] Nymphodoros, the Athenians' *proxenos* in that area, was successful in securing Sitalkes' promise of a Thracian army of cavalry and peltasts for the Athenians (2.29.5). He also brought Perdikkas over to the Athenian side, who subsequently fought along with Phormio in a campaign against the Chalkidians (2.29.6). Finally, in the autumn of 431, the Athenians invaded the Megarid with what was, according to Thucydides, "without doubt the largest army the Athenians had ever assembled, the state being still in the flower of her strength and yet unvisited by the plague" (2.31.2).

PERIKLES' FUNERAL ORATION, POLICY, AND THUCYDIDES' ASSESSMENT

In the winter of 431/0, Perikles was chosen to present the funeral oration for those who died in the first year of the war (2.35–46). Prevalent in his speech is the theme of Athens' *dunamis*. What is encompassed by the word? Judging from his discussion here as well as from his first speech (1.140–44) and his exhortation on the eve of war (2.13), *dunamis* does not connote simply the might of the city in an abstract or moral sense, or even its physical manifestation in fine, imposing buildings, but it also embraces tangible military power, money and ships.[6] Indeed, Perikles' frequent references to *dunamis* in this sense might appear odd,

---

5. On the alliance, cf. Luppino, *RSA* 11 (1981):1–14.
6. On δύναμις in Thucydides, see Rokeah, *RFIC* 91 (1963):282–86; Immerwahr, "Pathology of Power," 15–31; also, *Form and Thought*, 206–7, for comparison with Herodotos' usage; Bar-Hen, *SCI* 2 (1975):73–82.

especially in the Funeral Oration where the orator is extolling the spirit and grandeur of Athens, had he not already consistently used the word in reference to the result of superior financial resources and ships,[7] and had Thucydides himself not often presented this aspect of *dunamis* in his narrative. The argument of the Pentekontaetia, the speeches of Archidamos and Perikles, and the latter's catalog of Athens' resources in 2.13 can all be brought to mind as we read 2.36.2–3:

> And if our more remote ancestors deserve praise, still more do our own fathers, who added to their inheritance the empire which we now possess, and spared no pains to be able to leave their acquisitions to us of the present generation. Lastly, there are few parts of our dominions that have not been augmented (ἐπηυξήσαμεν) by those of us here, who are still more or less in the vigour of life; while the mother country has been furnished by us with everything that can enable her to depend on her own resources whether for peace or for war. (Crawley)[8]

We have already seen that an important theme in the *History* is inherited and subsequently increased power (cf. 1.9 [Agamemnon]; 1.96.1 [the Athenians]). Perikles alludes to this in 2.41.2, when he states "that this is no mere boast thrown out for the occasion, but plain matter of fact, the power [δύναμις] of the state acquired by these habits proves" (Crawley). Athens' *dunamis* was something acquired and increased.[9] Perikles' attitude toward the *dunamis* of Athens is most remarkably expressed further on: "You must look at the power of the city every day in its actuality and become its lover" (2.43.1).[10]

The relationship between money and the city's *dunamis* is understood implicitly in the Funeral Oration from all that has preceded in the *History*; there is not, and need not be, much stated explicitly or specifically about the city's financial resources, since the oration focuses chiefly on the *tropoi* that make Athenians unique and on the result, their *dunamis*. At the same time, the speech does offer important insight into an ideology of wealth and power that extends from private expenditure for individual political power to public expenditure for military power. For

---

7. 1.144.4; 2.39.3; 2.41.2 (which is not limited to, but includes, military might) and 41.4, where the emphasis is on δύναμις that comes from doing things and acquiring things, manifest mostly in military enterprises.

8. Cf. also 2.41.

9. Cf. also 2.62.3, which echoes these passages.

10. ἀλλὰ μᾶλλον τὴν τῆς πόλεως δύναμιν καθ' ἡμέραν ἔργῳ θεωμένους καὶ ἐραστὰς γιγνομένους αὐτῆς; the words ἔργῳ θεωμένους make it clear that the *dunamis* is visible and tangible. The ἐραστής metaphor is extraordinary in this context and would even seem peculiar were it not for the fervor with which Perikles believed that the strength of the city lay in its men, money, and ships. The metaphor is especially striking if the αὐτῆς in 43.1 refers to δύναμις and not πόλις; the Greek seems to me ambiguous.

Perikles cites the Athenians' attitude toward wealth as one of the admirable qualities of the polis: "Wealth is something we put to use, not boast about; nor do we think that poverty is a disgrace, but not to attempt to escape it is indeed shameful."[11] This comment is all the more meaningful because of its occurrence in a work which has demonstrated the significance of wealth used to attain power in the external, military sphere, and its lack of significance, by implication, if only displayed as a sign or manifestation of *dunamis*. Nowhere in Thucydides' work, least of all here, is there any sense of uneasiness about wealth, the kind of disquiet that pervades, among numerous other works, Herodotos' *History*. If Athens' great financial might were acquired for the sake of profit and display, then we might expect to find scattered evidence of concern alongside the *Real-* and *Machtpolitik* that form the milieu for Thucydides' treatment of financial resources—especially since questions of the morality and justice of the *arche* punctuate the work in key places (for example, 2.41.4; 2.63.2) and pervade the Melian Dialogue.

On the contrary, the similarities between the "wealth for expenditure-use" ethic stated in general terms in the Funeral Oration as well as argued and analyzed in other parts of the *History* and the idea of self-sufficiency and "natural" use of wealth found in Xenophon and Aristotle may help explain the "morally comfortable" place of wealth in Thucydides' work. The attitude parallels, to a great extent, ideas about the accumulation and (proper) expenditure of wealth and the economy of *charis* in the context of aristocratic power in the polis.[12] What is notable about the use of public wealth for military power is that it extends to the demos as a whole the ideology of expenditure for power traditionally held by a narrow aristocratic elite. It is the Athenians' own money, broadly speaking, that is spent on achieving their preeminence as a whole, not just in the confines of their polis but in the Greek world at large—just as athletic victory by an individual in international competition brings fame and glory to his native city.[13]

In his final speech to the Athenians (2.62–64), Perikles continues the theme of the city's *dunamis*, but with a different emphasis. The plague had hit Athens in the beginning of the second year of the war. Thucydides chose not only to juxtapose the Funeral Oration with his account of the catastrophic disease, combining clinical description and analysis

---

11. 2.40.1: πλούτῳ τε ἔργου μᾶλλον καιρῷ ἢ λόγου κόμπῳ χρώμεθα, καὶ τὸ πενέσθαι οὐχ ὁμολογεῖν τινὶ αἰσχρόν, ἀλλὰ μὴ διαφεύγειν ἔργῳ αἴσχιον; more literally (and circumlocutory), "We make use of wealth, regarding it as providing the opportunity actually to do something, not simply as something to boast about." The *logos/ergon* antithesis appears in both clauses.

12. See Introduction, pp. 18–19.

13. Davies, *Wealth*, 98; Kurke, *Traffic*, 170–74.

of the plague's destruction of spirit and *nomos* but also to follow it with the power of Perikles' *logos* and *gnome* for the final time in the *History*. Perikles tries to shift the Athenians' preoccupations at home to recognition of their external achievement of empire, unmarred by the plague, in the Greek world. To that end, he focuses specifically on the implications of naval superiority in a passage critical for providing a larger framework in which to place the contrast between Athens and all other land powers, as well as the ἀληθεστάτη πρόφασις.

> I shall explain something that you yourselves seem never to have realized, namely, an advantage with respect to the magnitude of your *arche*, but one that I have never noted in my previous speeches. Not even should I have made use now of what is a rather boastful claim, if I did not see you terrified unreasonably. It is this: you think that your *arche* is confined to power over your allies; but I assert that of the two manifest spheres in use, land and sea, you have absolute mastery of the last, to such an extent that it is over not only your present hold but also any extension you may wish for. There is no one, neither king nor any other race in existence today, who can prevent you, with your current naval *paraskeue*, from the use of the sea. This *dunamis* itself is not revealed by our ability to use our farms and land, the loss of which you consider so important. (2.62.2)[14]

This analysis of the nature of sea power stands out in the *History*, as the speech itself is conspicuous as well for its focus on empire.[15] Although thus far in the work Thucydides has given ample attention to Athens' *arche*—providing detailed analyses of its basis, evolution, its extraordinary success as *dunamis*, even, finally, suggesting its novelty and inherent superiority over land power—nevertheless, Perikles' remarks here in his last speech introduce a further characteristic that reinforces what has already been implied. Naval power of the extent of Athens' *arche* was a phenomenon so far out of the range of traditional experience that even explanations defied complete understanding.[16] The nature of Athens' *arche* was something that transcended mere rule of allies, unlike land powers, for it meant absolute mastery over the sea.

The breathtaking exaggeration in this comment is what immediately draws attention; but there is an important truth in it that should not be obscured. Perikles brings out the crucial distinction between land and

---

14. καὶ οὐκ ἔστιν ὅστις τῇ ὑπαρχούσῃ παρασκευῇ τοῦ ναυτικοῦ πλέοντας ὑμᾶς οὔτε βασιλεὺς οὔτε ἄλλο οὐδὲν ἔθνος τῶν ἐν τῷ παρόντι κωλύσει. ὥστε οὐ κατὰ τὴν τῶν οἰκιῶν καὶ τῆς γῆς χρείαν, ὧν μεγάλων νομίζετε ἐστερῆσθαι, αὕτη ἡ δύναμις φαίνεται.

15. de Romilly, *TAI*, 37.

16. Note Gomme's comment on this passage: "It has always been difficult to persuade others, whether allies or enemies, and especially the former, of the value of sea-power; and even the citizens of the country which exercises it have often to be reminded of its importance" (*HCT* 2:170). See also Momigliano, *CR* 58 (1944):2–3.

sea power: the latter allows the extension of power in an unparalleled way; its intrinsic potency is of an altogether different and greater scope than that of any land power, even Sparta. That polis was the acknowledged preeminent power on land, but others had control of their own territories, through which Sparta may have marched but which it could not be said to own (with the obvious exception of Messenia). By contrast, no one but Athens controlled whatever sea—in its range of experience—the Athenians sailed on. Perikles thus was making a fundamental point about the inherent *potential* of naval power that set it apart from land power per se, as much as Athens' current naval mastery set it apart from Sparta's land superiority.

Perikles' remarks here, which focus as much on the conceptual framework, the *mentalité*, underlying the unique significance of sea power as on the concrete element of Athens' *dunamis*, may cast light on the ἀληθεστάτη πρόφασις, whose full significance, I have suggested, the historian is gradually unfolding. The antithesis contained in 1.23.6, ἡ ἀληθεστάτη πρόφασις which is ἀφανεστάτη λόγῳ, concerns a phenomenon that is obvious in one sense and obscure in another, just as in 2.62 Perikles draws attention to the difference between the superficial appearance of the *arche* (control over allies) and its true nature (mastery of the sea). In 1.23.6, the obscurity of the "truest explanation" lies in the realm of articulation (λόγῳ); it is not that the πρόφασις simply did not come up in speeches but rather that it was least accessible to *understanding* and thus to verbal expression.[17] Likewise, in 2.62.2, Perikles suggests that the Athenians were not really conscious of what they had accomplished (ἐνθυμηθῆναι).

The ἀληθεστάτη πρόφασις concerns the potential for growth in power as much as Athens' current strength, hence the present participle γιγνομένους. For a single polis with that kind of apparently unlimited range of power, extension is always possible. Thus, the issue in 1.23.6 is not specific acts of extension—that is, not whether Athens in the 430s was expanding—but rather a concept: the very idea and potential of sea power on the scale of Athens' brings greatness. Accordingly, 2.62.2 continues to develop and elaborate on the definition of Athens' *arche* that was articulated earlier, in 1.118.[18]

Perikles devalues individual property as a decoration and ornament of wealth, insignificant compared to the polis's *dunamis* (2.62.3). The implications are clear and fundamentally disquieting to Athenians, for whom the measure of their worth and their power was those very things

---

17. It is significant, that is, that Thucydides omitted the definite article in 1.23.6 and refers simply to λόγῳ.

18. See above, p. 88.

now denigrated by the statesman. The harsh fact was the complete separation of polis power from the land resources of Attica and the corresponding devaluation of the agricultural *oikos*. The impact of these words would have been felt squarely by aristocrats and peasants alike.

The substitution of garden and ornament for home and property introduces implicitly the distinction between expenditure and display in the context of power: homes and land have no relevance to Athens' naval *dunamis*, and therefore, individual wealth is essentially a useless trifle;[19] this links up with the explicit and implicit demotion of display in the Funeral Oration and the exalting of expenditure (2.40.1). This is of great importance when set beside earlier, traditional conceptions of wealth and power; but it is also notable when placed in its late fifth-century context in which the display of wealth continued to be a crucial measure of prestige and power not only in the private sphere but in the public sphere as well.[20]

The elevation of expenditure culminates in 2.64.3, when the statesman proclaims that "the polis has the greatest name among all mankind ... because it has expended (ἀνηλωκέναι) more lives and energy than any other city, and has won the greatest power (*dunamin megisten*)." The connection between expenditure and fame, and expenditure and power, serves as the capstone of Perikles' vision of Athens and places the idea of expenditure almost in the realm of ideology, alongside the expression of the importance of using wealth in the Funeral Oration (2.40.1).

Let us return to 2.62.2. Perikles also reminds the Athenians that their *dunamis* was inherited and brings out the obligation and responsibility that accompany such "inheritances": to preserve their "gift" but also in turn to hand it down to the next generation[21]—here the language of the *oikos* is transferred to the public realm of the polis. The role of financial resources as the cornerstone of this extraordinary kind of military power is implicit here as it was understood in the Funeral Oration to be the means by which the Athenian τρόπος could achieve *dunamis*. Indeed, in any discussion of Athens' *arche* and *dunamis*, the intimacy of the link between *chremata* and *nautikon* that has been expounded and developed in the *History* guarantees the reader's conscious awareness of the underlying presence of surplus, revenue, and expense.

Perikles regarded the greatness of Athens in the external sphere as the result of the acquisitive, active nature of its citizens and of its military resources—money and ships. The value the statesman placed on financial resources and the control of the empire through *chremata* for *nauti-*

---

19. It is important to bear in mind that the first εἰσφορά still lies in the future (Thuc. 3.19.1).
20. See Introduction, pp. 18–19.
21. For the *topos*, see 1.71.7 and Hdt. 7.8α2.

kon is patent, as it is for Thucydides as well. Through his rendering of Perikles' several speeches, Thucydides depicts the statesman in such a manner as to instill confidence in the intelligence of Perikles' military policy and strategy, his ability to understand the prerequisites of naval power, and his vision of the true greatness of the *arche*. In choosing what to emphasize, the historian underscores what so manifestly impressed him: the statesman's combination of solid pragmatism and intellectual agility, reflected in his concrete assessments of the ingredients of power and the way in which such power is maintained, and his overall *gnome* and *pronoia* concerning both the Athenian empire and the nascent war.[22]

Thucydides' stress on Perikles' foresight (*pronoia*) allows a strong presumption that the course and end of the war confirmed to him that Perikles did understand and project accurately Athens' strength and needs that would enable the city to withstand even a protracted conflict; in other words, that Perikles did judge correctly the ultimate dependence of the city's *dunamis* on its financial resources. Indeed, this is clear from 2.65, the historian's assessment of Perikles' leadership of the city, which serves in its narrative context as a kind of advance obituary.

In this passage, written from a retrospective distance, long after the statesman's death, Thucydides observes that

> As long as Perikles presided over the polis in peacetime, he proved a moderate leader who maintained a secure watch over it; and owing to him the city had extraordinary power. Moreover, after the war broke out, he also in that circumstance manifestly judged accurately the city's *dunamis*. (2.65.5)

Thucydides contrasts Perikles' *pronoia* and ability to determine the best strategy for the war with his successors' inferior guidance, under which, in his view, the city deteriorated and ultimately lost the war. It is evident that, in the historian's perception, Perikles correctly gauged Athens' resources for the war and that if the Athenians had only followed his strategy, they would have won easily. The point is driven deeper by explicit reference to all of the major difficulties and setbacks that Athens encountered following Perikles' death: the lack of quality in Athens' subsequent leaders, the Sicilian expedition, internal faction, Persian *chremata* for the Lakedaimonians' *nautikon*, and revolts among allies. All of these debilitating factors, even *combined*, could not fatally deplete Athens' resources, because, as Thucydides concludes his entire discussion of Perikles' policy, "So abundant were the resources then, based on which

---

22. Rokeah, *RFIC* 91 (1963):282–86, notes Perikles' attention to *periousia chrematon* and the influence that his conception of the requirements of power and the ingredients of military success had on Thucydides.

Perikles predicted that the city would easily prevail over the Peloponnesians alone in the war."[23]

In other words, Athens' resources were great enough to withstand extraordinary odds; however, what turned the tide in the end was a factor that perhaps Perikles could not have predicted, Persian *chremata*, mentioned in 2.65.12 specifically in connection with building up a Lakedaimonian fleet. It is significant and indicative of Thucydides' own views that his closing comment on the statesman concerns the vastness of Athenian resources at the beginning of the war and the probability, or indeed, virtual certainty, of an Athenian victory over the Peloponnesians alone, that is, without the intervention of Persian gold.[24]

Thucydides, then, insists on the accuracy of Perikles' *pronoia* with respect to Athens' *dunamis*, the foundation of which was its financial resources. A fundamental part of Thucydides' historical argument concerns the importance of financial resources far exceeding what was required for any one operation or campaigning season—that is, surplus wealth, *periousia chrematon*. Naval power, thus, unlike land-based power, demands a farsighted approach, a clear understanding of the big picture. Thus, to ignore the paramount necessity of insuring that Athens maintain its reserve of centralized, public funds would be dangerous and destructive. Thucydides' treatment of Perikles, financial resources, and naval power raises some interesting questions about the historian's account of policy and strategy during the Archidamian War after Perikles' death.

Cawkwell asks, "Was Thucydides right?" about Perikles' strategy since it was implemented for such a brief period that "it cannot be thought to have been properly tested, and to commend it one is forced in some degree, like Thucydides, to argue the ineptitude of what replaced it."[25] Thucydides can provide negative testimony that Perikles' policy was not

---

23. τοσοῦτον τῷ Περικλεῖ ἐπερίσσευσε τότε Ἀηαφ' ὧν αὐτὸς προέγνω καὶ πάνυ ἂν ῥᾳδίως περιγενέσθαι τὴν πόλιν Πελοποννησίων αὐτῶν τῷ πολέμῳ (2.65.13). Connor, *Thucydides*, 63, regards this last sentence of 2.65 as more qualified and ambivalent in praise than do most scholars. He draws attention to the ambiguity of τοσοῦτον and notes the various interpretations which it has elicited. I agree with Connor, Crawley, and Classen-Steup, against LSJ and others (cf. de Romilly, *REG* 78 [1965]:563) that τοσοῦτον refers to "things," resources. Athens' resources, estimated by Perikles as more than sufficient, were what enabled Athens to hold on as long as it did. I do not see any ambiguity as necessarily a sign of tempered praise.

24. When Thucydides refers to the Peloponnesians "alone" (αὐτῶν), it seems most likely that there is an implied contrast to the Peloponnesians "with assistance," namely that from the Persians—but also, possibly, Alkibiades?

25. Cawkwell, *YCS* 24 (1975):53. Scholars disagree on the extent to which Perikles' strategy was followed or abandoned in the Archidamian War after his death; for recent discussions, see Knight, *Mnem.* 23 (1970):150–61; Cawkwell, ibid.; Holladay, *Historia* 27 (1978):399–427; Huart, *AFLN* 35 (1979):83–108.

followed because of flawed leadership; but in the end, his assessment of personal qualities has to remain a judgment call, which could be disputed. Moreover, how could it be proved that even if there were strict adherence to the statesman's strategy, the course of the war would have been different under Perikles' successors than under Perikles himself?

Perikles had noted that the combination of two elements, *gnome* and *periousia chrematon*, would bring military victory to the Athenians (2.13.2). In Thucydides' view, regardless of adherence to the strategy or policy outlined by the great statesman, one critical element necessary for military success was missing after Perikles' death, the *gnome* of Perikles himself. However, the other element, *periousia chrematon*, remained. It seems to me that the magnitude of the city's financial resources and their place as the guarantor of victory if mixed with *gnome* offered Thucydides a criterion by which to measure both the accuracy of Perikles' *pronoia* and strategy, and the inability of subsequent leadership to guide the city through the war. In 2.65.13, Thucydides gives the impression that, having scrutinized the whole war with attention to strategy and financial management, he judged Athens' financial reserves to have been sufficient to last through a long war and earn an Athenian victory, had not Persian money interceded—and had not Athens' subsequent leaders failed to exercise *gnome*. We shall want to test this theory about the usefulness of Athens' financial resources to make a point about Periklean strategy and *gnome*. For if correct, it bears directly on the prevailing view that the financial expertise of Athenian leaders increased after Perikles' death.[26]

Perikles does not appear in the *History* after the summer of 430, although the statesman did not die until autumn 429;[27] yet Thucydides suggests that during that period, or at least a good part of it, Perikles was still in control of the affairs of the city, since soon after the Athenians fined him, due to their ὀργή, they once again entrusted their affairs to him (2.65.4). Perikles' curious absence cannot, in my opinion, be explained easily by the view that nothing of importance involving him occurred. Even were that the case, one would expect Thucydides to mention Perikles' death in its proper place.[28] It is important, then, as we

---

26. E.g., Busolt, *GG* 3.2, 993; West, *CP* 19 (1924):124–46, 201–28; Andrewes, *Phoenix* 16 (1962):83; Kagan, *Archidamian War*, 250; Connor, *New Politicians*, 124–25; Ostwald, *Pop.Sov.*, 204.

27. ἐπεβίῳ δὲ δύο ἔτη καὶ ἓξ μῆνας, 2.65.6. The date of his death is inferred from Diod. 12.46.1; Athen. 271e; Plut. *Per.* 38. But cf. Connor, *Thucydides*, 75, n. 55, who thinks that the Greek is ambiguous and that Thucydides could be saying that Perikles lived on for two and a half years after his last speech. See also Stadter, *Commentary on Plutarch's Pericles*, 341–42.

28. Perhaps, however, the simple explanation is that Thucydides' rigid adherence to his subject prevents him from mentioning even important incidents when they occur outside

examine the following year or so in the war, to bear in mind that Perikles was still alive at that time; can we detect any reasons for his disappearance from Thucydides' narrative?

Perikles presents a clear, straightforward picture of what Athens must do to win the war; but as soon as he is removed from the *History*, events become more complicated. Indeed, Thucydides gives the impression that Athens began experiencing some difficulties right away, as we shall see. If, moreover, we recall that Perikles is not in fact out of the picture, but only out of Thucydides' narrative, the puzzle becomes more complex. Let us consider Thucydides' narrative following 2.65.

THE FALL OF POTEIDAIA

At the end of the summer of 430, the Peloponnesians sent an embassy to Persia to attempt to procure funds (*chremata*) from the King (2.67.1). They failed even to reach their destination: while they were in Thrace, attempting to lure Sitalkes away from his alliance with Athens and persuade him to send an army to Poteidaia, still under siege by the Athenians, their mission was thwarted by two Athenian ambassadors present at that time with the Odrysian king. It is important to note that already the Spartans seem to recognize that the level of resources required for the war with Athens was completely beyond what they could raise themselves. Equally significant, although they were aware to some extent of this primary need, they were nevertheless unable to address it for a long time.

In the winter of 430/29, the Poteidaians finally surrendered. The Athenian generals accepted their proposals, "seeing both the hardships endured by the army in such a wintry place and that they had already spent two thousand talents on the siege" (2.70.2). What can we extract of special significance from this passage? We should first note that Thucydides specifies the cost of the siege rather than simply commenting that the expense of the operation caused the generals to listen to the Poteidaians' proposals for an end to the operations.[29] Second, was it an unusually high expense, perhaps not anticipated? That it was especially costly compared to other sieges is confirmed later in another passage, where we learn that the soldiers at Poteidaia were paid at double the usual rate.[30] Moreover, the onerousness of the financial burden of the

---

of his main subject, the war itself. Because Perikles' death did not occur in battle, it properly lies outside the historian's purview. Also relevant here, Thucydides does not mention Archidamos' death, although he is another important (and admired) figure; Archidamos did not die in battle either.

29. Cf. Isok. 15.113 (twenty-four hundred talents).

30. 3.17.4. For the normal rate of pay for a soldier during this period, see Pritchett, *GSAW* 1:14–17.

siege, even before the war began, is suggested by the several allusions to it in Thucydides' narrative, always in connection with its expense (2.13, 2.70, and in 3.17).

Indeed, examining these allusions from a narrative standpoint proves instructive. Recall that Thucydides, in his editorial comment in 2.13.3, explicitly mentioned Poteidaia among the significant expenses that drained the reserve from ninety-seven hundred to six thousand talents. Among his aims in presenting this indirect speech was to demonstrate Perikles' financial knowledge and, implicitly, his role in Athens' acquisition of a vast reserve that could easily sustain large depletions like the building program and Poteidaia. The cost of Poteidaia that had built up already before the war is used to a positive effect in the portrayal of Periklean strategy: even with substantial outlays, Athens' *periousia chrematon* was enough to suggest invincibility in the coming war. Consider the different effect in the next allusion to the cost of the siege: Perikles has just been removed prematurely from the *History*, when Thucydides relates the fall of Poteidaia. The eulogy in 2.65 predisposes the reader henceforth to banish Perikles from the events of the war. Now the heavy expenditure required in the siege becomes a cause for concern, a factor in the Athenian commanders' decision to accept the surrender of the Poteidaians. Not only does Thucydides explicitly draw attention to the specific cost of the siege, but he also notes that right at this time, in the winter of 430/29, the Athenians dispatched six "money-collecting ships" to the region of Karia and Lykia (2.69). I shall discuss the purpose of these ships below; for now, what is important to note is that Thucydides mentions them explicitly just before recounting the fall of Poteidaia. It is not sufficient justification that he relates these events because they happened then; we must remember that he has chosen to include this information and to present it in a certain way.

On one level, then, immediately after Perikles is removed from the narrative, hints of financial distress surface. Yet, on another level, the proximity of Thucydides' presentation of Athens' tremendous financial strength, combined with his pronouncement on the accuracy of Perikles' *pronoia*, intentionally leads the reader to the conclusion that Athens could not in fact have been in financial trouble. Accordingly, the implication is planted for the first time, by means of Thucydides' treatment of financial resources, that leadership and guidance—that is, *gnome*—not money, was the problem.

The settlement of Poteidaia itself prompts some intriguing historiographical and historical considerations that also bear on the larger issue of decisions that were made about the city's financial basis, particularly regarding imperial revenue, after Perikles was apparently no longer at the helm. Thucydides tells us that the community was expelled, and the inhabitants were even allowed to leave with a certain amount of money to be used as a traveling allowance.³¹ Subsequently, Thucydides tells us, the Athenians sent out a colony to the site.³² This marks a clear departure from the usual procedure following a revolt that had been quelled at great expense: some patterns emerge from the cases provided by the historian. In the case of lengthy—and therefore costly—sieges, Thucydides consistently specifies the ways in which the Athenians defrayed the expense and derived financial gain from the defeated town. By contrast, in the instances not involving such financial losses, the establishment of an Athenian colony on the site, usually after the expulsion of the inhabitants, was not uncommon.³³ Thus Thasos, at the end of a three-year siege against it, was compelled to repay whatever money it could immediately and was made tributary for the future; in addition, the Thasians had to tear down their walls and surrender their ships.³⁴ Furthermore, Thucydides makes a point of mentioning that they handed over their rights to the mines under their control. After a nine-month siege of Samos ended its revolt, Thucydides mentions that an indemnity for the cost of the siege was imposed (1.117.3); we learn elsewhere that it well exceeded fourteen hundred talents.³⁵ Thus, Athens' imperial treasury benefited from revolts, since the Athenians not only recouped the expense of the siege but also acquired tribute for the future (and could gain some ships in the bargain as well). In other words, the public, centralized financial resources of the ruling naval city were strengthened, and therefore the *dunamis* of the city was not impaired or endangered in the long term.

The difference between these earlier instances and Poteidaia is glaring: in the latter case, no provision was made for any direct financial benefit to the Athenian polis, neither to replenish the losses already suffered nor to insure money to the treasury in the future. The settlement of Poteidaia provides the first example since the outbreak of war of the way that a polis might be treated after its revolt was suppressed. Al-

---

31. ἀργύριόν τι ῥητόν, 2.70.3.

32. One thousand settlers, according to Diod. 12.46.7. There is disagreement over whether the new settlement at Poteidaia was a colony, klerouchy (as was sent out in 362/1, schol. Dem. 6.20; 7.10; Diod. 16.8), or something in between; see Ehrenberg, *Aspects*, 116–43; Ehrenberg, *CP* 47 (1952):143–49; *ATL* 3:284–85; Alexander, *Potidaea*, 75–78; Meiggs, *AE*, 535. If a klerouchy, then the settlers may have been subject to *eisphorai* when levied; see Graham, *Colony*, 169–70, 189 (*eisphorai* levied on klerouchs in other cases); that it was a colony is suggested by [Arist.] *Oik.* 2.1347a 17–24, in which reference occurs to the inhabitants levying a tax on themselves; if a klerouchy, one would expect the demand to issue from Athens.

33. E.g., Histiaia, Thuc. 1.114.3; 7.57.2; Plut. *Per.* 23.2; schol. Ar. *Clouds* 213; cf. cases not following a revolt, e.g., Aigina, Thuc. 2.27.1; 7.57.2; 8.69.3; Notion, Thuc. 3.34.4.

34. 1.101.3; χρήματά τε ὅσα ἔδει ἀποδοῦναι αὐτίκα ταξάμενοι καὶ τὸ λοιπὸν φέρειν.

35. *IG* I³ 363; cf. Nepos *Tim.* 1.

though the community of Poteidaia was smaller than the combined poleis on the large islands of Thasos and Samos, its annual tribute of six talents suggests considerable wealth. More important, that the assessment was not only raised to fifteen talents but actually paid in 433/2 (*IG* I³ 279, II.70) is an important indication of the impressive resources under the polis's control.[36] Furthermore, the settlement imposed was not the result of a collective Athenian decision but rather of a decision made on the spot by the generals in charge, who were subsequently criticized for their independent action (2.70.4). It is not clear, however, whether the Athenians intended to demand any financial compensation for the expense that they incurred: Thucydides comments only that they thought they could have forced an unconditional surrender.

Whether they could have or not, the juxtaposition of the specific cost of the siege, the money that the Poteidaians were allowed to take with them, and the silence on any financial benefit accruing to the Athenians to recoup their losses, together with the removal of Perikles from the narrative immediately before, fuels speculation that the historian is not simply "telling the facts" in a neutral way but rather is constructing an account designed to make a point about the inadequacies of Athens' leadership, especially in regard to the city's financial resources. The implication emerges, therefore, that the absence of steps to insure revenue to offset both the loss of significant tribute and the heavy expense of the siege reflects poor policy, a failure to appreciate the requirements of military success, and decisions that Perikles would have neither advocated nor undertaken.[37]

THE THRACIAN "EXCURSUS" (2.95–101)

Thucydides begins his account of the third year of the war by relating the Spartan attack on Plataia and then moves to the simultaneous expedition by the Athenians against the Chalkidike, followed by Phormio's naval triumph in the Korinthian Gulf against the Peloponnesians on their way to Akarnania. During that winter, the Spartans, at the instigation of the Megarians, intended a surprise attack on the Piraieus, but "fearing the danger," they instead attacked Salamis and retreated when the Athenians came out in full force, in response to reports that their

---

36. The disruption of the polis and expulsion of the inhabitants make it difficult to assess its postrevolt economic potential, as Poteidaian silver coinage ends in 432; bronze coins may have started to be issued then; certainly many appear in Olynthos, and lesser quantities at other sites; see Alexander, *Potidaea*, 93–94; Kraay, *ACGC*, 138.

37. The editors of *ATL* believe that perhaps fifty talents came to the state from Poteidaia annually after the colony was founded but, curiously, offer no evidence in support, 3.345 and n. 101.

harbor had already been taken (2.93–4). In 2.95, Thucydides turns to the north.

Thucydides' narrative on activities in Thrace and Macedonia, introduced by the Odrysian king Sitalkes' plan to march against Perdikkas and the Chalkidians, is usually described as a digression with little importance for the *History*. Westlake, for example, includes it among the passages he calls "irrelevant," that is, of little or no significance in understanding the work or the progress of the war, and he is far from alone in this judgment.[38] By this view, Thucydides includes this digression simply because he was interested in Thrace and more knowledgeable about it than most Athenians; and, beyond confirming the historian's interest in this area, its only significance is to demonstrate that he is not so selective about choosing only material directly relevant to his subject as is usually thought.

Yet, as we shall see, this section of the work is not only relevant but also important in two respects: first, although it is true, as scholars have noted, that Sitalkes accomplished little in actual military terms, the relationship between Athens and Thrace and the former's need for Thracian support were both crucial in the war. Second, Thucydides sets out in this section to make several important arguments by means of comparison, one of his characteristic methods. Here, as elsewhere in making implicit or explicit comparisons between Athens and poleis or rulers, he focuses on power and wealth.

First, let us examine the significance of Sitalkes' activities in the progress of the war. To summarize, in the first year of the war, Athens successfully made an alliance with Sitalkes. Then, with the continuation of both the war and the siege of Poteidaia, the Athenians apparently gave high priority to securing strong support from the Odrysian kingdom. They clearly considered the situation in the region volatile and dangerous.[39] Perdikkas proved untrustworthy in his relations with Sitalkes, and this would affect the Athenians' interest in the area as well. Now, in winter 429, Sitalkes set out to fulfill his promise to the Athenians of ending the Chalkidian war in Thrace (2.95.2).

The Odrysian king's actions may have had little real or lasting effect in

---

38. Westlake, *Essays*, 14–16; cf. also, among others, Gomme, *HCT* 2:241: "Most of this is digression, and the whole of it might almost be so described; for the event narrated, Sitalkes' invasion of Macedonia and Chalkidike, is of very little importance"; Ziegler, *RhM* 78 (1929):58–67; Pearson, *CQ* 33 (1939):51; de Romilly, *Histoire et raison*, 47 n. 1; Ridley, *Hermes* 109 (1981):35, who, however, at the same time notes that "the basic purpose of this excursus is to show the greatness of the Thracian kingdom . . ."; Hornblower, *Comm.*, 371.

39. Cf. 2.29, in which Thucydides gives credit to Nymphodoros for bringing Perdikkas over to the Athenians; whereas, in 2.95.2, we are informed that it was Sitalkes who reconciled Perdikkas to the Athenians.

the end, but he was successful in his initial invasion of Macedonia: he captured or laid waste many cities and territories and negotiated with Perdikkas (2.100–101.1). By making a tremendous show of force, he succeeded in terrifying many cities.[40] Indeed, Sitalkes and his army could have done enormous damage; instead, they only caused fear. The explanation is plain enough: the Athenians did not come with a fleet as promised and, consequently, left Sitalkes' army with insufficient support to wage war against the Chalkidians. The reason, Thucydides comments, was that the Athenians did not believe that Sitalkes would actually hold up his end of the bargain and come.[41] The Athenians' behavior effectively points up the lack of strong leadership in Athens in the absence of Perikles' direction.[42] It is clear that, had they kept their promise to Sitalkes, they would most likely have secured the northern Aegean and Thraceward district against revolts and Peloponnesian interference. Thucydides' attention to Sitalkes' strength and to the wealth of the area underscores the Athenians' blunder in allowing their relationship to deteriorate. That the Peloponnesians were concerned about the Athenian alliance with Sitalkes, and thus regarded it as potentially dangerous, is obvious from their attempt to intervene and destroy it.

Thucydides' inclusion of the Thracian and Macedonian episode, then, is more than a simple manifestation of his interest in the area; it is clearly useful to his argument. His detailed treatment of the extent of resources concentrated in the hands of the Odrysian king not only highlights Athenian folly but also relates directly to his conception and analysis of power.

First, Thucydides describes the extent of both the Thracian tribes either subject to Sitalkes or able to be used in military campaigns and their territory. This provides the context in which to judge and appreciate what follows, a discussion worth quoting in full:

> The tribute (*phoros*) from all the barbarian regions and the Hellenic cities, as much as accrued in the reign of Seuthes, Sitalkes' successor, who brought it to its height, amounted to a *dunamis* of about four hundred talents of money (*arguriou*) in both gold and silver. No less a quantity came in in the form of gifts (*dora*) of gold and silver, besides woven and plain stuffs and other accoutrements, and not only for Seuthes but also for the lesser kings and nobles. . . . Thus the kingdom came to exert great strength: for

---

40. 2.101.2–4. Thucydides makes a point of alluding to the the fear with which Sitalkes was regarded.
41. 2.101.2. There does not seem to be reason to doubt this explanation; cf. Höck, *Hermes* 26 (1891):81 n. 2; Busolt, *GG* 3.2, 973; Adcock, in *CAH* 5, 206; Kagan, *Archidamian War*, 120.
42. Connor, *Thucydides*, 75–78. Connor considers Perikles dead by this point, but that is not certain, although he seems clearly to be out of the picture.

of all those in Europe between the Ionian Gulf and the Euxine, it was unsurpassed in revenue of money (*chrematon prosodo*) and in general prosperity, and second only in military strength and size of army to the Skythians. (2.97.3–5)

As is unsurprising by now, Thucydides' attention to *periousia chrematon* is focused and detailed: he supplies a specific figure, four hundred talents, for the amount of tribute coming in. He comments further that it is all money, *argurion*, consisting of both gold and silver.[43] He turns to gifts, indicating that their annual total was at least as much as the tribute; next, he elaborates on the importance of gifts as the essential mechanism for transacting business (οὐ γὰρ ἦν πρᾶξαι οὐδὲν μὴ διδόντα δῶρα, 2.97.4)—and thus, their regularity as a form of income.[44] Thucydides' interest in both gifts and income from tribute springs from the same source, as is evident from the sentence immediately following: ὥστε ἐπὶ μέγα ἡ βασιλεία ἦλθεν ἰσχύος. Furthermore, Thucydides specifies the tribute at its height, under Seuthes, although he is concerned in the narrative with Sitalkes, in part because of his interest in "greatests." This detail could also function, however, to emphasize the growth in wealth of the Odrysian kingdom at the very time when the Athenians, as it turned out, sorely needed a wealthy and powerful ally in the region.

The Odrysian king's *dunamis* is linked implicitly with his wealth in *phoros* and *dora* in a way that might remain almost Herodotean were it not for Thucydides' broader comparative purpose and previous analyses of power, such as those concerned with Minos and Agamemnon in the Archaeology, and in the evaluation of Athenian and Spartan power, where *phoros* has been a chief gauge.[45] By this point in the *History*, the reader who encounters a detailed description of revenue in tribute and gifts—much of it immediately employable—centralized under the control of the Odrysian kings readily thinks of actual and potential *dunamis* through the use of money in war. The wealth of the Odrysian kingdom, especially by Thucydides' specification of gold and silver money, meets

---

43. Does Thucydides' usage here suggest that when he writes ἀργύριον, he means simply "money" rather than strictly "silver," since both ἀργύριον and ἄργυρος occur here? It is difficult to be certain. When he uses ἀργύριον, sometimes he clearly means silver, e.g., in 1.27.1; 2.13.4; 4.116.2; probably in 3.50.2 and 6.8.1; other instances seem to me ambiguous without further exploration, 2.7.2; 2.70.3; 4.26.5; 4.65.1; 4.69.3; 5.49.5; 6.24.3; 6.60.4; 6.94.4; 7.16.2; 7.82.3; 8.76.6; since, however, silver coinage was the usual medium of exchange, it is quite likely that ἀργύριον in Thucydides generally means "silver money."

44. Thucydides is not concerned with the reciprocal aspect of the gift-exchange contract. On gift exchange, see M. I. Finley, *World of Odysseus*, passim; also see Mauss, *Gift*, for discussion of the function of gift exchange and potlatch in archaic Melanesian societies; cf. also Hornblower's comments, *Comm.*, ad loc.

45. A negative one in Sparta's case: 1.19, οἱ μὲν Λακεδαιμόνιοι οὐχ ὑποτελεῖς ἔχοντες φόρου τοὺς ξυμμάχους ἡγοῦντο; 1.80.3, in which Archidamos notes that the Athenians have (as) ξυμμάχους πολλοὺς φόρου ὑποτελεῖς, in contrast to the Spartans.

the criterion for extraordinary power. Yet Sitalkes does not wield naval power, at least not on any significant level; he has wealth but not a naval *arche* through which to project *dunamis* even more broadly. It is an easy step, however, to the view that the Athenians gravely erred in not following up on their alliance with Sitalkes, whom they initially wooed and cultivated in so determined a fashion.

Thucydides makes one final point in his comparative analysis of the northern empires. He notes in 2.97.6 that the Skythians were the largest group of people in Europe and that if they were united and made the wisest use of their resources (ξύνεσιν περὶ τῶν παρόντων), none would have been able to withstand them. Why, then, was the Odrysian kingdom more powerful than the Skythian, since the Skythians had great wealth and the advantage of being more numerous? The answer lay in their lack of unity. The Odrysian kings, on the other hand, succeeded in uniting many Thracian tribes, received and controlled large amounts of tribute and other wealth, and thus were extremely powerful.

The inferences that the reader draws from Thucydides' treatment of the Odrysian and Skythian empires are that greatness and power depend ultimately not on size or wealth itself but rather on unity and the concentration of wealth in the form of money so that it is readily expendable. But these alone may not be enough: wise counsel and intelligent use of resources are also essential elements in the formula for power. Thucydides' analysis of the Odrysian and Skythian empires readily fosters implicit comparisons and contrasts with Athens, both under Perikles and afterwards, and in different ways, Sparta.

THE SPEECH OF THE MYTILENAIANS AT OLYMPIA AND THE EXPENSE OF THE WAR

Sitalkes' invasion took place in the winter of 429; ultimately unsuccessful, he returned home (2.101.5). At the same time, the Athenian general Phormio made an expedition into Akarnania, which Thucydides treats in 2.102–3. Then, in the summer of 428, in the third year of the war, Mytilene on Lesbos revolted. The island of Lesbos was, along with Chios, one of the two remaining nontributary members of the Athenian empire. The Mytilenaians sought assistance from the Peloponnesians, first at Sparta and then at Olympia. Their speech at Olympia, as reported by Thucydides, opens with an allusion to the disparity in *paraskeue* and *dunamis* between the Athenians and themselves (3.9.2), and they urge the Peloponnesians to seize the opportunity that lay before them to attack the Athenians. They advocate a three-pronged strategy, involving both a land and sea invasion of Attica and assistance to the Mytilenaians (3.13.2–3). The time is right, they claim, because the Athenians are debilitated by the plague and by expenditure (*chrematon dapane*) (3.13.3). Indeed, the Mytilenaians attempt to emphasize even further the weakness of the Athenians by making the extraordinary suggestion that the Spartans attack Attica by land and sea (3.13.4).

The doubt cast on Athens' military vitality because of the plague has immediate credence, especially after Thucydides' lengthy description of the disease and its effects, both in Athens and abroad (that is, in Poteidaia); but what about the notion that expenditure has worn down the Athenians? Is there any substance to the Mytilenaians' allegations? There need not be, for it could be expected that the Mytilenaians would say anything necessary to persuade, even to the point of outright falsehood. Yet Thucydides' several accounts of Athens' great financial strength are still reasonably fresh in the reader's mind: Archidamos' and Perikles' speeches telling of Athens' enormous financial superiority, as well as the latter's detailed catalog of resources, including the concrete image of thousands of talents of silver on the Akropolis and removable gold from the chryselephantine statue—precious resources swelled continually by shiploads of tribute from the empire. Thus, the Mytilenaians' remark comes as something of a surprise.

There has been only one significant clue about the extent of the drain on the treasuries, that is, the cost of the siege of Poteidaia, at 2.70.2. Both that expense and the Mytilenaians' speech now foster uncertainty about the financial health of Athens in 428 and present a puzzle concerning Athenian war finance: how could the extraordinary financial resources outlined by Perikles at the beginning of the war have plummeted to a dangerously low level within a few years? As I have suggested earlier, Thucydides may have intended to create an impression of financial problems as soon as Perikles disappears from the *History*, despite the fact that, just two years into the war and with a good part of the expense of the revolt already incurred, Athens' financial position was still strong. The Mytilenaians' comment may be aimed at puncturing further an inflated image of Athens' financial might or, at least, at intensifying doubts about financial management and guidance.

The Mytilenaians follow their comment on the Athenians' depleted resources with a striking contrast: although they initially emphasized Athens' vulnerability, they now adjust their arguments to try to persuade the Peloponnesians that forming an alliance with the Mytilenaians will harm the Athenians. To make this tactic most effective, they now emphasize Athens' strength, which the Spartans can reduce by preventing Mytilene from falling tributary to the Athenians. Finally, they make a critical argument about the war and financial resources:

> It is not in Attica that the war will be decided, as one might suppose, but in those areas which benefit Attica materially: specifically, Athens' revenue is

drawn from the allies (*ton chrematon apo ton xummachon he prosodos*) and will become even larger if they reduce us, both because no one else will revolt [in the future], and because our resources will be added to theirs; and we would suffer far worse treatment than those who were previously enslaved. (3.13.5–6).

From this standpoint, both the strategy and the aim of the war are to destroy Athens' source of revenue, or rather, Athens' ability to maintain its control over the sources of revenue.[46] Pointing to the inevitable growth of *prosodos* (ἔτι μείζων) through the suppression of Mytilene suggests *auxesis*, that is, a direct connection with an increase in power. The Mytilenaians thus emphasize Athens' power by specific allusion to the result of a crushed revolt: they will have to pay *chremata*.[47] At the same time they make their appeal on an emotional level, which is perhaps more effective, given the Spartans' self-appointed role as liberator.[48]

The Mytilenaians anticipated that their claims about Athens would be convincing, and they were correct. The Peloponnesians decided to attack Attica by a strategy unlikely to have been attempted had they not been convinced of the extreme weakness of their enemy, and began their preparations (3.15). Thucydides then informs us that the Athenians were aware of these preparations and knew that they were based on the conviction that Athens was weak.[49] He continues:

[The Athenians], wishing to show [the Peloponnesians] that they were wrong, rather, that they were able, without moving the fleet against Lesbos, to defend themselves easily against those attacking them from the Peloponnese, manned a hundred ships with both citizens (except the Knights and Pentekosiomedimnoi) and metics; and putting out for the Isthmus, they put on a show, and descended upon the Peloponnese wherever they pleased. (3.16.1)

The language is strong and unequivocal: the Athenians want to make it clear (δηλῶσαι) that the Peloponnesians' conviction was incorrect (ὅτι οὐκ ὀρθῶς ἐγνώκασιν). They respond to the charge that they had suffered depletion of both men and money by easily (ῥᾳδίως) manning one hundred ships with citizens—and not nearly all of them, either—and metics.[50]

The Athenians counter all doubts about their strength by demonstrat-

---

46. I agree with Gomme, *HCT* 2, ad loc., that a colon is wanted, not a full stop, after ὠφελεῖται and before ἔστι δὲ τῶν χρημάτων, as I have done above. For the strategy, cf. 1.81.4; 1.122.1; 3.31.1.
47. Both an indemnity and *phoros* would be likely, but note below in 3.50.1 what actually happens after the revolt is suppressed.
48. δουλεύοντες, 3.13.6, with ἐλευθεροῦντες, 13.7; cf. 2.8.4.
49. διὰ κατάγνωσιν ἀσθενείας σφῶν, 3.16.1.
50. I.e., without having to hire foreign sailors.

ing their (still) enormous power for the Spartans to observe firsthand. Indeed, the Mytilenaians' assertion in 13.3 about Athenian weakness resulted in proof of quite the opposite condition,[51] as Thucydides emphasizes with the words δηλῶσαι . . . οὐκ ὀρθῶς ἐγνώκασιν . . . ῥᾳδίως . . . αὐτοί, and finally καὶ ἀποβάσεις τῆς Πελοποννήσου ᾗ δοκοίη αὐτοῖς. The Lakedaimonians are convinced, as we would expect; they return home, having failed in their plan, and the Athenian ships sail back to Athens, having concluded the demonstration of their *dunamis*.

THE AUTHENTICITY, PLACEMENT, AND MEANING OF 3.17

The preceding episode is followed by a chapter that has evoked great controversy, about both its authenticity and, if genuine, its placement in the text:

> If at the time that this fleet was at sea, Athens had almost the largest number of first-rate ships in commission that she ever possessed at any one moment, she had as many or even more when the war began. At that time one hundred guarded Attica, Euboea, and Salamis; a hundred more were cruising round Peloponnese, besides those employed at Poteidaia and in other places; making a grand total of two hundred and fifty vessels employed on active service in a single summer. It was this, with Poteidaia, that most used up her money—Poteidaia being blockaded by a force of heavy infantry (each drawing two drachmae a day, one for himself and another for his servant), which amounted to three thousand at first, and was kept at this number down to the end of the siege; besides sixteen hundred with Phormio who went away before it was over; and the ships being all paid at the same rate. In this way her money was used up at first; and this was the largest number of ships ever manned by her. (Crawley, adapted)[52]

This chapter has been the subject of much debate and controversy since Steup first pronounced it spurious in 1869.[53] Steup argued that it

---

51. MacLeod, *JHS* 98 (1978):67 (= *Collected Essays*, 91), notes the irony in this result of the Mytilenaians' claim.

52. καὶ κατὰ τὸν χρόνον τοῦτον ὃν αἱ νῆες ἔπλεον ἐν τοῖς πλεῖσται δὴ νῆες ἅμ' αὐτοῖς ἐνεργοὶ † κάλλει ἐγένοντο, παραπλήσιαι δὲ καὶ ἔτι πλείους ἀρχομένου τοῦ πολέμου. τήν τε γὰρ Ἀττικὴν καὶ Εὔβοιαν καὶ Σαλαμῖνα ἑκατὸν ἐφύλασσον, καὶ περὶ Πελοπόννησον ἕτεραι ἑκατὸν ἦσαν, χωρὶς δὲ αἱ περὶ Ποτείδαιαν καὶ ἐν τοῖς ἄλλοις χωρίοις, ὥστε αἱ πᾶσαι ἅμα ἐγίγνοντο ἐν ἑνὶ θέρει διακόσιαι καὶ πεντήκοντα. καὶ τὰ χρήματα τοῦτο μάλιστα ὑπανήλωσε μετὰ Ποτειδαίας. τήν τε γὰρ Ποτείδαιαν δίδραχμοι ὁπλῖται ἐφρούρουν (αὑτῷ γὰρ καὶ ὑπηρέτῃ δραχμὴν ἐλάμβανε τῆς ἡμέρας), τρισχίλιοι μὲν οἱ πρῶτοι, ὧν οὐκ ἐλάσσους διεπολιόρκησαν, ἑξακόσιοι δὲ καὶ χίλιοι μετὰ Φορμίωνος, οἳ προαπῆλθον· νῆες τε αἱ πᾶσαι τὸν αὐτὸν μισθὸν ἔφερον. τὰ μὲν οὖν χρήματα οὕτως ὑπανηλώθη τὸ πρῶτον, καὶ νῆες τοσαῦται δὴ πλεῖσται ἐπληρώθησαν.

53. Steup, *RhM* 24 (1869):350–61; cf. also *RhM* 27 (1872):637–40.

was the work of an interpolator, and many scholars have followed this line.[54] Many others have defended its authenticity.[55]

The main objections to the authenticity of the passage are (1) its often imprecise and obscure (and, therefore, "un-Thucydidean") form of expression;[56] (2) its probable corruption (ἐνεργοὶ κάλλει); (3) its conflict with statements made elsewhere by Thucydides, in particular, concerning the total number of ships in the Athenian fleet.[57] Although Steup rejected 3.17 *in toto*, his main objections were directed at the first sentence of the chapter, in which, by any view of the passage's authorship, there is obvious corruption (in the phrase ἐνεργοὶ κάλλει). But to reject the entire chapter essentially because of a sentence containing corruption and some usage which Steup found un-Thucydidean is unwarranted, and those who have defended the passage have demonstrated its inherently Thucydidean character.

But even after one has accepted the passage, the problem of placement remains. Some scholars have argued that the passage, while surely genuine, is incorrectly placed in the text. For example, Adcock suggests that it belongs in the year 430, and would move it between 2.56 and 57.[58] The impetus for this change derives from difficulty in accounting for the ship totals in section 2, if they apply either to the year 428 (emending section 1 by <ἢ> ἀρχομένου τοῦ πολέμου) or 431, in which case the 250 ships would be the total in that year (ἀρχομένου τοῦ πολέμου). Adcock found both of these years impossible and proposed the year 430 instead. Gomme agreed with him on the year, but suggested a way in which the passage could remain where it is and still refer to 430, taking ἀρχομένου

---

54. E.g., Hude, ad loc.; Stuart Jones, ad loc.; Müller-Strübing, *Thuk. Forschungen*, 112; Classen, ad loc.; Busolt, *GG*, 3.2, 870–71, n. 2; Westlake, *CR* 19 (1969):278 (interpolation or misplaced); Meiggs, *AE*, 259 ("a misplaced chapter of Thucydides' text which may possibly not be by Thucydides himself").

55. Including Arnold, *Thucydides*, 3d ed., ad loc.; Stahl, *RhM* 27 (1872):278; *RhM* 28 (1873):622; Herbst, *Philol.* 42 (1883):681–83; Böhme (ed. Widmann), ad loc.; Adcock, *Cambridge Historical Journal* 1 (1923–25):319–22; Gomme, *HCT* 2, ad loc.; Weil, *Thucydides III* (Budé) xxi, 86–87; Pritchett, *GSAW* 1:14–16; most recently, Hornblower, *Comm.*, ad loc.

56. In particular, the use of ἔπλεον without modification simply to mean "were sailing"; the use of ἐν τοῖς with the superlative, which Steup took in its "restrictive" sense, meaning "among the most" and consequently rejected on the grounds that there were no parallels for such a usage in Thucydides.

57. The numbers of ships at the beginning of the war and in 428/7 are nearly the same, according to chapter 17; yet detractors of the passage maintain that there were nowhere near 250 in 428/7; rather, from Thucydides' narrative, one comes up with only about 150. This is used to contribute to arguments either that the chapter is spurious or, if believed to be authentic, that it is misplaced.

58. Adcock, *Cambridge Historical Journal* 1 (1923–25):321–22. This, like other alternatives, requires some emendation (e.g., most notably, ἢ before ἀρχομένου τοῦ πολέμου).

τοῦ πολέμου in a looser sense.[59] I believe that, if the numbers are correct—not necessarily a valid assumption[60]—Adcock correctly concludes that a total of 250 ships is impossible (though "unlikely" is preferable) for the summer of 428, but not for the reasons he gives. As he has made the most comprehensive case for moving the chapter, and his conclusions therefore have consequence for our investigation, his arguments will be addressed in more detail in an appendix to this chapter. The main and fairly simple point that needs to be made here is that the arguments in favor of moving 3.17 seem primarily to be based on what scholars regard as probable or improbable; I believe that is insufficient justification for moving the chapter.[61]

A different approach from that based on examining ship numbers and textual problems is in order. In the case of a passage with no textual justification or argument drawn from ancient evidence to support a shift, the first priority is to establish whether it is out of place in the general context and in Thucydides' chain of thought, before scrutinizing individual items. In fact, this passage fits neatly where it is and continues the theme and argument that the historian has been developing.

We have already examined the Mytilenaians' speech, with its assertions of the Athenians' current financial and physical exhaustion, and the Spartans' decision to help the Mytilenaians and invade Attica by land and sea. In 3.16 Thucydides describes the Athenians' immediate and forceful response. Now he follows up in 3.17 with evidence to support and confirm the Athenians' performance; however, instead of presenting us with a detailed account of ship totals in 428, he draws a comparison with Athens' navy at a time when there was no doubt in anyone's mind that it was at its height. He thus achieves two results: first, he makes Athens' naval force in 428 seem all the more impressive by comparing it with the fleet at a time when Athenian sea power was inarguably at full strength. Second, by reminding us of the beginning of the war, he emphasizes similarity—but with a twist. We have been convinced that the Mytilenaians lied at Olympia about the Athenians' financial distress: the Athenians persuaded us otherwise in 3.16, and Thucydides has just underscored this point in 3.17 by referring to the beginning of the war, when Athens was manifestly at its height. Thucydides wants to convey the belief that all is the same, or nearly the same, as it was then.

59. Gomme, *HCT* 2, ad loc.
60. On numerical corruption in Thucydides generally, see Lewis, *Historian's Text*, 119–36 and nn.; cf. also the sound and apposite comments of Dover in *CR* n.s. 7 (1957):24–25.
61. It is probably worth bearing in mind that numerical conflict and inconsistency are a frequent problem in Thucydides but do not occasion a similar response as that to chapter 17. In particular, ship totals are a cause of concern in 3.16, the immediately preceding chapter, yet no one has suggested moving it.

Yet at the same time, he points out in 3.17 the war's tremendous drain on Athens' finances.[62] Is Thucydides supporting the Mytilenaians' statement in 3.13.3? He confirms one implication of their claim, that the Athenians were spending an extraordinary amount of money on the war. But his admission of this expense has a decidedly different purpose from that intended by the Mytilenaians. Section 3.17 is an elegant demonstration that expense and power are partners in naval war: power necessitates expense, and expense perpetuates power. Indeed, in chapter 16, Thucydides displays the Athenians' power, consisting in their navy; chapter 17 then confirms and explains it by relating ships to expense (*dapane*). Let us examine its contents.

It is notable, first of all, that Thucydides explains his statement in 3.17.3 with such a high degree of financial detail: he mentions the rate of pay for the hoplites at Poteidaia and specifies further that it was divided between themselves and their ὑπηρεταί.[63] He also notes that the ships which he refers to in 17.4 were also paid at the same rate. Thucydides provides such detailed information for a significant purpose: he is using it to explain why there was a special financial drain on Athens.[64]

Most striking, however, is the explicit linkage between the expense of money and ships and, in turn, their connection with power. In 3.17.1–2 Thucydides refers to the Athenians' naval strength by emphasizing the great number of ships which were navigable in 428 (αἱ νῆες ἔπλεον ἐν τοῖς πλεῖσται δὴ νῆες). Then, in 17.3–4, he turns to its precondition—the amount of money that was spent. He underscores the drain on Athens' financial resources by ring composition: καὶ τὰ χρήματα τοῦτο μάλιστα ὑπανήλωσε (17.3); τὰ μὲν οὖν χρήματα οὕτως ὑπανηλώθη τὸ πρῶτον, καὶ νῆες τοσαῦται δὴ πλεῖσται ἐπληρώθησαν (17.4). Most important, the historian's closing sentence is crucial for an understanding of his argument about finances and the war: he confirms emphatically that the enormous expense of the war began with its outbreak and, furthermore, was entirely expected, precisely because of the *dunamis* of the Athenian navy. The expense that Athens incurred was paradoxically a sign of its strength. Finally, by noting that the extent of the expense was anticipated and essential from the beginning (τὸ πρῶτον), Thucydides affirms again the *gnome* and *pronoia* of Perikles.

Nevertheless at the same time that such emphasis on the expense of the war signals Athens' *dunamis*, it also contributes to an impression of unease over the state of Athens' finances. Indeed, since removing

---

62. Note the repetition of the verb ὑπαναλίσκω, 3.17.3, 17.4.
63. Cf. Sargent, *CP* 22 (1927):201–12, and Jordan, *CSCA* 2 (1969):183–207, for contrasting views on who the *huperetai* were.
64. This chapter contains the earliest mention of a precise rate of pay for Athenian hoplites. See Pritchett, *GSAW* 1:14–17, for detailed discussion of this passage.

Perikles from the scene, the historian has chipped away at the image of the extraordinary magnitude of Athens' financial resources and *dunamis*, evinced by the statesman in 2.13. He has altered it with hints of financial trouble that, taken together, instill doubts about the city's financial strength: the cost of the siege of Poteidaia (2.70.2), the dispatch of ships to collect money (2.69.1), and the Mytilenaians' comment which, even if patently false, is still present in the reader's mind. Against this unsettledness stands Athens' impressive display of naval strength; but the effect is tempered by the sense that the Athenians were putting on a show (ἐπίδειξις) to alter the Peloponnesians' perception of Athens' *dunamis*, and by the fact that Thucydides does not give the total of Athenian ships in 428, but only at the beginning of the war.

The placement of 3.17, in my view, fits neatly into the progression of Thucydides' narrative and argument. It marks the climax of the preceding chapters in which Athens' financial strength has been at issue and the Athenians have convinced the Peloponnesians that the Mytilenaians' claim was false; but it also perpetuates the reader's traces of doubt that began with the siege of Poteidaia, the blunder in Thrace, and the remark of the Mytilenaians. Now Thucydides confirms, in his own person, the disquiet about Athens' financial resources. And as we wonder whether Athens truly is suffering financially, we soon reach 3.19, which concerns this directly. Thus 3.17 also prepares us for what follows. It therefore occupies an important place in Thucydides' developing argument and discussion about the resources of the war and makes perfect sense in its context. These are strong grounds against moving it.

THE εἰσφορά AND THE ἀργυρολόγοι νῆες OF 428/7 (3.19.1)

In 3.19, we read:

> The Athenians, needing additional money *chrematon* for the siege [of Mytilene], although they had for the first time levied a tax *esphoran* on themselves of two hundred talents, sent out twelve ships to collect money *argurologous naus* from their allies, with Lysikles and four others in command.[65] Lysikles sailed about collecting money from various places; then, going inland from Myous in Karia, across the Maiandrian plain up to the Sandian hill, he was attacked by the Karians and Anaiatans, and killed along with many in his army.

Here is the first explicit statement by Thucydides about a need for money over and above, apparently, that from regular revenues, and it is accordingly important to analyze its content carefully. The passage con-

---

65. Προσδεόμενοι δὲ οἱ Ἀθηναῖοι χρημάτων ἐς τὴν πολιορκίαν, καὶ αὐτοὶ ἐσενεγκόντες τότε πρῶτον ἐσφορὰν διακόσια τάλαντα, ἐξέπεμψαν καὶ ἐπὶ τοὺς ξυμμάχους ἀργυρολόγους ναῦς δώδεκα καὶ Λυσικλέα πέμπτον αὐτὸν στρατηγόν.

tains significant but problematic evidence of Athenian financial decisions and measures, and Thucydides' allusions to an εἰσφορά and the ἀργυρολόγοι νῆες have received a great deal of scholarly attention. Let us begin with the εἰσφορά.

At issue is the precise reference for τότε πρῶτον, "then, for the first time." Three possibilities have been raised: (1) "then, for the first time, they collected an εἰσφορά"; (2) "then, for the first time *during the war* they collected an εἰσφορά"; (3) "then, for the first time they collected an εἰσφορά which amounted to as much as two hundred talents." The second possibility need not detain us.[66] If Thucydides had meant to convey that it was the first time during the war that they had collected an εἰσφορά, he surely would have included the qualification as well. Τότε πρῶτον by itself is unambiguous and devoid of qualification. But this leaves the question of what was done "then, for the first time."

It is of considerable importance to note that the third possibility—that, although such taxes had been introduced long before, not until 428 did an εἰσφορά bring in as much as two hundred talents—was prompted only by the conviction that the Kallias Decrees or, more specifically, the second decree (B), contradicted Thucydides; these decrees, as we have noted earlier, are usually dated to 434.[67] That is, no one had taken τότε πρῶτον to refer to the two hundred talents until the Kallias Decrees were thought to date firmly to 434 B.C. This implies that Thucydides' sentence naturally reads another way: "then, for the first time (ever), the Athenians collected an εἰσφορά." While conceding at most the theoretical possibility of taking τότε πρῶτον with διακόσια τάλαντα (two hundred talents), the fact that τότε πρῶτον is surrounded by ἐσενεγκόντες and ἐσφοράν and is thus linked most directly with them, in my view, strongly militates against it.[68]

Most important here is Thucydides' characteristic interest in the first occurrence of a financial measure he deems significant. Thus, although the amount raised by this tax is certainly impressive, the real emphasis in the sentence likely lies in the comment that the Athenians taxed themselves (καὶ αὐτοί).[69] The significance of this surfaces upon recollection of

---

66. Though it has impressive backing, including, among others, Kirchhoff, *Abh. der Königlichen Akad. der Wiss. zu Berlin* (1876/77):27; Boeckh, *Public Economy*, 612, n. 2; Francotte, *Finances*, 27; Beloch, *GG*, 2.1, 317–18; Stevenson, *JHS* 44 (1924):1; Busolt and Swoboda, *GS* 2:1223 and n. 2; Gomme, *Historia* 2 (1953/54):17; Gomme, *HCT* 2, ad loc.; Merritt, *Hesp.* 23 (1954):223; Thomsen, *Eisphora*, esp. 139–46; Meiggs, *AE*, 519–20.

67. *IG* I³ 52. Reference to the εἰσφορά occurs in lines 17 and 19, both partially restored. See Kallet-Marx, *CQ* 39 (1989):94–113.

68. See Sealey, *TAPA* 114 (1984):77–80, for detailed discussion of Griffith's article on the first *eisphora*, *AJAH* 2 (1977):3–7, and fuller examination of the Greek.

69. Sealey, ibid., 79–80.

Perikles' remark in his first speech: "It is reserves *hai periousiai* that maintain wars rather than forced contributions *hai biaioi esphorai*;" (1.141.5); this comment, in turn, recalls Archidamos' admission that the Spartans not only lacked public wealth but even the capability to tax themselves (1.80.4). Perikles points out that not even that kind of measure answers the extraordinary financial needs of naval *dunamis*. Thucydides' statement in 3.19.1 clearly echoes Perikles' comment. Two inferences can be drawn, one more certain than the other. First, recourse to a property tax on Athenians suggests a lack of confidence in Athens' ability to extract necessary revenue from the empire and is perhaps the first significant evidence of the war's effect on Athens' control of its subjects. Second, the very fact that Perikles had previously explicitly noted the long-term ineffectiveness of the kind of ad hoc war financing that the Athenians themselves are now implementing prompts two reactions: that the εἰσφορά of 428 reflected poor financial management and foresight and that Perikles himself, had he still been alive, would not have resorted to such a measure.

Thucydides, then, notes that the Athenians in 428 took the measure of taxing themselves for the first time,[70] and he provides the precise total, two hundred talents. The second decree of Kallias is thought to contradict this. Yet the date of this decree is uncertain, and the references to an εἰσφορά are partially restored.[71] It therefore does not contradict Thucydides; it is more likely irrelevant.

Let us move on to the "money-collecting ships." Thucydides, after referring to the εἰσφορά, then mentions, in the main clause of the sentence, that twelve "money-collecting ships" were sent out. This is a measure for which the participial phrase indicates the circumstance, that is, "needing money for the siege." Thucydides juxtaposes it with the εἰσφορά: first, he told us that the Athenians taxed themselves (καὶ αὐτοί); next, he states how they procured money from the allies (καὶ ἐπὶ τοὺς ξυμμάχους, in which the καί is clearly adverbial). Furthermore, he specifies not only the number of ships sent out but also the number of generals: Λυσικλέα πέμπτον αὐτὸν στρατηγόν). Is this an exceptionally large number of both ships and generals? It is in comparison with the only previous mention of an expedition of "money-collecting" ships (2.69), where six ships and one general are dispatched. The context of 3.19,

---

70. It is clear from τότε πρῶτον that more followed; cf. Ar. *Knights* 924, which implies its regularity.

71. My own preference at this point for the date of the decree is 418, the date which Fornara proposed for both A and B, *GRBS* 11 (1970):185–96, since reference to the necessity for a vote of ἄδεια before the money can be used occurs in lines 16 and 18, and we have record of no such vote in connection with the sacred moneys until that year, from *IG* I³ 370.

which concerns measures to meet a financial need, lends support to the inference that the number of ships and generals in this case, in 428, was unusual.

The mission of these ships has been the subject of much debate, which has focused on whether they are (1) tribute-collecting ships, more specifically, ships dispatched to collect tribute arrears; (2) ships sent out in connection with tribute reassessments; or (3) ships not connected with tribute, but rather, sent out to collect extra money in time of need.[72]

Thucydides mentions the "money-collecting ships" four times, sent out in the early winters of 430/29, 428/7, and 425/4 and in the summer of 424 (2.69.1, 3.19.1, 4.50.1, 4.75.1). In none of these instances is there any specific mention of tribute. We shall see in the next chapter that the evidence to associate these ships with reassessments and tribute collection is, for all but one year, tenuous and problematic.[73] For the present, we need to assess the significance of these ships' mission in 428 as we try to determine the extent, if any, of Athens' overall financial problems. First, the ships sent out with Lysikles as one of the generals were likely not those that might be dispatched routinely to collect (arrears of) tribute: the context is rather one of exceptional need met by the decision both to institute an *eisphora* and to collect extra money from parts of the empire. Significantly, Thucydides carefully points out that the money was needed "for the siege," that is, not for the war generally.

The situation in 428, then, was one of temporary financial need, not widespread financial crisis. Indeed, the earlier mention of "money-collecting" ships in 2.69 supports the same conclusion: immediately following the dispatch of that expedition, the Poteidaians came to terms with the Athenians. The extraordinary expense connected with the siege of Poteidaia suggests a fuller context for the dispatch of "money-collecting ships" in anticipation of the siege of Mytilene. There is an important psychological element as well: the threat of a major siege, such as that of most of Lesbos, following so closely the siege of Poteidaia must have caused substantial fear, if not panic, about the expenditures required in the war. Consider the picture that Thucydides presents of Athens' decisions and activity abroad after the plague broke out.

The Athenians had let their alliance with Sitalkes lapse, despite the importance of an ally of such *dunamis* in that region (as proved later when Brasidas showed up in the north in 424).[74] Next, an expedition in search of money ended in disaster (2.69) and was followed by the surren-

---

72. Cf. Nesselhauf, *Klio* Beiheft 30 (1933):141; Meritt, *AJP* 55 (1934):285; Gomme, *HCT*, ad loc.; *ATL* 3:69–70; Meiggs, *AE*, 254, 307, 315; Schuller, *Herrschaft*, 56.
73. See below, pp. 160–64.
74. 4.78–88; 102–16; 120–5.12. Thucydides will not pass up the opportunity to remind us of the significance of the loss of Sitalkes (4.101.5).

der of the Poteidaians after a miserable two-year siege, settled by the generals on the spot on terms bringing no direct financial compensation to Athens and causing anger at home. Thus, in 428, when the Athenians learned of Mytilenaian preparations for revolt, Thucydides contrasts their reaction dramatically with their earlier response simply upon fearing a revolt by Poteidaia: at first they did not believe it, but when their envoys were repeatedly unable to persuade the Mytilenaians to stop their preparations, they became afraid, and then suddenly sprang into action.[75] The impression made by Thucydides' choice of words is one of wasted time, indecision, fear, and rash behavior. Had the Athenians acted immediately and forcefully, the siege might have come to an expeditious close, with less expense in the end.

The contrast to the Athenians' immediate action in 432 against the Poteidaian revolt could not be plainer. Now, in 428, Perikles was gone, the effects of the plague were lingering and debilitating, and Athens' leadership had proved unable to act firmly and consistently. Disbelief was a luxury that the Athenians could not afford, given the importance of Lesbos and the consequences of a revolt for the empire in that region as a whole; nevertheless, the response was unwillingness and inaction, followed by haste. It is against this general social and political background that we need to place the decisions and mood of the polis in 428, for it is a better explanation for the quick-cash schemes recorded by Thucydides than the hypothesis that the reserve had been exhausted and the money in general had run out. The financial decisions incorporated in 3.19, then, are intelligible purely from the standpoint of uneasiness about the idea of depleting the reserve and spending the regular revenue on variable, emergency operations such as sieges following the magnitude of the Poteidaian campaign and the failure to recoup its expense. The decisions suggest concern about the future based on their current difficulties rather than about any present financial crisis.

From the narrative and speeches of the beginning of the war, which abounded with references to, and evidence of, Athens' *dunamis*, *paraskeue*, and *periousiai chrematon*, Thucydides has shifted the tone considerably and altered the image of Athens' overwhelming financial might. Thucydides' narrative prompts the reader to attribute the change to the loss of Perikles' leadership and *gnome*, especially with respect to the management of the city's finances and alliance with Sitalkes. Thus, after Perikles disappears from the *History*, we can immediately discern the contrast between the statesman and subsequent leadership; we do not have to wait until Kleon's entry into the *History*.

---

75. οὐκ ἀπεδέχοντο . . . οὐκ ἔπειθεν . . . δείσαντες . . . ἐξαπιναίως, 3.3.1.

THE END OF THE REVOLT OF MYTILENE

We shall now complete our investigation of the early years of the war by examining the *History* to the end of the Mytilenaian revolt and the subsequent settlement. The attack on Plataia, occurring in the same winter, 428/7, is reported by Thucydides in 3.20–24, and he resumes the narrative of the revolt of Mytilene in 3.25. The siege continued through the winter until the Mytilenaians were forced to come to terms with the Athenians in the following summer, 427.

The Peloponnesian ships under the command of Alkidas wasted much time in coming to Mytilene (3.26.1, 29), and Thucydides minces no words in bringing this out.[76] They learned of Mytilene's fate while at Mykonos, and from there they went to Embaton in the Erythraia, arriving a full week after Mytilene surrendered (3.29.2). In subsequent discussions about the course of action to follow, some Ionian exiles and Lesbians in Alkidas' fleet urged him "to seize one of the cities in Ionia or Aeolic Kyme, that thereby, using it as a base, they might effect the revolt of Ionia" (3.31.1). Thucydides inserts an editorial comment noting the likelihood of the plan's success and continues with the proposal: if they did this, "they would deprive Athens of an area that provided the greatest source of revenue (*ten prosodon*); and, at the same time, if the Athenians blockaded them, they would incur expense (*dapane*)."[77]

Thucydides makes clear his own opinion of the extent of Alkidas' incompetence as a general and strategist by commenting that Alkidas did *not even* (οὐδέ) accept this proposal—that is, one so obviously advantageous to the Spartans—and by contrasting Alkidas' leisurely cruise to a critical theater of operation with his present desire to return to the Peloponnese ὅτι τάχιστα, "as quickly as possible."[78] In fact, the advice of the

---

76. The ships "which should have come to their aid in haste ... wasted their time and proceeded in a leisurely fashion for the rest of the voyage" (3.29.1).

77. καὶ τὴν πρόσοδον ταύτην μεγίστην οὖσαν Ἀθηναίων [ἣν] ὑφέλωσι, καὶ ἅμα, ἢν ἐφορμῶσι σφίσιν, αὐτοῖς δαπάνη γίγνεται, 3.31.1. Cf. Gomme, *HCT* 2, ad loc., who thinks that αὐτοῖς should include the Ionians; in my view, it more likely refers only to the Athenians. It does not make sense that the Lesbians and Ionians would be suggesting a way in which one of the possible and desirable results would be for their own lands to incur expense; rather, if Athens went against these cities to try to bring them back into the empire, it would have to incur great expense. This comment is especially apposite in light of what we have read about the siege of Poteidaia as well as the siege of Mytilene.

78. Cf. also 3.69: ὡς τότε φεύγουσαι διὰ τοῦ πελάγους. Adcock's suggestion (*Mélanges Glotz* 1:1–6), on the basis of his dating of ML 67 (*IG* V¹ 1 and 219) to 427, that Alkidas was an effective fund-raiser during his expedition in 427 is hard to reconcile with Thucydides, even taking into account exaggeration by the historian. The date of the inscription, recording contributions to the Spartan war fund, is problematic; see now W. T. Loomis, *The Spartan War Fund: IG V 1.1 and a New Fragment*. Historia Einzel. 74. Stuttgart, 1992, for

Ionians and Lesbians was sound: depriving Athens of its revenue was the best (and only) way currently available for the Peloponnesians to win the war, given the glaring inadequacy of their own resources. Thucydides presents advice proffered but never followed, given by former allies of Athens now taking refuge with the Spartans. It is characteristic of his careful research that he found out about the proposals made to Alkidas, and significant that he considered these arguments important enough to relate.

Indeed, Thucydides uses this particular episode as an egregious example of the Spartans' failure not only to deprive Athens of her revenue but even to grasp the significance of this strategy in the early years of the war. Furthermore, by focusing on Alkidas' fatuous behavior to explain why the revolt of Mytilene failed and why the Ionian cities were not incited to revolt, Thucydides deflects attention from the positive aspects (from an Athenian point of view): that the Athenians were able to force the surrender of Mytilene and that the Ionian cities did not take the Mytilenaian revolt as an opportunity to rise up against the Athenians themselves. Let us return to the contents of the plan proposed to Alkidas.

The Ionians and Lesbians claim that Ionia contributes "revenue which was the greatest of the Athenians',"[79] a statement at striking variance with the conclusions drawn from the tribute quota lists about the economic condition of Ionia in the fifth century.[80] It is regarded as fact that Ionia was an economic backwater in the fifth century, in a "Dark Age," in contrast to its great prosperity in the sixth century.[81] The case was argued fully by J. M. Cook in 1961 and has received much support.[82]

---

discussion and bibliography; cf. Roisman, *Historia* 36 (1987):385–421, who considers Thucydides' portrayal of Alkidas unfair.

79. τὴν πρόσοδον ταύτην μεγίστην οὖσαν Ἀθηναίων.

80. The Ionians and Lesbians are, of course, trying to persuade Alkidas to effect the revolt of Ionia; their statement could be outright exaggeration and falsehood, and certainly the description of Ionia's revenue μεγίστη, "the greatest," makes the Spartan general's subsequent refusal to act on their advice look especially bad. But it is notable that Ionia's revenue is called μεγίστη, rather than simply πολλή or the like. Even if the Ionians and Lesbians are exaggerating, it still is doubtful that if Ionia yielded insignificant amounts of revenue, they would stretch it to the "greatest" amount.

81. The ideas which follow were also presented at the January 1989 annual meeting of the APA, in a paper entitled "Was Ionia Impoverished in the Fifth Century, B.C.? The Evidence of Thucydides and the Tribute Quota Lists."

82. Cook, *PCPS* n.s. 7 (1961):9–18; cf., among others, Meiggs, *AE*, 269–72; Amit, *SCI* 2 (1975):38–72; Emlyn-Jones, *Ionians and Hellenism*, 165–66; Balcer, *Sparda*, 414; cf. Pritchett, *GSAW* 1:62–66, who addresses the problems in the evidence for Ionia and in particular, in correlating Thucydides' ἀτειχίστου οὔσης τῆς Ἰωνίας (3.33.2) with the archaeological evidence.

Disagreement has arisen over the causes of this decline, but belief in its existence remains intact.[83] Cook based his case partly on archaeological evidence, which has carried little weight because of the limited area excavated.[84] He also tried to determine the Greek-Persian frontier and concluded that the rich agricultural land of Ionia would either have been in Persian hands or have belonged to "oligarchic" Greeks who preferred to pay taxes to Persia rather than tribute to Athens.[85] But the chief support for the theory of profound economic decline in fifth-century Ionia is the tribute quota lists, in which the Ionian cities pay a consistently minor amount in comparison with other districts. In the words of one scholar, "the tribute lists unequivocally show the economy in decline."[86]

But are the tribute quota lists in fact an accurate measure of economic prosperity? Can we determine the general wealth of a city or district by reference exclusively to the amount of tribute that it apparently paid? If this were true, we would have to suppose that many cities within the empire were in a depressed economic state, cities known from other evidence to have been prosperous. Indeed, it is well known that the amount of tribute a city paid to Athens often depended on a variety of factors beyond its economic condition. For example, disaffection could result in lower or partial payments, as well as an indemnity following a suppressed revolt, or the settlement of a klerouchy in a city's territory.[87] All were circumstances that could affect both assessment and payment of tribute.

Another, and highly important, factor that could bear not only on the amount of tribute assessed and paid, but even on whether a polis had tributary status at all, is Athens' extraction of revenue over and above tribute from regions of the empire. In this regard, Amphipolis is noteworthy, a city that we know from Thucydides (4.108) supplied substantial revenue to Athens. That Athenian colony paid no tribute, but the

83. Cook, *PCPS* n.s. 7 (1961):9–18, argued that only a small coastal strip of Asia Minor was affected by the Athenian empire and that the cities' agricultural land was under Persian control, whereas Meiggs, *AE*, 269–72, saw the suppression of the Ionian Revolt as the decisive factor in the decline of Ionia.

84. See Meiggs, *AE*, 271.

85. The evidence does not appear very strong. It is largely extrapolated from the very beginning and end of the fifth century, i.e., when the Athenian empire was not yet in existence or had already weakened tremendously.

86. Amit, *SCI* 2 (1975):41; cf. also Balcer, *Sparda*, 414: "Ionian poverty is strongly noted among the records of the Athenian Tribute Lists."

87. The latter probably accounts for the reduction of tribute for Andros and Karystos. See the discussion on all of these circumstances by Meiggs, *AE*, 242–51; cf. also, *HSCP* 67 (1963):1–36; Fornara, *CSCA* 10 (1977):39–56. Plut. *Per.* 11.5 lists cities in which klerouchies were founded around the middle of the fifth century, and this can be used to help understand decreases in tribute.

example is useful nevertheless for indicating the wealth of an area that is not reflected in the tribute quota lists. We are fortunate to have Thucydides' valuable reference to Amphipolis' revenue and to know much about the richness of the area; but if we did not, would we have to suppose that Amphipolis was impoverished in the fifth century?

If the tribute quota lists were taken generally as an accurate (and the only) gauge of a region's economic condition, we would have an extremely distorted picture of many of the cities known to be members of the Athenian alliance. Skepticism is in order, therefore, about the notion of Ionia's supposed poverty in the fifth century, reliant as it is chiefly on the tribute quota lists. The issue, however, needs to be focused more sharply. For it is not so much that the region of Ionia had no considerable economic productivity: even Cook does not deny great agricultural richness in the district; he simply believes that its yield went to Persia because of the quota lists. Rather, the real question is, to whom did the wealth of the land go, leaving an impression of poverty? Let us return to 3.31.

The Ionians and Lesbians maintain that Ionia furnishes *he megiste prosodos* to the Athenians. According to Gomme, since "officially 'Ionian tribute' included 'Karian tribute' (from the R. Maiandros southwards) since 438, . . . Thucydides may have had this in mind."[88] But we cannot insist that Thucydides is rephrasing, and it is difficult to believe that the Ionians and Lesbians had the rubric from the quota lists in mind. We must admit that Ionia's tribute record apparently conflicts with the claim in 3.31 or that the latter has been misunderstood.

What do the Ionians and Lesbians actually claim? They do not refer to *ho megistos phoros*, but *he megiste prosodos*. Herein lies an answer to the apparent conflict between this comment and the quota lists and, more important, a clear refutation of the poverty of Ionia in the fifth century. Tribute was not the only form of imperial income: we have encountered references to other forms of revenue in Thucydides already (and shall continue to do so), for example, yield from mines (1.101.3), indemnities (Samos, 1.117.3), and other money collected from the empire over and above tribute (2.69.1; 3.19.1; cf. 4.50.1; 4.75.1); in addition, we shall find reference to revenue from klerouchies and sacred lands (3.50.2). From the allusions in Thucydides alone, it is reasonable to suppose that there are even more types of income beyond those that he records. Finally, we should recall that Perikles, in 2.13.3, refers to "six hundred talents of revenue coming in annually from the empire, for the most part consist-

---

88. Gomme, *HCT* 2, ad loc.; cf. Highby, *Erythrae Decree*, 40 and n. 3, who notes that Thucydides uses the terms Ἴωνες and Ἰωνία for the Ionians of the Asiatic mainland.

ing of tribute," that is, there was clearly not insignificant revenue apart from tribute.

I suggest that the reference in 3.31 to *prosodos* from Ionia is positive testimony that Ionia was supplying revenue to Athens in addition to tribute and that this might also account for the relatively low totals inferred from the tribute quota lists.[89] The archaeological record, inconclusive as it is, and Thucydides together suggest not that Ionia's economic resources had been severely weakened after the suppression of the Ionian revolt in 494 but rather that their financial yield went to Athens.[90]

THE SETTLEMENT OF MYTILENE

Following the Athenians' successful conclusion of the siege, the prisoners, consisting of the Spartan Salaithos and some Mytilenaians, were sent to Athens. Thucydides describes the actions and decisions reflective of their impassioned mood: they killed Salaithos immediately and passed a decree to kill all adult Mytilenaian males and enslave all the women and children (3.36.2). But the next day, the Athenians experienced a sudden change of mind and accordingly called a second assembly.

In the speeches presented by Kleon and Diodotos, the effect of the revolt (and of revolts in general) on the financial resources of Athens and the financial potential of the revolting polis proves to be one of the issues that both speakers use in support of their opposing proposals. Both Kleon and Diodotos explicitly connect money and naval power, each arguing that the revenue on which Athens' strength depends will be forfeited following the revolt's suppression. Kleon, as part of his rhetorical strategy to convince the Athenians to adhere to their original decision, argues that the poleis in the empire learn no positive lessons from the revolts of others and, in any case, Athens will have to spend money and lives on suppressing the revolts; moreover, even if successful, the Athenians will be unable to gain revenue "on which their strength depends" from the defeated polis, since its own resources will have been wasted.[91] Kleon, then, makes the familiar connection between money,

---

89. Low tribute might suggest either that Ionia was relatively "cash poor" but rich in other resources or that the cities were simply assessed a low amount of tribute because Athens derived other revenue from the area.

90. In his comment on 3.31, Hornblower, *Comm.*, cites Diod. 15.90.4, a passage which alludes to Ionian revenue (*prosodos*) as comprising half of the Persian king's take at the time of the Satraps' Revolt.

91. 3.39.7–8. Kleon echoes two phrases that we have encountered before: χρήματα καὶ σώματα, here, τὰ χρήματα καὶ αἱ ψυχαί (the former, 1.85.1, 2.53.2; cf. also 6.12.1; 8.65.3) and τῆς προσόδου, δι' ἣν ἰσχύομεν (cf. 1.81.4, 1.122.1; 2.13.2).

expense, and power in advocating harsh punishment as a deterrent to future revolts.

Diodotos argues that expediency dictates lenient treatment on the grounds that poleis that recognize the futility of their revolts will surrender before their resources have been drained and, therefore, will still be able to repay the expense (*dapane*) of the siege and tribute (ὑποτελεῖν) for the future. If, however, the polis is to be destroyed whether it comes to terms early or late, then it might as well hold out. In that event, Athens must endure the expense (*dapane*) of a long siege and, even if successful, receive a polis that is depleted financially (ἐφθαρμένην) and unable to pay the revenue (*prosodou*) "which constitutes our real strength" (3.46.2–4).

Diodotos argues for a moderate punishment, so that, thereby, "we shall be able to make use of the poleis that are strong in regard to money."[92] He ends his speech with what he apparently decided would be his most persuasive point, that the demos in the allied states is well-disposed toward the Athenians. His arguments succeed.

It is clear that, for both speakers, financial considerations regarding both imperial revenue and the city's hold on the *arche* were at the forefront of discussion. It is not difficult to surmise the combined effect of the two revolts, the plague, and the war on the Athenians. To what extent did palpable anxieties about financial resources translate into concrete measures designed to insure the continued flow of needed revenue to the centralized treasuries? As we saw, the city neither received compensation for the expense of Poteidaia nor demanded tribute for regular revenue in the future. The omission of both of these measures was highly unusual following a costly siege in a wealthy region. Let us look at the case of Mytilene.

Thucydides records the settlement decided upon by the Athenians in 3.50. He first relates the immediate arrangements, whereby those chiefly responsible for the revolt were to be killed, fortifications torn down, and ships surrendered (50.1).

> But afterwards, they [the Athenians] did not assess the Lesbians tribute; instead, they divided the land, except for the Methymnians', into three thousand lots; three hundred they selected as sacred to the gods, and the rest was distributed among Athenian klerouchs, who were sent out there. The Lesbians were assessed to pay two minai a year for each lot and worked the land themselves (50.2).[93] In addition, the Athenians took possession of

---

92. ταῖς πόλεσιν ἕξομεν ἐς χρημάτων λόγον ἰσχυούσαις χρῆσθαι, 3.46.4.
93. *IG* I³ 66 refers to a klerouchy, Mytilenaians, and land which is to be "given back," whether to the Mytilenaians or the Athenians is unclear. The decree is not dated and is in extremely fragmentary condition, but it is usually placed in 427 and associated with the settlement described in 3.50.1; cf., e.g., Meritt, *AJP* 75 (1954):359–68; Gauthier, *REG* 79

the fortified towns on the mainland which the Mytilenians had controlled and thereafter made them subject to Athens (50.3).

Thucydides' account of the details of this settlement is important and revealing, for its terms departed markedly from those imposed after earlier revolts. We noted the difference in the way that the Poteidaian settlement was handled; that case and the settlement of Mytilene suggest a change in the nature of settlements which has important consequences for the city's financial resources and, therefore, for the city's power. The revolt of Poteidaia cost Athens two thousand talents and many lives; the final terms imposed on the Poteidaians were expulsion from their polis and colonization of the land by Athenians. The terms laid on the Lesbians, and their implications for Athens, are somewhat similar: no tribute is assessed, but land is appropriated for the benefit of individual Athenians.

The purpose of the klerouchy is expressed in financial terms as the alternative to *phoros*.[94] What financial benefit did it yield? Ten talents would come in annually from the three hundred holdings set aside on sacred land. In addition, a total of ninety talents would be paid to individual Athenians every year, making the total financial gain an impressive one hundred talents a year.[95] The attempt to determine the purpose and significance of this measure yields considerable complexity of interpretation, suggesting both positive and negative ways in which the settlement can be viewed.

(1966):64–88. Its contents are too uncertain to have great significance, though Gomme sensed a "generous atmosphere" in the inscription and accordingly argued that it should not be connected with Thucydides 3.50.1, about which he commented, "short of total destruction a severer punishment could hardly have been inflicted" (*Studies Robinson* 2, 334–39; cf. also Gauthier, 83). The condition and absence of a firm date of the inscription necessitates caution. The possibilities that the klerouchs were absentee landowners or were on the spot in a garrison as hoplites have been suggested; see Gomme, *HCT* 2:328–33; Gauthier, 65; Hornblower, *Comm.*, ad loc. The notion of a garrison is highly speculative, since although the amount of rent (for each *kleros*) "more or less corresponds to hoplite pay" (Hornblower, *Comm.*, 440, after Gauthier), it is a figure that can be made to correspond to much else, even rents on land; see, e.g., Walbank's "Classification of Properties by Type and Rent" (Table 2) in *Hesperia* 52 (1983):212–13, for the range of average rents on various types of property; moreover, *IG* I³ 66 distinguishes between klerouchs and soldiers (e.g., lines 17, 19).

94. Though not necessarily suggesting any kind of equivalence; cf. Gauthier, *REG* 79 (1966):80, 84.

95. There seems to be a general assumption in the scholarship on this settlement that Athens as a *state* received one hundred talents annually, e.g., West, *TAPA* 61 (1930):225; *ATL* 3:345 (cf. 3.343, n. 87); Huxley, *PRIA* 83 (1983):199 (110 talents). But this is not what Thucydides says. At most ten talents would have gone into the sacred treasuries, as rent from the κλῆροι dedicated τοῖς θεοῖς; an individual Athenian klerouch would have collected two minai per year.

First, let us consider the possible positive goals of the settlement. The considerable sum of one hundred talents may have been presumed easier to obtain in the long run by means of a klerouchy rather than tribute: while the individual rents were not insignificant, neither were they oppressive in nature (two minai per year) nor did they have the symbolic undertones of tribute; and both of these factors may well have increased the probability of payment. The Lesbians, with the exception of the ringleaders, would have survived the revolt intact, would not be forced to leave their land, and would not be pressed into the subject status of virtually all other allies and forced into the repugnant and humiliating act of paying tribute. In short, the establishment of an Athenian klerouchy may have been a surer way of obtaining imperial revenues, especially since one thousand of Mytilene's leading citizens had just been executed, men who may well have been expected to bear the onus of an indemnity or tribute.[96]

The measure also permits a positive interpretation with respect to its effect on the Athenians. Still suffering the effects of the plague, property owners had just been taxed for the first time (3.19.1) and many had, in addition, seen their land in Attica ravaged by the Spartans. For those selected as klerouchs, the private advantage would have been most welcome; from the standpoint of leadership and policy, the measure would surely have been calculated to appease (which may have been the intention of the settlement of Poteidaia as well). Thus, the measure acquires a shrewd aspect, all the more so if Athens' strategists saw an increasing need for taxation as a form of war revenue.

One hundred talents of total financial gain every year, but dispersed among some three thousand Athenians, would have had both a financial and psychological benefit. This dispersal, however, also provides grounds for questioning the perspicacity and value of the settlement for Athens. For what matters most in the maintenance of naval power, especially in times of war, is centralized public wealth, *periousia chrematon*, that can easily be expended and continually replenished by revenue to the state and whose reserve is more than amply maintained. Scattered, private wealth and reliance on sporadic taxation cannot insure the necessary accessibility and quantity of wealth essential to success in war fought on the sea. The only direct benefit to Athens' public finances would have been rents from the sacred land, amounting to ten talents—

---

96. The division of all of Lesbos, except Methymnos, into klerouchies on which the previous owners now had to pay rent to use themselves is relevant to the issue of who bore the burden of tributary status in the subject cities, the demos as a whole or the wealthy, and therefore, who would have suffered most in the event of a failed revolt. In the cases of Poteidaia and Lesbos, the respective populations in their entirety were apparently made to suffer equally.

not an amount to be dismissed, but meager in comparison to the potential financial yield of the island.[97] Accordingly, evaluated squarely in the context of the war and the requirements for success, the financial result of the settlement looks increasingly negative. Moreover, the apparent psychological boon accompanying the measure, derived from its appeal to renewed morale through private benefit, can also seem like part of the typical stock-in-trade of the demagogue, an attempt to curry favor among the demos in order to maintain one's own power.

In any case, the Athenians chose not to change Mytilene to tributary status, although that would have been the expected result and one that would seem to be the best method of insuring systematic, centralized revenue. One immediate question, however, is whether the Mytilenaians would have been able to pay tribute after they had just experienced what was probably a significant depletion of their own resources. In the discussions in Athens about the fate of Mytilene, a prominent concern appears to have been the financial consequences of lengthy sieges against allies who had revolted. The sieges of Poteidaia and now Mytilene were raising serious questions about their erosive effects on Athens' lifeline, its financial resources, because of both the drain on the city's reserve and the damage done to the sources of revenue. The proposals of Kleon and Diodotos, especially the latter's, had as an important goal the preservation of the resources of the allies, the chief financiers of the war. But was Mytilene reduced to poverty by the siege and thus unable to pay tribute? That the form of punishment imposed by the Athenians was not dictated primarily by a practical inability on the part of the conquered city to produce an annual tribute is evident from the nature of the settlement, which Thucydides expresses as an alternative to tribute and which raised an impressive combined revenue.[98]

Moreover, it is not even clear that the Aktaian *polismata* opposite Lesbos on the mainland coast formerly under the control of Mytilene were made tributary themselves as part of the Mytilenaian settlement. Thucydides notes (3.50.3) that the Athenians took possession of these towns and thereafter made them subjects but does not explicitly state that they were made tributary. It is quite possible that a decision was made in this

---

97. It would help if we knew how many ships the Mytilenaians contributed to the League fleet and how much financial responsibility the men who were killed for their role in the revolt had; cf. Hdt. 6.8.2, who gives seventy ships as the Lesbians' contribution to the Ionian Revolt. It is impossible to determine whether the Athenians would have had to pay any sort of tax themselves on their income from the rent. If so, it would likely have been a tithe.

98. Important and interesting in the cases of both Poteidaia and Mytilene is the "egalitarian" nature of the settlements: all inhabitants were punished equally, and financial hardship was incurred by the demos as a whole, not simply the wealthy citizens.

case as well not to demand tribute—at least initially—but instead to derive revenue in other ways.[99]

The terms of the settlement, then, are conducive to subtle and complex interpretations; which is correct? Strictly from the standpoint of military strategy, the settlement was undeniably a mistake, failing to regard the city's *periousia chrematon* as the paramount issue and instead scattering wealth for the enrichment of individuals. Moreover, together with the settlement of Poteidaia, the terms for Mytilene indicate a pattern of decisions regarding Athens' *arche* and financial resources that directly contradict the policy advocated by Perikles for holding fast to the empire and winning the war. An argument that appeasement to individuals was justified and expedient at this point in the war would have been one stringently rejected by that statesman, even if to his temporary disadvantage.[100] His successors apparently judged otherwise. It is tempting to see in the settlement of Mytilene, and possibly in the eventual settlement of Poteidaia, tangible support for the charges of crowd-pleasing constantly lodged against such leaders as Kleon by the comic poets,[101] and by Thucydides in 2.65.7–8, whose hostile voices were raised against the demagogues' deployment of the demos as a political base. Can we try cautiously to infer Thucydides' judgment of the settlement of Mytilene?

First, it is intriguing and significant, I think, that Thucydides chose not to state the total number of talents to be extracted from Lesbos annually, for one hundred talents is an impressively large sum. The historian tends to relate both specific financial information and, in particular, significantly large amounts.[102] In this case, he provides the means to calculate the total by specifying the number of lots and the rent, but stops short of performing the calculation himself. It is reasonable to suggest that Thucydides did not judge the settlement as having a significant, positive effect on Athens' financial strength, for the simple reason that just ten percent of the grand total became centralized, public money, the only "useful" kind of wealth in the war. It is an easy step to infer a negative appraisal of the settlement, indeed, to suppose that Thucydides viewed the decision as a mistake, given his positive judgment of Periklean financial strategy and especially the necessity of centralized re-

---

99. The Aktaian *polismata* were assessed tribute in 425 (*IG* I³ 71, III.124–40) and in 422 (*IG* I³ 77, IV.14–27); there is no evidence that they ever paid, though the tribute quota record is so spotty for these years that lack of positive evidence does not mean much.
100. 2.65.1–4.
101. E.g., Ar. *Knights, passim; Peace* 756; Kock, *Com.Att.Frag.* 3, p. 400, no. 11 (see *Mor.* 806F–807A); Connor, *New Politicans*, 93.
102. E.g., the amount of the first assessment of tribute (1.96.2); wealth in treasuries (2.13.3–5); expense of the siege of Poteidaia (2.70.2).

serve for long-term military success. It is notable that he conspicuously introduces the terms of the settlement with a negative comment ("the Athenians did *not* assess tribute" on the Lesbians) and that he does not indicate the overall financial yield; totals of scattered, individual wealth are not significant factors in the emergency of war.[103]

There may be, then, some underlying criticism of the arrangements for Mytilene, though the point should not be pressed too far. But we can, from considering the implications of the settlement of Mytilene as well as that of Poteidaia, detect some important changes in leadership and imperial and financial policy after the death of Perikles. We shall consider them more fully in the final chapter. But here it is useful to suggest briefly how our exploration of these settlements informs and aids interpretation. First, their terms point distinctly to a move away from tribute as a means of extracting revenue. Second, however one judges these decisions in connection with the demagogic methods of Perikles' successors, they reveal a concentration on personal, individual benefit over that of the polis as a whole and thus have important consequences for our understanding of the differences in measures and outlook between Perikles and his successors. Perikles' belief in the primacy of the polis over the individual can be amply demonstrated by his policies and is brought out as well in Thucydides' presentations of his speeches. In the years after the statesman's death, there was a discernible shift away from this principle that reflected on the level of political and military policy, a development characteristic of Peloponnesian War society and culture in general, namely, growing individualism and rejection of public over private interest; this outcome is hardly surprising in such an environment of crisis, but pernicious to a city at war. The measures adopted in the war increasingly demonstrate these attitudes on the broader social level, reflecting a concern with private gain, even to the detriment of the polis as a whole. A failure to see that public and private were inextricably intertwined in crises such as war resulted in decisions which boded ill for the city and its citizens.

CONCLUSIONS

Beloch's judgment that, by 427, "der Kriegsschatz, auf dem hauptsächlich Athens maritime Überlegenheit beruhte, war bereits zum größten

103. It is interesting to speculate whether Kleon had a hand in the settlement. His initial proposed treatment of the islanders was overturned; but it is also makes sense that he would exert all efforts to repair the damage to his influence by coming up with a new suggestion after the demos voted to cancel the order to kill all adult males and enslave the women and children. His rhetorical agility at that time is suggested by Thucydides, who refers to him as τῷ τε δήμῳ παρὰ πολὺ ἐν τῷ τότε πιθανώτατος, 3.36.6.

Teile erschöpft,"[104] has been echoed by historians ever since. Some have tempered this view to a certain extent, but the general consensus remains that the Athenian "war treasury" was at a dangerously low level and soon to run out.[105] What support does Thucydides provide for this view?

The historian presents a picture of Athens during 429–428 that contrasts sharply with that at the beginning of the war. We sense trouble: some financial distress and problems of leadership. Indeed, Thucydides focuses on Athens' financial condition as a means of highlighting his analysis of the polis in the period following Perikles' death. This makes sense to the reader, since financial resources were a great concern to the Perikles we encounter in Thucydides' work. The historian may even be registering some disapproval at the way in which the city's war finances are being managed.[106] Thucydides conveys an overall *impression* of a state in trouble rather than anything more concrete. There are references to the expenses of the war and one indication that the Athenians decided that they needed money—not in general, but specifically for the siege of Mytilene—over and above that currently available to them. But we need to gain perspective on the degree of difficulties. We are still in the early years of the war, and Athens was well equipped in resources. While accepting that Athens was experiencing some financial problems in these years,[107] for which Thucydides provides evidence, we should nonetheless refrain as yet from supposing a crisis. At the same time, Thucydides makes it clear that it is precisely the expenditure of money that gives Athens her power. He seems to attribute to Perikles the (correct) *pronoia* concerning the extent of the expense that had been anticipated at the war's outset. He thus confirms that Perikles was not wrong when he maintained that Athens' financial resources could last through a long war with no difficulty whatsoever. But Thucydides demonstrates in his treatment of the period immediately following Perikles' death that, as the statesman himself had argued in 2.13.2, *periousia chrematon* had to be coupled with *gnome*.

APPENDIX: ON 3.17

Adcock (*Cambridge Historical Journal* 1 [1923–25]: 319) states that 428 "is impossible on grounds of *fact*" (my emphasis), but his arguments are

---

104. Beloch, *GG* 2.1, 316.
105. E.g., Busolt, *GG* 3.2, 984; Ferguson, *Proc.Mass.Hist.Soc.* 64 (1930–32):353; Knight, *Mnem.* 23 (1970):159–61; Meiggs, *AE*, 318; Hornblower, *Greek World*, 137–38; cf. Kagan, *Archidamian War*, 122; Cawkwell, *YCS* 24 (1975):53–54.
106. I would tentatively suggest this on the matter of ἐσφορά in 3.19.1, with 1.141.5; the terms of the Mytilenaian settlement.
107. For which the cause is unclear: serious depletion of reserves or inferior leadership?

drawn purely from probability. Thus, he notes (319–20), "If in 428 the Athenians had 100 ships guarding Attica and Euboea and Salamis, it would be easy to concentrate 70 ships in the Saronic Gulf to meet any Peloponnesian threat and the situation described in the preceding chapter [in which the Athenians man 100 ships anew] *could not possibly have arisen*" (my emphasis). But the Athenians wanted to make a show of force not in the Saronic Gulf but around the Peloponnese, and if ships had the command of guarding Attica, Salamis, and Euboea, they could not simply have sailed off to another area. The necessity to protect their lifeblood, wealth and men, would not have been taken lightly, especially after the plague. What makes it clear that Athens would not have removed ships from guard duty around Attica, Euboea, and Salamis in 428 is precisely that Thucydides has just informed the reader that the Spartans and their allies were preparing to invade Attica *by sea* (3.15), and the Athenians were aware of their preparations (3.16).

Adcock notes further that "nor is it *a priori* probable that after two years of the plague Athens could man 250 ships" (320). But even if we take the sentence giving the figure of 250 ships to refer to another, earlier year, for example, 431 or 430, that number was close enough in 428, for Thucydides writes παραπλήσιαι ("about as many"). Regardless of whether one emends the text by adding ἤ in section 1 (which would change the reference of παραπλήσιαι), two fleets are being contrasted and one is παραπλήσιαι in its number of ships to the other; thus, the fleet that does not have 250 ships still must have near that number. Adcock, of course, moves the entire chapter, but to do so, one first must establish its impossibility *in situ*. Moreover, it is not clear that we should assume that all 250 ships were manned by Athenians or metics. They may well have contained allied contingents serving as part of their obligation, as well as hired ξένοι (cf. 3.6.1 and also 1.121.3).

There is, however, a more compelling reason, in my view, why 428 cannot be the year referred to in section 2. If τήν τε γὰρ 'Αττικὴν . . . , etc. is describing the situation that pertains in 428, something is wrong: there were not just 100 ships περὶ Πελοπόννησον in that year, but 130, since the 30 sent out under Asopios in 3.3 were still themselves περὶ Πελοπόννησον at the same time as the 100 ships sent out later, as is clear from 3.16.2. Thus, if the numbers are correct, παραπλήσιαι δέ . . . διακόσιαι καὶ πεντήκοντα cannot refer to the total in 428.

CHAPTER FIVE

From the Kerkyraian Revolt to the Peace of Nikias (3.70–5.24)

We saw in the last chapter that as soon as Perikles disappeared from the *History*, the issue of Athens' financial strength for fighting the war and controlling the empire became clouded. This impression was fostered by Thucydides' development of the theme of the expense of war and *arche* and from his highlighting, partly through the treatment of financial resources, the decline in quality and πρόνοια of Athenian leaders after the death of Perikles. The historian's detailed presentation, moreover, has enabled us to fill out considerably our knowledge of the financing of the war and of the varieties of imperial revenue besides tribute. This evidence suggests that the war was having a palpable effect on the Athenians' ability to insure the steady influx of tribute and full payments of the poleis' assessments; in particular, recourse to taxation at home instills doubt in the city's power to exploit the resources of its *arche*. The financial decisions with respect to the war and the *arche* also raise questions about political leadership and the change in the relationship between leader and demos. In this chapter, we shall continue to explore the interplay in the text between financial resources, war, empire, and leadership, as we examine Thucydides' account of the final years of the Archidamian War.

With the exception of his detailed treatment of financial matters relevant to the origins of the Kerkyraian *stasis* (3.70), financial resources do not figure prominently in the *History* for the years 427–424. During these years, the war was fought primarily on land, as operations were conducted in Sicily and northwestern Greece, in the Megarid in summer 424 (4.66–77) and in Boiotia (4.78, 89–101). The lack of attention to financial resources accords well with the relative insignificance of money in warfare on land compared to that at sea.

Some naval activity, however, did occur during these years. Significantly, the Athenians did not respond to the relative relaxation of naval conflict by restricting expense to the bare necessities of naval defense. During the two years from summer 427 to summer 425, the Athenians sent out naval expeditions, some of which went well beyond the offensive naval strategy outlined by Perikles and were by no means necessary for the war with Sparta. They dispatched twenty ships to Sicily at the end of summer 427 in response to a request for help from the Leontinians; according to Thucydides, however, their real intent was to try to interrupt grain shipments to the Peloponnese from the west and to assess the possibility of conquering Sicily (3.86.4).[1] Then, in the following summer, while the twenty ships were still in Sicily, the Athenians sent out sixty ships and two thousand hoplites under Nikias' command to the island of Melos. Thucydides provides the reason for the expedition: "The Athenians wanted to bring the Melians over to their side, since they were islanders and wished neither to submit to the Athenians nor to enter into alliance with them" (3.91.2). The expedition failed in its aim, and Nikias subsequently brought the fleet over to Oropos and made raids in the area around Tanagra before returning home (3.91.3–6). In addition to these sixty ships, the Athenians sent out another thirty ships around the Peloponnese (3.91.1), as part of their usual strategy.

The decisions to undertake the naval expeditions both to Sicily and against Melos beyond those encompassed in Athenian military strategy have direct relevance for our understanding of Athens' financial condition at this time, so soon after the Mytilenaian expedition and not long after the siege of Poteidaia. The ad hoc financing that accompanied the operation against Mytilene was likely, as I suggested in the last chapter, a sign of concern about the future in the anxious climate following the end of the revolt of Poteidaia and amidst the ghastly effects of the plague. It does not attest to a general and extensive depletion of Athens' resources. The vitality of Athens' *periousia chrematon* is revealed by the polis's readiness to extend naval operations beyond the minimum, despite the expense involved.[2] Also relevant in this connection is the increasing archaeological evidence for public building throughout the 420s (and

---

1. Cf. Kagan, *Archidamian War*, 183, who, after Busolt, argues that the Athenian aim in Sicily was to forestall the possibility that Syracuse and others would provide ships and money to the Spartans and finds this conclusion "inescapable from [Thucydides'] own narrative" (n. 136); on the contrary, the fact that he did not point this out suggests that it was not a significant consideration at all. That the Athenian expedition to Sicily in 427 went beyond the scope of Periklean strategy is denied by Kagan but supported by Holladay, *Historia* 27 (1978):399–427.

2. Cf. Ampolo, *PP* 42 (1987):5–11, who dates *IG* I³ 291, contributions from Sicilian allies to Athens usually dated to the expedition of 415, to that of 427/6. If correct, there are significant sums—individual contributions in excess of fifty talents—to be added to Athenian funds.

beyond).[3] The natural inference to be drawn from the naval operations and building record of this period is that Athens' financial resources were not seriously diminished.

Allusion to expense occurs at the beginning of Thucydides' narrative of the Pylos episode. When Demosthenes revealed his plan to fortify Pylos to the generals Sophokles and Eurymedon, they responded sarcastically. "They said," comments Thucydides, "that there were many deserted headlands in the Peloponnese if, by occupying them, he wanted the city to incur expense" (*dapanan*) (4.3.3).[4] The word *dapanao* elsewhere in Thucydides simply means "spend" rather than "exhaust," and that is how I would interpret it here.[5] Nevertheless, the image of waste is put before the reader as a reminder of the expense of every operation. Following their victory at Pylos, the Athenians continued to have successes, in the Korinthia along the coast and at Methana with a fleet of eighty ships (4.42–45), also in summer 425/4. Thucydides then recounts events in Kerkyra with the arrival of Eurymedon and Sophokles (4.46–48), ending with the virtual annihilation of the anti-Athenian faction in the city.

At this time, Thucydides notes, Aristeides, one of the generals of the "money-collecting" ships sent out by Athens to the allies, captured in Eion on the Strymon River, Artaphernes, a Persian who was making his way to Sparta. He was taken to Athens, where (after, Thucydides bothers to point out, his messages had been translated from the Assyrian!), it was discovered that the Spartans had sent a number of embassies to Persia, the purpose of none of these missions clear, with each apparently asking something different from the one before (4.50.1–2).

Thucydides' conscientiousness in reporting such details as these, which may seem fairly unimportant per se, contributes to the cumulative picture of Athenian and Spartan strategy and policy concerning financial resources. In this case, we learn of another "money-collecting" expedition in an incidental context, which suggests that such expeditions were not unusual; furthermore, we learn that this one was in the Thraceward region, unlike the two mentioned previously (six ships to Karia and Lykia in 430/29 [2.69.2]; twelve to various places, including Karia in 428/7 [3.19.1]). Moreover, the capture of Artaphernes was important:

---

3. See Miles, *Hesp.* 58 (1989):221–35, for a good concise discussion of evidence and bibliography; Boersma, *Building Policy*, 82–96; Mikalson, *GRBM* 10 (1984):217–25.

4. οἱ δὲ πολλὰς ἔφασαν εἶναι ἄκρας ἐρήμους τῆς Πελοποννήσου ἢν βούληται καταλαμβάνων τὴν πόλιν δαπανᾶν. The syntax of the ἤν clause has troubled all commentators, as has the meaning of δαπανᾶν; cf. *Suidae Lexicon* 2 (ed. Adler), s.v. Δαπανᾶν; Classen-Steup, *Anhang* to Vol. 4, 265; Gomme, *HCT* 3, ad loc.; Arnold, ad loc.

5. Gomme, *HCT* 3, ad loc., maintains that "exhaust" is a late meaning. But cf. LSJ; Göller, ad loc.; Arnold, ad loc.

through it the Athenians learned of the many embassies sent by Sparta to the Persian king and the confused nature of their communication. Peloponnesian envoys had attempted, so Thucydides informs us, to request *chremata* for the war from the King in 429 (2.67.1); it is reasonable to include a request for money among the garbled messages of the Spartans here, given their inevitably heightened awareness of the need for money especially for naval operations.[6] Yet naval strategy still seems to have been a low priority for the Spartans, and they were still uncertain about its underpinnings as well as its execution. The confusion over the purposes of the embassies to Persia, in addition to, for example, Alkidas' failure to effect the revolt of Ionia and procure considerable money, attests to the Spartans' continued inability to understand the requirements of naval war.[7]

THE RANSOMING OF RHOITEION (4.52.2)

During the winter of 425/4, the Athenians forced the Chians to dismantle their walls (4.51). Thucydides' narrative of the next summer begins with the activities of the exiled Mytilenaians and other Lesbians who, along with hired local and Peloponnesian support, captured the city of Rhoiteion and then took the unusual step of handing it back unharmed in return for a ransom of two thousand Phokaian staters.[8] This episode is intriguing and unusual, and that, along with the fact that the ransom itself was substantial, surely accounts for Thucydides' specification both of the precise amount and the type of coinage used in the deal. Although not directly concerned with Athens' finances, it has necessarily become relevant indirectly through the association of the ransom money with Rhoiteion's tribute; moreover, the account provides a useful instance of the correlation and relative value of Thucydides and epigraphical evidence.

Scholars commenting on this passage have confined themselves to providing the equivalence of two thousand Phokaian staters in Athenian coinage, that is, eight Attic talents.[9] But the act of ransoming a captured

---

6. Though this awareness was apparently still rather vague; cf. Thucydides' comment (4.55.3–4) on the Spartan reaction to the loss of Kythera and the discussion below.

7. This point holds even if the Spartan embassies to Persia did *not* explicitly request money (they clearly did not bring up anything explicitly!), for then the question is "why not?" If they went so far as not only recognizing their need for assistance beyond what the Peloponnesian League could supply but even acting on it by sending envoys to Persia and yet did not include a request for financial assistance, then they still grossly misunderstood the requirements of the new warfare.

8. 4.52.2: λαβόντες δισχιλίους στατῆρας Φωκαΐτας ἀπέδοσαν πάλιν οὐδὲν ἀδικήσαντες.

9. E.g., Gomme, *HCT* 3, ad loc., who notes that this was "the sum at which Roiteion was

city is of considerable interest as well. There is no suggestion that the exiles intended to retain control of the polis, as they did, for example, in Antandros (4.52.3), nor to harm its inhabitants. Indeed, the point of capturing Rhoiteion may simply have been to raise money. The exiles, with grand designs in mind, had already hired soldiers: using Antandros as a base, they would liberate the Aktaian cities under Athenian control and construct ships with which to make raids on Lesbos and subdue the Aiolian towns on the coastal mainland (4.52.3). Thucydides, indeed, provides remarkably detailed information about the exiles' plans, of which the hiring of soldiers and the capture and subsequent ransoming of Rhoiteion are all important preparatory elements. Such elaborate naval plans, as the reader knows well by this point, require the extensive outlay of cash; significantly, Thucydides brings the issue of money explicitly into his account.

The plan, however, failed (4.75). Why is it related in such detail? The answer may be that the Lesbian exiles and their army were intending to put into effect exactly what Alkidas had been urged, but declined, to do;[10] the comparison is, I suggest, intended and pointed.[11] Also, the exiles from Lesbos waited three years before they attempted to regain control of the area and do harm to the Athenians. The delay may have been caused, in large part, by insufficient financial resources to implement the plan.

The practice of extorting money, not only at Rhoiteion but elsewhere during the war, suggests further the presence of considerable wealth in ready cash circulating, deposited in temples, or hoarded that would make such piratical attempts seem worthwhile.[12] The circumstances of the collection of the money at Rhoiteion, however, are generally connected with the annual tribute payment of that polis. Let us examine the evidence.

The editors of *ATL* specifically tied the ransom to the tribute reassessment of 425, for which we have the decree, *IG* I³ 71, and they write:

> In the early summer of 424 B.C. the Mytilenaian exiles on the mainland raided Rhoiteion and made their escape with 2000 Phokaian staters. . . . Reckoned at 24 drachmai to the stater this sum amounts to 8 talents, which is *precisely the assessment* [my italics] of Rhoiteion in A9 [the 425 reassessment

---

assessed in 425," a comment based on *ATL* 2:82; 3:88; but note the important qualification that he adds: "strictly, we should say 'probably assessed'."

10. Cf. Adcock, *Mélanges Glotz* 1:1–6.

11. This may derive support from the final sentence of Thucydides' account of the plan: καὶ οἱ μὲν ταῦτα παρασκευάζεσθαι ἔμελλον.

12. The finest example of the possibilities is the spectacular "decadrachm hoard"; see the articles by Fried, Kagan, and Spier in Carradice, *Coinage*, 1–42.

decree]. It looks very much as if the Mytilenaians timed their raid perfectly, and made off with Rhoiteion's tribute just when it had been gathered together for transportation to Athens.[13]

In fact, neither the connection between the ransom and reassessment of 425 nor the amount of the assessment is certain. The issue has importance not so much for our knowledge of the precise amount of tribute that one polis in the empire paid as for its broader application and significance in its methodological context of epigraphic restoration and reconstruction.

According to the editors of *ATL*, *IG* I³ 71, the 425 reassessment decree, shows that Rhoiteion was assessed eight talents in 425;[14] but they arrive at that figure through restoration. On the stele on which the decree and catalog of cities are inscribed, only a partial amount is extant in the preserved fragment: [. .]TT. Several totals are possible from these remains: four talents ([TT]TT); eight, as in *ATL* ([⊢T]TT); or thirteen ([⊢T]TT); or, for that matter, a number of even higher totals, the probability of which decreases with each increment. Furthermore, Rhoiteion itself is completely restored in col. III.126. Thus, the evidence for this city's "precise assessment" of eight talents is [. .]TT [. . . . . . .].

Moreover, not only is Rhoiteion restored but so are all of the cities on the new "Aktaian panel" made subject to Athens by the terms of the settlement of Mytilene, which had previously controlled these *polismata* (Thuc. 3.50.3). Fortunately, enough of the rubric ΑΚΤΑΙΑΙ ΠΟΛΕΣ survives to assure at least the certainty of the panel on the stone. But the fact remains that the debut of the Aktaian cities on any inscription whatsoever is here in *IG* I³ 71, in which *no* city's name is preserved; for nine entries, traces of the first letter in the name are visible.[15] Merritt and West restored the full panel by comparison with *IG* I³ 77, the assessment decree of 422/1, in which much of the Aktaian panel is preserved; it is this later decree which dictated the order in which Rhoiteion appears in *IG* I³ 71, immediately below Antandros, although the order of *IG* I³ 77 was not retained for many of the other cities listed in *IG* I³ 71. In view of such inconsistency, common in both quota lists and assessment decrees, the fact that Antandros and Rhoiteion head the list in *IG* I³ 77 does not assure that the same order was observed in *IG* I³ 71.

There is more. To the left of Rhoiteion in *IG* I³ 77, no figure is preserved; to the left of Antandros above it, however, [. .]TT appears.[16]

---

13. *ATL* 3:88.
14. Ibid.
15. Cf. the facsimile drawing in Plate II, in Meritt and West, *Assessment of 425*.
16. Only the left portion of the crossbar of the T survives, but is enough to insure the restoration.

Rather than supposing that *Antandros* should have been restored in Rhoiteion's place in *IG* I³ 71, which would have made the figure [. .]TT consistent, the editors of *ATL* decided that the mason inscribing this section made a mistake and erroneously inscribed Rhoiteion's tribute beside Antandros, and they restore [. .]TT as [TT]TT. The certainty, therefore, that (1) Rhoiteion was assessed eight talents, (2) the order of cities is correct, (3) the confused mason in 421 erred, and (4) Thucydides provides confirmation, is entirely unjustified.

There is a further important issue. Although Rhoiteion appears on one assessment list, that of the year 422/1 (*IG* I³ 77), and should reasonably be restored on *IG* I³ 71 (though not necessarily where it has been), there is no record that the polis ever actually paid tribute; one need only note the difference between assessment and collection, especially in connection with the 425 reassessment decree, in which even places such as Melos were registered as having been assessed. Nevertheless, let us suppose that the city did pay it. In what currency would it have done so? If one accepts the dating of the Coinage Decree (ML 45) to the mid-fifth century, as the editors of *ATL* did, then the citizens of Rhoiteion should have paid not in Phokaian staters but in Athenian silver coinage. This is not the place to enter the controversy over the date for this decree;[17] but if Thuc. 4.52.3 is to be connected with Rhoiteion's tribute, then its implications for the Coinage Decree need to be addressed: either it must have been passed after 425, or the decree was ineffective.

There is, then, no assurance that [. .]TT was Rhoiteion's assessment in 425. If it was, there is no certainty that it should be restored [ⲏ T]TT since we have no parallels from other assessment decrees or quota lists. Where then does this leave Thucydides 4.52.3? At the very least, there is no justification for assuming on the basis of the passage that Rhoiteion was on the verge of contributing its required *phoros* as directed in the new assessment of 425. Nor is there justification for associating the two thousand Phokaian staters with the city's tribute, again on the basis of 4.52.3.

It is fortunate when one can reconcile or find agreement between Thucydides and epigraphical evidence. But the case of Rhoiteion and the assessment decrees is one, I suggest, of false agreement. Rather, we should ask whether Thucydides' reference to the two thousand Phokaian staters conflicts with our knowledge that Rhoiteion was assessed an (unknown) amount, which could have been eight talents or a number of other possibilities in 425. The answer is that although the two pieces of evidence do not conflict, they also have little to do with each other; they

---

17. Cf. the discussion in ML 45; Meiggs, *AE*, 167–73; Lewis, "The Athenian Coinage Decree"; Mattingly, "The Athenian Coinage Decree and the Assertion of Empire."

are mutually irrelevant and supply only a specious connection. Thucydides 4.52.3 tells us nothing about tribute payment or assessment and thus bears no relation to the quota lists or assessment decrees.

Regardless of Rhoiteion's tribute assessment, the indications that Thucydides has provided thus far about the diverse means of exploiting the empire financially, for example in Ionia, allow the inference that Athens may well have obtained money from the Aktaian cities in ways other than or in addition to tribute. We know that, for example, "money-collecting" ships were operating in the area, and indeed, it was the generals of these ships who, in the same summer of 424, foiled the exiles' plans at Antandros (4.75–76.1). Thucydides' account of the ransoming of Rhoiteion offers another indication of the monetary wealth of but one polis in the area.[18]

THE CAPTURE OF KYTHERA

Thucydides leaves the Mytilenaian exiles with their plan untested and the result unknown. He turns to the Athenian operation against Kythera, off the southern coast of the Peloponnese, also in summer 424, involving sixty ships, two thousand hoplites, and some other forces under the command of Nikias (4.53). The island was taken with moderate ease, as the Kytheraians initially resisted but then came to terms with Nikias and the other generals; Thucydides reports the outcome as "quite advantageous" both for the present and future.[19] But the historian does not provide the actual details of these "quite advantageous terms" until 4.57.4, when, in another context, he refers to the prisoners the Athenians brought back to Athens, consisting of Aiginetans and some Kytheraians. We then learn that some Kytheraians who had been brought to Athens for their safety were to be resettled "on the islands," while the rest could remain on their own land and pay tribute amounting to four talents (4.57.4).

From Thucydides' account, we are to understand that both the imposition of four talents of tribute and the decision to allow the majority of the Kytheraians to remain on their land were considered "quite advantageous." The Athenians clearly had little to fear from the Spartans at this point, and the terms imposed on Kythera may reflect this. The Spartans' mood, as Thucydides describes it, was indeed pathetic: they were afraid (φοβούμενοι) of revolution in Sparta because of the "unexpected and great disaster" (τοῦ . . . πάθους ἀνελπίστου καὶ μεγάλου) at Sphak-

---

18. Relevant here is Thucydides' reference in the Pentekontaetia to the wealth brought in from Magnesia, amounting to fifty talents a year (1.138.5), a figure which, even if optimistic or exaggerated, still suggests a considerable amount.

19. 4.54.3: ἐπιτηδειότερον τό τε παραυτίκα καὶ τὸ ἔπειτα.

teria. Moreover, success in the war required swift action, and it was difficult to anticipate attacks; they were forced to act against their usual practice by sending cavalry and peltasts against Athens. Thucydides continues:

> And now, in their waging of war generally, they reached the highest peak of hesitation ever, having to deal with what was beyond the scope of their existing kind of preparation, namely, a naval contest, and that against the Athenians, people for whom not attempting an attack was always viewed as a failure to gain an achievement. (4.55.1–2)

In his analysis of the pathetic state of Spartan morale, Thucydides highlights both practical and conceptual difficulties faced by the Spartans in dealing with naval warfare. The virtual absence of Spartan *dunamis* on the sea and their failure even by 424, some seven years into the war, to confront the exigencies of naval war, are epitomized by their near paralysis as the island of Kythera, not distant but hard by the Lakonian coastline, was expeditiously conquered by the Athenians and given the humiliation of tributary status. Thucydides underscores the nature of and continuing disparity between Athens and Sparta by including a characterization of the Athenians to remind the reader of their unique τρόπος as a key to success in naval power and thereby to show that more than a difference in *paraskeue* is at issue.

The importance of the loss of Kythera to the Spartans has been noticed,[20] but we should not fail to appreciate the significance of making the island tributary from Athens' standpoint: imposing tribute on a Lakedaimonian city was an unprecedented event in the history of the war as well as significant proof of Athens' power. Thucydides notes at the beginning of the war that Athens had allies who were tributary (1.19; 2.9). Now, a city which was not an ally was being forced to pay tribute. That Kythera was a Lakedaimonian city is extraordinary testimony both to Athens' strength and Sparta's weakness at this time. The settlement of Kythera suggests that revenue was far more important to the Athenians than ξυμμαχία; we shall return to this below when we consider the Peace of Nikias, under the terms of which certain cities were made tributary without compulsion of alliance with Athens (5.18.5).

THE "MONEY-COLLECTING" SHIPS

In 4.75, Thucydides returns to the developments concerning the Lesbian exiles in summer 425/4. Their plan of fortifying Antandros was foiled by an Athenian and allied force, which retook Antandros. Thucydides' description of the nature of the Athenian contingent is of con-

---

20. E.g., Kagan, *Archidamian War*, 263; Holladay, *Historia* 27 (1978):405.

siderable interest to us, since he defines the leaders as "the generals of the Athenian money-collecting ships, Demodokos and Aristeides, who were around the Hellespont (the third general, Lamachos, had sailed with ten ships into the Pontos)" (4.75.1). Thus appears a further reference to the "money-collecting" ships, ἀργυρολόγοι νῆες, which is similar to that in 4.50.1, where Thucydides' primary concern was not so much with the fact that these ships were sent out as with the actions of their generals. In this case, Demodokos and Aristeides learned of the preparation of the exiles at Antandros, gathered an army, drove out the exiles, and restored the city to its inhabitants.

Nevertheless, here, as in the other examples mentioned previously, it is typical of both Thucydides' conscientiousness as a historian and his interest in the finances of the empire that he specifies the nature of the expedition occupying these ships when they waylaid the Lesbian exiles on Antandros; that he notes the presence of ten more in the Pontos with Lamachos; and that, after describing Demodokos' and Aristeides' successful campaign at Antandros, he returns to Lamachos, who was at first mentioned almost incidentally. Although that general lost all of his ships (Thucydides does not explain how or why), he and his men traveled on foot through Thrace, finally to reach Kalchedon at the mouth of the Pontos (4.75.2).

This expedition, like that of Demodokos and Aristeides, has been connected to the tribute reassessment of 425. Some scholars treat it as fact: "The Athenians also anticipated collection of tribute in the Euxine area, for in the summer of 424 Lamachos, in command of τῶν ἀργυρολόγων νεῶν, sailed with ten of the squadron into the Pontos and made his base at Herakleia, which had been assessed in A9 (Thucydides IV, 75 [T133])."[21] To account for the lateness of this "tribute-collecting expedition," Meritt wrote that

> the activities of tribute collection extended in this year later than usual, but we know also that the assessment was particularly severe and that the new levy was not proposed until the fourth prytany. Adjudication of claims was not completed until after the month of Poseideon and at the earliest the ships could not have left Athens before Gamelion. The fact that they were still occupied in the early summer is in part explained by this late departure from Athens.[22]

The view presented in *ATL* is generally accepted. It is certainly possible, but how secure is it? It rests on the assumption that the "money-collecting" ships in 4.75.1 were sent out to collect tribute as a result of the reassessment of 425. Moreover, though the editors do not state ex-

21. *ATL* 3:89.
22. Meritt, *AFD*, 20.

plicitly that they believe the amount assessed was actually collected, their discussion implies that the decree was implemented and effective. I shall discuss the decree of 425 in detail shortly; we need now to examine whether any of Thucydides' references to the ἀργυρολόγοι νῆες are associated with tribute collection and signify a reassessment.

The dates on which the historian mentions such ships—430 (2.69), 428 (3.19), 425 (4.50 and 4.75)—have been used to support the case for tribute reassessments in those years. What is the other evidence, and how firm is it? It will be clearest if we consider each year individually, beginning with the general remark that, of the tribute quota lists following the year 431, none can be dated with complete certainty; therefore, fluctuations in the quota cannot be pinned definitely on a particular year.

(1) Summer 430 (2.69): no assessment decree survives. Fluctuations in the quota lists suggest that there may have been an assessment in 431 or 430; the evidence does not allow preference of one year over another. (2) Summer 428 (3.19): no assessment decree survives. Although the dates of all the lists in the years following 431 are problematic, quota list 27 (*IG* I³ 283) is dated by the editors of *ATL* (and followed by most scholars) to 428/7, but this is uncertain.[23] The list is believed to reflect a new assessment, but if so, it may belong either in 428/7 or 427/6; there is no basis for preferring one over the other. (3) Winter and summer 425 (4.50, 75): *IG* I³ 71, the reassessment decree of 425.

We see, therefore, firm evidence of a reassessment in only one of the years in which Thucydides mentions the ἀργυρολόγοι νῆες, in 425. The evidence for the other two years, 430 and 428, is far weaker than it is commonly assumed to be; indeed, direct support is lacking for those years. Rather, the chief testimony in *ATL* is Thucydides' references to the ships; yet there must be evidence to associate the ships with tribute reassessments, not the reverse. Much circularity has resulted, as both Thucydides and epigraphical testimony, neither providing direct evidence in this case, have been used to support each other.[24] Meiggs commented that the connection between tribute reassessments and Thucyd-

---

23. *ATL* 3:70. The editors assert that this is the only year to which list 27 can be assigned; their reason is that the Aktaian panel does not appear on it, and therefore it must predate Athens' suppression of the Mytilenaian revolt, as a consequence of which the Aktaian cities were added to the empire. Yet one should bear in mind that the Aktaian panel does not appear on *any* tribute quota list, not even after the cities were assessed in 425; this considerably diminishes the certainty of their argument.

24. For example, the evidence to support the idea that the tribute reassessment of 425 was implemented and effective is the money-collecting expedition of 425 in Thucydides, 4.75.1. The only information that would constitute evidence that the assessment of tribute was effective would have to come from the tribute quota lists; it is one of the great frustrations of the period that these are all missing for the crucial years 425–421.

ides' "money-collecting" ships may be "mere coincidence."²⁵ We have decreased the "coincidences" considerably, down to one, that in 425.

There is, then, an inherent weakness in the alleged connection between Thucydides' ships and tribute reassessment. That Thucydides does not specify that the ships were on tribute-collecting missions is not necessarily a strong argument against it. In other cases where he clearly refers to tribute, he does not always use the explicit *phoros* but often simply writes *chremata*.²⁶

Yet why should we prefer to think that these ἀργυρολόγοι νῆες are tribute-collecting ships rather than simply "money-collecting" ships? As Meiggs noted, the word ἀργυρολογία does not itself imply any connection with tribute.²⁷ The word ἀργυρολόγος or the verb ἀργυρολογέω is most commonly used simply to refer to the (often extorted or forced) collection of money.²⁸ Indeed, such a usage actually occurs in Thucydides as well, in 8.3.1: Agis "collected money (ἠργυρολόγησεν) from the allies for the fleet."

All the same, Thucydides' references to ἀργυρολόγοι νῆες, even if not associated directly with tribute, may still indicate something important about tribute: the presence of these ships around the empire may suggest that tribute collection was yielding insufficient revenue; in that case, the historian's reference to these ships in his narrative could be a way of pointing up this problem.

Clearly, the temptation is strong to associate the "money-collecting" ships in Thucydides with tribute collection, and perhaps scholars are inclined to yield to it partly out of a desire to defend Thucydides against the charge that he omits important financial information; by pointing to 2.69, 3.19, and 4.50, they can exonerate the historian. Yet if we want to understand as fully as possible the role and treatment of finances in the historian's work, we must dismiss all our presumptions about what he

---

25. Meiggs, *AE*, 254.
26. This does not, however, seem to result simply from variation or a lack of precision for whatever reason. His determination of which word to use is, I think, explicable and consistent. In cases where he uses χρήματα, he clearly is interested in the actual money itself, not in what it is called (e.g., 1.99.3, in connection with ἀνάλωμα and δαπάνη; 1.101.3, connected with δαπάνη; 2.9.5; 2.13.2; 3.13.6; 3.46.4). By contrast, in 2.13.3, Perikles uses the word φόρος, because he is being precise in delineating sources of income. Here φόρος is appropriate, for types of revenue are being distinguished. 1.96.2 needs little explanation. Thucydides' point is the name for the payment of money. In 4.57.4, Thucydides specifies the amount of tribute, so he uses the word φόρος; it would make no sense to say "four talents 'of money.'"
27. Meiggs, *AE*, 254.
28. E.g., Xen. *Hell.* 1.1.8, 12; Plut. *Alk.* 30.3, 35.4; cf. Ar. *Knights* 1070–71; cf. also Aristeides, Εἰς 'Ρώμην 45, and Meiggs' discussion, *AE*, 254.

should have included. One such presumption is the insistence on a connection between the ἀργυρολόγοι νῆες, tribute collection, and reassessment.[29] Thucydides' text does not support the case for a reassessment in 430, in 428/7, or in 425, nor does it attest to the implementation of the 425 reassessment decree.

My conclusions about the relationship between Thucydides' ἀργυρολόγοι νῆες, the tribute quota lists, and *IG* I³ 71 are much the same as those in the case of Rhoiteion and the tribute quota lists: a direct connection is probably lacking. If Thucydides' text mentioning the "money-collecting" ships at 4.75.1 does not have any direct relation to the reassessment of 425, are we left with the idea that Thucydides omits important financial matters that are germane to his subject? I have been arguing that the historian is not only keenly interested in and knowledgeable about finances but, more important, that he makes them a crucial part of his conception of power in general, of his definition of Athenian naval power, and of his treatment of Athenian preparedness in the war. The absence from his work of reference to the reassessment, which modern scholars regard as one of the most significant measures taken by Athens with respect to the empire, apparently constitutes a damaging objection to our conclusions thus far. So let us explore in some detail one of Thucydides' most infamous "omissions," that of the 425 reassessment decree, in which the Athenians, in the midst of the Archidamian War, apparently trebled the tribute of their allies.

THE REASSESSMENT OF TRIBUTE IN 425

"The strangest of all omissions in Thucydides is that of the increase in the tribute in 425 B.C."[30] Gomme's famous pronouncement has been echoed by virtually all scholars everywhere, both those primarily con-

---

29. Gomme, *HCT* 2, on 2.69, 3.19, and pp. 202–3, also has doubted that the ships should be associated with tribute. An interesting passage in Aristophanes' *Knights* bears on the question of the nature of these ἀργυρολόγοι νῆες but unfortunately does not render a decision much easier. The Sausage-seller has just read an oracle περὶ τοῦ ναυτικοῦ to Demos (1067–69) and is explaining what it means: οὐ τοῦτό φησιν, ἀλλὰ ναῦς ἑκάστοτε / αἰτεῖ ταχείας ἀργυρολόγους οὑτοσί· / ταύτας ἀπαυδᾷ μὴ διδόναι σ' ὁ Λοξίας (lines 1070–72). Are there clues in ἑκάστοτε and/or αἰτεῖ? It is not clear to me that one can determine whether tribute collection or simply money collection from the empire is the purpose of these expeditions. The connection between these ships and tribute collection is generally assumed by commentators, e.g., Rogers, *The Comedies of Aristophanes* 1 (London, 1910), 149–50; Sommerstein, *Knights* (Warminster, 1981), 202; cf. the scholiast on ἀλλὰ ναῦς ἑκάστοτε: τὰς ἐκπεμπομένας ἀπὸ τῶν νήσων ἀναπράττεσθαι τοὺς φόρους. οἱ δὲ ἐκπεμπόμενοι πολλὰ ἐκέρδινον (1070), and on ταχείας ἀργυρολόγους: πολεμίας, τὰς συλλεγούσας ἀργύριον καὶ λήμματα αὐτῷ περιποιούσας. ἐλέγοντο δὲ πάραλοι καὶ σαλαμίνιαι (1071).

30. Gomme, *HCT* 3:500.

cerned with the epigraphic issues and those examining Thucydides from a historiographical standpoint.[31] Countless numbers of students of the historian have read M. I. Finley's similar judgment in the introduction to Warner's Penguin translation (p. 25):

> There are astonishing gaps and silences, whole chunks of history that are left out altogether.... Thucydides certainly knew that in 425 B.C. the Athenians, running short of funds, made a radical re-assessment of the tribute from the empire, more than trebling the total demanded; and it is impossible to believe that he thought the action less significant than thousands of minor details he rescued from oblivion. Yet there is not even a hint of the decree in the book.

Not only is it regarded as the "strangest" of all omissions but also one of the most serious, for which there is no adequate excuse or explanation. Gomme notes that later ancient writers mention an increase in the tribute in the years after the war began, though he finds it "equally remarkable" that Aristophanes omits reference to it both in the *Knights* and the *Wasps*.

Let us first consider the evidence for the increase in assessment and then turn our attention to Thucydides. The decree recording the measure of 425, *IG* I³ 71, was published fully by Meritt and West.[32] Our knowledge of its contents comes from the large number of fragments associated by Meritt and West, and extensive and impressive restoration based chiefly on parallels with the tribute quota lists and other assessment decrees. The section judged so damaging to Thucydides is that supplying the grand total of the reassessment, of which only part survives. The first figure is missing; it could be either ₣ or 𐅆 , which would make the total 960–1,000 or 1,460–1,500 talents, respectively. Meritt and West argued that the higher figure must be correct, on the basis of the district totals which do survive, and they have generally been followed.[33]

As Meiggs notes, however, "how spectacular an increase this represents depends on the figures for 430 and 428, and for the latter we have very little evidence indeed,"[34] as I have noted above as well. Moreover, it is not clear that the lower total is ruled out absolutely by the surviving district totals, because such a judgment is based on the premise that all

---

31. For discussion and references to modern scholarship, see Meritt, "Kleon's Assessment," 89–93; *IG* I³ 71; ML 69; Meiggs, *AE*, 324–39; *ATL* 3:70–89; for general discussion of both the inscription and Thucydides and further bibliography, see Gomme, *HCT* 3:500–505; Woodhead, *Mnem.* 13 (1960):289–317; de Romilly, *TAI*, 92; Kagan, *Archidamian War*, 249–51.

32. Meritt and West, *Athenian Assessment*; see also *ATL* 3:70–89.

33. *Athenian Assessment*, 64–90.

34. Meiggs, *AE*, 325.

increases were proportionately the same (and all restorations correct), and there is no certainty about this. How firm are the grounds for supposing that the tribute was increased dramatically even in 425? Plutarch (*Arist.* 24.3) is of little help; he does not mention the 425 assessment in particular, though he does comment that the demagogues raised the total gradually (κατὰ μικρόν) to thirteen hundred talents. There is, however, no reference to a date. Nor can implications from later sources (Andok. 3.9; Aisch. 2.175) of tribute increases be pinned on 425. The evidence of the quota lists is so poor that we can just as easily claim that the tribute had been raised even to eight hundred talents prior to 425 as that the assessment of 425 was a dramatic increase.[35]

Thus, firm evidence that the decree attested to a trebling of the tribute in 425 appears to be lacking. We do not know the level of previous assessments with any degree of certainty; thus, the total estimated in the decree of 425 may have been reached more incrementally and less dramatically than previously thought. We cannot even insist absolutely on the higher total, but let us grant that it is more probable, although it will not affect the present argument.

So much for the assessment. What about the effects of the decree? The editors of *ATL* argue that it was, by and large, implemented effectively. They suggest that the Athenians probably collected about one thousand talents annually in the years following 425.[36] Yet no quota lists for the years immediately after the assessment have been found; there are a few, extremely fragmentary, lists after the Peace of Nikias, but these are of no help in determining whether the total or near the total of the assessment was actually collected. Positive evidence is believed to come from the *Wasps*, lines 656–60, in which Bdelykleon gives a recitation of Athens' revenues:

αἰ πρῶτον μὲν λόγισαι φαύλως, μὴ ψήφοις, ἀλλ' ἀπὸ χειρός,
τὸν φόρον ἡμῖν ἀπὸ τῶν πόλεων συλλήβδην τὸν προσιόντα·
κἄξω τούτου τὰ τέλη χωρὶς καὶ τὰς πολλὰς ἑκατοστάς,
πρυτανεῖα, μέταλλ', ἀγοράς, λιμένας, μισθοὺς καὶ δημιόπρατα·
τούτων πλήρωμα τάλαντ' ἐγγὺς δισχίλια γίγνεται ἡμῖν.[37]

West took this passage quite literally, as did the editors of *ATL*.[38] Indeed, it was on the basis of this passage that the estimate of the annual total of

35. Ibid.
36. *ATL* 3:345. Gomme regarded it as effective as well, *HCT* 3:500.
37. "Then listen my own little pet Papa, and smooth your brow from its frowns again. / And not with pebbles precisely ranged, but roughly thus on your fingers count / The tribute paid by the subject states, and just consider its whole amount; / And then, in addition to this, compute the many taxes and one-per-cents, / The fees and the fines, and the silver mines, the markets and harbours and sales and rents. / If you take the total result of the lot, 'twill reach two thousand talents or near" (trans., B. B. Rogers).
38. West, *TAPA* 61 (1930):223–28; *ATL* 3:344–45.

tribute following 425 was made. Objections to this approach are obvious. Aristophanes is, after all, a comic poet, not a historian; yet this passage is treated in exactly the same way as if it had come from Thucydides or Xenophon, and as if Aristophanes composed with account books beside him. Or, "[a]s though Aristophanes ... was thus nicely calculating, and remembering to reckon not the assessment, but what actually reached the Athenian treasury."[39] Aristophanes here, as elsewhere, is exaggerating as much or as little as he thought would achieve the desired effect. In this case, Bdelykleon is trying to convince Philokleon in no uncertain terms how little of the state's income goes to jury pay and, by comparison, how much goes to Kleon and others. To make Kleon appear as venal as possible (which seems to be the goal), he surely will exaggerate the disparity in money. Second, even if two thousand talents were near the mark of the state's yearly income, it includes much besides *phoros*.

We are left, then, with less than satisfactory evidence about the real effect of the assessment. In short, we have an impressive document with insufficient information to judge either its significance or its effect. On the negative side, we have Thucydides' silence (as well as Aristophanes'). Can the results of our investigation into Thucydides' treatment of financial resources help us answer the question of why the historian makes no reference to the inscription? I have argued that the decree of 425 may not be so dramatic a document in its purpose and effect as scholars assume it to be. But for the sake of argument, let us suppose that it did prescribe an increase in the tribute to 1,460 talents and that the total was two or three times as great as previous assessments. Would we expect Thucydides to have mentioned it?

The historian informed us about the assessment of 478. Does this indicate an interest in assessments per se? Thucydides mentions the assessment of 478 because it was the first (πρῶτος), and he demonstrates his interest in "first occurrences" in his *History*. Indeed, in 1.96–98 there are several "firsts": the 478 assessment (1.96.1–2); the establishment of the office of Hellenotamiai by the Athenians (1.96.2); the statement that the allies were autonomous at first (1.97.1); the first expedition that the Athenians undertook (the capture and subjugation of Eion) (1.98.1); the first enslavement of a polis (Naxos) (1.98.4). Clearly, Thucydides is carefully reconstructing the financial machinery of the League and the initial steps toward Athens' increase in power. Hereafter, he mentions no reassessments at all,[40] and this is important to bear in mind in connection with his "failure" to mention that of 425. Rather, he is interested in first

---

39. Gomme, *HCT* 3:504.
40. In recording the terms of the Peace of Nikias, he mentions the tribute "in Aristeides' time" (5.18.5).

instances of significant decisions. We should not be any more surprised by the lack of reference to this assessment than to any other: that he does not mention it means that he did not judge it to be significant. This leads us back to the question of the decree's effect.

As we have seen, there is no positive evidence of the extent to which the assessment was realized. If it was ineffective in stimulating payments considerably above the levels collected during the previous years of the war, then we would not expect Thucydides to mention it; as we have seen, he was not concerned with assessments per se. In the area of finances, Thucydides was manifestly interested in results, in the actuality of *chremata*, not its potential (except in 1.96, where he mentions the 478 assessment because it was the first). Thus, he focuses on the tangible financial resources of Athens in the war, the revenue from tribute, the actual financial benefits that the city derived from the empire, and, in addition, particular expenditures. We can detect these interests in passages such as 2.13.3–5; 2.70.2; 3.17.3–4; 3.19.1. This attention expands to "cash transactions" of a significant nature, for example, 1.27.1; 4.26.5; 4.52.2; 4.65.1. By contrast, mere attempts, if unrealized, to do something of a financial nature (such as voting to raise tribute) are unimportant because they do not contribute concretely to naval *dunamis* and *paraskeue*.

Let us now suppose that the assessment of 425 was a great success and that the editors of *ATL* were correct in their hypothesis that Athens received about one thousand talents a year in tribute, the highest amount ever. Would we then expect Thucydides to have mentioned this result of the reassessment if not the reassessment itself? The answer is surely yes. Thucydides reveals a keen and consistent interest in significant quantities of money, and he often specifies such amounts.[41] More than that, however, the historian is as interested in "greatest" instances as he is in first instances.[42] Of particular relevance here is Thucydides' reference to Odrysian tribute at its height in the reign of Seuthes.[43] Similarly, he notes that Athens' resources were at their height (ἀκμάζοντες, with reference to both Athens and Sparta, 1.1.1) in 431, and he includes Perikles' speech as evidence. Accordingly, if Athens' tribute had reached its height as a result of the reassessment of 425, it seems to me that Thucyd-

---

41. E.g., the first assessment (1.96.2); the tribute of Magnesia (1.138.5); Athenian resources on the eve of war (2.13.3–5); the siege of Poteidaia (2.70.2); the first *eisphora* (3.19.1); the ransoms of Kerkyraian prisoners (3.70.1), and Rhoiteion (4.52.2), to give just a few examples.

42. The most obvious example of a "greatest" is the war itself, the *megiste kinesis*, 1.1.2; cf. Macleod, "Thucydides and Tragedy," for an interesting discussion of the tragic function of some superlatives in the *History*.

43. This comment is especially striking because Thucydides is writing about Sitalkes, not Seuthes, his successor (2.97.3).

ides would have remarked on this fact.[44] The evidence that tribute reached its highest point would not have been included simply as a detail for the purpose of thoroughness, but rather because it would have been central to the historian's argument about Athens' *dunamis*.

The conclusions to which we are heading should be clear by now. The fact that Thucydides does not mention that tribute reached its height in 425 strongly suggests that the decree had no especially significant effect, and this absence should also be considered alongside the negative testimony we examined in the beginning of this discussion (that is, without previous assessments and with only fragmentary tribute records, we cannot tell whether the assessment in 425 was in any way dramatic or unusual). Is it surprising that the decree may not have achieved its intended result? It should not be. Assessment and collection were two separate and distinct activities; furthermore, no one supposes that Athens ever received the total of its assessments. This decree is no exception. The possibility of a greater disparity between assessment and collection in 425 than at other times should not be unduly worrisome; nor should we feel compelled to adjust the estimates of collection to correspond more closely to the assessment totals.

Finally, does the probability that the reassessment decree was largely ineffective conflict with Thucydides' testimony about Athens' financial resources in the war? If the argument developed here is correct—that the efficacy of tribute as a stable source of imperial revenue was declining, in contrast to its central role in accumulating a reserve necessary for the development of Athens' naval *arche* during the Pentekontaetia—then the 425 reassessment decree has intriguing implications. The decree illuminates this very difficulty,[45] though the reasons behind it are less easy to determine. Was imperial revenue more forthcoming and reliable when demanded in another form and name than tribute? Or should we leave the idea of "willingness" completely out of the picture and suppose that Athens was better able to enforce regular payment of other types of imperial revenue than of tribute? Did the Athenians learn a lesson from the siege of Poteidaia that tributary states would revolt and the cost of suppression would be too high in the long run during a war? These are all possibilities; in any case, the decree makes clear that the Athenians had been unable properly and regularly to enforce full payment and collection but that they were now toughening their stance.[46]

---

44. But cf. Gomme, *HCT* 3:501; Proctor, *Experience*, 19, 209, both of whom suggest that Thucydides would have remedied the omission if he had had time.

45. As does other epigraphical evidence, to be discussed in chapter 6.

46. Support comes from the section (lines 34–38) ordering for the future regular four-year assessments under heavy penalty to the *prytaneis* for failure to do so, which suggests that previous assessments had not been regularly undertaken.

The decree of 425, however, imposing heavy-handed and rigid restrictions on both Athenians and allies, was not the right answer.

On the other hand, to accept the possibility that the decree of 425 was not effective in reality is not to deny its significance in a psychological and symbolic respect. Purely from a physical standpoint, the document was meant to impress, inscribed on a marble stele looming some twenty feet high. It presented a powerful symbol of Athens' extraordinary confidence in the aftermath (whatever the precise timing of the decree) of Sphakteria and the capture of Kythera, and other successes, which helped to reaffirm the sense of Athens' *dunamis* after the plague, Poteidaia, and Mytilene. Likewise, the expedition to Sicily confirmed the changed atmosphere of the city. The stele recording the new assessment testified to Athens' recovery, and the Athenians would doubtless have expected the allies to be suitably affected. The monument would have demonstrated and reaffirmed to the allies their subject status to the imperial ruler.[47]

BRASIDAS' NORTHERN CAMPAIGNS

The Athenians' optimism and apparent invincibility, now confirmed by their spectacular victories, refusal to make peace with the Spartans, and decisions to strengthen their hold on the allies, had a palpable effect on the Spartans and Athenian allies alike. In the very summer in which Athens' fortunes improved so dramatically, the Spartan general Brasidas set off northward to Thrace, and Thucydides describes his journey through Thessaly in north-central Greece. He indicates how widespread the view was that Athens had the upper hand in the war: not only did the Spartans feel dismayed at the present superiority of Athens following Pylos, but the inhabitants of the Athenian-held cities in the Thraceward area, especially those in the Chalkidike, did as well, fearing that Athens would attack them next (4.79.2). A Spartan army had been requested both by the allies and by Perdikkas, the Macedonian king, who was himself at odds with the Athenians.

Thucydides' discussion of the circumstances under which Brasidas went north raises some important considerations: the unrest in the Thraceward area, brought out well by the historian, and the significance of this area to Athenian interests bring home the clumsy handling of the alliance with Sitalkes, which would affect relations between Athens and Seuthes, his successor to the throne. It is not difficult to recall the massive resources at the disposal of the Odrysian king, which were near their height at this time. Now the allies were restive, Perdikkas was maneuver-

---

47. Cf., e.g., 4.87.3, where Brasidas equates tribute with slavery.

ing, and, with the exception of the Thessalians to the south, there was no strong pro-Athenian support in the area. The loss of Sitalkes as a firm ally, then, comes to mind as we read Thucydides' narrative of the Thracian towns in revolt and Perdikkas' activities. At this point, Sitalkes is still alive; and, although he has not figured in the narrative since the end of book 2, Thucydides judges it important to inform us of his death in 4.101.5. Why? Most likely, his intention is to underscore implicitly, as he had done earlier, Athens' loss of a powerful friend with enormous resources in the very region now threatened by Brasidas.

Thucydides makes a point of noting that the Spartan army was sent out largely at Brasidas' own request (4.81.1). If true, this is a telling detail, for it suggests that Spartan leadership as a whole had still not grasped the necessity of developing a strategy that would effectively strike at the source of Athens' power, its financial resources from the empire, by aiding or fomenting revolts of poleis that provided revenue to the Athenians. We have already noted that the problem was twofold: the Spartans had failed to obtain the necessary funds themselves to build a fleet adequate to meet the Athenians on their own terms; moreover, they seem to have been unable to understand that this war could not be won in the traditional way.[48]

Thus, even though Brasidas was to have enormous success in the north in depriving Athens of allies that contributed sizable revenue, the strategy and the victory were exceptional, reflecting not official Spartan policy but rather the shrewdness of an individual, Brasidas. Thucydides shows a great deal of interest in Brasidas' expedition. He describes the general's character and the high regard in which he was held by the Greeks in the area; indeed, Thucydides believed that Brasidas was chiefly responsible for a pro-Spartan attitude among Athens' allies after the Sicilian expedition. In characteristic fashion, he notes that Brasidas was the first to be sent out in this way (4.81.3), an implicit reminder of the Spartans' laggardness.

As a result of Brasidas' appearance in the north, the Athenians declared war on Perdikkas and guarded the area more closely (4.82.1), which suggests that the Athenians took Brasidas' expedition seriously and responded promptly. After Brasidas negotiated with Arrabaios, son of Bromeros, king of the Lynkestians (4.83), he marched against Akanthos with the Chalkidians and spoke before the assembly (4.84–87). The general's speech is remarkable for the number of times he refers to the "liberation" of Greece within such a brief space.[49] He speaks of the con-

---

48. Cf. the insight given by Thucydides into the Spartans' thinking at the end of the Archidamian War, 5.14.3.

49. He brings it up eight times in a speech comprising hardly more than two OCT pages: 4.85.1, 85.5, 85.6, 86.1, 86.4, 87.2, 87.4, 87.6.

sequences of the Akanthians' potential refusal to submit to Sparta, in which context he refers to the tribute which they pay to Athens. He makes some perceptive observations about the nature and source of Athenian power, arguing (somewhat sarcastically, it seems) that the Akanthians need to submit to Sparta; goodwill alone is of no benefit:

> You Akanthians may be well-disposed toward us, but we will still be harmed by the money which you are paying (*tois chremasi pheromenois*) to Athens. I will have to attack for two reasons: first, if you refuse to join us, lest, by your goodwill (and not joining us) the Lakedaimonians will be harmed; second, so that the Greeks will not be prevented by you from throwing off their slavery. (4.87.3)

The sting is clear: you are our friends, but what kind of friends are these who would harm us? The issue at hand is unmistakable and explicit: it is the money that the allies pay to Athens that is the source of concern and must be removed, not the allies themselves. In other words, if the allies were not providing Athens with its money, then a well-disposed attitude toward Sparta, without actively joining it, would be satisfactory.[50] Furthermore, Brasidas' comment that paying money to Athens also keeps the other Greeks in slavery is striking for its apparent implication that an argument based on concern for others' lot would have force.

Brasidas has come to Thrace with a direct and specific goal: to stop the flow of *chremata* from the Thraceward region into Athens and thus to put an end to Athens' *arche*. The general's remarks attest to his clear understanding of the necessary measures for military success; he not only appreciates what is required to damage Athenian power but is ready to take the steps to implement the necessary strategy. Moreover, by connecting the payment of *chremata* with slavery (*douleia*) and by advertising his intention to liberate poleis in the area, he uses his powerful and emotive rhetoric for maximum effect.[51] Indeed, his words persuade, though Thucydides pointedly notes the Akanthians' fear for their fruit (4.88) as a factor by no means negligible, and Akanthos revolts against Athens.

THE FALL OF AMPHIPOLIS

After Akanthos' revolt, the polis of Stagiros followed suit (4.88.2). Then, in the winter of 424, Brasidas marched against the Athenian colony of Amphipolis. Thucydides' account of its fall and his role in the events as one of the two generals responsible for the area has been thoroughly unsatisfying to virtually all modern scholars. Although some have come

---

50. Brasidas knows that the Spartans do not need more manpower.
51. He was, Thucydides notes, "not a bad speaker for a Lakedaimonian" (4.84.2).

to the historian's defense,[52] more have viewed his account as an apologia, written from the perspective of someone conscious of his guilt who aimed at self-exculpation but who offers little in the way of real explanation.[53] Indeed, even Gomme believed that Thucydides was conscious not only of his failure but also of his partial responsibility and that "responsible commanders should not allow themselves to be surprised by the enemy."[54] Many candidates emerge as potential winners in the competition for the most scathing appraisal; but perhaps J. R. Ellis put it most bluntly, accusing the historian of writing a "loaded and misleading version whose inadequacies are very simply explained in terms of a wish on his part to represent his own delinquency in a more favourable light."[55]

Virtually all scholars agree that Thucydides fails to provide an adequate explanation for his inability to anticipate Brasidas' arrival at Amphipolis.[56] On the contrary, as we shall see, the historian does address the situation squarely in the very passage that has received much attention but whose purpose in the narrative has not been fully appreciated; Thucydides' portrayal of his role in the loss of Amphipolis turns out to have much to do with his conception of the relationship between wealth and power. Let us survey the account.

In 4.102, Thucydides begins his description of Brasidas' march against Amphipolis. He underscores the importance of the region by noting all the attempts to found the colony,[57] impressing on the reader the extent to which the Athenians coveted the area. They had made numerous attempts to colonize Amphipolis, finally succeeding in 437; now, Brasidas arrived in the area in the wake of his success in the district. As

52. E.g, Delbrück, *Strategie*, 177–78; Meyer, *Forschungen*, 343; *Geschichte*, 120, n. 1; Grundy, *Thucydides*, 30.

53. E.g., Busolt, *GG* 3:1154–55, n. 4; Adcock, in *CAH* 5:244–45; Westlake, *Essays*, 123–37; Kagan, *Archidamian War*, 300–302; Roberts, *Accountability*, 117–18, 128–32. See also Bauman's recent discussion, *Political Trials*, 57–60.

54. Gomme, *HCT* 3, on 4.108.7; Gomme, *Greek Attitude*, 162; see also Finley, *Thucydides*, 200.

55. Ellis, *Antichthon* 12 (1978):28–29.

56. For Roberts, *Accountability*, 130, the "staggering omission" is of any explanation why Thucydides was on Thasos at all. As she notes, Thucydides' location was known to Eukles, and there is no reason to assume there was something amiss with his being there. The issue is not why Thucydides was on Thasos but why he could not get to Amphipolis in time to save it. Interestingly, Thucydides lays no blame on Eukles, who, after all, was on the spot and therefore should have been the one against whom anger was directed; this suggests Thucydides' conscious attempt at detachment from whatever personal judgments he may have had.

57. This is, in my view, his purpose in mentioning all of the attempts to colonize the place, rather than simply demonstrating his interest in chronology, as some scholars have argued, e.g., Ridley, *Hermes* 109 (1981):37.

the Spartan general moved toward Amphipolis, Eukles, the Athenian commander on the spot, sent for Thucydides, the other general in the Thraceward region, currently on Thasos, whose intention was "to reach Amphipolis before it yielded at all, but, failing that, to secure Eion" in advance of the Spartans (4.104.5). Upon learning that Thucydides was coming to lend assistance to Amphipolis, Brasidas' reaction was fear and haste, since he was aware that Thucydides

> held the contract for the gold mines in that part of Thrace and because of that had great power among the leading men there on the mainland; accordingly, Brasidas sped to gain possession of the polis before Thucydides, if possible, fearing that should Thucydides arrive first, the majority of the Amphipolitans, expecting that he would bring allies from the sea and from Thrace to save them, would no longer come over to his side. (4.105.1)[58]

In this well-known passage, Thucydides supplies a rare piece of biographical information; indeed, the very fact that the historian, loath to bring himself overtly into the narrative, has done so alerts the reader immediately to its importance. Although scholars have remarked on Thucydides' allusion to his own κτῆσις, they have not seen in it much more than a precious autobiographical comment. In fact, Thucydides' "possession of the contract for the gold mines in that part of Thrace" is a significant part of the reason for Brasidas' concern and helps account for the historian's failure to reach Amphipolis.

Brasidas' reaction to the news of Thucydides' approach differed significantly from what it would have been if anyone else had been coming to give assistance, for he knew that Thucydides had great influence among the leaders in the region. Thucydides' personal *dunamis* in that area resulted from his κτῆσις. It is necessary both to recall the historian's views on the importance of wealth as a source of power and to appreciate the fact that he has explicitly linked his own wealth and power with Brasidas' concern and consequent expeditious arrival at Amphipolis. Brasidas reasoned that Thucydides would be better able to levy troops, and to do so more quickly, than any other general because of his influence.[59] The historian is thus explaining why it was significant that he, Thucydides, was the particular general summoned. Although another general might conceivably have arrived in time, Thucydides was unable to. Put

---

58. ἐν τούτῳ δὲ ὁ Βρασίδας δεδιὼς καὶ τὴν ἀπὸ τῆς Θάσου τῶν νεῶν βοήθειαν καὶ πυνθανόμενος τὸν Θουκυδίδην κτῆσίν τε ἔχειν τῶν χρυσείων μετάλλων ἐργασίας ἐν τῇ περὶ ταῦτα Θρᾴκῃ καὶ ἀπ' αὐτοῦ δύνασθαι ἐν τοῖς πρώτοις τῶν ἠπειρωτῶν, ἠπείγετο προκατασχεῖν, εἰ δύναιτο, τὴν πόλιν, μὴ ἀφικνουμένου αὐτοῦ τὸ πλῆθος τῶν 'Αμφιπολιτῶν, ἐλπίσαν ἐκ θαλάσσης ξυμμαχικὸν καὶ ἀπὸ τῆς Θρᾴκης ἀγείραντα αὐτὸν περιποιήσειν σφᾶς, οὐκέτι προσχωροίη.

59. As Bauman notes, *AClass* 11 (1968):170–78, Brasidas viewed Thucydides' arrival as crucial.

another way, whereas Brasidas would not have hastened so to anticipate any other Athenian general, he saw the need for special celerity in Thucydides' case. This explanation, with its focus on the historian's special influence in the endangered area, is in effect a response to those who apparently doubted that he did in fact hurry to Amphipolis as fast as possible, and who therefore considered him responsible for the loss of the city. Thucydides argues that the situation had special circumstances and provides the reasons in 4.105.1: given the fact that Brasidas knew that it was he, Thucydides, who was coming to help, it was impossible for Thucydides to have arrived in time to save the city.

Thucydides seldom provides autobiographical detail; indeed, its absence from the work suggests that he believed it inappropriate to his *History*. The very fact that he drew attention to his κτῆσις is a sign, in my view, that he regarded it as an essential piece of information in his narrative.[60] The loss of Amphipolis' revenues had a direct effect on Thucydides; it is ironic that the writer who so consistently stresses the importance of *chremata* in naval empire and war was blamed for the loss of one of the valuable and profitable cities within the empire.

Amphipolis fell into Spartan hands. Thucydides describes the reaction in Athens:

> When they heard that Amphipolis had been taken, the Athenians plunged into great fear (ἐς μέγα δέος), especially because the polis was useful to them both in the supplying of timber for shipbuilding and in revenue of money (*chrematon prosodo*), and because, although up to the Strymon the Lakedaimonians had an avenue to Athens' allies if the Thessalians led them, they [the Spartans] could not advance beyond it as they did not control the bridge, since there was a large lake above the town, and toward Eion, Athenian triremes were blocking them. They [the Athenians] also were afraid that their allies would revolt. (4.108.1)

We already knew of Amphipolis' importance to the Athenians in general terms. Now Thucydides comments specifically that the loss of the city caused great fear, especially because it supplied Athens with timber for shipbuilding and *chrematon prosodos*. What kind of revenue? Amphipolis itself was not tributary; therefore, Thucydides is alluding to another kind of imperial revenue.[61] We can safely draw two inferences. First, wealth from Amphipolis flowed into Athens regularly, since Thucydides refers to it as *prosodos*. Second, it was clearly substantial, since the

---

60. If there is an element of apologia in Thucydides' account, it is probably to be found in his statement that he set out with the intention of reaching Amphipolis, or at least of holding Eion, that is, making Eion part of his original plan.

61. I agree with Gomme, ad loc., that the phrase does not refer to tribute that Athens was able to collect from the surrounding area by virtue of its control of Amphipolis.

loss of revenue and timber is cited as the chief reason for the Athenians' "great fear" at the loss of the colony.[62] Revenue may have accrued from sacred precincts,[63] but the bulk likely derived from the gold and silver mines for which the area of Mount Pangaion was famous, possessing the "richest mineral deposits" of the entire Thraco-Macedonian region.[64] Without Thucydides' explicit testimony, however, we would not have had firm evidence that Athens successfully exploited the abundant wealth of the region on a regular basis over and above receiving tribute from poleis in that area.[65]

In 4.108.2, Thucydides tells us that Athens now feared a wave of revolts in the area as a result of the fall of Amphipolis, prompted by Brasidas' apparent moderation and generous employment of the catchword and rallying cry ἐλευθερία. Indeed, other cities began to call in Brasidas, each, Thucydides comments rather cynically, wanting to be the first to revolt (4.108.3). He continues: "for they thought that this seemed a safe thing to do, and their mistaking of the extent of Athens' *dunamis* was shown later to be as great as that power itself, a miscalculation based on obscure intentions rather than steadied foresight" (4.108.4).[66] This strongly worded statement affirming Athenian *dunamis* in 424 warrants the inference that the city's financial resources were not by that time severely depleted; it is significant that when the armistice between the two powers was concluded shortly after, Athenian loss of power was not one of the reasons given for it.[67]

---

62. In *ATL* 3:339, n. 58, an estimate of seventy to seventy-five talents annually is given, though without specific explanation.

63. As in the case of *kleroi* set aside "for the gods" on Lesbos (3.50.2); also at Brea, for which the foundation decree refers to τεμένη (*IG* I³ 46.14–15); cf. the discussion of revenue-bearing sacred land in colonies by Malkin, *Chiron* 14 (1984):44–45, esp. n. 9, and *RCAG*, 156; see also Parker, *Miasma*, 160–63.

64. Hammond in *Macedonia* 2:69; also 70–73; Hammond, *Macedonia* 1:13; J. H. Healy, *Mining and Metallurgy in the Greek and Roman World* (London, 1978), 46. J. Ramin, *La technique minière et métallurgique des Anciens* (Brussels, 1977), conveniently lists the ancient sources attesting to the richness of the mines in the Mount Pangaion area, Appendices I, III.

65. Cf. also Thucydides' remark about the mines which fell under Athenian control following the suppression of the revolt of Thasos, 1.101.3.

66. καὶ γὰρ καὶ ἄδεια ἐφαίνετο αὐτοῖς, ἐψευσμένοις μὲν τῆς Ἀθηναίων δυνάμεως ἐπὶ τοσοῦτον ὅση ὕστερον διεφάνη, τὸ δὲ πλέον βουλήσει κρίνοντες ἀσαφεῖ ἢ προνοίᾳ ἀσφαλεῖ, εἰωθότες οἱ ἄνθρωποι οὗ μὲν ἐπιθυμοῦσιν ἐλπίδι ἀπερισκέπτῳ διδόναι, ὃ δὲ μὴ προσίενται λογισμῷ αὐτοκράτορι διωθεῖσθαι; on the problematic ἐψευσμένοις see Dover, *CQ* 4 (1954):81; Gomme, *HCT* 3, ad loc.

67. Gomme believes that the sentence καὶ γὰρ καὶ ἄδεια ἐφαίνετο αὐτοῖς, etc., belongs to a time later in the narrative, "after 410, in all probability" (*HCT* 3, ad loc.), but this does not seem to be a necessary hypothesis. Thucydides here, as in his account of the Kerkyraian stasis, is looking ahead to revolts generally, but with the revolts in the Thraceward area in mind as well. In Thucydides' view, the calculations of the cities that revolted or

ARMISTICE BETWEEN ATHENS AND SPARTA

After the fall of Amphipolis, Brasidas marched against the cities on the promontory of Akte, most of which came over to him (4.109), and from there against Torone, which was betrayed to him from within (110–14). Next, he attacked the Athenian fortifications at Lekythos and succeeded in taking it, although most of the Athenians escaped (115–16).

Then, in spring 423, the Athenians and Spartans agreed on an armistice for one year. Thucydides describes the reasons for, as well as the terms of, the agreement (4.117–18). Both sides seemed to regard the armistice as a hopeful prelude to a general and lasting peace treaty (4.117). The Athenians were, as Thucydides presents them, motivated by the desire to halt further Spartan successes in the north; the Spartans knew this and believed that they were therefore in a favorable position for negotiating the release of the Spartan prisoners taken from Sphakteria. Implicit in the Athenians' desire to forestall further revolts in the area and to increase their level of preparedness in order to deal most effectively with Brasidas was the need to guard against future losses of imperial revenue; but Thucydides is silent on any present concern for the condition of Athens' reserves which might have affected their decision in 423.

One of the points in the agreement made by Sparta and its allies, and approved by the Athenians, treated the sacred moneys of Pythian Apollo at Delphi:

> Concerning the *chremata* of the god, we shall take care to determine who has done wrong, in the case of both sides, adhering to our ancestral laws correctly and justly, and any others who wish may do so, according to their ancestral laws. (4.118.3)

It is unclear to what extent this clause refers to a specific instance of borrowing from the sacred treasures of Apollo. Parke and Wormell considered it "too unsafe to argue that the Peloponnesians actually made use of the sacred treasures," but they suggest the possibility that such a use might have occurred in 426, to hire Arkadian mercenaries for an attack on Naupaktos (3.101.1; cf. 109.2).[68]

They do, however, regard the relevant clause in the armistice agreement as a specific reference to offenses (alleged or otherwise) in the "management of the sacred treasury."[69] It is further unclear whether the clause refers directly to the discussion preceding the war about the use

---

contemplated doing so following the fall of Amphipolis were not based upon a correct assessment of Athens' *dunamis* at that time (in 424), any more than were those later.

68. Parke and Wormell, *Delphic Oracle* 1:191–92.
69. Ibid., 196.

of sacred money by the Peloponnesians.[70] Regardless of actual guilt or innocence, it would have been easy for the Athenians to make such a charge, in that the whole issue of the use of sacred treasures from Olympia and Delphi seems to have originated on the Peloponnesian side; it would therefore have been more in Athenian than in Spartan interests to have the matter investigated.

There is no subsequent mention of this charge in the terms of the Peace of Nikias. Is it because the Athenians were satisfied that action had been taken against the wrongdoers (as Steup believed) or because, after further Athenian losses in Thrace and also after the death of Kleon, the Athenians "quietly dropped" the matter (as Gomme suggested)?[71] Certainty is, of course, impossible. But it is likely either that the Athenians were satisfied that the problem had been cleared up and would not arise again (insofar as the clause looks both backward and forward) or that it was not among the issues of greatest concern in the ensuing peace treaty, to which we will now turn.

THE PEACE OF NIKIAS

Between the armistice and the Peace of Nikias occurred the revolts of Skione and Mende and the battle of Amphipolis.[72] After the battle, Thu-

---

70. Cf. Gomme, *HCT* 3, ad loc., who discusses the various hypotheses proposed by previous scholars on this point.

71. Steup, ad loc.; Gomme, *HCT* 3, ad loc.

72. Significant financial activity was restricted to the hiring of mercenaries, as Thucydides mentions several times. In two cases, interestingly, the failure of these mercenary forces to arrive at the crucial moment is notable. In the first instance, Illyrian mercenaries were supposed to join Perdikkas, who in turn was to help Brasidas (τοὺς Ἰλλυριοὺς μένοντες, οἳ ἔτυχον τῷ Περδίκκᾳ μισθοῦ μέλλοντες ἥξειν, 4.124.4). The latter felt it imprudent to move against Mende without them; they were crucial, in his view, to his success against the Athenians. As it turned out, the Illyrians betrayed Perdikkas and joined forces with Arrabaios. On the other hand, the Athenians took possession of Mende, aided by, among others, one thousand Thracian mercenaries (4.129.2). In the second case, Kleon, while based at Eion, sent to Polles, the king of the Odomantians, and asked him to bring "as many Thracian mercenaries as possible" (ἄξοντας μισθοῦ Θρᾷκας ὡς πλείστους, 5.6.2). These also never arrived. In both instances, Thucydides emphasizes ineffective leadership and problems of unreliability. The loss of the Illyrian mercenaries had a direct effect on the outcome of Brasidas' plan to capture Mende before the Athenians; the latter's success was aided in part by a thousand Thracian mercenaries. In contrast to Kleon's ineffectiveness at raising a large mercenary force (and Thucydides attributes his inactivity directly to his decision to wait for the mercenary force to arrive), Brasidas immediately raised fifteen hundred Thracian mercenaries and called up the entire Edonian army of cavalry and peltasts (5.6.4). Thucydides' mention of mercenaries, among other troops, is not so much a direct illustration of the necessity of financial resources as of effective leadership to engage them promptly. But it is implicit in the discussion that large quantities of money, along with effective leadership, are at issue as well. Finally, it is noteworthy that the side on which mercenaries formed a substantial part gained victory.

cydides tells us, both Athens and Sparta began to negotiate for peace (5.14.1). The Athenians had lost the confidence with which they had carried on the war after Pylos, and they also feared revolts from their allies; the Spartans, for their part, had a number of compelling reasons for making peace, among which was the realization that the war had turned out to be utterly different from what they had imagined—they had thought that they would be able to destroy the *dunamis* of Athens in a few years simply by laying waste its land. The Spartan surrender at Sphakteria was an unprecedented blow; their territory was being invaded by the Athenians, and there were other reasons as well (5.14.2–4). Both sides, then, judged peace to be in their self-interest. Thucydides notes, however, that the Spartans had the most to gain by it, "because of their desire to recover the men who had been captured on Sphakteria, among whom were Spartiates" (5.15.1).

This analysis of the considerations in the belligerents' minds fully accords with what we have seen emerge thus far in the *History*. The underlying thread developed by Thucydides, that the Spartans faced a fundamental problem of expectation and understanding as much as of necessary resources, is reinforced here. It is not the temporal miscalculation that is at issue but rather the assumption that this war, like earlier wars, would be decided along traditional lines of preparation and strategy. Despite Archidamos' arguments and the actual course of the war, the Spartans did not seem fully aware of the realities and implications of fighting a naval power. That this is not simply Thucydides' unsubstantiated opinion is borne out by the narrative of events, in which decisions, actions, and results demonstrate its accuracy.

Also significant is Thucydides' comment that the Spartans had the most to gain from peace, chiefly the retrieval of the soldiers captured on Sphakteria; that is, Sparta's loss of these men was a more significant factor than Athens' loss of its own resources. This line of thinking suggests that Athens' financial resources were not a major factor in their deliberations about the advantages of the treaty. At the same time, however, the northern campaigns of Brasidas had taken a heavy toll on the Athenians; just as the Spartans may well have begun to appreciate the preconditions and consequences of naval war, the Athenians too, having received the first real blow to their lifeline at the hands of the Spartans (as opposed to revolts emanating from the allies themselves), had reason for concern. Indeed, in a sense, it is not entirely perverse to state that the war really began, not ended, in 422, as both sides perhaps only now realized the potential destruction and magnitude of this kind of war.

Thucydides presents the decision for peace largely in personal terms: the impetus came from individuals whose motives stemmed from individual honor and achievement. It is clear from his narrative that what brought the two sides to consider peace seriously were the personal motives of Nikias and Pleistoanax, not the exhaustion of their respective resources (although Thucydides implies that the Spartans' ability to wage effective land war was affected significantly by the capture of their military elite). This point is crucial: for although individual self-interest need not exclude serious military factors, and we expect such focus on personal motives from an ancient author, it is nonetheless noteworthy that significant depletion of the essential requirement for making war is not brought up as one of the compelling factors for peace.

Thus, we find no evidence that the state of Athens' financial resources necessitated peace; peace at this time was expedient, not essential. In response to scholars who have argued that the Athenian treasury was virtually empty by the end of the Archidamian War, Kagan notes:

> If they are right it is truly amazing that Thucydides, who makes so much of the critical role of money in waging war and takes such pains to describe the precise condition of Athenian finances in 431, does not mention the lack of money as a motive for making peace ten years later.[73]

The absence of such a motive in Thucydides implies that Athens' finances were by no means dangerously low. We may briefly now turn to the peace treaty.

For our purposes, we need to examine only the clauses in the treaty relevant to financial resources. The first clause that concerns us is the following:

> The Lakedaimonians and their allies shall return Amphipolis to the Athenians. But as many cities as the Lakedaimonians handed over to the Athenians, let them go wherever they wish, keeping their own possessions; and the cities shall be autonomous, paying the tribute of Aristeides. (5.18.2)

We want to keep at a minimum our entry into the tangle of complexities that the clause has raised pertaining to the cities handed over by the Spartans to the Athenians.[74] Put simply, debate over this section of the treaty concerns whether the "tribute of Aristeides" is to be applied only to the specific cities mentioned in the clause, namely, Argilos, Stagiros, Akanthos, Skolos, Olynthos, and Spartolos, or whether a general extension is implied. The larger question is whether the Peace of Nikias marks a general softening in Athens' stance toward its allies. Those who hold that view argue for a broader application of the clause concerned with the tribute of Aristeides.[75] Aside from the questions raised in chapter 2

---

73. Kagan, *Archidamian War*, 336.
74. See Gomme, *HCT* 3, ad loc.; *ATL* 3:346–58; Meiggs, *AE*, 340–43.
75. Elaborated by West, *AJA* 29 (1925):135–51; *ATL* 3:347–53. They have argued, on the basis of the assessment of 421, *IG* I³ 77, that all tribute was reduced as near as possible to the Aristeidean level, not just that of the cities listed in 5.18.5. Yet, as Meiggs points out,

about the "moderation" of the first assessment of tribute,[76] the idea that Athens reduced the tribute of all of its allies as a result of the peace is not supported by extant fragments of a quota list most likely dating to 418;[77] but it is also clear that one cannot draw unilateral inferences about the treatment of allies by looking at tribute, for some areas seem to have been decidedly better off than others (for example, the islands). It makes most sense, and is most defensible, to suppose that the tribute of Aristeides held only for the few poleis at issue.[78]

Indeed, assuming a general application first requires demonstrating that it would have been in Athens' interest to extend the terms to other poleis, even though not specified by the treaty. Athens was by no means a weak party to the peace; accordingly, the Athenians would have lowered everyone's tribute to its level at the outset of the League only if they considered it to be a useful concession. Yet reducing the allies' financial burden, which had come to be so closely associated with their "slavery," would not make them feel less subjugated, nor would it have been worthwhile for Athens from the practical standpoint of maintaining power.[79] In any case, it is exceedingly unlikely that Athens would go beyond what was required by the terms of the peace and voluntarily decide to reduce tribute generally.

In the treaty, as noted, Athens appears to have a strong position: the clause of 5.18.5 is a case in point, whereby the grant of autonomy (and neutrality, if desired) to the six poleis is counterbalanced by their obligation to pay tribute. The combination is reminiscent of the situation at the beginning of the Delian League as Thucydides describes it: certain allies were tributary; all were "at first" autonomous (1.97.1). This arrangement was acceptable initially; but as soon as a polis reneged on its obli-

---

AE, 340–42, the evidence of the assessment list is far from certain. There are, on the contrary, indications that the assessment was far closer to the 425 level and not reduced. Furthermore, its date could be either 422 or 421; thus, it might not reflect the Peace of Nikias at all.

76. There may be a crucial distinction between 1.96.2, in which Thucydides discusses the first assessment of 460 talents, and 5.18.5. The former was an assessment alone; it is possible that, if it differed widely from what was actually paid in the early years of the League, the reference in 5.18.5—in which the cities are simply to pay the *phoros* in the time of Aristeides, not necessarily the *phoros* of the original assessment—might be to a lower figure. But additional considerations may help to assess better the nature of Aristeides' assessment.

77. *IG* I³ 287.

78. So Bauslaugh, *Neutrality*, 137–40.

79. The notion that its allies might be less likely to revolt if their tribute requirements were decreased is not immediately convincing; the argument could always be used that such reductions implied weakness on the Athenians' part and therefore would foster as many revolts as previously.

gations of money or ships, it lost its autonomy. Similarly, the six poleis specified in the treaty of 421 were to be autonomous and pay tribute, but force was allowed by the terms of the treaty if they refused.[80] The compatibility of tribute and autonomy thus has a precedent.[81] More interesting is the following stipulation. The treaty states that the cities which are to pay the *phoros* they did in the time of Aristeides are not to be allies of the Athenians—unless they themselves choose to be.[82] Refusal to pay tribute seems to be the only basis on which the Athenians could justly attack them; not, that is, on the grounds of their neutrality.[83] This term seems to be novel,[84] and it strongly suggests that revenue was more important than allies to Athens; this must have been increasingly apparent as the purchase of manpower became more commonplace. The treatment of Kythera (4.57) is relevant here: it was rendered tributary but not brought into the League as a compulsory ally. Both cases suggest the possibility of an emerging pattern different from the standard formula of tributary, subject ally. In both cases, we can see one effect of the large-scale introduction of money into the military sphere on Athenian practice in relationships with weaker parties; indeed, these examples continue the trend begun when a system of exchange involving money for survival and protection was instituted by the Athenians. The difference between the situation described by Thucydides in 1.99 and that toward the end of the Archidamian War is that the Athenians came to judge the bond of alliance unnecessary.

The six Chalkidian poleis specified in the peace regarded the terms as disadvantageous; indeed, they refused to agree to the provisions (5.21.2). The offer of *autonomia* can hardly have offended; less clear is their reception of the option to ally with Athens.[85] Certainly, neutrality could put a polis in an uncomfortable and insecure position. Perhaps

---

80. Whether this was true when the Delian League was established is less clear.

81. Ostwald, *Autonomia*, 28; Raaflaub, *Freiheit*, 187–89; Bauslaugh, *Neutrality*, 137–40. A neat distinction is not always maintained, however, especially in the case of tributary poleis that were regarded as ὑπήκοοι, without αὐτονομία, which comprised most of the League's membership.

82. ξυμμάχους δ' εἶναι μηδετέρων, μήτε Λακεδαιμονίων μήτε Ἀθηναίων· ἢν δὲ Ἀθηναῖοί πείθωσι τὰς πόλεις, βουλομένας ταύτας ἐξέστω ξυμμάχους ποιεῖσθαι αὐτοὺς Ἀθηναίοις (5.18.5).

83. ὅπλα δὲ μὴ ἐξέστω ἐπιφέρειν Ἀθηναίους μηδὲ τοὺς ξυμμάχους ἐπὶ κακῷ ἀποδιδόντων τὸν φόρον, ἐπειδὴ αἱ σπονδαὶ ἐγένετο. It is not clear to me whether the longer-term consequence of a failure to pay tribute was permanent loss of *autonomia*. This seems to have occurred in other instances (Ostwald, *Autonomia*, 28), but in the Peace of Nikias, the difference is that violence on the part of the Athenians is justified by the terms of the treaty.

84. Bauslaugh, *Neutrality*, 139.

85. Cf. Bauslaugh, *Neutrality*, 139–40, who implies that neutrality would have been the issue of concern.

THE KERKYRAIAN REVOLT TO THE PEACE OF NIKIAS   183

these cities had hoped for a Spartan alliance with full Spartan protections—if so, they would only have been disappointed. In any case, it is reasonable to suppose that the continued payment of tribute would have been objectionable, alliance or not. It is unfortunately impossible to determine whether the amount of tribute expected from these cities was a factor in their refusal to accept its terms.

Following the ratification of the peace by Athens and Sparta, but not by all of Sparta's allies, the two cities also concluded an alliance for fifty years, and with that Thucydides ends his account of the Archidamian, or "first," War.

CONCLUSIONS

At the end of chapter 4, which took us through the Mytilenaian settlement, I argued that Thucydides, while supplying firm evidence of the need for (additional) money, nevertheless seemed to be creating an impression of significant financial distress. This, I suggested, was more a result of the historian's argument concerning the inferiority of Athenian leadership after Perikles than evidence of a real financial crisis. Does Thucydides' analysis of the rest of the Archidamian War give further evidence of financial trouble, which would help us to assess whether Athens' financial resources at the beginning of the war were indeed great enough to sustain even a prolonged conflict of ten years?

In this chapter, we have investigated Thucydides' handling of the financial problems faced by Athens, some of the financial measures taken to meet the needs of war and to insure revenue, and the general role that the city's financial condition played in affecting the course of the war and political decisions made. We also scrutinized some of the key epigraphical evidence on imperial finances in conjunction with Thucydides to understand better not only the value of each kind of evidence but also the historical context. In general, the results fail to support the orthodoxy on Athens' finances during the Archidamian War, that is, that the treasuries were virtually depleted by its end. They do, however, shed light on the history of the war as it affected and was affected by the financial resources of the Athenian polis. In the next chapter I shall address more broadly Athens' financial status in the Archidamian War, with special attention to the evidence of Thucydides.

CHAPTER SIX

Athens' Financial Resources in the Archidamian War

When war broke out between Sparta and Athens in summer 431, Athens' financial resources were at their height: Perikles, in a speech to the Athenians shortly before the outbreak, assured his fellow citizens of their capacity to wage a successful war against the Peloponnesians and encouraged them by recounting in detail their assets, revenue, and reserve. Thucydides, undoubtedly present on the occasion, judged Perikles' ideas integral to the analysis of power that he was developing in his work, and thus he included the statesman's detailed *expliqué* of the city's financial status in his *History* (2.13.3–5). Not only were the Athenian treasuries stocked with reserve, ever replenished by revenue from the empire, but the fleet also had its largest complement (2.13.8); moreover, the empire had been under firm control without any serious recalcitrance for nearly a decade. This had allowed the recovery of the reserve, whose height at ninety-seven hundred talents, probably in the mid-fifth century, had diminished due to the building program and the expenses necessitated by the revolts of the early 440s and, most recently, Poteidaia (2.13.3–4). By 431, however, the Athenians had succeeded in replenishing the treasury of Athena by three thousand talents, bringing the reserve on the Akropolis to six thousand talents;[1] shortly thereafter, the moneys of the local gods and goddesses of Athens and Attica were likely concentrated on the Akropolis as well, further increasing the city's accumulated capital.[2]

The centralization of all immediately usable financial resources of the Athenian polis formed the cornerstone of Periklean strategy. The states-

---

1. *IG* I³ 52A.3–4; Thuc. 2.13.3.
2. Thuc. 2.13.5; *IG* I³ 52A with Kallet-Marx, *CQ* 39 (1989):94–113.

man recognized that the foundation of Athens' *dunamis* was its wealth, not its manpower, which was Sparta's strength: for Athenian naval mastery rested on the extraordinary, continual expenditure of money; thus, its success required substantial annual revenue and centralization of financial resources, to facilitate immediate disbursement and effective management of funds. These were the two essential components of Athens' financial strength: *periousia chrematon* supplemented by reliable *prosodos*. The idea of surplus as a *necessity* for naval mastery that is central to Thucydides' analysis of power stems directly from the dramatic increase in the expenditure of money in the sphere of military affairs due to the emergence of naval *dunamis*.

The Athenians' expectations at the outset of the war are difficult to judge, but it is likely that only when a Lakedaimonian force under King Archidamos actually marched into Attica and ravaged the territory of Acharnai did the majority of the citizens fully appreciate the implications and consequences of adopting the Periklean strategy. One response, to set aside an "iron reserve" of one thousand talents in case of emergency (2.24.1), clearly reflects their acknowledgment of the potential scale and gravity of the struggle now upon them, as it demonstrates their awareness of the crucial role of expense in the war. Moreover, the decision to create a special reserve was made solely with naval operations in mind, unambiguous testimony to the Athenians' fundamental understanding of the connection between money and the fleet, and especially of the absolute necessity of surplus. It is unclear to what extent they anticipated a lengthy struggle; however, after the first round of opposing strategies was played out, it became evident that a quick decision was unlikely.[3] Accordingly, the cost of the struggle would have been expected to be potentially enormous and unprecedented, but not unimaginable. For the Athenians were no strangers to the degree of expense a war could require, especially while maintaining an empire (and vice versa): their experience from the 470s through the 440s had been instructive. Moreover, two recent sieges against their own allies, one against Samos in 440/39 and the other currently under way against the town of Poteidaia in the Chalkidike, had repeated the lesson. Perikles' calculations in summer 431 would have included the need to keep a firm check on the allies, to avert the possibility of further revolts and sieges, and to conduct operations against the Spartans and their allies.

Finally, in winter 430–29, the Poteidaians surrendered to the Athenians (Thuc. 2.70.1). According to Thucydides, the siege had cost the Athenians two thousand talents (a good part of which had already been

---

3. Cf. the Spartans' view in 5.14.3 that the war would be wrapped up within a few years; however, this view was apparently not shared by Archidamos, 1.81.6.

spent before the outbreak of war) and inflicted great suffering on both Poteidaia and Athens. Uneasiness about their financial losses is perhaps further suggested by a naval mission to extort money from Karia and Lykia (2.69.1) which occurred just before the surrender of Poteidaia—and which Thucydides makes a point of noting right before he relates Poteidaia's fall. The tremendous cost of the siege renders the terms of the settlement all the more surprising. The generals on the spot abolished the community of Poteidaia but allowed the former inhabitants to take money with them and settle where they would; the site of the former polis was later colonized by Athens. The Athenians consciously gave up the profits of war in bodies and financial resources: most important, there is no record of any financial reparation made directly to the state in the form of continued tribute or an indemnity.

It is difficult to assess the Poteidaian decision because of the apparent disagreement it engendered in Athens (2.70.4); nevertheless, it marks a departure from previous settlements following the suppression of a revolt in that the Athenians did little or nothing to recover the cost of the siege by imposing an indemnity, nor to insure revenue to the polis for the future by, in this case, continuing to demand tribute, even if at a lower assessment than the prerevolt level.[4] It is indeed possible that the eventual colony indirectly facilitated the flow of revenue to Athens through taxation, for example; but whatever direct financial gain derived from the new *apoikia* most likely benefited individual colonists alone, not the public coffers of the mother city. There is no doubt that colonies and klerouchies make good strategic sense in trouble spots;[5] but such an approach raises important questions: How significant was the loss to the centralized financial resources of the state? Is there a pattern in the post-Periklean years of private benefit (however one assesses the indirect public gain) over public? What light do these changes, if detectable, shed on the relationship between leader and demos and on the effectiveness of political leadership in general in a city with an *arche* and a war? The settlement of Lesbos is of great importance in connection with these issues.

In 428/7, two years after the fall of Poteidaia, with the war now in full force and Athens debilitated by the plague, Mytilene (and much of Lesbos) revolted. The city had been one of Athens' most important and strongest allies and had enjoyed the nearly singular honor of retaining

---

4. Cf. Thasos (1.101.3) and Samos (1.117.3; *IG* I³ 363), both lengthy and costly sieges. Poteidaia's tribute had just been dramatically increased from six to fifteen talents (*IG* I³ 279, II.70, 433/2).

5. Although if maintaining order were the primary goal, it is unclear why a colony and not a garrison would have been established in the area; but cf. Mattingly, *CQ* 11 (1961), 161, with Meiggs' criticisms, *AE*, 535.

its own fleet; it was, that is, an autonomous ally with the means of defense, not a relatively powerless tributary subject, as Thucydides makes clear.[6] But the Athenians' reaction contrasted sharply with their earlier response upon merely suspecting disaffection by the Poteidaians in 433. At that time, they responded immediately and swiftly, recognizing the threat to their revenues; now, in 428, with Perikles dead and the plague still raging, reaction was laggardly and suspicious. When at last they accepted the truth and were forced into action by fear, they dispatched forty ships to the scene, but too late: Mytilene and all of Lesbos except Methymna had already revolted against Athens (3.2–3).

The Athenians were now faced with a new siege, only two years after Poteidaia came to terms. The length, cost, and hardship involved in quashing that revolt were still fresh in their minds; and unlike the timing of the revolt of Poteidaia,[7] now they were at war with Sparta and suffering from a devastating plague. The Athenians' next move is instructive: they levied a tax on propertied citizens for the first time and dispatched ships, as they had done in the winter of 429, to collect money from the empire (Thuc. 3.19.1). These measures must be considered in the general context of events at the time. The atmosphere in Athens no doubt approached panic; decisions were made hastily through fear, and without the luxury of careful forethought and intelligent planning.[8] Indeed, such emergency ad hoc financing was exactly what Perikles had insisted was not the way to win wars (1.141.5).

What is important to appreciate is that the Athenian treasury at this time, in 428/7, was far from empty: the cost of the siege of Poteidaia had been sizable, even unusually high,[9] but probably a good part of this had already been spent before summer 431 and, therefore, was taken into account by Perikles in his speech on Athens' resources on the eve of war. Accordingly, the decisions made in 428/7 may betoken more a collective psychological insecurity and the lack of sound financial and political management in an anxious atmosphere than a serious depletion of cash.[10] When Thucydides points out that "then, for the first time" the Athenians levied an *eisphora* on themselves of two hundred talents, his

---

6. 3.3.1; Thucydides notes the special strengths of the Mytilenaians (their fleet and "power in full force" [δύναμιν ἀκέραιον]).

7. I.e., in 433, before the war broke out.

8. Thucydides notes the manner in which the Athenians reacted to the reports of the revolt: their refusal to believe them, despite the importance of Mytilene to the empire, their fear (δείσαντες), and their hasty action (ἐξαπιναίως) when they realized the truth of the reports about Mytilene's intended revolt (3.3.1–2).

9. Thucydides notes elsewhere (3.17.4) that the soldiers had been paid at twice the normal rate.

10. Note that Thucydides specifies that additional money was needed "for the siege" (ἐς τὴν πολιορκίαν), i.e., not in general.

emphasis may in part be explained by the desire to contrast the policy and actions of Perikles with those of leaders who gained prominence after his death. Only then, that is, and not while Perikles was in command, did the Athenians take an action which that general and strategist would neither have approved of nor judged necessary. Moreover, the phrase, which points ahead to the continued use of a war tax in the course of the Peloponnesian War,[11] raises serious questions both about the stability of imperial revenue and about financial management. For the decision once again to plunder the empire as well as to impose a war tax on Athenian citizens suggests concern about the adequacy of normal revenues, chief among which was tribute, to satisfy the requirements of naval war and maintenance of the empire.

The decisions affecting Athens' financial resources made in the years immediately following Perikles' demise demonstrate at the very least a changed conception of the city's financial capability and a markedly different view of the proper methods for insuring the influx of revenue; this is patent not only from the decision to levy an *eisphora* but also from the terms of the settlement of Mytilene following the suppression of the revolt. For just as in the case of Poteidaia, tribute was not imposed on the defeated, although this would have been the usual procedure for a polis that had revolted and had not paid tribute previously; nor was an indemnity slapped on it. Thus, for the second time early in the war (though obviously it would not have seemed so at the time), the Athenians departed from their normal practice of insuring financial gain to the polis through the previously reliable system of tribute. Coming during a war, this trend toward rejecting tribute as both a punitive and necessary financial measure is surprising from a purely financial standpoint. The land of Lesbos, except that belonging to Methymna, was divided into 3,000 *kleroi*, 300 of which were set aside for the gods, while the remaining 2,700 became an Athenian klerouchy. From rent on the sacred land, the Athenian state derived ten talents a year, but the bulk of revenue, an impressive ninety talents annually, was spread among individual Athenians; it is important to underscore that the latter sum was not public revenue and that the Athenians chose to accept their leaders' proposal not to extract revenue from the island in the form of tribute for the public war fund.[12]

In the cases of both Poteidaia and Mytilene, the immediate question arises whether these communities would have been able to pay tribute

11. Ar. *Knights* 924 also implies its regularity.
12. Two years later, however, in 425, with a considerably improved atmosphere in Athens, there seems to have been great confidence in the prospect not only of stabilizing tribute but even of increasing the burden on the allies. I shall discuss the nature and significance of the tribute reassessment of 425 below.

after having experienced severe depletion of their own resources in the sieges. Poteidaia is problematic, for the issue is as much the community's hypothetical ability to pay tribute had it been allowed to survive intact as it is the colony's ability to exploit the region's financial potential and guarantee Athens state revenue. The revival of the polis under new inhabitants, however, combined with the wealth of the region, makes it reasonable to assume that Athens could have derived revenue from Poteidaia.[13]

An important part of the discussions at Athens after the revolt of Mytilene was quelled concerned the effect of revolts on the financial resources of the allies, and consequently, of the Athenian polis.[14] Kleon argued that a siege, leaving the conquered city a wasteland, would render it unable to bear any subsequent financial burden. But Mytilene was hardly reduced to poverty by the siege as is clear from the total financial yield of the settlement, nine-tenths of which, however, was scattered among private individuals and not accruing to the state.

As the settlement of Lesbos suggests that the Athenians could have imposed tribute but did not, their decision must have been based on choice, not necessity. What explains the fact that individual Athenian citizens, rather than the polis as a whole, reaped the reward of the Mytilenaian settlement? It may have been motivated by a genuine desire to placate especially those Athenians suffering from confinement in the city; but it resulted in the reduction of the amount of revenue that would have joined the war reserve and thus cut away at the polis's *periousia chrematon* necessary for ultimate victory. More broadly, it indicates a shift away from Perikles' view that the polis commands the highest allegiance, outweighing individual gain and self-interest, and that benefiting the polis does the greatest good to individuals in it, while catering to individuals brings harm to the polis. Thucydides allows Perikles to make this point abundantly clear in his last speech (2.60), at a time when personal hardship was at its height.

Against this background, the settlements of Poteidaia and Mytilene start to reflect an ominous development in the 420s, as they appear designed for individual gain at the expense of the welfare and strength of the polis, which depended on surplus concentrated wealth. These decisions shed important light more on Athenian political leadership and personal power than on financial, military strategy. For after the death of Perikles, appealing to the material and physical losses, lately relentless, suffered by the citizenry offered an easy formula for political success

---

13. Cf. [Arist.] *Oik.* 2.1347 a17–24, which allows for sufficient wealth to require an *eisphora*, or head tax, on every inhabitant.

14. See above, pp. 143–49.

and encouraged a style of political leadership which promoted the idea of personal gain, often by example. The increase of money in Athens, its constant association with Athens' new leaders, and its negative effect on society are depicted with the venom of late fifth-century comedy[15] and also by Pseudo-Xenophon (*Ath.Pol.* 3.3). Even Thucydides, normally reticent about details of this kind, judges it relevant to comment on the reputation and character of Perikles' successors, leaders who instilled in the citizenry by example a venal and mercenary individualism (2.65.7). Benefits accruing to individuals from the empire as the direct result of political decisions rather than of private initiative fit into this context. At the same time, however, the settlements of Poteidaia and Mytilene raise an additional consideration about the cohesion of the Athenian citizenry as a whole with respect to the empire and thus to the war. Wealthy Athenians had profited from the empire to a considerable extent,[16] a fact that no doubt engendered support for the continuation of the *arche*.[17] Colonies and klerouchies were among the means—apart from military service—of extending the exploitation of the empire to a broader group below the elite; these settlements were, in effect, a method of distributing the spoils of war to selected individuals among the citizenry.[18]

It is impossible to offer a definitive interpretation of the settlements that we have been examining. But it is clear that Athens, as a matter of policy, was steering away from the imposition of tribute on allies who had revolted. This raises an important question: how successful and effective in general was the collection of tribute during the war? For if there was growing difficulty in collecting *phoros*, which decreased its reliability and, hence, its value as a source of income, then the settlement of Mytilene could be regarded as a sensible approach to the problem of imperial revenue (though perhaps only if the Athenians had now begun to institute a fairly regular practice of taxing themselves). In conjunction with regular taxation, the klerouchy on Lesbos might be a fairly effective, though certainly circuitous, way of insuring regular revenue from the empire to the state by raising the income level of some individual Athenians. Unfortunately, the tribute quota lists, the best gauge for estimating tribute totals, are virtually useless on this question for the 420s, given their con-

---

15. E.g., *Acharnians*, lines 31–6, 65–67, 90, 137, 167, 602, 608ff., 618–19; *Knights*, lines 435ff., 442ff., 575ff., 773ff., 834–53; *Wasps*, lines 518–20, 655–724; cf. also works cited by Davies, *Wealth*, 69–70.

16. See Davies, *Wealth*, 55–64.

17. This aspect should not be exaggerated, however. It is fallacious to argue that members of the Athenian elite would have been against naval *arche* because it necessarily gave a stronger role in the polis to the masses than an aristocrat would have desired. Disliking a consequence of power would not have made an individual or group oppose the preservation of that power itself.

18. See Pritchett's discussion in *GSAW* 5:445–47.

dition of survival.[19] But there are other useful indicators suggesting that the amount of revenue coming to Athens in the form of tribute was declining.

First, that tribute collection was a matter of concern even early in the war can be inferred from an inscription dated ca. 430, *IG* I³ 60, which, although in extremely fragmentary condition, clearly deals with tribute. It is reasonable to suppose that underlying this inscription were problems in tribute collection serious enough to warrant a decree in response. If tribute was indeed proving much more difficult to collect in wartime, which would not be surprising, what were the responses to the problem? The inscription just mentioned is not helpful on this matter, beyond its probable testimony to the existence of a problem. More interesting and substantial is other epigraphic evidence, some clearly and some only possibly dated to this period, which suggests a tightening of the screws in a rather heavy-handed and likely unrealistic way. The decree proposed by Kleonymos, *IG* I³ 68 (dated to 426), calling for the appointment of tribute collectors, strongly indicates difficulties with tribute collection, concerned as it is with insuring that the cities make their full payments.[20]

The most famous of the epigraphic evidence concerned with tribute during the 420s is the inscription recording the assessment of 425, *IG* I³ 71. This reassessment, but one in a long line of reassessments since the formation of the Delian League in 478, occupies a special place because it is thought to have raised the tribute more drastically than all its predecessors; it is, moreover, extremely valuable as evidence of the "tribute problem" of the 420s, but in a more complex way than the inscriptions noted above. Leaving aside for the moment the total of the reassessment, the inscription testifies to continuing trouble with collection, and thus to the ineffectiveness of the previous measures mentioned. Moreover, it suggests that the problem emanated not only from the subject cities but, to a certain extent, from Athens itself: the decree orders future assessments every four years, with stiff penalties levied for the failure of the responsible *prytaneis* to do so (lines 26ff.), suggesting that recently assess-

---

19. Lists 25–28, *IG* I³ 281–84; Meiggs, *AE*, 531–37.
20. See ML 68, for commentary and bibliography. Similar in purpose is *IG* I³ 34, the decree of Kleinias, which also aimed at tightening up tribute payment. Although a date in the 420s used to be considered most likely, the decree is now generally thought to have been passed at an earlier time, in the mid-century. But the arguments against a later date are not decisive, and a date in the 420s is still possible, as it is also for the Coinage Decree, on which see the recent discussions of Lewis ("Coinage Decree") and Mattingly ("Coinage Decree and Assertion of Empire") in Carradice, *Coinage*, 53–64, 65–71; cf. also Meiggs, *AE*, 167–72; 599–601. Both of these inscriptions, however, since undated, are not useful as evidence for the present discussion.

ments had not been carried out on a regular four-year basis.[21] Like previous measures concerned with tribute, this document lays down stringent terms and penalties designed to raise more money, culminating with the list of the new assessment, which may have totaled more than fourteen hundred talents. This would mean a two- to three-fold increase for most cities in the empire since the assessment of 434, the last one for which we have any knowledge of the total. That assessment seems to have totaled approximately 430 talents, though our knowledge is incomplete.[22]

Thus, it appears that even though the Athenians' previous measures to insure the collection of tribute were by no means "soft," they had been less than successful. Yet in 425, the Athenians not only maintained their tough stance but even demanded greater amounts of tribute than previously assessed—despite their having failed to collect the lesser amount. What are we to infer from the measure of 425 in the light of our knowledge of the Athenians' continuing difficulties in obtaining tribute?

At the outset, we need to note, as discussed in the last chapter, the high uncertainty whether the assessment of 425 was indeed as sharp an increase as is commonly believed.[23] That the document, itself physically imposing, was intended to impress and intimidate the allies is obvious. How realistic it was, seen against the background of the war and the evidence we have been considering, is another matter.

The fortunes of war had, by 425, switched to Athens, as the city had made a spectacular recovery from the heavy cumulative toll of the plague and the revolts of Poteidaia and Mytilene: the cream of the Spartan army surrendered on Sphakteria, which gave the Athenians both a military and psychological advantage over their enemies. Indeed, insult was added to injury shortly after when an Athenian naval squadron captured the island of Kythera, a Lakedaimonian polis, and forced it to pay tribute.[24] The corresponding psychological effects on the Spartans and on the Athenians must have been extraordinary, as is evident from the Athenian decision just after Sphakteria alone to reject, no doubt on Kleon's proposal, Spartan peace overtures.[25] In this context, the reassessment of 425 reveals much about Athens' self-image at that time, constituting an unmistakable illustration of the projection of power; however, it tells us remarkably little by itself about what actually ended up in the treasury.

21. See the discussion in ML 69.
22. Meiggs, *AE*, 527.
23. See above, pp. 165–66.
24. Thuc. 4.54, 57.4.
25. Thus. 4.41.3; cf. 4.39 for Thucydides' description of the general Greek reaction to the Athenian victory on Sphakteria.

The effect the intimidating nature of the inscription had on the practical and concrete level, that is, on the amount of money consequently collected, is difficult to determine. To be sure, Athens' successes, especially that on Sphakteria, must have impressed Athens' allies as well: their would-be "liberator" had now been humiliated. Perhaps the majority of Athenians thought the victory was sufficient to cow the allies into greater obedience and compliance with their obligations, indeed, even increased ones. But shortly thereafter, in 424, the tables turned when Brasidas succeeded in wooing away a number of subject cities in the north, most important of which was Amphipolis, and Athens' attention was focused once again on revolts. It is not likely that the allies would have obediently met their (increased) financial obligations to the city. One of the most unfortunate losses in the epigraphic evidence is the record of quota for the years immediately following the reassessment; in fact, for the remainder of the 420s, nothing survives that could have indicated the success of the measure.

Arguments from silence are by themselves not compelling; but it has always caused some discomfort to scholars that Aristophanes is silent on a spectacular increase in tribute, given his penchant for exploiting the financial aspect of Athens' empire to comic effect, especially in the *Knights* and *Wasps*, and frequently in connection with Kleon, who may well have had a hand in the assessment of 425.[26] In particular, the absence of any allusion to the decree in the *Knights* of 424 is noteworthy. Thus, considering the topicality of Aristophanes' plays and his fondness for using as fodder for slander and humor the financial aspect of the empire as it affected Athenian politics and society (in particular, the efforts of Athens' leaders to fill their pockets around reassessment time), it is a bit odd, to say the least, to find no specific mention of a spectacular increase in tribute. It is less peculiar if the increase was neither as dramatic nor as effective as commonly believed.

As for Thucydides' omission of the assessment, we saw earlier the tenuousness of the position that we should expect to find explicit mention of a reassessment in the *History*: the only time he explicitly refers to an assessment is at its first occurrence, in 1.96. If the assessment of 425 was the highest yet, there is still no reason to expect Thucydides to mention it; he was not interested in decisions (in this case, assessments) per se. Only if the decree had in fact been effective—causing tribute to reach its highest peak and making an important impact on Athens' resources—would it be surprising to find no allusion to it in the text.

26. E.g., references to Kleon in connection with tribute: *Knights* 311–12; embezzlement and bribery: *Acharnians* 6; *Knights* 435–36, 438, 834–35; *Wasps* 759; general association with finances of empire: *Knights* 773ff., 801ff., 1070–17. Cf. also, on tribute generally, e.g., *Wasps* 670–71, 707, 1100–1101.

The reassessment of 425 was unexceptional if it was less dramatic than a doubling or trebling of the previous assessment; if it was as extraordinary an increase as usually presumed, then it was a striking piece of propaganda, testifying to and symbolizing the *dunamis* of Athens, a monument serving to bolster Athens' self-image and Athenian identity rather than a solid piece of realistic wartime financial planning.[27] However we interpret the significance of the decree of 425, underlying its passage is the growing problem of the proportion of revenue derived from tribute. The dispatch of the money-collecting expeditions may also signify trouble and point to a further method designed to offset a decline in tribute. The indications and evidence we have been exploring lead to the distinct possibility that tribute was becoming an insufficient source of cash for Athens. Thucydides' frequent attention to tribute earlier in the work, manifest in 1.96 and in discussions of arrangements imposed on the allies, contrasts with his relative silence about tribute in writing about the course of the Archidamian War. Indeed, the implications in his work about the declining reliability and importance of tribute as a form of revenue compared to the prewar years and the corresponding attention to other types of imperial revenue should be taken as an intentional and significant reflection of the historical reality of Athens' financial condition during the war.[28]

The general and, to some extent, expected difficulty in collecting tribute and the resulting decline in its usefulness as the chief source of imperial revenue are both explicit and implicit in the evidence under our purview. Does the evidence, however, signify that the total of imperial revenue was declining? More important, does it support the view that the Athenian treasuries were virtually drained in the course of the Archidamian War? We need to consider this second question before turning to the first.

An important piece of evidence for this question is the accounts of the Logistai, from the years 433–423. The inscription recording these ac-

27. Inscriptions as Athenian monuments helping to foster civic identity may be added to the institutions and monuments discussed by Hölscher, "City of Athens: Space, Symbol, Structure."

28. Yet even if tribute was declining in real importance, in another respect it retained its previous significance: for at the same time that it seems to have been a decreasingly reliable source of imperial income, its symbolic significance as a sign of *douleia*, brought up several times in speeches in Thucydides preceding the war (e.g., 1.80.3, 121.5) likely persisted throughout the war (cf. *Knights*, passim; *Peace* 621; cf. also Isok. *Panath*. 63; Plut. *Kim.* 11). There are, consequently, two distinct levels on which the issue of tribute is manifest in Thucydides' account of the war. They are, however, intimately related; it is doubtful that, without the persistence of the pejorative connotations of *phoros*, the collection of tribute would have been such a serious problem.

counts, *IG* I³ 369, reveals extensive borrowings from the sacred treasuries and has been largely responsible for the view that Athens depleted its financial resources during the Archidamian War. If correct, it has important implications for our assessment of Perikles' strategy in the conduct of the war as well as for the statesman's optimistic judgment about Athens' financial ability to succeed in a long struggle. The question is whether the conclusion is warranted. What precise information can we glean from the document, and what inferences can we safely draw?

Before addressing these questions, let us establish the extent of the body of evidence by which to estimate total reserve and revenue and therefore to judge the effect of the borrowings attested in the Logistai inscription: first, we have Perikles' totals of revenue and reserve in 2.13.3–5; no continuing record exists of total revenue accruing to the state from domestic sources and abroad, and no record of total reserve in the various treasuries for the period in question (or any period). Second, we have the Logistai's accounts, presenting evidence of outstanding loans in 423 dating back to 433. Finally, we have Thucydides' history of the Archidamian War.

What are the definite implications of heavy borrowing from the sacred treasuries of Athens? One clearly is the existence of substantial coined reserves to enable loans of this scale, and this accords with Thuc. 2.13. Further, the extensive borrowing corroborates in specific terms the degree of expense necessitated by the war and demonstrated in the *History*. It is important to note that the Logistai inscription is not useful on the question of whether any repayments of loans between the years 433 and 426 occurred, although there are indications that none were repaid between 426 and 423.[29] Moreover, it casts no light on how much money came in to the sacred treasuries in the form of revenue (for example, rents on sacred land) or dedications. The picture, therefore, which emerges from this document is skewed: it is illuminating only in the area of expenditure but leaves us completely in the dark about income and reserve.

So much is clear. When we move to the level of interpretation, however, we reach less secure ground. The natural emphasis of the inscription on expenditure makes it tempting to infer a drastic depletion of the reserve in the sacred treasuries. However, since we have only half of the picture, we cannot fairly arrive at such a conclusion without other support. Another approach to the significance of these loans is required, beginning with these questions: Why did the Athenians have such recourse to loans in the Archidamian War? Does such activity betoken a

---

29. Kallet-Marx, *CQ* 39 (1989):102–3.

dearth of other funds in some "war chest"? Is it correct to assume financial strain? Answers to these queries may lie in the realm of attitudes as much as economic practice—indeed, the two are surely linked.

In the modern world, it is customary to assume that the presence of loans denotes insufficient funds from the borrower's usual source. Yet it is a mistake to apply this assumption to ancient Athens or other Greek cities, where recourse to loans was a regular, normal practice, not a last resort.[30] Most important, the funds available in the sacred treasuries were those which the Athenians normally, though not exclusively,[31] used in wartime because these repositories held the majority of Athens' wealth, receiving annual revenue from various sources. That withdrawals from the sacred treasuries were a regular form of financing is clear from Thuc. 2.13 as well as from the epigraphic evidence of payments from these sources.[32] At the beginning of the Peloponnesian War, virtually all of the sacred treasure belonging to almost all of the gods and goddesses of Athens and Attica was housed on the Akropolis, concentrated there on the motion of Kallias (*IG* I³ 52A). As Perikles made clear to the Athenians (Thuc. 2.13.3–5), money in the treasuries was to be used by the Athenians in the coming struggle; one of the reasons for centralizing the treasures was to have an immediately accessible reserve continually supplemented by income, to meet the ensuing expenditures. The idea of the loan is necessary, for the treasures properly belonged to the gods. The central point is that these were the Athenians' own gods, and the money was the Athenians'.

Since we do not have any details about precise amounts under the control of the Hellenotamiai in any given year, nor total income beyond the evidence of 2.13.3–5, nor proportions of available moneys in the various treasuries, sacred and "imperial," that is, tribute, we cannot be specific about the state of the reserve in the course of the Archidamian War. We can only be confident that loans do not imply lack of funds. There are other, more intriguing, issues that remain unanswerable: for example, the reasons underlying decisions to withdraw from one source or another and, in particular, for withdrawing from a sacred treasury rather than from the Hellenotamiai's fund. For there was clearly an element of choice involved.[33] This raises the further question of attitudes

---

30. Migeotte, *L'Emprunt*, 357.

31. I argue elsewhere, *CA* 8 (1989):252–66, that tribute except for the *aparche* was under the control of the Hellenotamiai in a separate fund from that of Athena's treasury.

32. Any conditions placed on certain expenditures do not vitiate this conclusion, e.g., the vote of ἄδεια in the second "Kallias Decree," *IG* I³ 52 B.16. The Athenians were accustomed to earmarking funds for specific purposes; see Andreades, *HGPF*, 366.

33. There are indications of borrowings from the treasury of Athena at a time when the Hellenotamiai had ready cash of their own available: see Wade-Gery, *CQ* 24 (1930):38; Ferguson, *Treasurers of Athena*, 153, 161–62.

toward interest.[34] Here we must draw a distinction between interest from exchange in private transactions and interest on loans from sacred treasuries and other public loans. Aristotle's repugnance at the idea of interest in private exchange stems from the misuse of money inherent in usury: money, he asserts, came into use as a necessary medium of exchange, not for the purpose of producing more money—so that the process begets "money, son of money." For Aristotle, this fell into the category of "unnatural" exchange (*Pol.* 1258 b3ff.).[35]

When we consider the question of the significance of interest on public loans, we lack any direct assessment of its purpose. Some scholars have argued that interest on loans was a way of discouraging recourse to sacred moneys, thus safeguarding the sacred funds against indiscriminate use.[36] For others, it may instead reflect normal practice or piety.[37] It is perhaps significant that in 2.13 there is no trace of religious scruples over the use of sacred moneys; Perikles only reminds the Athenians of the obligation to repay in full the forty talents of gold from the statue of Athena if they were ever so hard-pressed as to make use of it. Introducing the notion of piety into the concept of interest on sacred loans does not, however, require the idea of restraint; rather, it may be a natural development from gift exchange between the divine and human in which the loan/gift must be repaid with something with enhanced value. Indeed, surplus deposits in the fifth century were called "gifts."[38]

The existence of heavy borrowing, then, need not signify more than a normal method of financing, given that the moneys recorded in the inscription of the Logistai formed part of the city's reserve. But the document does attest to heavy expenditure, therefore returning us to the question of whether revenue was sufficient to offset such expenses. Were

---

34. See Millett, *Lending and Borrowing*, esp. 91–108.

35. There is a decidedly paradoxical flavor to Aristotle's discussion of the perversity of interest when he alludes explicitly to the meaning of the term τόκος, "offspring." Money that gives birth is unnatural, since it no longer corresponds to the value of the thing(s) for which it is the medium of exchange but becomes something with intrinsic value. Aristotle's ideas about money and profit reflect a profound ambivalence about money discernible in elite Athenian society, manifest in the scorn accorded moneymaking, trade, and commerce as professions and in the lavish expenditures of the wealthy as a form of *charis* in the attainment of power and prestige; see Davies, *Wealth*, esp. 88–114; cf. Connor, *New Politicians*, 151–63. For comparisons between Greek and Jewish attitudes toward interest, see Gordon, *Hist. of Political Economy* 14 (1982):406–26; see also Millett, *Lending and Borrowing*, 100–103.

36. So Stevenson, *JHS* 44 (1924):9; Gomme, *HCT* 2:435.

37. E.g., ML, p. 215; I take "normal practice" to convey a mechanical, purely economic transaction rather than a transaction with enhanced subjective value due to the fact that it was sacred wealth.

38. Andreades, *HGPF*, 368, n. 5.

the Athenian treasuries virtually depleted by the end of the Archidamian War?

By examining Thucydides' treatment of financial resources as a whole, we can obtain a considerably fuller and more diverse financial picture of the economic benefit that the Athenians derived from their *arche* than is usually appreciated. In questions of imperial finance, attention has usually focused on tribute, and Thucydides has not been thought to contribute much in this area. However, in conjunction with the evidence of the tribute quota lists, Thucydides' *History* provides a more accurate picture of Athenian public finance as it was affected by the empire. The historian attributes great importance to tribute in the development of the Athenian *arche,* and it is clear that at the beginning of the Peloponnesian War, tribute comprised the bulk of imperial revenue (2.13.3). But as we have seen, after the war broke out, the intake of tribute declined, for the reasons discussed above. What should not be overlooked or obscured, however, is that this decline may have been offset by other, additional types of revenue extracted from the empire, about which Thucydides provides valuable evidence, especially if, as seems likely, the alternate sources were relied upon to a greater extent than in the past. What other financial benefit have we observed in the *History* that would have gone into Athenian state coffers rather than into individual hands?

One of the most important examples is revenue from Amphipolis, for which Thucydides is our only source (4.108.1). He does not specify its nature, but it surely consisted largely of income from the gold and silver mines around Amphipolis. Nor does he specify its amount, except to make clear that it was substantial, since its loss accounted in part for the reaction in Athens upon hearing that Brasidas had gained control of Amphipolis. That the colony did not pay tribute but nevertheless supplied important revenue to the polis should alert us to the possibility that other colonies benefited the state as well as the individual colonists, whether or not they also paid tribute.[39] From the same northern area came additional revenue from mines, those on Thasos and on the mainland coast opposite the island, which came under Athenian control as a result of the successful suppression of the Thasian revolt in 463 (1.101.3); this revenue was over and above the estimated thirty talents which Thasos paid in tribute. The total income that could be generated from the mines around and on Thasos ranged from an impressive two hundred to three hundred talents per annum.[40]

39. E.g., Skyros, 1.98.2; Poteidaia, 2.70; cf. also 1.103.3, Naupaktos.

40. Hdt. 6.46. Of relevance is the case of Siphnos, an island so rich in both silver and gold mines (Hdt. 3.57–58; Paus. 10.11.2) that it was able to pay one hundred talents to the Samians upon their demand (Hdt. 3.57). The mines flooded sometime after the sixth cen-

Revenue of an unspecified nature additional to tribute is attested in Thucydides not just from Amphipolis but also farther east, from Ionia, which we learn of in the account of Alkidas' Aegean cruise after Mytilene fell, when some Ionians suggested that the Spartan general liberate Ionia, said to supply "the greatest revenue" to Athens (3.31.1). As the tribute record appears to show that Ionia's totals were rather low compared to other districts, this testimony, despite likely exaggeration, suggests the possibility that this area also supplied the empire considerable nontribute revenue. In the case of both Amphipolis and Ionia, specific reference to revenue (*prosodos*) suggests the regularity of money coming in to Athens, which therefore should be reckoned into the estimate of total income and reserve.

Also providing regular imperial revenue were rents from sacred lands throughout the empire, testimony of which appears in Thucydides for the island of Lesbos (3.50.2). Supplemental evidence as well as common sense confirms that these references in Thucydides to rents (as well as other revenue) are representative, not comprehensive;[41] they reveal a glimpse of the modes of exploitation rather than a panorama, but they allow important inferences about both the nature and extent of imperial revenue that reflect more accurately the economic picture.

Finally, we come to the category of sporadic revenues of which Thucydides provides important evidence, that, in some instances, can be supplemented by other evidence. For example, one quite restricted type was indemnities following the suppression of revolts, which enabled Athens to recoup the often extraordinary expense entailed by a naval siege. We learn that both Thasos and Samos were forced to bear the cost of the sieges against them (1.101.3, 1.117.3). Thucydides does not specify the costs involved, but an inscription recording the expenses of the operations against Samos shows that they amounted to nearly fifteen hundred talents.[42] We have seen, however, that the Athenians stopped imposing

---

tury (Paus. 10.11.2), divine retribution, so Pausanias notes, for the Siphnians' neglect of the gods. Herodotos in recounting the wealth from the mines does not mention any such catastrophe, and his silence led Frazer (ad loc.) to suggest a post-Herodotean date; this may be supported by recent geological work, for complete bibliography on which see Francis and Vickers, *JHS* 103 (1983):56; but on the problems of their proposed chronology on this basis, cf. Boardman, *JHS* 104 (1984):161–63; Cook, *JHS* 109 (1989):164–70. If indeed the mines were operative in the fifth century, we would have another example of likely financial exploitation by Athens over and above tribute, since extant fragments of the quota lists from 449, 447, 443, 440, and 432 suggest that Siphnos paid only three talents per annum. But this is far from certain.

41. See Osborne, *Chiron* 18 (1988):281–304, 323, on the leasing of public property and its lucrative nature: "In all of the cities examined property leasing [both public and private] was financially of very great importance" (323).

42. *IG* I³ 363; cf. Nepos *Timoth.* 1; Diod. 12.28; Isok. 15.111.

indemnities (or even tribute) on vanquished poleis during the Archidamian War and turned instead to other avenues of revenue raising. For example, they taxed themselves, an expedient that Thucydides states was first imposed at the time of the revolt of Mytilene, with the clear implication that the measure was repeated subsequently.[43] They also had periodic recourse to another method of raising money that is intriguing and important for the light it sheds on the nature of Athenian imperialism; it is also highly problematic. I refer to the money-collecting expeditions sent out—how often is unclear—to parts of the empire.

I argued in the last chapter that these expeditions were probably not connected with tribute, although most scholars make that association, following the editors of *ATL*.[44] Thucydides mentions such expeditions four times (2.69, 3.19.1, 4.50, 4.75), attesting to dispatches of varying sizes and numbers of generals, and to diverse locations lining the north and west coasts of the Aegean and into the Pontos. Two of the expeditions mentioned by Thucydides involved forays into the Karian hinterland, and this is important: it suggests that the money-collecting expeditions were directed not only at poleis and regions firmly within the *arche* but also beyond, and raises doubts about the hypothesis that the ships were on routine missions of collecting tribute or arrears. Furthermore, the manner in which Thucydides mentions these expeditions, sometimes casually or incidentally, other times with greater emphasis, points to the likelihood that these instances are representative, not comprehensive. What are the implications of these expeditions to collect money?

As we observed in the last chapter, the term ἀργυρολογία by itself conveys nothing about tribute but rather is a word which most often refers to extortions of money (and certainly is used in this sense later in Thucydides' work: 8.3.1).[45] Indeed, the money-collecting expeditions sent out by the Athenians look very much like a kind of state piracy, officially authorized and organized plundering raids. Among the fundamental types of brigandage in the ancient Greek world categorized and described by Garlan is one which is regulated and controlled by the state; in all the instances of this kind of piracy, he notes, "on constate donc un lien 'structurel' entre la piraterie et l'Etat: la piraterie y faisait plus ou moins figure d'institution publique, d'industrie d'Etat."[46] There are both

---

43. Cf. εἰσφοραί elsewhere in the empire: Poteidaia, [Arist.] *Oik.* 2.1347 a17–24; cf. also *IG* I³ 41.38, which appears to contain a reference to an εἰσφορά demanded of the Histiaians.
44. See above, pp. 160–64.
45. See Andreades, *HGPF*, 24; Lowry, *Archaeology of Economic Ideas*, 131. By contrast, a reference in *IG* I³ 34, lines 26–27, to tribute-collecting ships contains the phrase "swift triremes"; cf. Ar. *Knights* 1071.
46. Garlan, *DHA* 4 (1978):4. Cf. also Haas, *Historia* 34 (1985):29–46.

important differences and similarities between Garlan's typology and the Athenian money-collecting expeditions. In the former, the ruling authority or collective group, for example, the Illyrians or Kretans, is strong enough to exert control over and use to its own profit what otherwise reverts to a kind of "private enterprise." The remarkable feature in the case of the Athenian *arche* is a considerably more advanced stage of state piracy, authorized by the Athenian demos, and headed by Athenian generals. But the basic nature of the financial extortion and exploitation is consonant with that among peoples such as the Illyrians and Aitolians.

This leads us back to where we began in this study, Thucydides' Archaeology. There the historian accords great importance to naval piracy and its effectiveness, if unchecked, in acquiring great wealth; if checked, it pointed the way to the exploitation of resources by any ruler strong enough to turn the profits reaped by pirates into revenue for the extension of power. For Thucydides, as Garlan notes, piracy is tied directly to the affirmation of a "state power."[47] Thucydides' discussion of piracy makes it clear that he regarded it as a natural (though not necessarily commendable) development in the history of power, as indeed Aristotle in the *Politics* classed piracy as a natural mode of acquisition (1256 a37). This sort of attitude is hard for modern readers to reconcile with their construct of the advanced Athenians, operating an empire which gave legal rights to its subjects and which was so systematic in its approach as to seem, somehow, fair, rather than exerting power like some arbitrary despotism; but as Chester Starr has pointed out in his comments about modern attitudes to Athens' empire, we are grossly misled if we fail to recognize the predatory and oppressive nature of the *arche*.[48] The innovative system of exploitation and control that the Athenians developed in the course of the fifth century B.C., includes, then, a natural adoption and extension to the public sphere of the long traditional pursuit of piracy and plunder.

Let us return to the money-collecting expeditions. It is frustrating not to know whether money-collecting expeditions went out before, or only during, the Peloponnesian War; it would help us to assess whether they were prompted by special pressure or were simply a routine way of extracting as much as possible from the Aegean world under Athenian control, supplementing more regular imperial revenue such as tribute, rents, yield from mines, and so forth. If they were sent out only after the war began, then they suggest a response to special stress caused by war,

---

47. Garlan, *DHA* 4 (1978):10; Thucydides also links piracy to the development of collaborative but unequal power relationships between, first, pirate and needy, and later, stronger authority and weaker individuals and communities (1.5).

48. Starr, *CJ* 83 (1987/88):114–23.

of which we have seen signs in Thucydides. Certainly the expedition dispatched in 428 (3.19) was designed to meet a temporary emergency.

The idea of the state's extorting money from the empire on marauding expeditions may receive some support from Aristophanes. His attention to the financial resources of the empire, the venality of politicians, and the pervasiveness of a "money mentality" in Athenian politics and society as a direct result of the Athenian empire makes him a valuable source for evidence concerning financial matters. There are frequent allusions to extortive practices on the part of the state and its leaders that could apply solely to tribute itself, and certainly there is continual focus on tribute in the plays. But general references to and jokes about the extent to which Athens squeezed the empire for money (and other goods) may well include practices that went beyond the collection of tribute to other ways of extracting revenue.[49] Moreover, a passage in *Knights* (1070–71), which refers to the "money-collecting ships" that Paphlagon is continually requesting, identifies them as triremes which are called in an oracle "hound-foxes" (κυναλώπηξ, line 1069), because they are swift like a hound and the troops "scour the farms and eat the grapes." This allusion brings out nicely the plundering character of such expeditions; even if these "money-collecting ships" were involved in tribute collection, it is reasonable to suppose that piratical-type raids were common to them as well.

Thus, the scope and nature of imperial revenue cuts a wide swath, and it is through Thucydides' *History* that we are able to enrich our knowledge of the diverse methods of financial exploitation which the Athenians employed before and during the Peloponnesian War, the period in which his testimony has been most useful for highlighting a shift in financial and imperial policy. Such evidence as Thucydides provides has, of course, not gone unnoticed but generally has been appreciated only in individual instances and not accorded its cumulative weight and implications. We still cannot arrive at a total for revenue beyond tribute; nevertheless, we should not for that reason downplay its significance, and I have attempted to give it a proper balance alongside tribute. Together this combined revenue provides important indications that the Athenian treasuries were not seriously depleted at two crucial times in question, 428 and 422.

Despite the questionable decisions made after Perikles was gone, despite the Spartans' successes in the north, the Athenians' financial capability to wage war was not severely threatened, though the defection of

---

49. E.g., *Wasps* 520; cf. 924–25; *Knights* 773ff., 801ff., 839ff., *Peace* 639–40; for the courts or the threat of prosecution as a lucrative means of profit for politicians, see Ostwald, *Popular Sovereignty*, 210–11.

tributary states and the loss of revenue from Amphipolis caused substantial alarm. Nevertheless, there is no doubt that by 424, Athens' financial resources had been sharply cut into because of problems in compensating for lost revenue: no indemnities came in from the costly siege of Poteidaia or from Mytilene; on top of that, Amphipolis and other Thraceward poleis were lost, though some only temporarily. But it is noteworthy that Thucydides gives no hint that the treasury was exhausted, nor does he include financial insufficiency among the reasons for the decision first to make a truce and then to make peace with Sparta. It is of great relevance that the Athenians did not touch their "iron reserve" until after the Sicilian expedition. Moreover, as we have seen, the naval expeditions sent out just after a time when the treasury is assumed to have been gravely low (when the revolt of Lesbos occurred) were neither necessary to Athenian war strategy nor particularly modest in nature.[50] Finally, the continued expenditure on domestic building projects through the 420s is another important indication that the reserve had not reached a dangerous low, either in 428 or in 422.[51]

We have summarized the chief historical results to which this examination of Thucydides has led. Let us conclude by noting some of the other, more strictly historiographical, issues relating to Thucydides' treatment of financial resources, first, its value for understanding more fully the historian's portrayal of Perikles and his "successors."

Thucydides presented Perikles as being fully attuned to the extraordinary potential expense of the war; moreover, the historian's treatment of Perikles indicates his own approval of the statesman's understanding of finances and strategy, and he set out to confirm the accuracy of Perikles' πρόνοια and strategy with respect to Athens' financial resources in two ways: first, not by downplaying but by accurately emphasizing the great expense of the war; and, second, by implying that such expense was not unanticipated and that Athens had ample funds to meet it. At the same time, it is implicit in the *History* that both intelligent judgment and surplus financial resources were necessary. In the remaining years of the Archidamian War after Perikles' death in autumn 429, Thucydides presents a picture of Athens in some disarray, under the control of leaders who were unable to make intelligent use of the city's resources or to project accurately the city's financial needs in the war.

In short, Thucydides believed that Athens was now guided by men who lacked the foresight and judgment of Perikles, necessary qualities for handling something so critical to success as Athenian public finance. Nevertheless, he presents an implicit case that the city's financial re-

50. To Melos, with thirty ships, Thuc. 3.91; to Sicily, with twenty ships, Thuc. 3.86, 115.
51. Miles, *Hesp.* 58 (1989):227–35.

sources were extensive enough even to withstand poor judgment, at least during the Archidamian War. Therefore, passages in which the historian specifically draws attention to financial strictures do not signify serious financial problems; they are rather intended to create a general impression of financial trouble and mismanagement. The historian does not castigate explicitly but allows the reader to judge various measures with an awareness informed by his presentation of Perikles' financial strategy, acumen, and *pronoia*, and by his treatment of the role of financial resources in general. The historian's attitude toward Perikles, thus, is revealed through his analysis of financial resources in the war.

Thucydides' treatment of Athenian financial resources constitutes almost an apologia for the statesman who was generally held responsible for what became the most devastating event in Athens' history. This does not mean that the historian's analysis of Athenian finances should be discounted: rather, his attention to this aspect reveals a desire to explain, to provide evidence for his confidence in Perikles' foresight. Beyond that, Thucydides' analysis helps to clarify and indeed to refine our understanding of his objections to Athenian leaders after Perikles' death. His judgment of their inferiority to Perikles in their management of affairs and in their relationship to the demos is obvious in a general way; but we have been able to point out more specifically one area of disapproval, that is, the political decisions under their leadership which gave higher priority to individual interests and benefits than to the safeguarding of the city's surplus and imperial revenue.

The Spartans, too, were targets of Thucydides' censure in the course of his narrative of the Archidamian War. He argues implicitly that the Spartans failed to grasp one of the most important and basic lessons that he imparts in his *History*, namely, the significance of *chremata* to the war. Before the war began, Archidamos explained it to them in the most elementary terms, yet at the time his words had no effect. Even though they lacked sufficient financial resources, they voted to go to war anyway, and Thucydides remarks on the relative speed with which the Spartans made their preparations, while the Athenians had been building up and consolidating their own resources for almost fifty years.[52] The Korinthians understood Archidamos' arguments, but nevertheless, the Peloponnesians under Spartan leadership failed to effect a strategy which would deprive Athens of its revenue or increase their own until 424, when Brasidas marched north to Thrace with the express intention of terminating Athens' profit from its *arche*. Thucydides repeatedly draws attention to the Spartans' difficulty in meeting the demands of the new kind

---

52. 1.125.2; see above pp. 91–93.

of war in which they were involved and their basic ignorance about the role of financial resources in it.[53]

Finally, let us summarize Thucydides' essential contribution to the history of ideas and the historiographical tradition. The historian's treatment of financial resources forms part of his interpretation and analysis of *dunamis*. He contests and rejects ideas about wealth and its relation to "state power" that had persisted since Homer, demonstrating a conspicuous lack of interest in the morality of profits and prosperity; rather, his concrete analysis focuses on the role that money played in the development of *dunamis, auxesis*, and naval *arche*. He argues in effect that the rise and fall of naval empires depend upon monetary flow, from revenue to reserve to expense (*prosodos, periousia chrematon*, and *dapane*), and not upon hubris or fate, not, that is, upon the gods or abstract moral forces governed and manipulated by them; nor, in turn, on the physical prowess, courage, and technical ability of a soldier. To Thucydides, *dunamis* had decisive, concrete components: as Perikles put it, *dunamis* was something the Athenians could actually see (2.43.1); it was partly composed of talents on the Akropolis and ships in the Piraieus, with the importance of the former lying exclusively in its expenditure on the fleet. *Dunamis*, therefore, was something tangible and mortal, susceptible to precise and concrete definition.[54]

Thucydides' treatment of the role of financial resources in his *History* through the end of the Archidamian War constitutes, in its breaking away from a long and venerable tradition of ideas about wealth and power, a central aspect of his originality as a historical analyst. He does not stand alone among his contemporaries in recognizing the significance of money to naval power; Athens' exploitation of the wealth of the empire as a crucial key to the city's *dunamis* was patent to every Athenian and was clearly "in the air" in discussions preceding the outbreak of war (in Sparta as well as Athens). Rather, he was the first to formulate in writing a fundamentally new definition of the relation of wealth to power; his rejection of traditional concepts of possession and display as a measure of power and worth would have clashed not only with earlier

---

53. They heeded Sthenelaidas rather than Archidamos, 1.87; their embassies to Persia failed either to get there (2.67) or, more damaging, to make their wishes clear (4.50.1–2); they failed to follow the Mytilenaians' advice upon meeting with resistance (3.13–16); they failed to effect a revolt of Ionia when presented with an easy opportunity (3.30–32); the eventual expedition to foster revolt in the north was led by Brasidas "on his own wishes," i.e., not as a result of changing strategy to combat the Athenians more effectively by depriving them of revenue (4.81.1); finally, they thought that they could wrap up the war within a few years, (5.14.3), and it is implicit that they expected to do so using conventional strategy.

54. As I have suggested above, however, *arche* was much harder to define.

but also with prevailing aristocratic values, which placed great emphasis on display as well as expenditure. Thucydides' contribution to the history of thought about power extends to his exploration into the very nature of sea power and its intrinsic superiority to land power, which forms a part, I suggested, of his "truest explanation" of the need for war; underlying his ideas about sea power may be a sense of the potential for the limitless extension of power that occurs when money becomes the enabling force behind military might.[55] Thus, Thucydides' work, especially his treatment of financial resources, reveals the tension between discordant values and mentalities between Athens and Sparta and within Athens itself, and between traditional and new attitudes to the way that military power is achieved and projected, all of which permeate the social, political, and military fabric of late fifth-century Greece.

55. This is an issue that I shall be examining more closely in the next project on Thucydides and financial resources.

ABBREVIATIONS

ACGC   Kraay, C. M. *Archaic and Classical Greek Coins*. London, 1976.
AE   Meiggs, R. *The Athenian Empire*. Oxford, 1972.
AFD   Meritt, B. D. *Athenian Financial Documents*. Ann Arbor, 1932.
ATL   Meritt, B. D., H. T. Wade-Gery, and M. F. McGregor, eds. *The Athenian Tribute Lists*. Princeton, 1950.
ESHAG   Austin, M. M., and P. Vidal-Naquet. *Economic and Social History of Ancient Greece*. Berkeley and Los Angeles, 1977.
GMS   Parke, H. W. *Greek Mercenary Soldiers*. Oxford, 1933.
GSAW   Pritchett, W. K. *The Greek State at War*. Vols. 1–5. Berkeley and Los Angeles, 1971–91.
HCT   Gomme, A. W. *A Historical Commentary on Thucydides*. Vols. 1–3. Oxford, 1950–56.
HGPF   Andreades, A. M. *A History of Greek Public Finance*. Translated by C. N. Brown. Cambridge, Mass., 1933.
LSJ   Liddell, H. G., and R. Scott. *A Greek-English Lexicon*. 9th ed. Revised by H. S. Jones. Oxford, 1968.
ML   Meiggs, R., and D. M. Lewis, eds. *Greek Historical Inscriptions to the End of the Fifth Century B.C.* Rev. ed. Oxford, 1988.
OPW   Ste. Croix, G. E. M. de. *The Origins of the Peloponnesian War*. London, 1972.
PPHT   Hunter, V. *Past and Process in Herodotos and Thucydides*. Princeton, 1982.
PPT   Allison, J. W. *Power and Preparedness in Thucydides*. Baltimore, 1989.
RCAG   Malkin, I. *Religion and Colonization in Ancient Greece*. Leiden, 1987.
TAI   de Romilly, J. *Thucydides and Athenian Imperialism*. Oxford, 1963.

BIBLIOGRAPHY

Adcock, F. E. "On Thucydides III, 17," *Cambridge Historical Journal* 1 (1923–25):319–22.
———. "Alcidas ἀργυρολόγος." *Mélanges Gustave Glotz* 1, 1–6. Paris, 1932.
———. "The Archidamian War, 431–404 B.C." *Cambridge Ancient History*, vol. 5, 193–253. Cambridge, 1940.
Alexander, J. A. *Potidaea: Its History and Remains*. Atlanta, 1963.
Allison, J. W. "ΠΑΡΑΣΚΕΥΗ. Process-product Ambiguity in Thucydides VI." *Hermes* 109 (1981):118–23.
———. "Pericles' Policy and the Plague." *Historia* 32 (1983):14–23.
———. "Sthenelaidas' Speech: Thucydides 1.86." *Hermes* 112 (1984):9–16.
———. *Power and Preparedness in Thucydides*. Baltimore, 1989. (= *PPT*)
Amit, M. *Athens and the Sea*. Brussels, 1965.
———. "The Athenian Empire in Asia Minor." *SCI* 2 (1975):38–72.
Ampolo, C. "I contributi alla prima spedizione ateniese in Sicilia (427–404 A.C.)." *PP* 42 (1987):5–11.
Anderson, J. K. *Military Theory and Practice in the Age of Xenophon*. Berkeley and Los Angeles, 1970.
———. "Hoplite Weapons and Offensive Arms." In *Hoplites: The Classical Greek Battle Experience*, edited by V. D. Hanson, 15–37. London, 1991.
Andreades, A. M. *A History of Greek Public Finance*. Translated by C. N. Brown. Cambridge, Mass., 1933. (= *HGPF*)
Andrewes, A. "Thucydides on the Causes of the War." *CQ* n.s. 9 (1959):223–39.
———. "The Mytilene Debate: Thucydides 3.36–49." *Phoenix* 16 (1962):64–85.
Arnold, T. *Thucydides*. 2 vols. Oxford, 1840.
Atmore, A. E. "The Extra-European Foundations of British Imperialism: Toward a Reassessment." In *British Imperialism in the Nineteenth Century*, edited by C. C. Eldridge, 106–25. London, 1984.
Austin, M. M., and P. Vidal-Naquet. *Economic and Social History of Ancient Greece: An Introduction*. Berkeley and Los Angeles, 1977. (= *ESHAG*)

Aymard, A. "Le partage des profits de la guerre dans les traités d'alliance antiques." *Revue historique* 217 (1957):233–49. (= *Etudes d'histoire ancienne*. Paris, 1967, 499–512)
Badian, E. "Thucydides on Rendering Speeches," *Athenaeum* 80 (1992): 187–90.
Balcer, J. M. *Sparda by the Bitter Sea*. Brown Judaic Studies 52. Chico, Calif., 1984.
Bar-Hen, E. "les sens divers du mot δύναμις chez Thucydide." *SCI* 2 (1975): 73–82.
Baudrillard, P. *Pour une critique de l'économie politique du signe*. Paris, 1972.
Bauman, R. "A Message for Amphipolis." *AClass* 11 (1968):170–81.
———. *Political Trials in Ancient Greece*. London, 1990.
Bauslaugh, R. A. *The Concept of Neutrality in Classical Greece*. Berkeley and Los Angeles, 1991.
Beloch, K. J. *Griechische Geschichte* 2.2. Strassburg, 1916.
Biraschi, A. M. "L'auxesis 'diversa' dell'Attica. A proposito di Tucidide I 2, 6." *PP* 39 (1984):5–22.
Bizer, F. *Untersuchungen zur Archäologie des Thukydides*. Tübingen, 1937.
Blackman, D. "The Athenian Navy and Allied Contributions in the Pentekontaetia." *GRBS* 10 (1969):179–216.
Bloedow, E. F. "The Speeches of Archidamus and Sthenelaidas at Sparta." *Historia* 30 (1981):129–43.
———. "Archidamus the 'Intelligent' Spartan." *Klio* 65 (1983):27–49.
———. "Sthenelaidas the Persuasive Spartan." *Hermes* 115 (1987):60–66.
———. "Athens' Treaty with Corcyra: A Study in Athenian Foreign Policy." *Athenaeum* 79 (1991):185–210.
Boardman, J. "*Signa tabulae priscae artis*." *JHS* 104 (1984):161–63.
Boeckh, A. *The Public Economy of the Athenians*. Translated by A. Lamb. Boston, 1857.
Boersma, J. S. *Athenian Building Policy from 561/0 to 405/4 B.C.* Groningen, 1970.
Bogaert, R. *Banques et banquiers dans les cités grecques*. Leyden, 1968.
Boulding, K., and T. Mukerjee, eds. *Economic Imperialism*. Ann Arbor, 1972.
Bourdieu, P. *Outline of a Theory of Practice*. Translated by R. Nice. Cambridge, 1981.
Brunt, P. A. "Spartan Policy and Strategy in the Archidamian War." *Phoenix* 19 (1965):255–80.
———. "Athenian Settlements Abroad in the Fifth Century B.C." In *Ancient Society and Institutions: Studies Presented to Victor Ehrenberg*, edited by E. Badian, 71–92. New York, 1967.
Busolt, G. *Griechische Geschichte* 3.2. Gotha, 1904.
Busolt, G., and H. Swoboda. *Griechische Staatskunde* 2. Munich, 1926.
Canfora, L. "La Préface de Thucydide et la critique de la raison historique." *REG* 90 (1977):455–61.
Carradice, I., ed. *Coinage and Administration in the Athenian and Persian Empires*. BAR International Series 37. Oxford, 1987.
Cawkwell, G. "Thucydides' Judgment of Periclean Strategy." *YCS* 24 (1975): 53–70.
Centre Nationale de la Recherche Scientifique. *Armées et fiscalité dans le monde antique*. Paris, 1977.

Chambers, M. "Four Hundred Sixty Talents." *CP* 53 (1958):26–32.
———. "Studies on Thucydides, 1957–1962." *CW* 57 (1963):6–14.
Classen, J. *Thukydides*. Berlin, 1873.
Classen, J., and J. Steup. *Thukydides*. Berlin, 1963.
Cogan, M. *The Human Thing*. Chicago, 1981.
Connor, W. R. *The New Politicans of Fifth-Century Athens*. Princeton, 1971.
———. "Tyrannis Polis." In *Ancient and Modern. Essays in Honor of Gerald F. Else*, edited by J. H. D'Arms and J. W. Eadie, 95–109. Ann Arbor, 1977.
———. *Thucydides*. Princeton, 1984.
———. "Narrative Discourse in Thucydides." In *The Greek Historians: Literature & History Papers Presented to A. E. Raubitschek*, edited by M. Jameson, 1–17. Stanford, 1985.
Cook, J. M. "The Problem of Classical Ionia." *PCPS* n.s. 7 (1961):9–18.
Cook, R. M. "The Francis-Vickers Chronology." *JHS* 109 (1989):164–69.
Cornford, F. M. *Thucydides Mythistoricus*. Reprint edition. Philadelphia, 1971.
Davies, J. K. *Wealth and the Power of Wealth in Classical Athens*. Salem, N.H., 1981.
Delbrück, H. *Die Strategie des Perikles*. Berlin, 1890.
Donlan, W. "Scale, Value, and Function in the Homeric Economy." *AJAH* 6 (1981):101–17.
Dover, K. J. "The Palatine Manuscript of Thucydides." *CQ* 4 (1954):76–83.
Doyle, M. W. *Empires*. Ithaca, 1986.
Eddy, S. K. "Four Hundred Sixty Talents Once More." *CP* 63 (1968):184–95.
Ehrenberg, V. *Aspects of the Ancient World*. Oxford, 1946.
———. "Thucydides on Athenian Colonization." *CP* 47 (1952):143–49.
Eldridge, C. C., ed. *British Imperialism in the Nineteenth Century*. London, 1984.
Ellis, J. R. "Thucydides at Amphipolis." *Antichthon* 12 (1978):28–35.
Emlyn-Jones, C. J. *The Ionians and Hellenism: A Study of the Cultural Achievement of the Early Greek Inhabitants of Asia Minor*. London, 1980.
Erbse, H. "Zur Geschichtsbetrachtung des Thukydides." *AA* 10 (1961):19–34.
———. "Über das Prooimion (1, 1–23) des thukydideischen Geschichtswerkes." *RhM* 113 (1970):43–69.
Ferguson, W. S. "Causes of Wars in Ancient Greece." *AHA* (1915):113–21.
———. "Athenian War Finance." *Proc. Mass. Hist. Soc.* 64 (1930–32):347–63.
———. *The Treasurers of Athena*. Cambridge, Mass., 1932.
Finley, J. H., Jr. *Thucydides*. Cambridge, Mass., 1942.
———. *Three Essays on Thucydides*. Cambridge, Mass., 1967.
Finley, M. I. *The Ancient Economy*. 2d ed. Berkeley and Los Angeles, 1985.
———. *The Use and Abuse of History*. London, 1975.
———. "The Ancient City: From Fustel de Coulanges to Max Weber and Beyond." *Comp. Stud. in Soc. and Hist.* 19 (1977):305–27. (= *Economy and Society in Ancient Greece*, 3–23.)
———. *The World of Odysseus*. New York, 1977.
———. "The Fifth-Century Athenian Empire: A Balance Sheet." In *Imperialism in the Ancient World*, edited by P. D. A. Garnsey and C. R. Whittaker, 103–26. Cambridge, 1978. (= *Economy and Society*, 41–61.)
———. *Economy and Society in Ancient Greece*. London, 1981.
———. *Ancient History: Evidence and Models*. New York, 1986.

Fliess, P. J. *Thucydides and the Politics of Bipolarity.* Nashville, 1966.
Fornara, C. W. "The Date of the Callias Decrees." *GRBS* 11 (1970):185–96.
———. *Herodotus.* Oxford, 1971.
———. "*IG* I² 39.52–57 and the 'Popularity' of the Athenian Empire." *CSCA* 10 (1977):39–56.
———. *The Nature of History in Ancient Greece and Rome.* Berkeley and Los Angeles, 1983.
Francis, E. D., and M. J. Vickers. "*Signa priscae artis:* Eretria and Siphnos." *JHS* 103 (1983):49–67.
Francotte, H. *Les finances des cités grecques.* Rome, 1964.
French, A. "The Tribute of the Allies." *Historia* 21 (1972):1–20.
———. "Athenian Ambitions and the Delian Alliance." *Phoenix* 33˙ (1979):134–41.
———. "Thucydides and the Power Syndrome." *G&R* 27 (1980):22–30.
———. "The Guidelines of the Delian Alliance." *Antichthon* 22 (1988):12–25.
Fried, S. "The Decadrachm Hoard: An Introduction." In *Coinage,* edited by I. Carradice, 1–20. BAR International Series 37. Oxford, 1987.
Frost, F. *Plutarch's Themistocles.* Princeton, 1980.
Gabba, E. "True History and False History." *JRS* 71 (1981):50–62.
Garlan, Y. *Recherches de poliorcétique grecque.* Paris, 1974.
———. *War in the Ancient World.* Translated by J. Lloyd. London, 1975.
———. "Signification historique de la piraterie grecque." *DHA* 4 (1978):1–16.
———. *Guerre et économie en Grèce ancienne.* Paris, 1989.
Garland, R. "A First Catalogue of Attic Peribolos Tombs." *BSA* 77 (1988):125–76.
Gauthier, P. "Les clérouques de Lesbos et la colonisation athénienne au Vᵉsiècle av. J-C." *REG* 79 (1966):64–88.
Giovannini, A., and G. Gottlieb. "Thukydides und die Anfänge der athenischen Arche." *SBHeidelberg,* Phil.-Hist. Klasse, no. 7 (1980):7–45.
———. "Le Parthénon, le trésor d'Athéna et le tribut des alliés." *Historia* 39 (1990):129–48.
Gomme, A. W. *A Historical Commentary on Thucydides.* Vols. 1–3. Oxford, 1950–1956. (= *HCT*)
———. "*IG* I² 60 and Thucydides III 50.2." *Studies Presented to David Moore Robinson* 2, edited by E. Mylonus and D. Raymond, 334–39. St. Louis, 1953.
———. "Thucydides ii 13,3." *Historia* 2 (1953/54):1–21.
———. *The Greek Attitude to Poetry and History.* Berkeley and Los Angeles, 1954.
Goodman, M. D., and A. J. Holladay. "Religious Scruples in Ancient Warfare." *CQ* 36 (1986):151–71.
Gordon, B. "Lending at Interest: Some Jewish, Greek and Christian Approaches, 800 B.C.–A.D. 100." *Hist. of Political Economy* 14 (1982):406–26.
Graham, A. J. *Colony and Mother City in Ancient Greece.* 2d ed. Chicago, 1983.
———. "Thucydides 7.13.2 and the Crews of Athenian Triremes." *TAPA* 122 (1992):257–70.
Griffith, J. G. "A Note on the First Eisphora at Athens." *AJAH* 2 (1977):3–7.
Grundy, G. B. *Thucydides and the History of His Age.* 2 vols. Oxford, 1948.
Haas, C. "Athenian Naval Power before Themistocles." *Historia* 34 (1985):38–39.

Hammond, N. G. L. "The Arrangement of Thought in the Proem and Other Parts of Thucydides I." *CQ* n.s. 2 (1952):127–41.
———. "The Origins and the Nature of the Athenian Alliance of 478/7 B.C." *JHS* 87 (1967):41–61.
———. *A History of Macedonia*. Vol. 1. Oxford, 1972.
Hammond, N. G. L., and G. T. Griffith. *A History of Macedonia*. Vol. 2. Oxford, 1979.
Hanson, V. D. *Warfare and Agriculture in Classical Greece*. Pisa, 1983.
———. *The Western Way of War*. New York, 1989.
———, ed. *Hoplites: The Classical Greek Battle Experience*. London, 1991.
Herskovits, M. J. *Economic Anthropology*. New York, 1952.
Highby, L. I. *The Erythrae Decree*. Klio Beiheft 36. Leipzig, 1936.
Höck, A. "Das Odrysienreich im fünften und vierten Jahrhundert v. Chr." *Hermes* 26 (1891):76–117.
Hölscher, T. "The City of Athens: Space, Symbol, Structure." In *City States in Classical Antiquity and Medieval Italy*, edited by A. Molho, K. Raaflaub, and J. Emlen, 355–80. Stuttgart, 1991.
Holladay, A. J. "Athenian Strategy in the Archidamian War." *Historia* 27 (1978):399–427.
Holladay, A. J., and M. D. Goodman. "Religious Scruples in Ancient Warfare.," *CQ* 36 (1986):151–71.
Hornblower, S. *The Greek World, 479–323*. London, 1983.
———. *A Commentary on Thucydides*. Vol. 1. Oxford, 1991.
How, W. W., and J. Wells. *A Commentary on Herodotus*. 2 vols. Oxford, 1928.
Huart, P. "Les événements de l'année 429 dans l'histoire de Thucydide." *AFLN* 35 (1979):83–108.
Hude, C. *Thucydides Historiae*. 2 vols. Leipzig, 1910.
Hunter, V. *Thucydides: The Artful Reporter*. Toronto, 1973.
———. "Thucydides and the Uses of the Past." *Klio* 62 (1980):191–218.
———. *Past and Process in Herodotos and Thucydides*. Princeton, 1982. (= *PPHT*)
Huxley, G. L. "Thucydides on the Growth of Athenian Power." *PRIA* 83 (1983):191–204.
Immerwahr, H. *Form and Thought in Herodotus*. Cleveland, 1966.
———. "Pathology of Power and the Speeches of Thucydides." In *The Speeches of Thucydides*, edited by P. Stadter, 15–31. Chapel Hill, 1973.
Jackson, A. H. "The Original Purpose of the Delian League." *Historia* 18 (1969):12–16.
Jacoby, F. *Atthis*. Oxford, 1949.
Jaeger, W. *Paideia*. Vol. 1. Oxford, 1939.
Jordan, B. "The Meaning of the Technical Term *Hyperesia* in Naval Contexts of the Fifth and Fourth Centuries B.C." *CSCA* 2 (1969):183–207.
———. *The Athenian Navy in the Classical Period*. University of California Publications: Classical Studies. Berkeley and Los Angeles, 1975.
Kagan, D. *The Outbreak of the Peloponnesian War*. Ithaca, 1969.
———. *The Archidamian War*. Ithaca, 1974.
Kagan, J. H. "The Decadrachm Hoard: Chronology and Consequences." In *Coinage*, edited by I. Carradice, 21–28. BAR International Series 37. Oxford, 1987.

Kallet-Marx, L. "Did Tribute Fund the Parthenon?" *CA* 8 (1989):252–66.
———. "The Kallias Decree, Thucydides, and the Outbreak of the Peloponnesian War." *CQ* 39 (1989):94–113.
Kelly, T. "Thucydides and Spartan Strategy in the Archidamian War." *AHR* 87 (1982):25–54.
Kennedy, P. *The Rise and Fall of British Naval Mastery*. London, 1976.
———. *The Rise and Fall of the Great Powers*. New York, 1987.
Kirchhoff, A. "Zur Geschichte des athenischen Staatsschatzes im fünften Jahrhundert." *Abh. der Königlichen Akad. der Wiss. zu Berlin* (1876/77).
Kitto, H. D. F. *Poiesis*. Berkeley and Los Angeles, 1966.
Kleingünther, A. ΠΡΩΤΟΣ ΕΥΡΕΤΗΣ. *Untersuchungen zur Geschichte einer Fragestellung*. New York, 1976.
Knight, D. W. "Thucydides and the War Strategy of Perikles." *Mnem.* 23 (1970):150–61.
Kraay, C. M. *Archaic and Classical Greek Coins*. London, 1976. (= *ACGC*)
Kurke, L. *The Traffic in Praise: Pindar and the Poetics of Social Economy*. Ithaca, 1991.
Larsen, J. A. O. "The Constitution and Original Purpose of the Delian League." *HSCP* 51 (1940):175–213.
Lenardon, R. J. "Thucydides and Hellanikos." In *Classical Contributions: Studies in Honour of Malcolm Francis McGregor*, edited by G. S. Shrimpton and D. J. McCargar, 59–70. Locust Valley, N.Y., 1981.
Lewis, D. M. "Toward an Historians' Text of Thucydides." Ph.D. diss., Princeton University, 1952.
———. "The Athenian Coinage Decree." In *Coinage*, edited by I. Carradice, 53–64. BAR International Series 37. Oxford, 1987.
———. "Public Property in the City." In *The Greek City*, edited by O. Murray and S. Price, 245–63. Oxford, 1990.
Linders, T. *The Treasurers of the Other Gods in Athens and Their Functions*. Meisenheim am Glan, 1975.
———. "Gifts, Gods, Society." In *Gifts to the Gods*, edited by T. Linders and G. Nordquist, 115–22. Boreas 15. Stockholm, 1987.
Lowry, S. T. *The Archaeology of Economic Ideas*. Durham, 1987.
Luppino, E. "La ξυμμαχία tra Atene e Sitalce: Un episodio del primo anno della guerra del Peloponneso (Thuc. II, 29, 1–7)." *RSA* 11 (1981):1–14.
McDonald, B. R. "Ληιστεία and λήζομαι in Thucydides and in *IG* I³ 41, 67, and 75." *AJP* 105 (1984):77–84.
McGregor, M. F. "Athenian Policy, at Home and Abroad." In *University of Cincinnati Classical Studies*, 53–84. Norman, 1973.
Macleod, C. M. "Reason and Necessity: Thucydides III 9–14, 37–48." *JHS* 98 (1978):64–78. (= *Collected Essays*. Oxford, 1983, 88–102.)
———. "Thucydides and Tragedy." In *Collected Essays*. Oxford, 1983, 140–58.
Mahan, A. T. *The Influence of Sea Power upon History, 1660–1783*. Boston, 1890.
Malkin, I. "What Were the Sacred Precincts of Brea? (*IG* I³ 46)." *Chiron* 14 (1984):43–48.
———. *Religion and Colonization in Ancient Greece*. Leiden, 1987. (= *RCAG*)
Marshall, M. H. B. "Urban Settlement in the Second Chapter of Thucydides." *CQ* 25 (1975):26–40.

Mattingly, H. B. "The Methone Decrees." *CQ* 11 (1961):154–65.
———. "The Financial Decrees of Kallias (*IG* I² 91/2)." *PACA* 7 (1964):35–55.
———. "Athenian Finance in the Peloponnesian War." *BCH* 92 (1968):450–85.
———. *AJP* 105 (1984): 355–57.
———, "The Athenian Coinage Decree and the Assertion of Empire," In *Coinage*, edited by I. Carradice, 65–72. BAR International Series 37. Oxford, 1987.
Mauss, M. *The Gift: Forms and Functions of Exchange in Archaic Societies*. Translated by I. Cunnison. London, 1970.
Meiggs, R. "The Crisis of Athenian Imperialism." *HSCP* 67 (1963):1–36.
———. *The Athenian Empire*. Oxford, 1972. (= *AE*)
Meiggs, R., and D. M. Lewis, eds. *Greek Historical Inscriptions to the End of the Fifth Century B.C.* Rev. ed. Oxford, 1988. (= ML)
Meritt, B. D. *Athenian Financial Documents*. Ann Arbor, 1932. (= *AFD*)
———. "Athenian Covenant with Mytilene." *AJP* 75 (1954):359–68.
———. "Indirect Tradition in Thucydides." *Hesperia* 23 (1954):185–231.
———. "Kleon's Assessment of Tribute to Athens." In *Classical Contributions. Studies in Honour of Malcolm Francis McGregor*, edited by G. S. Shrimpton and D. J. McCargar, 1983.
Meritt, B. D., H. T. Wade-Gery, and M. F. McGregor, eds. *The Athenian Tribute Lists*. Vol. 3. Princeton, 1950. (/*ATL*).
Meritt, B. D., and A. B. West. *The Athenian Assessment of 425 B.C.* Ann Arbor, 1934.
Merkelbach, R., and E. Varinlioglu. "Die Einwohnerzahl von Keramos." *ZPE* 59 (1985):264.
Meyer, E. *Forschungen zur alten Geschichte* 2. Halle, 1899.
———. *Geschichte des Altertums* 4. 5th ed. Basel, 1956.
Meyer, H. D. "Vorgeschichte und Gründung des delisch-attischen Seebundes." *Historia* 12 (1963):405–46.
Migeotte, L. *L'Emprunt public dans les cités grecques*. Quebec, 1984.
Mikalson, J. D. "Religion and the Plague in Athens." *GRBM* 10 (1984):217–25.
Miles, M. M. "A Reconstruction of the Temple of Nemesis." *Hesperia* 58 (1989):131–249.
Millett, P. *Lending and Borrowing in Ancient Athens*. Cambridge, 1991.
Momigliano, A. "Sea Power in Greek Thought." *CR* 58 (1944):1–7.
Müller-Strübing, H. *Thukydideische Forschungen*. Vienna, 1881.
Murray, O. "Ο ΑΡΧΑΙΟΣ ΔΑΣΜΟΣ." *Historia* 15 (1966):142–56.
Murray, O., and S. Price, eds. *The Greek City: From Homer to Alexander.* Oxford, 1990.
Nesselhauf, H. *Untersuchung zur Geschichte der delisch-attischen Symmachie*. Klio Beiheft 30. Leipzig, 1933.
Newman, W. L. *The Politics of Aristotle*. Vol. 1. Oxford, 1887.
Nixon, L., and S. Price. "The Size and Resources of Greek Cities." In *The Greek City*, edited by O. Murray and S. Price, 137–70. Oxford, 1990.
Ober, J. "Thucydides, Pericles, and the Strategy of Defense." In *The Craft of the Ancient Historian: Essays in Honor of Chester G. Starr*, edited by J. W. Eadie and J. Ober, 171–88. New York, 1985.
Oliver, J. H. "Thucydides II, 13, 3." *AJP* 79 (1958):188–90.

Osborne, R. "Social and Economic Implications of the Leasing of Land and Property in Classical and Hellenistic Greece." *Chiron* 18 (1988):279–323.
Ostwald, M. *Autonomia: Its Genesis and History.* Chico, Calif., 1982.
———. *From Popular Sovereignty to the Sovereignty of Law.* Berkeley and Los Angeles, 1986.
———. *ANAΓKH in Thucydides.* American Classical Studies 18. Atlanta, 1988.
Owen, R., and R. Sutcliffe, eds. *Studies in the Theory of Imperialism.* London, 1972.
Parke, H. W. *Greek Mercenary Soldiers.* Oxford, 1933. (= *GMS*)
Parke, H. W., and D. E. W. Wormell. *The Delphic Oracle.* 2 vols. Oxford, 1956.
Parker, R. *Miasma.* Oxford, 1983.
Parry, A. "Thucydides' Historical Perspective." *YCS* 22 (1972):47–61.
Parry, J., and M. Bloch, eds. *Money and the Morality of Exchange.* Cambridge, 1989.
Pearson, H. W. "The Economy Has No Surplus." In *Trade and Market in the Early Empires,* edited by K. Polanyi, C. M. Arensberg, and H. W. Pearson, 320–41. Glencoe, Ill., 1957.
Pearson, L. "Thucydides and the Geographical Tradition." *CQ* 33 (1939):48–54.
———. *The Local Historians of Attica.* Philadelphia, 1942.
Polanyi, K. "Aristotle Discovers the Economy." In *Trade and Market in the Early Empires,* edited by K. Polanyi, C. M. Arensburg, and H. W. Pearson, 64–94. Glencoe, Ill., 1957.
Pouncey, P. *The Necessities of War.* New York, 1980.
Pritchett, W. K. *The Greek State at War.* Vol. 1. Berkeley and Los Angeles, 1971. (= *Ancient Greek Military Practices* 1) (= *GSAW*)
———. *The Greek State at War.* Vol. 5. Berkeley and Los Angeles, 1991. (= *GSAW*)
Proctor, D. *The Experience of Thucydides.* Warminster, 1980.
Raaflaub, K. "Beute, Vergeltung, Freiheit? Zur Zielsetzung des delisch-attischen Seebundes." *Chiron* 9 (1979):1–22.
———. *Die Entdeckung der Freiheit.* Vestigia 37. Munich, 1985.
Rabel, R. J. "Agamemnon's Empire in Thucydides." *CJ* 80 (1984):8–10.
Rawlings, H. R., III. *A Semantic Study of Prophasis to 400 B.C.* Hermes Einzelschr. 33. Wiesbaden, 1975.
———. "Thucydides on the Purpose of the Delian League." *Phoenix* 31 (1977):1–8.
Redfield, J. M. "The Economic Man." In *Approaches to Homer,* edited by C. A. Rubino and C. W. Shelmerdine, 218–47. Austin, 1983.
Rhodes, P. J. "The Athenian Empire." *G&R New Surveys in the Classics* 17 (1985).
———, ed. *Thucydides, History II.* Warminster, 1988.
Ridley, R. T. "Exegesis and Audience in Thucydides." *Hermes* 109 (1981):25–46.
Roberts, J. T. *Accountability in Athenian Government.* Madison, 1982.
Robertson, N. D. "The True Nature of the Delian League." *AJAH* 5 (1980):64–96, 110–33.
Robinson, R. "Non-European Foundations of European Imperialism: Sketch for a Theory of Collaboration." In *Studies in the Theory of Imperialism,* edited by R. Owen and R. Sutcliffe, 117–40. London, 1972. (= "Collaboration")
Roisman, J. "Alkidas in Thucydides." *Historia* 36 (1987):385–421.
Rokeah, D. "Περιουσία χρημάτων: Thucydides and Pericles." *RFIC* 91 (1963):282–86.
Romilly, J. de. *Histoire et raison chez Thucydide.* Paris, 1956.

———. "La crainte dans l'oeuvre de Thucydide." *C&M* 17 (1956):119–27.
———. *Thucydides and Athenian Imperialism*. Translated by P. Thody. Oxford, 1963. (= *TAI*)
———. "L'optimisme de Thucydides et le jugement de l'historien sur Periclès (Thuc. II. 65)." *REG* 78 (1965):557–75.
———. "Thucydide et l'idée de progrès." *ASNP* 35 (1966):143–191.
———. *The Rise and Fall of States According to Greek Authors*. Ann Arbor, 1977.
Rubincam, C. R. "Qualifications of Numerals in Thucydides." *AJAH* 4 (1979): 78.
Ruschenbusch, E. "Tribut und Bürgerzahl im ersten attischen Seebund." *ZPE* 53 (1983):125–43.
———. "Das Machtpotential der Bundner im ersten attischen Seebund." *ZPE* 53 (1983):144–48.
———. "Modell Amorgos." In *Aux origines de l'hellénisme: La Crète et la Grèce. Hommage à Henri Van Effentere*. Paris, 1984, 265–71.
———. "Die Zahl der griechischen Staaten und Arealgröße und Bürgerzahl der 'Normalpolis'." *ZPE* 59 (1985):253–63.
Ste. Croix, G. E. M. de. *The Origins of the Peloponnesian War*. London, 1972. (= *OPW*)
Salmon, J. B. *Wealthy Corinth*. Oxford, 1984.
Sargent, R. L. "The Use of Slaves by the Athenians in Warfare II." *CP* 22 (1927):201–12.
Schneider, C. *Information und Absicht bei Thukydides*. Göttingen, 1974.
Schuller, W. *Die Herrschaft der Athener im ersten attischen Seebund*. Berlin, 1974.
Sealey, R. "P. Strassburg Verso." *Hermes* 86 (1958):440–46.
———. "The Origins of the Delian League." In *Ancient Society and Institutions: Studies Presented to Victor Ehrenberg*, edited by E. Badian, 233–55. Oxford, 1966.
———. "The Causes of the Peloponnesian War." *CP* 70 (1975):89–109.
———. "The Tetralogies Ascribed to Antiphon." *TAPA* 114 (1984):71–85.
Simmel, G. *The Philosophy of Money*. Translated by T. Bottomore and D. Frisby. London, 1978.
Snodgrass, A. M. *Archaic Greece*. London, 1980.
Spence, I. G. "Perikles and the Defence of Attika During the Peloponnesian War." *JHS* 110 (1990):91–109.
Spier, J. "Lycian Coins in the 'Decadrachm Hoard.'" In *Coinage*, edited by I. Carradice, 29–42. BAR International Studies 37. Oxford, 1987.
Stadter, P. "The Motives for Athens' Alliance with Corcyra (Thuc. 1.44)." *GRBS* 24 (1983):131–36.
———. *A Commentary on Plutarch's Pericles*. Chapel Hill, 1989.
Stahl, H.-P. *Thukydides. Die Stellung des Menschen im geschichtlichen Prozess*. Zetemata 40. Munich, 1966.
Stahl, J. M. "Zu Thukydides." *RhM* 27 (1872):278–83.
———. "Zu Thukydides." *RhM* 28 (1873):622–24.
Starr, C. G. "Athens and Its Empire." *CJ* 83 (1987/88):114–23.
Steup, J. "Ein Einschiebsel bei Thukydides." *RhM* 24 (1869):350–61.
———. "Noch einmal das angebliche Capitel III, 17 des Thukydides." *RhM* 27 (1872):637–40.

Stevenson, G. H. "The Financial Administration of Pericles." *JHS* 44 (1924): 1–9.
Strasburger, H. "Herodot und das perikleische Athen." *Historia* 4 (1955):1–25.
Stuart Jones, H. *Thucydidis Historiae.* 2 vols. Oxford, 1942.
Stupperich, R. *Staatsbegräbnis und Privatgrabmal im klassichen Athen.* Münster, 1977.
Täubler, E. *Die Archäologie des Thukydides.* Leipzig, 1927.
Thompson, W. E. "Notes on Athenian Finance." *C&M* 28 (1967):216–39.
———. "The Chronology of 432/1." *Hermes* 96 (1968):220–23.
Thomsen, R. *Eisphora.* Copenhagen, 1965.
Tuplin, C. "The Administration of the Achaemenid Empire." In *Coinage,* edited by I. Carradice, 109–66. BAR International Studies 37. Oxford, 1987.
Unz, R. K. "The Surplus of the Athenian Phoros." *GRBS* 26 (1985):21–42.
Vernant, J.-P., ed. *Problèmes de la guerre en Grèce ancienne.* Paris, 1968.
Vickers, M. "Metalwork and Athenian Painted Pottery." *JHS* 105 (1985):108–28.
Vidal-Naquet, P. "Temps des dieux et temps des hommes." *Revue de l'histoire des religions* 157 (1960):65–69.
Wade-Gery, H. T. "The Year of the Armistice, 423 B.C." *CQ* 24 (1930):33–39.
Wade-Gery, H. T., and B. D. Meritt. "Athenian Resources." *Hesperia* 26 (1957):163–97.
Walbank, M. B., "Leases of Sacred Properties in Attica, Part IV." *Hesperia* 52 (1983) 207–31.
Wallinga, H. T. "The Ionian Revolt." *Mnem.* 37 (1984):401–37.
West, A. B. "Pericles' Political Heirs, II." *CP* 19 (1924):201–28.
———. "Aristeidean Tribute in the Assessment of 421 B.C." *AJA* 29 (1925): 135–51.
———. "Cleon's Assessment and the Athenian Budget." *TAPA* 61 (1930): 217–39.
Westlake, H. D. *Essays on the Greek Historians and Greek History.* Manchester, 1969.
Winton, R. I. "Thucydides 1, 97, 2: The '*arche* of the Athenians' and the 'Athenian Empire.'" *MH* 38 (1981):147–52.
———. "Thucydides 1.99.1: A Conjecture." *Eranos* 80 (1982):171–72.
———. "Thucydides 1.19." *MH* 41 (1984):146–51.
Woodhead, A. G. "The Institution of the Hellenotamiai." *JHS* 79 (1959): 149–52.
———. "Thucydides' Portrait of Cleon." *Mnem.* 13 (1960):289–317.
———. *Thucydides on the Nature of Power.* Cambridge, Mass., 1970.
———. "West's Panel of Ship Payers." In *ΦΟΡΟΣ: Tribute to Benjamin Dean Meritt,* edited by D. W. Bradeen and M. F. McGregor, 170–78. Locust Valley, N.Y., 1974.
Ziegler, K. "Der Ursprung der Exkurse in Thukydides." *RhM* 78 (1929):58–67.

GENERAL INDEX

Acharnai, 110, 185
Achrematia, 28–30, 56
Acquisition. See *Ktesis*
Agamemnon, 27–30, 57–58; wealth and power of, 13, 28
Aigina/Aiginetans, 32, 68, 111, 122n33, 159
Akanthos, 171–72, 180–82
Akropolis, 101–3
Aktaian cities, 145, 147–48, 156, 157, 159
ἀληθεστάτη πρόφασις, 13n44, 15, 37, 39, 58, 86, 88, 107, 114–15, 206
Alkidas, 139–40, 156
Alliances: Athens with Sitalkes, 124–27; Delian League as, 44–45; Korinthian/Kerkyraian conflict, 77–78; land vs. naval, 44–45; Peloponnesian, 12, 33
Allies: Athens' *auxesis* and, 60–62, 81–89; Athens' in Macedonia and Thrace, 171–72; Athens' treatment of, 61, 65–66, 68, 180–82, 186–87; Delian League origins and, 40–42; financial obligations and, 44–47, 50, 52–54, 172; military service and, 64; motives of, 9–10, 53–54; revolts of, 60–61, 68, 78–80, 120, 127, 138–39, 172, 177; settlements with, 68, 120, 143–49, 186–87; as subjects, 182
Amphipolis, 141–42, 193; fall of, 172–76; as source of revenue, 175–76, 198
Andros, 141n87
Antandros, 156, 157, 160–61

Archaeology, 57–58, 201; financial resources in, 3; financial terminology and, 35–36; purpose of, 33–34, 37
Arche, 13, 15, 16, 19–20, 32, 43, 48, 56, 58, 68–69, 85, 88, 113, 148, 152, 190, 204; allies and, 39, 62, 64, 67; in Archaeology, 33–35; *chremata, nautikon* and, 3, 6, 28, 70, 143–44, 172, 175; *dapane* and, 67; definition of, 6; development of, 80–81; economic and/or financial benefits of, 8–9, 198, 201; establishment of, 59; financial exploitation of, 4, 198–202; Minos and, 25–27; motives of, 7–8; nature of, 10–15, 201; Perikles on, 114–17; threats to, 78–80; tyranny and, 30–31; wealth and, 7, 190, 198
Archidamian War, 4–5, 86–87, 182–83, 194–96, 200, 203–5
Archidamos, 80–87, 91, 94, 96, 128, 204
Argilos, 180
Argurion, 74, 122, 125, 126
Aristeides, 50–52, 180. See also *Phoros*, of Aristeides, first assessment of
Aristeides, general during Archidamian War, 154, 161
Aristophanes, 165–67, 193, 202; *Knights*, 193, 202; *Wasps*, 166–67
Aristotle, 17, 113, 197, 201
Arrabaios, 171
Artaphernes, 154
Artayktes, and sanctuary of Protesileos, 52–53

219

INDEX

Athens/Athenians: armistice with Sparta, 177–78; character of, 15–16, 58, 80, 116–17; compared with Sparta, 5–6, 81–89, 94–96, 160; development of, 32; development of *dunamis*, 40–43; financial health of, 128–29, 132–34, 180, 198–203; financial resources on eve of war, 96–107; leadership after Perikles, 117–20, 125, 136, 138, 146, 149–50, 186–90, 202–3; military might of in 428/7, 129–30; Peace of Nikias and, 178–83; relations with Thrace, 124–25
Atthidographers, 34
Autonomy, 180–82, 187
Auxesis, 23–24, 205; allies and, 60–62, 64, 67; centralization of money and, 55–56, 57; as part of cause of Peloponnesian War, 39; *phoros* and, 57; power and, 23–24, 38–39; *prosodos* and, 129

Booty, 11, 52–53
Brasidas, 137, 170–76, 193
Building, public, 42, 96, 121, 153–54

Chalkidike/Chalkidians, 111, 123, 124–25, 170, 171, 182
Charis, 9, 66; expenditure and, 113; moral aspects of, 19
Chios/Chians, 64n71, 155
Chremata/money, 32, 43, 44, 48–49, 53, 81, 93, 95, 120, 129, 133, 134, 155, 177, 204; Agamemnon and, 28–30; in Archaeology, 33–36; *arche* and, 3, 6, 143–44, 172, 175; Athens' and Sparta's compared, 81–89; definition/compositon of, 29–30, 35–36, 49, 84, 100, 163n26; development and, 23–24; *dunamis* and, 3, 6, 107; *eisphora* and, 134–36; Epidamnian colony and, 73–74; first assessment of *phoros* and, 49; Kerkyra and, 71–72; Minos and, 26–27; *nautikon* and, 3, 28, 30, 67, 70, 75, 76, 83, 89–90, 91, 110, 116, 117, 185; Perikles on, 112–13; *phoros* and, 100, 163; war and, 11–14, 75, 84–85, 175, 204. See also *Argurion; Dapane;* Financial resources; *Misthos; Periousia chrematon; Prosodos*
Civilization, development of, 23–24
Coinage Decree, 158
Coined money, 36, 73–74, 96, 195; first assessment of *phoros* and, 50. See also *Argurion*
Colony/colonization: of Amphipolis, 173; metropolis/colony/founder relationship, 71–72; Minos and, 25–26; in Pentekontaetia, 60; Poteidaian settlement and, 122; sieges and, 186
Croesus, 14, 47n29, 72

Dapane/expenditure, 6, 94, 108, 128, 139, 197–99, 205; in 420s, 153–54; in Archaeology, 36; *arche, auxesis* and, 67; Athens' financial condition and, 104, 128, 133, 195–98; *dunamis* and, 6, 96, 116, 133, 205; in Korinthian/Kerkyraian conflict, 77–78; link between *chremata* and *nautikon*, 67, 76, 78, 83, 84, 89, 90, 91, 106, 108, 110, 116, 133, 143–44, 205; meaning of, 154; moral aspects of, 17–19; *nautikon*, power and, 61, 89–90, 92, 185, 205; Perikles on, 113, 116; of sieges, 104, 120–23, 139, 144; as sign of strength, 121, 133; war and, 11–14, 78, 84, 94, 127–30, 185
Darius, 14n49, 47n29
Dasmos, 48
Delian League, 41–50, 53–56, 60–62; coercion of members, 60–62; members' motives in creating, 8–9, 40; treasury of, 54–56
Delphi: borrowing from, 89–90, 95, 177–78; Korinthian/Kerkyraian conflict and, 71
Demodokos, 161
Demosthenes, 154
Diodotos, 143–44
Dunamis/power, 3, 6, 13, 22–23, 28, 39, 40, 42, 57, 58, 61–62, 77, 80, 87–89, 107, 111–16, 117, 118, 122, 130, 133, 134, 137, 170, 176, 179, 185, 205; Agamemnon and, 28; allies and, 61; in Archaeology, 33–35; Athens and Sparta compared, 81–89; *chremata/periousia chrematon* and, 3, 6, 28, 31, 58, 107, 125–27, 133, 134, 169, 185, 205; *dapane* and, 6, 133; development of, 14, 22–23, 40–43, 61–62, 66–69; financial resources and, 3; increase in Athens', 61–62, 80; Kerkyra and, 71–72; meaning of, 111–12; Minos and, 24–27; nature of, 205; naval *arche* and, 10–15;

revenue and, 91; Sparta and, 33; of Thucydides, 174–75; tyranny and, 30–31; wealth and, 13–14, 28, 72, 174, 205. *See also* Power

Eion, 60, 154, 167, 175, 178n72
Eisphora/εἰσφορά, 14, 116n19, 122n32, 134–36, 187–88, 200
Empire, naval. See *Arche*
Emporia: development and, 23; Korinth and, 31
Epidamnos, 71, 73–74
Euboia, 111, 130, 151
Eukles, 174
Eurymedon, 154
Expenditure. See *Dapane*
Extortion, 11, 42, 46, 52–53, 156, 163; as source of revenue, 202. *See also* Money-collecting ships; Piracy

Fear, 37, 39, 86–87, 138, 159, 172, 175
Financial resources, 149–50, 176, 180; abundance of Athenian, 117–18; Athens' and Sparta's compared, 81–89; centralization, 55–56, 103–7, 184–85; *gnome* and, 96, 107, 117, 121; power and, 3; in Thucydides, 1–2. See also *Periousia chrematon*
Fleet. See *Nautikon*
Funeral Oration, 15, 18–19, 111–13

Gifts, 125–26, 197
Gnome, 96; of Perikles, 117, 119, 121, 133, 138, 150
Growth. See *Auxesis*

Hatred/μῖσος: as causal factor, 40–41, 42, 43, 71–73
Hellanikos, 40, 59
Hellenic League, 40, 47
Hellenotamiai, 43, 49, 167, 196
Herodotos, 40–42, 46, 63; on Aristeides, 51; on Korinth/Kerkyra, 72; on wealth, 13–15, 73
Histiaia, 122n33, 200n45
Hubris, 15, 20, 72

Imperialism, 3, 6–7; collaborative theory of, 8–10; Delian League and, 56–57; economic, 7; Minos and, 26–27

Indemnities, 68, 122, 142; as source of revenue, 199–200
Inscriptions/epigraphic evidence, 2, 105–7, 157–58, 162–66, 191–94; *IG* I³ 19, 20n72; *IG* I³ 34, 191n20, 200n45; *IG* I³ 41, 200n43; *IG* I³ 46, 74n10, 176n63; *IG* I³ 52, 105–7, 135–36, 184, 196n32; *IG* I³ 60, 191; *IG* I³ 66, 144–45n93; *IG* I³ 68, 191; *IG* I³ 71, 148n99, 156–58, 162–67, 191–94; *IG* I³ 77, 148n99, 157–58, 180n75; *IG* I³ 156, 20n72; *IG* I³ 267, 79n28; *IG* I³ 269, 79n28; *IG* I³ 270, 79n28; *IG* I³ 272, 79n28; *IG* I³ 278, 79n28; *IG* I³ 279, 79n28, 123, 186n4; *IG* I³ 281–84, 191n19; *IG* I³ 283, 162; *IG* I³ 287, 181n77; *IG* I³ 291, 153n2; *IG* I³ 363, 122n35, 186n4, 199n42; *IG* I³ 369, 194–97; *IG* I³ 370, 136n71; *ML* 5, 74n10; *ML* 20, 74n10; *ML* 45, 158; *ML* 67, 139n78
Ionia, as source of revenue, 139–43, 199
"Iron reserve," 110–11, 185, 203
Ischomachos, 17

Judgment. See *Gnome*
Justice, 72, 86

Kallias Decrees, 105–7, 135–36, 184
Karia, 134, 154, 186, 200
Karystos/Karystians, 60, 141n87
κέρδος, 27, 54
Kerkyra/Kerkyraians, 71–78
Kleon, 143–44, 189; in *Wasps*, 167
Kleonymos, 191
Klerouchies, 122n32, 141, 142, 144–48, 186, 190
Korinth: Kerkyra and, 71–78; *nautikon* and, 31–32; Poteidaia and, 78–80
Krete. See Minos
Ktesis, 29; Delian League and, 55, 66; of Thucydides, 174–75; tyranny and, 31–32
Kythera, 159–60, 182, 192

Lakedaimonians. *See* Peloponnesians; Sparta/Spartans
Lamachos, 161
Leontini/Leontinians, 153
Lesbos/Lesbians, 155–56, 160, 186–87. *See also* Mytilene/Mytilenaians

Liberation of Greeks, theme of, 129, 171–72
Loans, 89–90n44, 195–98
Logistai, 194–95
Lykia, 121, 154, 186

Macedonia, 124–25, 170–71
Magnesia, 159n18, 168n41
Megara/Megarians, 111, 123, 152
Melos, 64, 153, 158
Mende, 178
Mercenaries, 10, 75–77, 90, 95, 156, 177, 178n72
Mines, 68, 176, 198
Minos, 24–27, 33, 35, 60, 66
Misthos, 29n23, 75, 130, 178n72
Money. See *Chremata*
Money-collecting ships/ἀργυρολόγοι νῆες, 121, 134–38, 154, 159, 160–64, 187, 200–202
Mytilene/Mytilenaians: end of revolt, 139–43; Rhoiteion and exiles from, 155–57, settlement of, 100, 143–49, 186–90; speech at Olympia, 127–30; *See also* Lesbos/Lesbians

Naupaktos, 177
Nautikon, 3, 28, 30, 38, 43–44, 61, 67, 93; Agamemnon and, 28; *arche* and, 3; *chremata* and, 3, 28, 30, 61, 67, 70, 75, 76, 83, 89–90, 91, 110, 116–117, 185; *dapane* and, 61, 67, 185; Kerkyra and, 71–72, 76; Korinth and, 31–32, 75; Minos and, 24–26; size of Athens', 130–32, 150–51; tyranny and, 30–31
Naval *arche*. See *Arche*
Naval power/mastery, 10–12, 15–16, 16n55, 92, 114–15. See also *Arche*; *Dunamis*
Navies. See *Nautikon*
Naxos/Naxians, 60–61, 63
Neutrality, 181–82
Nikias, 153, 159, 180
Nymphodoros, 111

Oaths, 58; Agamemnon and, 28; Delian League and, 43, 58
Odrysians, 111, 120, 124–27, 137, 168, 168n43, 170–71
Oikos, 16–17, 19, 116

Olympia, 127, 132; borrowing from, 89–90, 177–78
Olynthos, 180

Papyrus Decree, 102
Paraskeue/preparedness, 3, 92, 114, 127, 168; development of, 22–23; Kerkyra and, 72; in Korinthian/Kerkyraian conflict, 71, 79; of Peloponnesians, 91–93, 98n61; Perikles on, 114; of Sparta, 85–86; tribute and, 56; Trojan Expedition and, 30
Pausanias, 40–42
Peace of Nikias, 178–83; first assessment of *phoros* and, 50, 180–82
Peloponnesian invasion and preparation for, 91–93, 110–11
Peloponnesians: Mytilene and, 127–30, 139–40; Persia and, 120. *See also* Sparta/Spartans
Pelops, 28, 33
Pentekontaetia, 93, 98; ἀληθεστάτη πρόφασις and, 37–39; purpose of, 37–39, 59
Perdikkas, 111, 124–25, 170–71
Perikles, 15, 128; death of, 119–20; early removal from *History*, 119–20; financial acumen of, 107, 121, 133; policies/financial and war strategy of, 103–7, 109–10, 148–49, 153, 184–85, 188, 195, 203–4; on the nature of naval power, 114–15. See also *Gnome*; *Pronoia*
Periousia chrematon/financial resources, 12, 18, 23, 26, 29, 38, 55, 58, 66, 68, 94, 104, 118–19, 121, 126, 136, 146, 153, 185, 189, 205; in Archaeology, 33–35; centralization of, 55–56, 104–7, 126, 127; *dunamis*/power and, 3, 6, 92, 125–27, 185; on eve of war, 96–107; Korinth and, 31–32; in mid-420s, 153–54, 195, 202–3; moral aspects of, 17–18; Mytileneaian settlement and, 148–50; war and, 12–14, 74, 94, 96, 118–19, 136, 138, 146–47, 189. See also *Chremata*; Financial resources; Wealth
Persia/Persians, 60; *chremata* from, 117, 120, 155; Ionia and, 141; Spartan embassies to, 154–55; tribute payment and, 47–48
Persian Wars, loss of ships and, 63–64

Phokaian staters, 155–59
Phormio, 111, 123, 127, 130
Phoros/tribute, 6, 33, 79; allies' conversion to payment of, 9–10, 62–66; allies' status and, 60–62; of Aristeides, 167n40, 180–82; Athens' *auxesis* and, 57, 67; barbarian despotism and, 47; called *chremata*, 163; collection of, 166–69, 190–94; composition of, 99–101; first assessment of, 49–53, 57, 167, 168, 180–82; institution of, 43–49, 52–53, 56–57; insufficiency as a form of revenue, 163, 169, 190, 194; justification of, 43–45, 48, 52–53, *see also* πϱόσχημα; from Kythera, 159–60; as a measure of prosperity, 141–42; not demanded from allies after revolt, 122–23, 144–45; place of in Thucydides' treatment of *auxesis* and power, 56–57; as punishment after sieges, 68, 122, 144, 188; reassessment of 421, 157–58; reassessment of 425, 156–59, 161–62, 164–70, 191–94; of Rhoiteion, 155–59; as sign of *douleia*, 47–48, 90, 170n47, 172, 181, 194n28; to Sitalkes and Seuthes from Thrace, 125–26; vs. *apophora*, 46–47; who paid, 9, 45n24, 146; without ξυμμαχία, 160, 180–83
Piracy, 11, 18, 26n17, 31, 52–53, 60, 66, 156; Korinth and, 31–32; Minos and, 25–26; moral aspects of, 18; in Pentekontaetia, 60; Rhoiteion and, 156; as source of revenue and power, 200–202. *See also* Money-collecting ships
Piraieus, 123
Plague, 113–14, 128, 187
Plataia, 139
Pleistoanax, 180
Plunder, 11, 52–53
Polykrates, 14, 24n11
Poteidaia: expense of siege, 104, 134, 137, 145, 187; fall of, 120; rate of pay of soldiers at, 120, 130, 133; revolt of, 78–79, 187; settlement of, 120–23, 138, 185–86, 188–90
Power: in Archaeology, 33–35; inherited, 28, 35, 68, 112, 116; stronger and weaker, 8–10, 26–27, 61–62, 66, 201n47; cf. 80. See also *Dunamis*
Preparedness. See *Paraskeue*

Pronoia, of Perikles, 117–19, 121, 133, 150, 203–4
Prosodos/revenue, 38, 79, 83, 91, 96, 98–101, 126, 129, 185, 187–88, 190, 198–203, 205; in 425, 166–67; from Amphipolis, 141–42, 175–76, 198; in Archaeology, 32, 33, 36; Athens', 98–101; *dunamis* and, 91, 92, 144, 185, 187–88, 200, 205; from *eisphora*, 134–36; from indemnities, 68, 199; from Ionia, 139–43, 199; from klerouchies, 145–46; Korinth and, 31–32; from mines, 68, 176, 198; Minos and, 25; from "money-collecting" expeditions, 121, 134–38, 154, 159, 160–64, 187, 200–202; Mytilenaian settlement and, 143–49; revolts and loss of, 139–40; from sacred lands, 145, 176, 199; from tribute, 61, 68, 96, 194. See also *Phoros*
πϱόσχημα, 43–45, 46, 48, 52, 60
Public building, in Athens, 153–54
Public vs. private enrichment, 145–49, 186, 189–90, 204
Pylos, 154, 170

Ransom, 155–59
Reassessment of 425, 2, 156–59, 161–62, 164–70, 191–94
Revenue. See *Prosodos*
Revolts, 61, 68, 139–40, 141, 143, 178; benefit to Athens from, 122–23, 129, 168; of Mytilene, 127, 138–40; of Poteidaia, 78–80; settlements of, 68, 121–23, 129, 138, 143–49, 186–90
Rhoiteion, 155–59
Rowers, 64, 95

Sacred lands, 142, 144–46, 176, 199
Sacred treasures: at Delphi, 89–90, 95, 177–78; at Olympia, 89–90, 95, 178. *See also* Treasuries
Salaithos, 143
Salamis, 123, 130
Samos, 68, 104, 122, 142, 199; expense of siege, 122
Self-sufficiency, 19
Sestos, 52, 63
Seuthes, 125–26, 168
Ships: contributors of to Hellenic and Delian Leagues, 62–64; totals of in Athen-

Ships (*continued*)
  ian fleet, 131–32, 151. See also *Nautikon*
Sicily: ships sent to in 427, 153; tyranny and, 31
Sieges: *dapane* and, 52–53, 120–23, 137, 144, 147, 185–86; of Mytilene, 134; of Poteidaia, 120–23; of Sestos, 52–53
Siphnos/Siphnians, 63, 198–99n40
Sitalkes, 111, 120, 124–27, 137, 168n43, 170–71
Skione, 178
Skolos, 180
Skyros, 60, 66
Skythians, 127
Sophokles, 154
Sparta/Spartans, 10, 123, 170, 204; armistice with Athens, 177–78; compared with Athens, 5–6, 81–89, 94–96, 160; development of power of, 32–33; Kythera's capture and, 159–60; lack of public wealth, 55, 81–82; Peace of Nikias and, 178–83; Persia and, 154–55; reasons for voting for war, 39–40, 42; understanding of role of money in war/nature of Peloponnesian War, 85–87, 120, 139–40, 155, 160, 171, 204–5. *See also* Alkidas; Archidamos; Brasidas; Peloponnesians
Spartolos, 180
Speeches: of Archidamos, 80–89, 96; of Kleon and Diodotos, 143–44; in Korinthian/Kerkyraian conflict, 77–78; of Korinthians, 80, 89–91; of Mytilenaians, 127–30; of Perikles, 93–107, 111–16; of Sthenelaidas, 86–87. *See also* Funeral Oration
Sphakteria, 159, 177, 179, 192
Stagiros, 180
Sthenelaidas, 86–87
Suntaxis, 48
Surplus. See *Periousia chrematon*

Taxation. See *Eisphora*
Thasos, 68, 122; as source of revenue, 198–99
Themistokles, 32, 39, 42, 46
Thrace, 111, 120, 123–27, 137, 168, 168n43, 170–76
Thucydides, 172–75; on Athens' leadership, 117–20, 125; epigraphical evidence and, 2, 155–59, 162–70, 193–94
Torone, 177
Treasuries: Athenian, 4, 20, 101–3, 187; centralization of, 103–7, 196; of Delian League, 54–56; of Other Gods, 103–6; sacred, borrowing from, 89–90, 177–78, 195–97
Tribute. See *Phoros*
Tribute quota lists, 99–101, 190; first assessment of *phoros* and, 50–51; Ionia and, 140–43; reassessment of 425 and, 162–66; Rhoiteion and, 158–59. *See also* Inscriptions/epigraphic evidence, *IG* I³ 279, *IG* I³ 281–84, *IG* I³ 287
Trireme, 32, 64
Trojan Expedition, 27–30; Thucydides' account of the Delian League and, 56
Trophe, 29–30, 36
Tropos/τρόπος, 39, 59n61, 80, 112, 116, 160
Tyranny, 30–31

Unity: in Archaeology, 23–24, 30–31, 33–35, 58; centralization of resources and, 55–56; Delian League and, 65–66; Odrysians and, 127; tyranny and, 30–31

War/warfare: *dapane* of, 78, 84, 127–30, 133–34; effect of on Athens' *arche* and revenue, 136, 147; naval, 110–11, 152–53; wealth and, 10–15
Wealth, 3–4, 6–7, 113; Athenian collective attitude toward, 113; Athens' and Sparta's compared, 81–89; *chremata* and, 26–27; Delian League and, 66; display vs. expenditure of, 113, 116, 205–6; *dunamis* and, 13–14, 28, 72, 174, 205; excess/surplus, see *Periousia chrematon*; Kerkyra and, 71; moral aspects of, 15–19; of Odrysians, 125–27; private, 16–17, 186, 187, 189, 190; private, Perikles on, 115–16; private, in Sparta, 81–82, 94, 136; private vs. public, 114–16, 136; sources of Athens', 66–67, 81, 83, 96, 99, 101, see also *Prosodos*; war and, 10–15, 72. *See also Chremata*; Financial resources; *Ktesis*

Xenophon, 17, 113

INDEX OF PASSAGES IN THUCYDIDES

Book 1
1: 21, 33
1–23: 21
1.1: 33n28, 168
1.2: 38, 98, 107, 168n42
1.3: 22, 24
2: 24n10
2.1: 22
2.2: 23, 29, 36
2.4: 23
2.4–6: 24
3: 24
4: 22n5, 108
4.1: 24–25
5: 201n47
5–8: 26
5.1: 26
7: 29, 36
8.2–3: 26
8.2–9.2: 66
8.3: 9n26, 20n73, 26–27, 30, 36, 54, 66, 81
8.3–4: 29
9: 58, 108
9.2: 36
9.3–4: 28
10: 28
11: 30, 56
11.1: 36
11.1–2: 28–29
11.2: 36
12.2: 100n70

13: 30, 108
13.1: 30–31, 36
13.2: 73n6
13.2–4: 31
13.5: 31, 36, 73n6
13.6–14: 24n11, 32
14.3: 32, 80n30
15.1: 32, 36
17: 30, 32
18: 32–33
19: 32–33, 35–36, 126n45, 160
19.1: 108
20: 22
22: 75–76n18
22.4: 81n32
23.6: 13n44, 15, 37–38, 58, 88, 107, 115
24–25.2: 71
24–55: 108
25.4: 71, 72n4, 108
26.1: 74n11
27.1: 73, 110n4, 126n43, 168
27.2: 74, 78n22
29.5: 78n22
30.2: 75, 108
31.1: 75, 77, 90n46, 93, 108, 109n1
33.2: 76
35.4: 76
39.7–8: 143
41.2–3: 39n5
44.1: 77
45: 78, 109n1

225

Book 1 (*continued*)
46.1: 78n22
48.1: 109n1
49.4: 78n24
53: 78
54.2: 77
56.1: 78n25
56.2: 79
57.1: 78n25
57.5: 79
57.6: 79, 109n1
59: 79
60.1: 79, 109n1
61.1: 109n1
67: 205n53
68–71: 80, 81
70: 80
70.1: 39n5
71.7: 116n21
72.1: 80
73–78: 81
73.4–74.2: 80n30
75: 18n68, 81
75.2: 48n33, 62n64
76.2: 8, 48n33, 62n64, 81
80–86: 80–89
80.3: 126n45, 194n28
80.3–4: 81
80.4: 55, 74n13, 81n34, 94, 136
81.4: 83, 91n47, 108, 129n46, 143n91
81.6: 185n3
82.1: 83, 108
83.2: 61, 78n23, 84, 108
85.1: 84n37, 143n91
86.3: 86, 108
86.5: 86
87: 205n53
88: 38–39, 86, 88
89: 32n2, 39
89–93: 39
89–96: 59
89.1: 59n61
89.2: 63n69
93: 39, 95n55
94: 40
94–95: 58
94–99: 66
94.1: 40n7
95: 40
95–96: 10n27, 40, 45n19, 62
95–99: 80n31

95.1: 40n7
95.2: 41
95.3: 40n7
95.5: 40n9
95.7: 42–43
96: 2n2, 40, 43–44, 54n52, 56–58, 72n3, 168, 193, 194
96–98: 167
96.1: 40
96.1–2: 167
96.2: 54, 100, 148n102, 163n26, 167, 168n41, 181n76
97: 54n51, 59
97.1: 167, 181
97.2: 40, 48, 59
98: 60
98.1: 167
98.2: 198n39
98.4: 167
99: 9n26, 45n24, 62–65, 182
99.2–3: 61
99.3: 65, 81, 100n68, 163n26
101.3: 68, 122n34, 142, 163n26, 176n65, 186n4, 198, 199
102.4: 45n19
103.3: 198n39
103.4: 72n3
108.4: 68
114.3: 122n33
115.3: 73n8
117.3: 68, 122, 142, 186n4, 199
118: 88, 115
120–24: 89–91
121.3: 95, 151
121.3–4: 89, 108
121.5: 20n73, 90, 194n28
122.1: 91, 129n46, 143n91
122.2: 20n73
125.2: 91–93
130.2: 40
138.5: 159n48, 168n41
139.3: 93
140–44: 93–96, 111
141.2: 94
141.3: 95n56
141.5: 74n13, 83n36, 95n56, 136, 150n106, 187
142.1: 83n36, 94, 95n56
143.1: 89–90n44, 95, 110n4
143.1–2: 83n36
143.3–5: 96n58

143.4: 96
143.5: 109n2
144.4: 112n7

Book 2
7: 96
7.2: 87n42, 126n43
8: 96, 129n48
9: 160
9.5: 163n26
11.1: 96
13: 2n2, 111–12, 121, 134, 195–97
13.2: 96, 105, 109, 119, 143n91, 150, 163n26
13.3: 55, 100, 103, 121, 142, 163n26, 184n1, 198
13.3–4: 184
13.3–5: 15, 18, 96–107, 148n102, 168, 184, 195–96
13.4: 103, 126n43
13.5: 18, 103, 184n2
13.8: 184
19: 110
19.2: 110
21.1: 110
21.2: 110
23.2: 111
24.1: 95n55, 185
24.1–2: 110
26.1: 111
27.1: 111
29: 111, 124n39
29.5: 111
29.6: 111
31.2: 111
32: 26n17
35–46: 111
36.2–3: 112
36.3: 19
36.4: 39n5
39.3: 112n7
40.1: 18, 113, 116
40.4: 66
41.2: 112
41.4: 113
43.1: 112n10, 205
52–53: 81n32
53.2: 143n91
56–57: 131
60: 189
62–64: 113–17

62.2: 15–16, 109n2, 114, 116
62.3: 109n2, 112n9, 115
63: 20n73
63: 20n73, 113
64.3: 116
64.5: 72n3
65: 117–20, 121
65.1–4: 148n100
65.4: 119
65.6: 119n27
65.7: 109n2, 190
65.7–8: 148
65.12: 118
65.13: 119
67.1: 120, 155
69: 121, 136, 162–63, 164n29, 200
69.1: 26n17, 134, 137, 142, 186
69.2: 154
70: 121, 198n39
70.1: 185
70.2: 104, 120, 128, 134, 148n102, 168
70.3: 122n31, 126n43
70.4: 123, 186
93–94: 124
95: 124
95–101: 123–27
95.3: 168n43
97.3–5: 125–26
97.6: 127
100–101.1: 125
101.2–4: 125n40, 125n41
101.5: 127
102–3: 127

Book 3
2–3: 187
3.1: 138n75, 187n6, 187n8
6.1: 151
9.2: 127
10.3: 44n18
13–16: 205n53
13.2: 127
13.3: 127–28, 130, 133
13.4: 128
13.5–6: 128–29
13.6: 163n26
13.6–7: 129n48
15: 129, 151
16: 132, 151
16.1: 129
17: 121, 130–34, 150–51

INDEX

Book 3 (*continued*)
17.3–4: 168
17.4: 120n30, 187n9
19.1: 2n2, 94n53, 134–38, 142, 146, 150n106, 154, 162–63, 164n29, 168, 187, 200–202
20–24: 139
25: 139
26.1: 139
29: 139
29.2: 139
30–32: 205n53
31: 142–43
31.1: 129n46, 139, 199
34.4: 122n33
36.2: 143
36.6: 149n103
37.2: 20n72
39.8: 91n47
43.2: 9n25
46.2–4: 144
46.4: 163n26
50: 144–45
50.1: 100, 129n47, 144
50.2: 126n43, 142, 144, 176n63, 199
50.3: 145, 147, 157
51.2: 26n17
67.5: 72n3
69: 139n78
70: 110n4, 152, 168n41
82.2: 81n32
86.4: 153, 203n50
91.1: 153, 203n50
91.2: 153
91.3–6: 153
101.1: 177
102: 73n8
109.2: 177
114.1: 106n87
115: 203n50

Book 4
3.3: 154
9.1: 26n17
26.5: 126n43, 168
39: 192n25
41.3: 192n25
42–45: 154
46–48: 154
50: 162–63, 200
50.1: 137, 142, 161
50.1–2: 154, 205n53
51: 155
52.2: 155–59, 168
52.3: 156, 158–59
53: 159
53.3: 26n17
54: 192n24
54.3: 159n19
55.1–2: 160
55.3–4: 155n6
57: 182
57.4: 159, 163n26, 192n24
65.1: 126n43, 168
66–77: 152
67.3: 26n17
69.3: 126n43
75: 156, 160, 162, 200
75–76.1: 159
75.1: 137, 142, 161, 162n24, 164
75.2: 161
78: 152
78–88: 137n74
79.2: 170
81.1: 171, 205n53
81.3: 171
82.1: 171
83: 171
84–87: 171
84.2: 172n51
85.1: 171n48
85.5: 171n48
85.6: 171n48
86.1: 171n48
86.4: 171n48
87.2: 171n48
87.3: 20n73, 170n47, 172
87.4: 171n48
87.6: 171n48
88: 172
88.2: 172
89–101: 152
98.5: 95n55
101.5: 137n74, 171
102: 173
102–16: 137n74
104.5: 174
105.1: 174–75
108: 141
108.1: 26n16, 175–76, 198

108.2: 176
108.3: 176
108.4: 176
109: 177
110–14: 177
115–16: 177
116.2: 110n4
117: 177
117–18: 177
118.3: 177
120–5.12: 137n74
124.4: 178n72
128.5: 72n3, 126n43
129.2: 178n72

Book 5
6.2: 178n72
6.4: 178n72
14.1: 179
14.2–4: 179
14.3: 87n42, 171n48, 185n3, 205n53
15.1: 179
18.2: 180
18.5: 50n42, 110n4, 160, 167n40, 180n75, 181, 182n82
21.2: 182
26: 5
27.2: 72n3
49.5: 126n43
107: 100n70

Book 6
8.1: 126n43
12.1: 143n91
17.6: 72n3
22: 64n70
24.3: 8n19, 126n43
30.1: 64n70
44.1: 64n70
46.4: 100n70
60.4: 126n43
76.3–4: 44n18
94.4: 126n43

Book 7
7.3: 64n70
16.2: 126n.43
17.3: 64n70
18.4: 64n70
19.3: 64n70
57.2: 122n33
82.3: 73n9, 126n43

Book 8
3: 73n8
3.1: 163, 200
15.2: 64n71, 95n54
40.2: 95n54
65.3: 143n91
69.3: 122n33
76.6: 126n43

Designer: Ina Clausen
Compositor: Graphic Composition, Inc.
Text: Baskerville, Greek
Display: Baskerville